SEEKING A SANCTUARY

Seeking A Sanctuary

Seventh-day Adventism and the American Dream

Malcolm Bull
and Keith Lockhart

1817

HARPER & ROW, PUBLISHERS, SAN FRANCISCO

New York, Grand Rapids, Philadelphia, St. Louis
London, Singapore, Sydney, Tokyo, Toronto

SEEKING A SANCTUARY: *Seventh-day Adventism and the American Dream.* Copyright © 1989 by Malcolm Bull and Keith Lockhart. All rights reserved. Printed in the United States of America. No part of this book may be used or reproduced in any manner whatsoever without written permission except in the case of brief quotations embodied in critical articles and reviews. For information, address Harper & Row, Publishers, Inc., 10 East 53rd Street, New York, NY 10022.

FIRST EDITION

Library of Congress Cataloging-in-Publication Data

Bull, Malcolm.
  Seeking a sanctuary.

  Bibliography: p.
  Includes index.
  1. Seventh-day Adventists—United States.
2. Adventists—United States.   3. Seventh-day Adventists
—Doctrines.   4. Adventists—Doctrines.   I. Lockhart,
Keith.   II. Title.
BX6153.2.B85 1989   286.7'73   88-45981
ISBN 0-06-250108-9

89 90 91 92 93 HC 10 9 8 7 6 5 4 3 2 1

*For
Simon and Esther
and
in memory of
Ernest Merchant*

Contents

Preface

Seventh-day Adventism is one of the most subtly differentiated, systematically developed and institutionally successful of all alternatives to the American way of life. A nineteenth-century religious sect that observes the seventh-day Sabbath, proclaims the imminent end of the world, and practices health reform, Seventh-day Adventism now has more than 5 million members worldwide and is one of the fastest growing Protestant groups.

Despite being one of the most important religious movements native to the United States, Seventh-day Adventism has been unjustly ignored. Unlike the Mormons and the Jehovah's Witnesses, Adventists have never gained notoriety through open opposition to the state. But neither do they form part of the Protestant mainstream that sustains the national religious identity. In this, as in other respects, Adventism seems ambiguous. This book argues that the ambiguity of Adventism's relationship to America is the source of its identity and success.

If the American dream can be defined, it would include the following elements: (1) the belief that the American revolution created a state uniquely blessed by God in which human beings have unprecedented opportunities for self-realization and material gain; (2) the conviction that the American nation, through both example and leadership, offers hope for the rest of the world; and (3) the assumption that it is through individual, rather than collective, effort that the progress of humanity will be achieved.

In their formative years, the Seventh-day Adventists rejected the essentials of the American myth. They did not accept that the republican experiment would lead to the betterment of humanity or that it would be a lasting success. They consigned America to eventual destruction, and in place of the nation, they daringly substituted themselves as the true vehicle for the redemption of the world. America had offered sanctuary to generations of immigrants from Europe; Adventism sought to provide a sanctuary from America. By presenting itself as an alternative to the Republic in this way, the church rapidly came to operate as an alternative to America in the social sphere as well, as Adventists replicated the institutions and functions of American society.

This book examines the Adventist experience in the light of the church's response to the American nation. As such, it has two aims: (1) to give an accurate, up-to-date account of all aspects of Adventist belief and practice and (2) to provide, for the first time, a framework within which the complexities of the Adventist tradition can be understood. After an introductory review of the images of Adventism disseminated by the media, the argument is developed in three stages. In part one, the main developments in Adventist theology are chronicled in an effort to define the ideological boundaries between the church and the world. Part two deals more directly with Adventism and America and argues that many aspects of the church—its organizational and financial structure, its vast institutionalization, its evangelistic success, its attitude toward health, its dealings with the state, and the character of its art—reveal its ambiguous position in American society. In part three, the various groups that comprise the church are examined in more detail, while the concluding chapter relates the diversity within Adventism to the church's deviant response to the American dream.

The book draws on a great variety of published and unpublished sources. Research commenced in 1984 and was conducted mainly in the libraries and archives of the denomination's colleges and universities in America and Britain. The summer of 1985 was spent interviewing dozens of Adventist leaders, hospital administrators, laymen, and representatives of the church's various institutions and groups. In addition, the authors both have many years of participant observation on which to draw. One of the authors, although not himself an Adventist and never a baptized member of the church, was born into an Adventist family. The other was also brought up as an Adventist and was educated in Adventist institutions in Britain and America. In an attempt to do justice to the full range of the Adventist experience we have adopted an interdisciplinary approach. We hope the book will be useful both to the academic specialist and to the general reader.

As a social and historical phenomenon, Adventism is of unusual, but largely unrecognized, importance. The object of the book is to draw attention to that phenomenon.

Malcolm Bull
Keith Lockhart

March 1989

Acknowledgments

The authors are grateful to all whose assistance enabled them to complete this book. One of the authors enjoyed the hospitality of the Ecole Normale Supérieure de Fontenay-aux-Roses and, later, of Wolfson College, Oxford; both benefited from the facilities provided at Newbold College, Bracknell. William Schomburg and Hugh Dunton, the librarians of Newbold College were particularly helpful, as was Gilberto Abella of Loma Linda University Library, California.

Harry Leonard and several other members of the faculty of Newbold College read and commented on portions of the manuscript in its early stages. Bryan Wilson, Michael Pearson, Roy Branson, and Jonathan Butler read the first draft in its entirety and offered many valuable criticisms. Davis Bitton gave of his time to act as a guide to Salt Lake City and the history of the Latter-day Saints. Giles Darkes assisted with research for chapter 9. Carola Parker and Marla Matthews typed the manuscript. Robin Helps, Jill Foulston, Kenneth Newport, Julian Lethbridge, Kevin Ringering, Michael Battle, John Hughes, and Sarah Womack all provided accommodation and friendship when it was most needed.

SEEKING A SANCTUARY

CHAPTER 1

Introduction: Public Images

In a Gallup poll conducted in the United States in 1986, 30 percent of those questioned said that they had not heard of Seventh-day Adventism. Of those who had, four-fifths were able to provide further information.[1] Most were aware that Seventh-day Adventists were religious, and many knew that Saturday was observed as the Sabbath. Four percent confused Adventists with Mormons, and 1 percent mistook them for Jehovah's Witnesses. When asked what they liked best about Seventh-day Adventists, half did not reply, and one-fifth said "nothing in particular." When asked what they liked least, the response was identical. Apart from the Saturday Sabbath, popular awareness of the church's beliefs and practices was vague. Although perceived as an extremely rigorous group with peculiar eating habits, the details of particular taboos were hazy. Some presumed Adventists to be opposed to conventional medicine, while others commented favorably on Adventist hospitals. Historical facts were also conspicuous by their absence, and in a similar survey conducted in 1970, it was Mormon rather than Adventist history that came to mind.[2]

This is not the profile of a religious group that has captured the popular imagination. After almost one and a half centuries of rapid growth, Adventism is still largely unknown, and the public appears indifferent to its existence. Further exposure to Adventism appears unlikely to excite enthusiasm. A 1977 Gallup poll revealed that of those who held an opinion, 27 percent disliked Seventh-day Adventists, a negative rating significantly higher than those of mainstream Protestant groups (4 to 8 percent) and marginally greater than that given to the Mormons.[3] Increased familiarity with Adventists does not necessarily engender more positive feelings. A small-scale study of public attitudes toward Adventists compared a town with only thirty-five Adventist church members to a town with an Adventist institution.[4] The study revealed that the large Adventist presence was associated with a markedly higher level of public hostility. In sum, the public is ignorant of Adventism but inclined to view the church negatively relative to other Christian groups.

This is hardly surprising. Adventism is a small sect with firm moral and religious standards, and the public seems to view churches more negatively the more rigorous they are. In this respect, Adventism appears to be only partially distinguishable from several other groups at the margins of American religion. Public perceptions are derived not only from direct contact with Adventists who are friends, relatives, or engaged in evangelism but also indirectly from non-Adventist accounts of Adventism given by the media and other churches. In many ways, the latter sources seem more likely to shape public opinion, for they provide a context within which Adventism can be related to the rest of society. As most people's direct experience is too limited to provide an alternative, this is probably the framework that informs the popular understanding of Adventist practices.

The picture of Adventism disseminated by the media draws on a long tradition rooted in the newspaper coverage of the Millerites in the 1830s and 1840s. William Miller was a farmer from Low Hampton in upstate New York. He fought in the War of 1812 but lost his faith in patriotism and endured a profound spiritual crisis. He was converted from deism to Christianity in 1816 and joined the Baptist church. Devoting himself to Bible study, he gradually became convinced that the prophecies of Daniel would reach their final fulfillment in the Second Advent of Christ around 1843. Commencing in 1831, he preached throughout New England, slowly building up a widespread network of lecturers and followers who also proclaimed his message. In this he was assisted by Joshua Himes, minister of the Chardon Street Chapel in Boston and a man with a unique talent for religious propaganda. As the date drew near, the Millerites rallied support at a series of camp meetings.[5]

Although Miller himself was an unassuming man, the alarming nature of his message and the numerous publications sponsored by Himes naturally attracted popular attention. Reactions varied. Derision came easily, but there was also a sense of unease, for the idea that the history of the world was approaching its final culmination was popular. Most, however, expected this ending to involve the progressive perfection of the existing world rather than its annihilation. The Millerites warned of destruction at the very time that most Americans anticipated progress. It was an unsettling combination.[6] The poet John Greenleaf Whittier commented on the incongruity after a visit to a Millerite camp meeting:

How was it possible in the midst of so much life, in that sunrise light, and in view of all abounding beauty, that the idea of the death of Nature—the baptism of the world in fire—could take such a practical shape as this? Yet here were sober, intelligent men, gentle and pious women, who, verily believing the end to be close at hand, had left their counting-rooms, and work-shops, and household cares to publish the great tidings, and to startle, if possible, a careless and unbelieving generation into preparation for the day of the Lord and for that blessed millennium—the restored paradise—when, renovated and renewed by its fire-purgation, the earth shall become as of old the garden of the Lord, and the saints alone shall inherit it.[7]

Whittier realized that Miller's message was not a novelty but just the most recent manifestation of the long Millenarian tradition. But he remained skeptical: "The effect of this belief in the speedy destruction of the world and the personal coming of the Messiah, acting upon a class of uncultivated, and, in some cases, gross minds, is," he observed, "not always in keeping with the enlightened Christian's ideal of the better day."[8]

Miller had argued that the world would end sometime between March 21, 1843, and March 21, 1844. It did not. But Miller believed his calculations to be substantially accurate, and the enthusiasm of his followers could not be quenched. On August 12, 1844, a Millerite minister, Samuel Snow, interrupted a camp meeting to announce that he had discovered the true date of the Second Advent—October 22 of that year. The new date was quickly adopted, and preparations for it were undertaken with renewed zeal.[9] Millerism was now seen to exemplify a second type of incongruity. Earlier reports had concentrated on the peculiarity of a movement that prophesied catastrophe in an everimproving world; during 1843 and 1844, the focus changed. The essential characteristic of the Millerites was perceived to be their absurd attempt to prepare for heaven in the trivializing surroundings of this world.[10]

Reports dwelt on the Millerites' supposedly careless indifference to worldly goods. It was, for example, widely rumored that Abraham Riker, a well-known shoe dealer of Division Street, New York, was scattering his goods in the street and that crowds gathered nightly at his door until his son had him committed to an asylum. Riker was later said to have committed suicide.[11] The newspapers published many similar tales, some even more bizarre. The case of Mr. Shortridge was an early example of the genre. "In Pelham, New Hampshire, Mr. Shortridge formally enrobed himself in a long white dress, and climbed into a tree, to be prepared to ascend, believing that the Second Advent was to take place on that day—in attempting to *rise* he fell to the ground and broke his neck."[12]

The Shortridge story included an element of particular significance to the popular perception of Millerism: the ascension robe. From early in 1843, the press reported that Millerites had taken to wearing peculiar garments in readiness for their ascent to heaven. The New York correspondent of the *National Intelligencer* stated that "several believers in Miller's theory were nearly frozen to death last Wednesday, on the heights of Hoboken, sitting in the snow in their ascension robes."[13] The description given of these robes varied. The *Gazette* of Springfield, Massachusetts, commented that "these ascension robes have created a great demand for drab Mackintosh cloth, and other draperies suitable for the liveries of the saints."[14] Another paper implied that the robes were of more expensive material, noting that Millerites in one town had ordered "$5,000 worth of silk."[15] A further alternative was suggested by a Bowery dry-goods store that had a sign in its window reading, "Muslin for Ascension Robes."[16]

All of these traditions about the Millerites were brought together in the reports of Millerite activities in Philadelphia on October 22, 1844.[17] It was said that several hundred Millerites had left the city on the morning of October 21 to set up camp outside in anticipation of the end of the world. As they left, one of them threw away money in the streets. Once at the campground, the Millerites were ill prepared for the elements. On October 24, one newspaper reported that "four of the converts to the Miller humbug who went to the encampment near Darby are dead from the effects of over-excitements and exposure. We understand that one of the female believers gave birth to a child in one of the tents."[18] The *Pennsylvania Inquirer* quickly conflated the two stories, reporting that "two little children were found in the encampment, perfectly cold, stiff and dead."[19] As if this were not bad enough, two days later the *United States Saturday Post* noted that the leaders of the expedition had absconded with large sums of money.[20] Forty years later, historians added the detail that the unfortunate Millerites had all been "clad in thin white 'ascension robes.' "[21]

There is no firm evidence for this or any of the other embellishments to the story. As F. D. Nichol demonstrated in *The Midnight Cry*, his defense of the Millerites published a century after the Great Disappointment of October 22, 1844, the rumors of the time were mostly unfounded. Mr. Shortridge, the man reported to have broken his neck after climbing a tree in an ascension robe, had written to the newspapers complaining about reports of his death.[22] Abraham Riker, the shoe dealer, had been able to discount reports of his suicide when the coroner called at his house to hold an inquest.[23]

Despite their slender basis in fact, the tales of Millerite madness did not disappear. On the contrary, they were perpetuated. There had been about 50,000 active Millerites, and their beliefs were well known and widely reported. Numerous writers reflected on the significance of the movement.[24] In 1843 Nathaniel Hawthorne had written a romance entitled *The New Adam and Eve*, based on the supposition that Miller's prophecies had come true.[25] Ralph Waldo Emerson had contacts with Millerites that he noted in his journals,[26] and the transcendentalists Theodore Parker, Bronson Alcott, George Ripley, and Christopher Cranch all visited a Millerite meeting.[27] Later writers continued to explore Millerite themes. In Henry Wadsworth Longfellow's *Kavanagh*, published in 1849, there is a fictional account of a Millerite camp meeting that emphasizes the pessimistic aspect of the movement and culminates in the suicide of an orphan who drowns herself in a river in the belief that she is damned.[28]

The most important literary account of Millerism is Edward Eggleston's realist novel *The End of the World*.[29] Set in Indiana in 1842–44, the book recounts the adventures of two young lovers, Julia Anderson and August Wehle, who are eventually united on the very day, August 11, that the world is expected to end. The contrast between the Millerite experience and the assumptions and routines of everyday life is made clear in order to explain the attraction of the apocalyptic message: "Now in all the region about Sugar Grove school-house there was a great dearth of sensation. . . . Into this still pool Elder Hankins [the Millerite preacher] threw the vials, the trumpets, the thunders, the beast with ten horns, the he goat, and all the other apocalyptic symbols understood in an absurdly literal way. The world was to come to an end in the following August. Here was an excitement worth living for."[30] The author points out that this enthusiasm led to irresponsible behavior: "This fever of excitement kept alive Samuel Anderson's [Julia's father] determination to sell his farms for a trifle as a testimony to unbelievers. He found that fifty dollars would meet his expenses until the eleventh of August, and so the price was set at that."[31] But the Millerite message was unable to suppress natural human optimism. As August Wehle asks after his marriage to Julia on the fateful day: "Can it be possible that God, who made this world so beautiful, will burn it up tonight? It used to seem a hard world to me when I was away from you, and I didn't care how quickly it burned up. But now—"[32]

It would be wrong to disregard the literary and journalistic traditions about Millerism. They may contain little accurate historical information, but they are invaluable sources for understanding the relationship between the Millerites and the rest of society. Almost all of the stories hinge on the idea that Millerism reversed customary patterns of behavior. The accounts present images of a group whose logic is inverted: a shopkeeper who throws his goods onto the street, a man who climbs a tree hoping to take off like a bird, farmers who do not plant their crops, people who sit in the snow wearing flimsy clothing. In Edgar Allan Poe's "Eureka," the author refers to "one Miller or Mill" as the cleverest of logicians.[33] It is a telling juxtaposition. John Stuart Mill, the British philosopher and exponent of utilitarianism, sought the amelioration of society; William Miller predicted its destruction. As Whittier had noted, the essential peculiarity of Millerism was its insistence, at a time when many other people considered society to be approaching perfection, that the world would be destroyed. The reversal of established beliefs seemed to position the Millerites outside contemporary culture, almost beyond the boundaries of civilization itself.[34]

This situation is reflected not only in the frequently repeated tales of the Millerites' self-destructive behavior but also in the tradition that the Millerites behaved irrationally in all possible ways. Because they were seen to have placed themselves in opposition to conventional assumptions about the future, the Millerites were presumed to be muddled in other spheres of life. The humor of the stories about the Millerites is grounded in this supposed peculiarity. There is no real evidence that the Millerites suffered from such confusions, but because they stood outside the general cultural optimism of the period, they were imagined to be innocent of the basic scientific and moral beliefs that structured life for society in general. The Millerites were probably normal in all respects save their Millerism; because of their Millerism, they were deemed abnormal in every other respect as well.

Seventh-day Adventism emerged in the years after the Great Disappointment. Its earliest leaders, Joseph Bates, James White, and Ellen Harmon, were all former Millerites. For the first seven years, adherents to the movement were drawn virtually exclusively from those who had waited in vain on October 22, 1844; salvation was considered impossible for those who had not waited. Adventism thus originated not from within wider society but from a disintegrating tradition that was considered thoroughly antisocial in its beliefs and practices. The Adventists did not attempt to shake off the legacy of Millerism. By reinterpreting the significance of October 22, 1844, they enshrined the date and Miller's movement as an important episode in salvation history. It was, Adventists came to believe, on that date that the judgment of saints and sinners began in heaven. The Second Advent, meanwhile, was expected to take place at some unspecified but imminent time after the judgment had been completed. The other major innovation in Adventist thinking was the belief that God's law required the observance of the Sabbath on Saturday rather than Sunday. This doctrine owed much of its prestige within Adventism to the authority of Ellen Harmon, from 1846 the wife of James White, whose visions were accepted as revelations of God's will. Inspired by Ellen White and organized by her husband, the Adventist community expanded from about one hundred in 1849 to a membership of 3,500 at the time of the church's formal incorporation in 1863.[35]

Initially, of course, the denomination was too small to attract public attention. But as the church grew, references to Adventists once more found their way into literature.[36] Their image differed from that of the Millerites only in the absence of a clearly defined theological context. Everyone had known what Millerites believed. The only thing that appeared to characterize Adventists was their marginality to the mainstream of society. They are presented as just one amidst a host of deviant orientations. In *Elmer Gantry*, a novel by the Nobel prize winner Sinclair Lewis, one character complains to another that "It's fellows like you who break down the dike of true belief, and open a channel for higher criticism and sabellianism and nymphomania and agnosticism and heresy and Catholicism and Seventh-day Adventism and all those horrible German inventions!"[37] In Jerome Charyn's novel *On the Darkening Green*, a rabbi comments that although no black Jews attend his synagogue, he does have "Seventh-day Adventists and Abyssinian Baptists up here for sermons. And occasionally a Holy Roller."[38] The English novelist Lawrence Durrell places Adventists in different, but comparably obscure, company in *Balthazar*, the second volume of the *Alexandria Quartet*: "Alexandria is a city of sects . . . groups akin to the one concerned with the hermetic philosophy . . . Steinerites, Christian Scientists, Ouspenskyists, Adventists."[39]

The black novelist Richard Wright grew up in the 1920s and 1930s. He lived for a time with his grandmother. His autobiography, *Black Boy*, gives a personal account of life at the margins of society:

Granny was an ardent member of the Seventh-Day Adventist Church and I was compelled to make a pretence of worshipping her God, which was her exaction for my keep. The elders of her church expounded a gospel clogged with images of vast lakes of eternal fire, of seas vanishing, of valleys of dry bones, of the sun burning to ashes, of the moon turning to blood, of stars falling to earth, . . . a salvation that teemed with fantastic beasts having multiple heads and horns and eyes and feet.[40]

Like Whittier, Wright found the Adventist vision incompatible with what he saw around him: "While listening to the vivid language of the sermons I was pulled toward emotional belief, but as soon as I went out of the church and saw the bright sunshine and felt the throbbing life of the people in the streets I knew that none of it was true and that nothing would happen."[41] When he left church school to attend public school, Wright sensed acutely the discrepancy between the values of his home and those of the world outside. Forbidden to work on Saturdays, Wright had less money than his schoolmates:

I could not bribe Granny with a promise of half or two-thirds of my salary; her answer was no and never. Her refusal wrought me up to a high pitch of nervousness and I cursed myself for being made to live a different and crazy life. . . . To protect myself against pointed questions about my home and my life, to avoid being invited out when I knew that I could not accept, I was reserved with the boys and girls at school, seeking their company but never letting them guess how much I was being kept out of the world in which they lived.[42]

Wright's account of his experience picks up many of the themes prominent in the work of Whittier, Eggleston, and other authors. Like the Millerites, Adventists are portrayed as adherents of a bizarre religious system expressed in lurid, apocalyptic symbols. Their beliefs are perceived to alienate them from, and to be incompatible with, a normal, healthy appreciation of the world. Wright emphasizes that while forced to live as an Adventist, he was trapped within a deviant subculture so alien that he could not even risk explaining his predicament to his friends. He presents Adventism as an enclosed world of dark delusions that evaporate when brought into the clear light of day.

The sinister element implicit in this understanding of Adventism was brought dramatically to the surface in Australia in the 1980s. Lindy Chamberlain, the wife of a Seventh-day Adventist pastor, reported that her nine-week-old baby had been carried off by a dingo while she and her family were camped at Ayers Rock. Mrs. Chamberlain was later imprisoned for the murder of her child. The long-running legal battle that led to her eventual acquittal became the most famous in Australian history, made headlines all over the world, and was the subject of the 1988 film "A Cry in the Dark." The name of the child was Azaria, which was widely, but incorrectly, believed to mean "sacrifice in the wilderness." The rumor quickly spread that the Chamberlains were following their religious beliefs in practicing sacrificial murder. Adventists became the object of suspicion and derision.[43]

Evil Angels, the account of the Chamberlain case written by the Australian lawyer John Bryson, opens not at Ayers Rock but on October 22, 1844, in Pennsylvania, with a description of the Great Disappointment.[44] All the old Millerite traditions are repeated. Some characters are portrayed as dressed in white muslin ascension robes; there is an empty space reserved for the late Mr. Shortridge who fell out of the tree; the two dead babies lie frozen under a dray. These are the images that the author, himself sympathetic to Lindy Chamberlain's defense, felt to be most pertinent to an appreciation of modern Adventism. Whether such images contribute directly to an understanding of Adventism is doubtful. But it is certainly true that they inform the public responses to the church, illustrate the way in which Adventism is conceived by outsiders, and illuminate the relationship between the denomination and the world. Adventism is seen as a group that does not share the cultural assumptions that bind society together. Adventism's values are presumed to be the very opposite. All "normal" people take particular care to preserve the lives of young children; thus Adventists, being by definition "abnormal," may be supposed to be indifferent or hostile to the welfare of infants.[45] It is a crude logic, but it is one that has governed public reactions to the Adventist movement from its inception and is firmly embedded in the collective memory of the Millerite Disappointment.

That this picture is incomplete, even as a characterization of public perceptions, is evident from the Gallup polls. Few seemed to register the kind of hostility that is detectable in most of the literature on Adventists. It may be that fear of Adventist peculiarity is latent because of the church's low public profile. Certainly, when opposition is aroused, the language used tends to be extreme. In 1979, for example, a city council candidate in Riverside, California, who was opposed to the church's local political influence, compared Adventism to the People's Temple cult responsible for the mass suicide in Jonestown, Guyana.[46] But there is another factor in the generally muted response to Adventism: the existence of an alternative image of the church, one completely at odds with the picture of apocalyptic fanaticism.

Hints of this alternative image are evident in the responses given to the Gallup polls, which revealed that very few people are aware that Adventists are unusually concerned with the end of the world. What emerged clearly in the 1986 poll was the public's strong association of Adventists with health. Of those who were aware of the church, 25 percent knew of the practice of temperance, 13 percent had heard of Adventist health food products and the church's medical school at Loma Linda, California, and 12 percent were acquainted with the Adventists' five-day plan to stop smoking.[47] Such activities are very different from the otherworldly obsessions often thought to characterize Adventists. Adventist concerns are seen as this-worldly in emphasis, concerned not with the end of life on the planet but with its improvement.

To trace the development of this alternative image of Adventism, it is necessary to return once again to the nineteenth century. The subject of health reform was widely discussed in the world in which the Millerites lived. Throughout the 1830s, Sylvester Graham, inventor of the famous graham cracker, lectured on the benefits of temperance and vegetarianism. Although some Millerites were sympathetic to his cause, the more pressing question of the Second Advent remained uppermost in their minds. Seventh-day Adventists, however, had more time in which to contemplate the correct way to live on this earth. In 1863 Ellen White had a vision that revealed that the health reform movement was correct in its insistence on abstinence from alcohol, tobacco, meat, and rich foods and in its advocacy of natural cures by fresh air and water. Three years later, the church put these ideas into practice with the opening in Michigan of the Western Health Reform Institute, later renamed the Battle Creek Sanitarium. In 1876 a young Adventist doctor, John Harvey Kellogg, was appointed medical director. From that time onward, the development of Adventism's interest in health was largely Kellogg's responsibility. He expanded the sanitarium and hospital, founded a school of nursing, and in 1895 was instrumental in creating the American Medical Missionary College for the education of Adventist physicians. During this period, he also edited the journal the *Health Reformer* (later *Good Health*) and wrote several voluminous books. In the early years of the twentieth century, Kellogg disputed with other church leaders the control of medical institutions and the orientation of the church's message. As a result, Kellogg retained control of the sanitarium but lost his church membership. However, the medical emphasis in Adventism was now well established, and the church opened an alternative center for medical training in Loma Linda. The range of medical and health services provided by the church continued to expand, with the result that by the 1980s Adventist Health Systems had become one of America's leading suppliers of medical care.[48]

The growth of the Adventist interest in health has not gone unobserved. Kellogg himself was an ardent publicist. In 1876 he exhibited health literature at the Centennial Exhibition in Philadelphia; at the Columbian exhibition in Chicago, the sanitarium ran a cooking school; at the St. Louis World Fair of 1904, September 29 was officially proclaimed Battle Creek Sanitarium Day.[49] At the end of his life, Kellogg estimated that his work had brought him into personal contact with a quarter of a million people.[50] Some were famous. The sanitarium was visited by state governors, tycoons such as John D. Rockefeller Jr., Arctic explorer Roald Amundsen, composer Percy Grainger, U.S. Attorney General George Wickersham, and many others. Its 100,000th patient was former President William Howard Taft, and at the institution's jubilee celebrations in 1916, former Secretary of State William Jennings Bryan delivered the major address.[51]

Kellogg was something of a celebrity. The historian Will Durant considered Kellogg's book *The New Dietetics* to be one of the hundred best books ever published. Henry Finck, editor of the New York *Evening Post*, thought Kellogg worthy of a Nobel prize.[52] Kellogg's books sold over a million copies, and his *Plain Facts for Old and Young* was perhaps the most significant sex manual of the late nineteenth century.[53] Phenomenally creative, Kellogg not only invented cornflakes and numerous other health food products but also patented several mechanical devices. In the early 1920s, he produced for the Columbia Gramophone Company what must have been one of the first exercise records.[54]

Although Kellogg left the denomination in 1907, he continued to keep the Sabbath, strongly advocated all Adventist health principles, and often invited church leaders to hold their meetings at Battle Creek. Kellogg's religious interests were not hidden. In 1906 he was featured in a series on "The Spiritual Life of Great Men" by the *New York Magazine of Mysteries*.[55] Kellogg established an alternative frame of reference within which Adventists could be viewed. It was his dream that "the whole Seventh-day Adventist denomination would sometime become . . . the medical missionary people of the world."[56]

Despite his estrangement from the denomination, Kellogg's vision has been realized. In a speech at Loma Linda delivered in 1971, U.S. President Richard Nixon recalled that in 1953

Mrs. Nixon and I took a trip clear around the world. And as we visited the countries of southeast Asia and southern Asia, we saw several hospitals run by various organizations. The most impressive ones were the ones run by the Seventh-Day Adventists, people who were dedicated. There were doctors, there were nurses, there were others who were giving their lives for the purpose of helping those people in those poor countries to develop a better system of medicine. . . . I [can] think of nothing that does more to make friends for America abroad than that kind of selfless service by people like those from Loma Linda who have gone out through the world.[57]

In 1960 the popular writer Booton Herndon celebrated Adventist missionary endeavor in similar terms, noting that "in some countries, particularly the Near and Far East . . . the Adventist hospitals are by far the largest and best."[58] Herndon, however, went further in emphasizing that Adventism had something to offer to America as well as to the Third World.

By almost any criterion of the Western world for human happiness, the . . . members of the Seventh-Day Adventist church . . . must be rated as one of the most fortunate groups on earth. . . . Their children will enjoy better health, and enjoy it longer, than the children of their non-Adventist neighbors, they will be singularly free of such killing diseases as lung cancer, and they will have less than half the amount of tooth decay of their playmates (and their parents will have commensurately lower dental bills to pay!).[59]

In the 1970s and 1980s, this picture of Adventists as an insurance company's dream was further elaborated. For an increasingly body conscious society, Adventism began to sound like an attractive option. Scientific studies, mainly conducted at the denomination's Loma Linda University, began to show that Adventists were relatively unaffected by various forms of disease.[60] In 1984 the *Saturday Evening Post* ran a feature that described Adventists as "the healthiest group of people in the country." It reported that male Seventh-day Adventists aged 35 to 40 had a life expectancy 6.2 years longer than the national average, that female life expectancy was 3.1 years greater, and that the Adventist cancer rate was 50 percent less than that of the general population.[61]

It would be difficult to exaggerate the discrepancies between this picture of Adventism, which is rooted in the achievements of John Harvey Kellogg, and its alternative, which draws on the legacy of William Miller. The discrepancy is not due simply to the differing standpoints of the commentators. One image is not the exclusive preserve of the church's critics, and the other is not confined to sympathizers. The differences are more fundamental. The two pictures represent two independent traditions; they are grounded in different historical events, focused on different aspects of the church's work, sustained by different types of information, and propagated in different sectors of the media. At one extreme, Adventists are seen to be at odds with socially accepted values, obsessed with the end of the world, and pessimistically inclined to self-destructive behavior. At the other extreme, they are perceived to endorse social norms and to be peculiarly successful in attempting to realize life-enhancing goals. The first picture was drawn in the 1840s and is retouched whenever new stories of Adventist eccentricity occur. The second was based on the success of the Battle Creek Sanitarium and is enlarged by reports of Adventist achievements in overseas missions and in the health field. Of the two pictures, the former is the more colorful, appealing to the popular press, creative writers, and the ministers of rival denominations; the latter is prosaic, by comparison, having immediate relevance to foreign travelers and health professionals, with, until recently, a more limited impact on others.

The tension between these two images of Adventism was most clearly seen in the worldwide publicity surrounding the Baby Fae operation. On October 26, 1984, Dr. Leonard Bailey, a Seventh-day Adventist surgeon at Loma Linda University Medical Center, replaced the defective heart of a twelve-day-old baby girl with that of a baboon. It was the first such operation on a human child, and it attracted massive news coverage. At first, the event was interpreted in a manner compatible with the picture of Adventists as leaders in the field of health. The *New York Times* described the operation as "a bold surgical effort that could have a wide impact on the treatment of failing hearts."[62] On November 5, the *Philadelphia Daily News* commented that "as the days go by and Baby Fae's new heart keeps pumping blood through her tiny body, Bailey's accomplishment is losing its unbelievable air and making the names of this obscure researcher and his obscure institution into household words."[63] The *San Bernardino Sun* had already reported that Bailey was described as "visionary," noting his colleagues' belief that "they would not be surprised to see [him] win the Nobel Prize in medicine."[64] And the *Sacramento Bee* suddenly discovered that Loma Linda was "the state's top producer of doctors," remarking on how "the Seventh-day Adventist institution continues to grow as University of California medical schools cut back enrollment."[65]

It was not long, however, before the newspapers began to connect the operation with the alternative picture of Adventists as deviant and socially marginal. Early criticism had focused on animal rights and the question of whether a suitable human heart might have been used. But objections soon emerged that dealt with the more specific issue of the suitability of the surgeon and his institution. On November 6, the *New York Times* argued, in an extended discussion, that "Loma Linda's public account of the course of events leading up to the landmark surgery has been one of confusion and, at times, outright misstatements of fact." The paper observed that "the institution has not been noted as a research leader" and made much of reports that some of Dr. Bailey's earlier work on animal transplants had been denied publication in scientific journals. The article concluded that to some he seemed "a maverick who relished working in a sheltered place like Loma Linda."[66]

Baby Fae died on November 15. On the following day, the *San Francisco Examiner* quoted an expert who considered the operation "a scientifically unjustified leap into the dark."[67] On November 17, the *Washington Post* printed the comments of Dr. Adrian Kantrowitz, the first American to transplant a human heart. Regretting the absence of preliminary publications, he said: "That's a shortcoming. They deprived themselves and their patients of peer review."[68] The *Boston Globe* quoted another expert: "The Loma Linda research was not plugged into the research system in any way. Frankly, Bailey was essentially an unknown quantity. Not many places would have let him do that [baboon transplant]. It would not happen at any first-line center."[69]

Such comments drew implicitly on the tradition that pictured Adventists as being outside the boundaries of society, out of touch with everyday reality. Bailey's apparent failure to obtain scientific or financial backing from outside the Adventist system was interpreted as evidence of his professional marginality. On the other hand, the very fact that Loma Linda attempted the operation with a relative degree of success revealed the unanticipated sophistication of Adventist medicine and gave further weight to the belief that Adventists were in the vanguard of health improvement.

As a single event of worldwide interest, the Baby Fae operation was interpreted within both of the two traditions that have governed the public perception of the church, and it was the discrepancy between these two traditions that, at least in part, sparked the debate that surrounded the case. In general, however, the two streams of images do not flow together, but run separately: the one dark and heavy, carrying visions of the midnight disappointment of the Millerites, the strange beasts of the apocalypse, and the sinister currents of the dingo baby case; the other reflecting images of light: Dr. Kellogg dressed entirely in white, the cleanliness of hospital wards, the bright sun overhead at the mission.

The public is too dimly aware of Adventism to be perplexed by this apparent discontinuity. Most people are likely to have only occasional contact with the church, and for them there is no need to form a coherent picture. But for Adventists seeking to appreciate their own heritage and for non-Adventists who wish to understand the character of Adventism, the tasks of drawing these diverse strands together has proved perplexing. Several approaches have been tried. The simplest is to deny outright the validity of one of the two traditions. This is the position adopted by both the critics and the apologists of the church. The critics focus on the apocalyptic tradition, perceiving Adventists as deluded fanatics who persistently resort to dishonesty to cover their past mistakes.[70] For the apologists, however, Adventists have always been rational people, behaving in a socially acceptable fashion and out-doing their fellow men in health, vitality, and generosity.[71]

More sophisticated commentators usually perceive that historical change accounts for the discrepancy between the two traditional images of Adventism. In the nineteenth century, it is argued, Adventists took more radical positions that, with the passage of time, have been mod-ified to bring Adventist doctrine into alignment with the beliefs of other Christians. This line of reasoning informs the work of Le Roy Edwin Froom, Adventism's greatest apologetic historian, and the non-Adventist evangelicals, Walter Martin and Donald Barnhouse, who in the late 1950s took it on themselves to welcome Adventism into the evangelical fold.[72]

Non-Adventist sociologists who examine Adventism in a social, rather than a religious, context note a similar development. Gary Schwartz suggests that becoming a medical missionary was the goal of an Ad-ventist work ethic that promoted upward social mobility among church members.[73] Robin Theobald, a British sociologist, suggests that Adven-tism's increasing concentration on health and welfare work was prompted by the need to modernize and adapt to urban environ-ments.[74] For Bryan Wilson, the Oxford sociologist who studied Adven-tism in the mid 1970s, the process of change is seen as denomination-alization, the move from a hostile and sectarian response to the world to an accommodating position akin to that of more established churches.[75]

All of these interpretations are illuminating in that they highlight the process of change and reveal the range of views and experience that Adventism has encompassed. But insofar as they are attempts to yoke together the seemingly divergent traditions of apocalypticism and health reform, these interpretations are distinctly incomplete. The pub-lic images of Adventism do not reflect the whole picture. The two tra-ditions are only partially representative. Not only is Adventism a little-known group, but the historical figures most closely associated with it were not even lifelong church members. Miller was never a Seventh-day Adventist; Kellogg ceased to be one thirty-six years before his death. The central figure in Adventism has remained largely out of public view. Ellen White, Adventism's prophetess and founder in all but in name, is the crucial missing link between Miller and Kellogg. She was a devoted follower of the former and the spiritual guide of the latter. Her life and thought shaped the characteristic features of Adventism. To understand how and why Adventism has impinged on the public consciousness, a detailed analysis of Adventist theology and

Ellen White's writings is necessary. Tracing the public traditions about Adventism to their sources does not uncover the heart of the church's message. A more direct approach is essential. To understand how the public thinks about Adventists, it is vital to grasp the way in which Adventists conceive of themselves and the world in which they live.

Part 1

ADVENTIST THEOLOGY

CHAPTER 2

Authority

Born in 1827, the daughter of a hatter from Gorham, Maine, Ellen Harmon had an uneventful childhood, until, at the age of nine, she was accidentally hit on the head by a stone, and her injuries prevented further formal education. In 1843 she and her family were disfellowshipped from the Methodist Church because of their Millerite associations. Her first vision occurred two months after the Great Disappointment of October 22, 1844. She was to continue to have visions until 1878, although the frequency declined markedly in the 1860s and she probably did not have more than about two hundred altogether. She married James White in 1846. Together they worked for the Seventh-day Adventist denomination until James's death in 1881. After this, Willie, one of Ellen's two surviving sons, became her closest confidant. Having spent most of her life in the northeastern United States, she visited Europe from 1885 to 1887 and spent the years between 1891 and 1900 in Australia. Throughout her long career, Ellen White wrote and spoke for Adventist audiences, who received her in the belief that she was the "spirit of prophecy" identified in Revelation (19:10).

Even those who accept religious experiences as genuine rarely accept them as authoritative. To understand how Mrs. White became an authority within the church, it is worth looking more closely at her religious development and the intellectual context in which she operated.[1]

As a teenager, Ellen White's religious experience started to follow a pattern similar to that of many previous mystics. In 1842 she went through a "dark night of the soul" occasioned by her inability to pray in public: "I remained for three weeks with not one ray of light to pierce the thick clouds of darkness around me. I then had two dreams which gave me a faint ray of light and hope."[2] In one of these, she ascended a stairway. At the top she was brought to Jesus. Like other female mystics, she was so impressed with his beauty that she knew she could not be mistaken. But, like St. Teresa, she still had to be reassured before being able to experience the full joy of his presence.[3] Shortly after this dream, Ellen White managed to overcome her fear of public prayer. During her prayer, she experienced an overwhelming sense of love for Jesus: "Wave after wave of glory rolled over me, until my body grew stiff." Just as St. Teresa had written of her transverberation that her soul could not "be content with anything less than God," so Mrs. White wrote, "I could not be satisfied till I was filled with the fullness of God."[4] This intense desire for experience of the divine presence is an aspect of Mrs. White's experience that is often overlooked. Her exceptional religious propensities originated not from a search for doctrinal or ethical information but from a simple desire to feel the love of Jesus.

The physical manifestations that accompanied this and similar experiences were fundamental to her acceptance as God's messenger within the emergent Seventh-day Adventist denomination. When in a trancelike state, she appeared not to breathe and seemed, because of the cessation of normal bodily functions, to be "lost to the world." This phenomenon was very important to her contemporaries, who made a concerted effort to establish her indifference to earthly things. They covered her nose and mouth, held a mirror up to her face, pinched her, felt her chest, pretended to hit her, and shone bright lights in her eyes, all in an effort to see if she would breathe, flinch, or blink. To perceive these actions as indignities is to miss a fundamental point. Mrs. White was not being tormented, but tested.[5]

The attempt to establish that Ellen White was lost to this world was based on the implicit understanding that if she were, she would be more open to the spiritual world.[6] In her first vision, she had experienced heaven so directly that afterward she wept and felt homesick for the better land she had seen.[7] This ability to see the heavenly world was vital to the early Adventists who, after the Great Disappointment, had begun to doubt that what was visible on earth revealed eternal truth. Thus, through her vision of heaven, Ellen White could inform the faithful what ought to be believed on earth. The most literal example of how this worked was Mrs. White's vision of the Ten Commandments in the most Holy Place, the heavenly sanctuary. Reading them, she observed that God had not changed the wording of the fourth commandment in favor of the first day of the week. Therefore, she concluded that God required the observance of the seventh-day Sabbath on earth.[8]

It was some time before the "Testimonies," as her writings became known, led rather than followed the group to which they were addressed. For the first ten years, she confirmed belief rather than admonished believers. Indeed, the quantity of her output was regulated by the attitude of the community. As she herself noted in 1855, "The reasons why visions had not been more frequent of late, is, they have not been appreciated by the church."[9] In practice, the extent to which the visions could be appreciated by the church was dependent on the frequency of their publication. As the Adventist denomination expanded, its chief means of communication became the press. Mrs. White's religious experience, once validated to the scientific satisfaction of her peers, became the raw material on which a publishing industry was based. The financial and technological development of Adventist publishing may not have influenced Mrs. White's experience, but it certainly determined the extent and form in which that experience could be communicated.

The nineteenth century witnessed a revolution in American publishing, and the Adventist press followed the general trend.[10] As technology improved, it became easier to produce longer books. This advance also necessitated a constant flow of copy, an example of which can be seen in the books dealing with the "great controversy" theme—Mrs. White's classic exposition of the ongoing battle between good and evil. The central idea of the great controversy is a cosmic struggle between Christ and Satan, which the prophetess traced from its origins in heaven to its final resolution at the close of the millennium. The great controversy theme first appeared in the first volume of *Spiritual Gifts* in 1858. Material from the *Spiritual Gifts* series was expanded to form the four-volume *Spirit of Prophecy* series in 1870–84. Between 1888 and 1917, this series was transformed into the *Conflict of the Ages* series that comprised five books: *Patriarchs and Prophets* and *Prophets and Kings* (accounts of Old Testament history), *Desire of Ages* (a biography of Christ), *Acts of the Apostles* (an account of early Christianity), and the *Great Controversy* (which related the battle between Christ and Satan from the destruction of Jerusalem in AD 70 to the millennium at the end of time). In the course of this process, the content and style of the books underwent significant changes.[11]

Some idea of the stylistic changes may be gained by comparing the account of the fall of man given in volume one of *Spiritual Gifts* (1858) with the accounts found in volume one of the *Spirit of Prophecy* (1870) and in volume one of the *Conflict of the Ages* series, *Patriarchs and Prophets* (1890).

Mrs. White's writing in 1858 reveals both the deficiencies in her education and the intensity of her experience. The narrative style is simple but compelling. The account is given in the past tense, not so much because the events described happened in the past as because the visions were in the past. By 1870 Mrs. White had acquired many of the techniques of contemporary religious novelists.[12] Making much use of the vivid present, she emphasizes narrative detail and the emotional state of the characters involved. The short sentences found in *Spiritual Gifts* are filled out by abundant adjectives and adverbs and expanded by additional clauses. Thus the angels that in 1858 "gave instruction to Adam and Eve" in 1870 "graciously and lovingly gave them the information they desired."[13] While in 1858 Eve simply "offered the fruit to her husband," in 1870 "she was in a strange and unnatural excitement as she sought her husband, with her hands filled with the forbidden fruit."[14]

In 1890 a much more sophisticated writer appears, concerned not with narrative details but with moral exhortation. The vivid present is replaced by past or future tenses, depending on when the events described took place. The simple connectives used in 1870 give way to dependent clauses of time and purpose. Abstract nouns make an increasing appearance, along with the passive voice and impersonal constructions. So the vivid statement that "Satan assumes the form of a serpent and enters Eden" gives way to the observation that "in order to accomplish his work unperceived, Satan chose to employ as his medium the serpent—a disguise well adapted for his purpose of deception."[15] Mrs. White also cuts back on the superfluous use of adverbs in favor of a richer vocabulary. So the serpent that in 1870 "commenced leisurely eating" is in 1890 "regaling itself" with the same fruit.[16]

While there is no doubt that these developments indicate an increase in the literacy of both Mrs. White and the assistants who aided in the preparation of manuscripts, it would be quite wrong to assume a commensurate improvement in literary quality. On the contrary, Ellen White's earliest work shows an intuitive awareness of the dramatic potential of narrative that is obscured by the sentimental and moralizing tone of her later books. This diminution in the power of her language is, however, partly explained by the fact that her books decreasingly represented her unique experience. As the demands on her time increased, she relied on her assistants to do research and prepare copy. Further, the outlines of her narratives were frequently supplemented by material drawn from other writers. This is particularly true of the *Conflict of the Ages* series. *Patriarchs and Prophets* and *Prophets and Kings* owe something to Daniel March's *Night Scenes of the Bible* and to books by Alfred Edersheim. The *Desire of Ages* owes much to both of these authors and to William Hanna's *Life of Christ*. The *Acts of the Apostles* takes much from a book by William Conybeare and John Howson, *The Life and Epistles of the Apostle Paul*, as well as drawing material from two of Mrs. White's favorite authors, John Harris and Daniel March. The *Great Controversy* contains substantial sections from the historians J. A. Wylie and Merle D'Aubigné.[17]

In the mid-nineteenth century, "new publishers encouraged high productivity in their authors," as they felt that "to keep up demand, the public must be constantly reminded that a particular writer existed."[18] Adventist publishing was no exception, and Mrs. White's increasing use of sources enabled the press to engage in the almost continuous publication of "new" material. This, in turn, enabled the church to disseminate her somewhat diluted influence more widely. Thus, the authority accorded to Mrs. White by the small circle familiar with her visions expanded to encompass a much wider audience. Since many of these people had no contact with Mrs. White as an individual, her writings were the focus of their recognition of her as God's messenger.

By acknowledging Mrs. White's statements as divinely inspired, the church thereby understood God as having two authorized channels of revelation: the Bible and the Testimonies. The human intellect was not considered a reliable source of knowledge. Mrs. White herself confirmed this view, arguing that "to man's unaided reason, nature's teaching cannot but be contradictory and disappointing. Only in the light of revelation can it be read aright."[19] In taking this position, Adventists distanced themselves from the Millerites, who had placed great faith in "unaided reason" and placed "no reliance whatever upon any visions or dreams, mere impressions, or private revelations."[20]

It was, after all, William Miller's sense of obligation to the requirements of rationality that prompted his study of the Bible. He had had an emotional conversion in which he had said he felt the loveliness of a Savior. "But the question arose How can it be proved that such a being does exist?" Considering that "to believe in such a Savior without evidence would be visionary in the extreme," he turned to the Bible as the only source of information. Miller reasoned that since the Bible "must have been given for man's instruction," it "must be adapted to his understanding." And he resolved to remain a deist if he could not harmonize all the apparent contradictions.[21]

This deference to reason was not just the legacy of the Enlightenment skeptics Miller had read twelve years previously. It is better understood in the context of the Common-Sense philosophy that was becoming popular in nineteenth-century New England. The Scottish philosophy, as it was also known, was a form of realism, and its reliance on individual common sense appealed to American Protestants as a bulwark against doubt. Although the philosophy derived from the work of Thomas Reid, the seventeenth-century philosopher Francis Bacon was seen as the founder of the school. The Scottish philosophy denied that anything intervenes between the mind and its apprehension of external facts. If the systematic study of these facts was undertaken by a mind unprejudiced by theory, it was believed that knowledge of a limited certainty would be obtained. In a religious context, Baconianism became identified with the Reformation principle of *sola scriptura*, and it was later influential in the dispensationalist school of prophetic interpretation that divided past and future biblical events into distinct eras.[22]

Baconianism was not alien to the Millerite world. The Disciples of Christ, who founded Bacon College in 1836, disseminated a popularized version of the philosophy for every level of society. Their leader, Alexander Campbell, considering that "skepticism was founded upon 'Assumption' and Christian faith upon 'Experience,'" appealed to Bacon as having laid "the foundation of correct reasonings."[23] Campbell, who took a close interest in the 1,260- and 2,300-day prophecies in the book of Daniel, had been introduced to Boston audiences by Miller's publisher Joshua Himes and was one of the Millerites' most sympathetic critics.[24]

Whether or not Miller had any direct contact with advocates of the Scottish philosophy, it is known that he had spent time reading in the library of the Scotsman Alexander Cruikshanks.[25] Whatever the source, Miller echoed Bacon's injunction "to proceed regularly and gradually from one axiom to another" when, as he recalled, "I determined to lay aside all my prepossessions, to thoroughly compare Scripture with Scripture, and to pursue its study in a regular and methodical manner."[26] The result of this endeavor was Miller's conclusion that the Second Advent would occur around 1843. Making his motto "Prove all things; hold fast to that which is good," Miller accumulated scriptural and historical facts to support his conclusion. Like the contemporary revivalist Charles Finney, Miller spoke as if to a jury, gradually building up the evidence for his case.[27] This approach appealed to exponents of the Common-Sense philosophy. As Alexander Campbell noted, Miller benefited from his critics' unBaconian arguments, which far transcended "the oracles of reason and the canons of common sense."[28]

Despite Miller's careful methods, he was disappointed in both 1843 and 1844. For Miller, there was nothing to do but add this rather disconcerting fact to all the others and to reassess his conclusions. The Baconian doctrine of "restraint," which asserted that no belief should transcend observable facts, was not followed by all in the Millerite movement. Some in the radical wing could not tolerate the prospect of revising their calculations. For them, it proved easier to renounce Miller's methodology than to abandon the specific date for which they had suffered. The Great Disappointment was a watershed in the thinking of this group. October 22, 1844, was to have been the ultimate conclusion to which all the carefully assembled facts of scripture and history pointed; it became an unassailable premiss to which all future knowledge must conform.[29]

The first conclusion of the radicals was that since no extraordinary phenomena had been observed on October 22, observation was not the best way to monitor such events. Reassurance came in the form of direct, and often ecstatic, religious experience. When these groups, which included the future founders of the Seventh-day Adventist Church, held meetings, they fell on the floor, groaned, shouted, and sang. It was in this atmosphere that Ellen White rose to prominence.[30] Her ability to receive direct communications from God was of particular value because the Great Disappointment had shown more established channels—such as human reason—to be flawed.

Yet the acceptance of Mrs. White's visions was also facilitated by two aspects of the Common-Sense philosophy that underlay the early Adventist view of the world. First, the realist theory of perception emphasized that the apprehension of objects was direct and not influenced by mental constructs. So it was quite possible to believe that Ellen White literally saw what was written on the Ten Commandments. Second, it was presumed that language was perspicuous, that it was the servant rather than the master of thought, and that words corresponded directly to objects. Language could be trusted. (When Mrs. White had a vision of heathens and Christians gathered under their respective banners, the Christian banner bore words; the banner of the heathens, symbols.) Accordingly, when Mrs. White related her visions, it was assumed that what she had seen determined the words she used. Her accounts were as authoritative as what she had experienced.[31]

Thus the process by which the mystical proclivities of a teenage girl were recognized as the revelations of an authoritative prophet was aided at every step by the underlying philosophical assumptions of the Adventist community. Unlike the Mormon prophet Joseph Smith, Ellen White did not proclaim her revelation and gather a following; rather, she had a particular kind of religious experience that came to be accepted as authoritative within an existing group. The prophetic ministry of Ellen White was an aspect of Adventist social experience, not just the psychological experience of a single individual.

Throughout the process in which Miller's original emphasis on the priority of reason was overturned, the one constant was the Bible. From 1844 onward, Adventist publications are replete with statements to the effect that the Bible is God's word and is the only rule of faith and practice. Similarly, the priority of the Bible over any other revelation was reiterated in church publications on countless occasions. The statement made by the church president George Butler in 1883 was typically categorical:

The Scriptures are our rule to test everything by, the visions as well as all other things. That rule, therefore, is of the highest authority; the standard is higher than the thing tested by it. If the Bible should show the visions were not in harmony with it, the Bible would stand and the visions would be given up.[32]

It would be difficult to find an official statement from any period that contradicted this one. However, the history of any denomination is not simply that of its creeds. The statements about any one source of authority are only informative in the context of contemporary statements about other potential sources. The undeviating official line on the Bible may thus disguise some underlying shifts in the balance of authority.

For Miller, the Bible had been completely perspicuous to reason. It was "a system of revealed truths so clearly and simply given that the 'wayfaring man, though a fool, need not err therein.' "[33] For the Adventist pioneers, Biblical interpretation proved a great deal more problematic. As Mrs. White recalled, "Again and again these brethren came together to study the Bible, in order that they might know its meaning, and be prepared to teach it with power."[34] Although they sometimes spent the entire night searching the scriptures, there were in 1848 "hardly two agreed. Each was strenuous for his views, declaring that they were according to the Bible." Understandably, these frustrated students came to the point where they said, "We can do nothing more."[35]

Ellen White, meanwhile, found all these discussions somewhat above her head. "During this whole time I could not understand the reasoning of the brethren. My mind was locked, as it were, and I could not comprehend the meaning of the scriptures we were studying."[36] Fortunately for her and the Adventist community, aid came from another source. She would be taken off in vision and given clear explanation of the passages under consideration. Her accompanying angel would indicate who was right and who was wrong, explaining "that these discordant views, which they claimed to be according to the Bible, were only according to their opinion of the Bible, and that their errors must be yielded."[37]

William Miller, for whom the Bible was "a feast of reason," would have found this conflict unwarranted and its supernatural resolution distasteful. Among the early Adventists, however, such guidance was obviously a practical necessity. Without it, the fledgling church would have been stranded in the disintegrating nest of Millerism. In later years, things appeared rather differently. The reason given in 1871 for the existence of the Testimonies was the neglect of the Bible rather than the inability of its students to agree on the correct interpretation.[38] But the principle remained the same. When the church needed doctrinal or practical guidance, it could, during her lifetime, turn to Mrs. White for advice specifically related to the question at issue. The Bible contained truths of eternal validity, but it was not always clear how they applied in a particular case. The Bible might set the agenda for discussion, but Mrs. White usually had the last word. The reason for this was not that the Bible was deemed incomprehensible but that Adventists, as a group, were unable to reach complete agreement on its meaning.

In practice, however, the significance of this distinction proved difficult to convey to the church's membership. As the church president A. G. Daniells remembered, it was not long before some preached that "the only way we could understand the Bible was through the writings of the spirit of prophecy." Daniells denounced this view as "heathenish," although the president would not have been far from the truth if he had replaced his "could" with a "did."[39] By the time of her death in 1915, Ellen White functioned as the acknowledged interpreter of scripture for the Adventist church. She might not be considered as infallible, but most Adventists preferred to suspend judgment rather than admit her error on any specific point. The relative methodological importance of reason, the Bible, and visionary authority was now the reverse of what it had been for the Millerites. Reason had once tested and expounded the Bible and discounted individual revelation; it was now considered unfit to test or expound either scripture or the spirit of prophecy. The authority of Mrs. White's visions, however, could define the meaning of the Bible and the status of reason. Certainly, the Bible was supposed to test the prophet, but if it could not be understood without the prophet, such an investigation would be hard to initiate. Thus, although Mrs. White was never accorded theological primacy, her methodological priority made her position inviolable. The church's social boundaries reflected this position. As W. W. Prescott remarked, "if a man does not believe in the verbal inspiration of the Bible, he is still in good standing; but if he says he does not believe in the verbal inspiration of the Testimonies, he is discounted right away."[40]

For a century, the Bible had seemed securely fixed at the center of the seesaw of reason and prophecy. In the 1920s, events in the wider world threatened to dislodge the scriptures from the pivotal position they had enjoyed in the world view of most nineteenth-century Protestants. The higher critical approach to the Bible had influenced academic circles in the previous century, but during World War I, the modernists became more vocal. In particular, they resented the upsurge of premillennialist thought occasioned by the war and attacked the millenarian fundamentalists for lacking both patriotism and theological sophistication. While Adventists were not directly accused, their views were similar to the ideas of those who were. Understandably, when the fundamentalists counterattacked in the early 1920s, the Adventist response was very similar.[41]

The broad-minded A. G. Daniells was replaced as church president in 1922. Under his successor, W. A. Spicer, the church, which had been divided on such questions as the verbal inspiration of the Bible, aligned itself firmly with the fundamentalist cause. In 1924 William G. Wirth, an Adventist Bible teacher, published *The Battle of the Churches: Modernism or Fundamentalism*, a book designed to "help the reader, if he be inclined to favor Modernism, to see the weakness of its claims."[42] The same year, the popular Adventist writer Carlyle B. Haynes, echoed the conservative Baptist E. Y. Mullins in the title of his pamphlet *Christianity at the Crossroads*. Its cover depicted a man faced with signs labeled "fundamentalism" and "modernism" pointing in opposite directions. The tone of the book left little doubt as to which route was considered preferable.[43] This peripheral involvement in the fundamentalist-modernist controversy had far-reaching consequences. Although the question of Mrs. White's authority was not involved, the defense of the Bible resulted in greater insistence on its inspiration and inerrancy. Along-side this concentration on the Bible came a revival in the rhetoric of Baconianism. It was once again emphasized that the Bible was a col-lection of readily comprehensible facts. Similarly, it was argued that unless confused by the hypotheses of the liberals and evolutionists, the evidence of nature was clear. It was, as the Adventist creationist George McCready Price had written in 1913, because "the current geology has never used a trace of sound Baconian science" that it had been fallen into evolutionary thinking.[44]

But the Baconianism of the 1920s differed from that popular a cen-tury earlier. In the 1820s Baconianism had been directed against the skeptics who felt they could know nothing. In the 1920s it was directed against the scientist who claimed to know too much.[45] The basic thrust of the new Baconianism was antiintellectual. It was to an audience of Seventh-day Adventists in 1924 that William Jennings Bryan, the an-tievolution crusader, proclaimed: "All the ills from which America suf-fers can be traced back to the teaching of evolution. It would be better to destroy every other book ever written, and save just the first three verses of Genesis."[46]

From the 1920s to the 1950s, the attitude toward authority found within Adventism was more or less static. The Bible and Mrs. White existed in symbiosis. Mrs. White's writings clarified and elaborated the scriptures; the scriptures confirmed and clarified her prophetic role. In keeping with this understanding, F. D. Nichol, the editor of the *Seventh-day Adventist Bible Commentary*, made it a policy that no inter-pretation given in the *Commentary* should appear to conflict with a state-ment by Ellen White.[47] Although some Adventists would have been wary of affirming verbal inspiration in either case, the universal use of the proof-text method, in which isolated passages from both sources were used to prove specific doctrines, indicated that, in practice, verbal inspiration was assumed. With such a wealth of material from which to draw, there was hardly a single human experience on which some sentence from the Bible or Mrs. White did not have bearing. The need to use human reason, thus, rarely arose.

The stability afforded by this structure of authority obviated the ne-cessity of engaging in any major doctrinal discussions between 1919 and the next Bible Conference in 1952. Ironically, it was the alignment with fundamentalism that prompted a reassessment of the situation. Adventists might be pleased to carry the fundamentalist banner, but few fundamentalists were enthusiastic about having Adventists shelter under it. The embarrassment of this situation was acutely felt by men like Le Roy Edwin Froom, who represented the church in the scholarly world. An opportunity to remedy the situation presented itself in the mid 1950s in the form of Walter Martin and Donald Barnhouse, two evangelicals who approached the denomination hoping to establish whether it was a Christian church or a heretical cult. In discussions with Barnhouse and Martin, a select group of Adventist scholars forcefully repudiated the accusation that Mrs. White was put on the same level as the Bible.[48] This was not a new position, but its implications were not unanimously welcomed within the church.[49]

In the 1960s the church's prolonged theological dispute with Robert Brinsmead, the leader of a dissident Adventist movement in Australia, started to reveal the difficulties of using the proof-text method with the statements of Mrs. White. Each side was able to produce quotations that appeared to support their conclusions concerning the doctrine of salvation.[50] It was obvious that an appeal to Mrs. White was not a sure way to resolve doctrinal conflict. The situation was analogous to that of the 1840s, except that on this occasion, the disputants were searching the Testimonies rather than the Bible. While in 1848 the supernatural authority of visions had settled discussion, in the 1960s there seemed to be no court of appeal. It was clear that the Bible and the Testimonies were by themselves incapable of producing answers that would satisfy more than one section of the church.

It was in this climate that two Adventist academics, Roy Branson and Harold Weiss, published an appeal to make Ellen White "a subject for Adventist scholarship." The motivation for this plea was to find a means of solving the confusion generated by the indiscriminate use of the proof-text method and to "recapture Ellen White's original intentions and the absolute truth of what she meant."[51] So now reason, shaped by the tools of historical scholarship, was called to clarify Mrs. White's pronouncements just as she had once clarified the Bible.

As it turned out, the only thing that was clarified was the difficulty of using Ellen White as an authority at all. The research of the 1970s did little to establish what she meant. Rather, it demonstrated that not everything she had written was of her own invention, let alone of God's direct revelation. It was evident that she changed her mind on various questions and that she held a number of beliefs about history and science with which no contemporary scholar would agree.[52] Reason was allowed to judge the Testimonies on questions of history, but the Bible was still the only rule for judging Mrs. White's theology. In the early 1980s the work of the Adventist professor Desmond Ford on the significance of the Great Disappointment of October 22, 1844, was to reveal the potential for conflicts in this area as well.[53] In 1985 Harold Weiss looked back on the fifteen years of Ellen White scholarship and concluded: "Mrs. White's formal authority—the readiness of her readers, that is, to accept what she said as true just because a prophet said it—has in fact been shattered. From now on no one should be able to end a theological dialogue by giving a quotation from Mrs. White."[54]

It is wrong to assume that Weiss's conclusion will necessarily be accepted by succeeding generations. Scholars, like prophets, live and think within a particular historical framework. When the framework changes, the most acrimonious of academic pursuits can appear trifling and irrelevant. Plagiarism, for example, is only an issue within the context of a romantic theory of authorship, which emphasizes the creativity of a single individual. Other literary theories, such as new criticism and structuralism, are interested only in the text itself, not the person who produced it.[55]

The history of modern biblical scholarship provides a good example of how academic fashions can change. Nineteenth-century critics doubted the Bible's historical accuracy to a degree greater than twentieth-century archaeological discoveries warranted, and their more speculative hypotheses were adjusted accordingly. This development was watched closely by Seventh-day Adventists, who had heeded F. D. Nichol's call of 1936 to "establish more fully the truth of the Bible."[56] Following the lead of the archaeologist W. F. Albright, Adventists looked to recent discoveries to buttress the Bible. *The Spade Confirms the Book* was the title of a book by Adventism's first professional archaeologist Siegfried Horn.[57] Horn later led an Adventist excavation of the presumed site of Biblical Heshbon, hoping to confirm that the city was captured during the Exodus. The previously unbridled enthusiasm for archaeology was tempered by the failure to find the anticipated evidence, but Adventists continued to affirm archaeology's positive contribution to Biblical study.[58]

The far-reaching implications of higher criticism have, however, always been anathema. Specific doctrines have anchored Adventist scholars to a conservative position: the Sabbath demands the historicity of the Pentateuch; prophetic interpretation requires a sixth- (rather than the customary second-) century date for the book of Daniel. Similarly, the traditional reliance on proof texts has led Adventists to be wary of any doctrine of inspiration, which suggests that the Bible is not a compendium of revealed propositions but simply an expression of its authors' encounters with God.[59] Thus in Old Testament studies, Adventist scholars have concerned themselves with archaeology and chronology, and in the New Testament, they have concentrated on linguistic and textual criticism.[60] In neither area has it been possible for them to do substantial literary or theological work, as their conservative presuppositions are not shared by most of the academic world.

Some Adventist scholars clearly affirm that God's word should not be questioned. Gerhard Hasel argues that "man's understanding of himself and the world around him is dependent upon God and revelation that comes from Him."[61] This means that with regard to the boundaries of the Biblical canon, man should accept that "God's providence provided the origin of the sixty-six biblical books and their selection and presentation over a long period of time. Hence, the number of OT and NT books is what it is; no more and no less."[62] To other

Adventist scholars, there might seem to be a short circuit in this reasoning. For Harold Weiss, "to equate God's word with a book is the
work of a corrupted faith which sets up for itself an idol."[63] Few church
members would endorse Weiss's opinion, but Adventists have publicly
dissociated themselves from fundamentalism. As early as 1966, the *Seventh-day Adventist Encyclopedia* complained that "fundamentalists have
ignored or rejected valid findings of Biblical scholarship."[64]

The idea of "limited inerrancy" has been suggested as a way of avoiding vulnerable dogmatism while retaining a truly biblical faith.[65] Limited inerrancy could prove an elastic concept. What is to determine the
limits, if not the judgment, of contemporary scholarship? The employment of this concept suggests that reason has taken the place of
Mrs. White as the source that clarifies the meaning of the scriptures.
The yoking together of the Bible and scholarship may make a more
wayward team than the Bible and the Testimonies. The spirit of prophecy was once seen as a buffer between the Bible and the corrosive
effects of higher criticism.[66] Now that Adventist scholars have sharp-
ened their critical tools on Mrs. White, their application of these tools
to the Bible might have radical consequences. Mrs. White clearly envisaged such a sequence of events: "It is Satan's plan to weaken the
faith of God's people in the Testimonies. Next follows skepticism in
regard to the vital points of our faith, the pillars of our position, then
doubts as to the Holy Scriptures, and then the downward march to
perdition."[67]

It certainly appears that the structure of authority within Adventism
has, from the time of Miller to the 1980s, come full circle. For Miller,
reason came first; it expounded the Bible, and visions were disregarded. The Great Disappointment inverted this order; visions expounded the Bible, and reason was disregarded. The spread of Mrs.
White's published work then allowed this order to stabilize, with the
Testimonies clarifying the scriptures. The modernist challenge to the
Bible aligned Adventism with fundamentalism, further downgraded
the intellect, and made the Bible and the Testimonies mutually ex-
planatory. The Adventist encounter with fundamentalism, both outside
and inside the denomination, created embarrassment and frustration
about the way the Testimonies were used. In the 1970s an open season
on Ellen White research made reason and the Bible her two judges. In
the 1980s this restructuring was contested by some, while others prepared to give scholarship license to test the Bible itself.

These developments were all prompted by specific historical events,
but it is possible to observe several patterns. A restructuring of authority usually takes place when existing sources of authority fail to
generate clear-cut answers, as was the case in the 1840s and 1960s. The
rise of an alternative source of authority is usually facilitated by appeal
to the one that is being disregarded. Thus, the early Adventists sub-

jected Mrs. White to empirical investigation, and contemporary scholars quote Mrs. White's statement on the need for "new light" in the church.[68] This dependence of new authorities on the old builds instability into the system. If one source fails to provide the answers, it can always be undermined by the source that gave it authority in the first place.

What these patterns reveal is not only the capacity of external events to promote changes in authority structure but also the extent to which Adventist ideology is a clearly defined system with its own distinct sources that have a limited number of ways to recombine. In the 1980s the primacy of any source of authority would seem to point in directions unattractive to many Adventists: reason to liberalism; the Bible to fundamentalism; Mrs. White to sectarianism. In order to control the balance between these existing elements, new sources may intervene, for if the church is to maintain its sense of identity, its sources of authority must be clearly defined.

CHAPTER 3

Identity

William Miller had no desire to found a church; he hoped that his message would be received by members of all denominations. Millerite publications were circulated widely, but Millerite lecturers were drawn predominantly from Methodist or Baptist backgrounds.[1] Although Miller's teaching focused on a single theme that transcended sectarian differences, it was inevitable that those who believed the Second Advent to be only a few years distant felt more solidarity with fellow Millerites than with their coreligionists. Some Millerites freed themselves of their previous affiliations; others, like the Harmon family, were expelled from the churches they were attending.[2] A gulf emerged between the Millerites and the Protestant denominations from which they were drawn.

In 1843 the Millerite leader Charles Fitch published a sermon "Come Out of Her, My People" in which he concluded that "[Babylon] is everything that rises in opposition to the personal reign of Christ on David's throne, and to the revealed time for his appearing: and here we do find the professed Christian world, Catholic and Protestant, on the side of Antichrist."[3] This application of the concept of Babylon—traditionally used by Protestants for the Roman Catholic Church—to non-Millerite Protestantism was a dramatic step. It was a move inspired by the experience of rejection. As Fitch commented: "Speak to them about the coming of Christ . . . and they show themselves sufficiently disgusted to spit on your face. Ask them to read anything on the subject and they put on every possible expression of scorn."[4] Those who believed Miller's predictions should, Fitch argued, separate themselves from other religious groups: "Just remember then what must be the consequence of refusing to receive the truth and abide by it. Babylon must be destroyed and you with it."[5] His final appeal was direct: "Come out of Babylon or perish."[6]

This belief in the imminent Second Advent was enough to distinguish the Millerites from other religious movements of the time. The Millerites were derided, and they in turn consigned their opponents to eternal destruction. After the Great Disappointment, the dividing line was blurred. It had been expected that saints and sinners would be forever parted on October 22, 1844. But no visible division had taken place. Where now was the promised destruction of Babylon? The Great Disappointment not only appeared to undermine Millerite theology, it also threatened the identity of the movement itself.[7] The initial reaction was to reassert that the world had been irrevocably but invisibly divided on October 22. It was argued that the door of mercy had been shut and that only faithful Millerites could wait for the delayed Second Advent with any hope. As Miller himself wrote on the eighteenth of November: "We have done our work in warning sinners, and in trying to awake a formal church. God in his providence had shut the door; we can only stir one another to be *patient*; and be diligent to make our calling and election sure."[8] Some leading Millerites, notably Joshua Himes, rejected the Shut Door and soon persuaded Miller to renounce the idea as well. But among the radicals, the idea persisted. Their basic idea was summarized thus: "A wicked world, and a corrupt apostate, world-loving church, no longer shares our sympathies, our labors or our prayers. Their doom is sealed and it is just."[9]

The criterion by which the Adventist movement identified itself was thus reinterpreted. Before the Great Disappointment, the movement was united by a common belief. After October 22, the shared experience of the Disappointment became a further identifying characteristic. A movement that first defined itself with reference to the future began to perceive itself also in terms of the past. But what of the present? How could those who believed in the Shut Door distinguish themselves from their fellow Millerites who did not? Both groups had passed through the Great Disappointment; history did not separate them. It was to differentiate themselves that many who believed in the Shut Door sought some hitherto neglected commandment that could be observed as a token of complete loyalty to the divine will.[10]

One of the commandments that the Shut-Door believers reinstituted was Jesus' directive that his disciples should wash one another's feet. As one correspondent wrote to the *Day Star*, the journal of the radical Millerites: "This, I believe, is the last test for the little children, but every *little* child can stand it."[11] Associated with the foot washing was the practice of the holy salutation: sacramental kissing. Neither practice was undertaken lightly. As another correspondent, Benjamin Spaulding, reported in an early Adventist paper the *Hope of Israel*: "Washing the *Saints'* feet and the 'holy' salutation are also being observed. Some at first rather shrank away from these Bible duties; but after investigating the matter with mature deliberation, they cannot say they are not binding."[12] These practices, in which both men and women engaged, provoked criticism. As Himes's paper, the *Morning Watch*, commented: "It is a singular and mournful fact that fanaticism inevitably runs into acts that are in the first stage, *doubtful*, and in the next, *licentious*."[13] But those who practiced foot washing and kissing were not easily deterred: "We FEEL the reproach, we know the shame, and have counted the cost, but still we dare not disobey what we believe to be the will and purpose of God in us, as we follow the Lamb whithersoever he goeth."[14]

The other major test on which some Adventists focused was the keeping of the seventh-day Sabbath. This practice was also seen as a means of distinguishing the saints. One correspondent of the *Day Star* described how he saw the purpose of these tests: "The *spirit of Elijah* has been sifting, fanning, and purging out all the dross and chaff, and the Lord has taken his own way to sanctify us 'through the TRUTH' by the different sieves of feet-washing, the holy salutation, keeping the Sabbath."[15]

In her first vision, Ellen White concentrated on foot washing and kissing as the distinguishing characteristics of the saints: "The 144,000 [the number of the righteous described in the book of Revelation] were all sealed and perfectly united. . . . Then it was that the synagogue of Satan knew that God had loved us who could wash one another's feet and salute the brethren with a holy kiss, and they worshipped at our feet."[16] In subsequent visions, Sabbath keeping was presented as the unique characteristic of the saints. As she wrote in 1847, "the holy Sabbath is, and will be, the separating wall between the true Israel of God and unbelievers; and that the Sabbath is the great question to unite the hearts of God's dear, waiting saints."[17] Despite this, she continued to regard kissing and foot washing as defining characteristics of the group to which she belonged. As late as 1851 she exultantly described how one Brother Baker had "a baptism of the Holy Ghost . . . [and] has come into the salutation and washing the saints feet which he never believed in before."[18]

As far as the mainstream of the Millerite movement was concerned, all tests were abhorrent. At the Albany Conference of April 29, 1845, where Miller, Himes, and others who opposed the Shut Door met to decide future policy, it was resolved

That we have no fellowship with any of the *new tests* as conditions of salvation. . . . That we have no fellowship for Jewish fables and commandments of men, that turn from the truth, or for any of the distinctive characteristics of modern Judaism. And that the act of promiscuous feet-washing and the salutation kiss, as practiced by some professing Adventists *as religious* ceremonies . . . are not only unscriptural, but subversive—if persevered in—of purity and morality.[19]

The radical Adventists had distanced themselves from the rest of the world by the Shut-Door doctrine. By the adoption of tests, they distinguished themselves from Open-Door Adventists. Their identifying characteristics were highly specific. Not only was belief in Second Advent required but also the experience of the Great Disappointment and the observance of neglected commandments. The founders of the Seventh-day Adventist church were thus known as Sabbatarian Shut-Door Adventists, a name resembling a botanical specimen that enabled identification to be made according to genus and species.

The seventh-day Sabbath had been introduced as one of a number of tests designed to separate faithful from unfaithful in the brief period prior to the Second Advent. In the words of one hymn:

The *Sabbath* is a sign
A *mark* which all may see
And sure will draw a line
When servants all are sealed
And while destruction's in the land
This *mark* will guard the waiting band.[20]

When, in the early 1850s, the Shut-Door theory was finally abandoned, the focus broadened. The Sabbath was viewed as more than a mark that labeled a particular subgroup of former Millerites. In the first volume of *Spiritual Gifts*, published in 1858, Ellen White developed the idea that the Sabbath was at the center of the controversy between Christ and Satan. In heaven, before the creation of the earth, Satan had rebelled against God's immutable law, knowing that "if he can cause others to violate God's law, he is sure of them; for every transgressor of his [God's] law must die."[21] Accordingly, he then "led on his representatives to attempt to change the Sabbath, and alter the only commandment of the ten which brings to view the true God, the maker of the heavens and the earth."[22] The Sabbath appears here as a memorial of creation and the continuing symbol of loyalty to God's law. The early Adventists came to believe that to observe the seventh-day Sabbath was to value the Bible above the authority of the papacy, which they held responsible for the change of the fourth commandment. For Seventh-day Adventists, the Sabbath was the logical expression of the Protestant tradition. In 1859 J. N. Andrews, a young Adventist scholar, published a substantial tract, the *History of the Sabbath and First Day of the Week*, in which he quoted a Catholic source to show that it was contradictory for Protestants to observe Sunday: "The word of God commandeth the seventh day to be the Sabbath of the Lord, and to be kept holy: you [Protestants] without any precept of scripture, change it to the first day of the week, only authorized by our traditions."[23] The argument is clear. To observe Sunday is to be a crypto-Catholic. Adventists later developed this idea to show how, before the end of the world, this implicit acknowledgment of papal authority would become explicit through the enforcement of Sunday laws, which "will be a virtual recognition of the principles which are the very cornerstone of the Romanism."[24] As Ellen White commented: "When our nation shall so abjure the principles of its government as to enact a Sunday law, Protestantism will in this act join hands with popery."[25]

Although Adventists continued to regard the Sabbath as a badge of identity, the context of this belief shifted. In the 1840s the Sabbath was understood to be a "present test" for those who had passed through the Great Disappointment.[26] The Sabbath divided one group of Adventists from the others. After the Shut-Door doctrine had been given up, the Sabbath was seen as not a present but a future test and one of universal applicability. It would, it was argued, only become a test when Sunday laws were enforced, which would make public the division between those who obeyed the laws enacted by the American government and those who remained loyal to God's law. The Sabbath would thus eventually separate Seventh-day Adventists from other Americans who followed Satan's representative, the pope. Given the Sabbath's significance, it was not surprising that the Adventist pioneers thought the precise manner of keeping the day was highly important. After some years of disagreement as to when the Sabbath should begin and end, it was decided in 1855 that the correct period of Sabbath observance was between sundown on Friday and sundown on Saturday. Thereafter, Adventists regarded this time as holy time. As such, the day was to be devoted strictly to the worship of God and to meditation on his word. All secular work, activity, and entertainment were to be given up for twenty-four hours.[27]

After the Shut-Door period, it was no longer considered necessary to have passed through the Great Disappointment in order to be saved. But another experience was considered necessary—the experience of repentance and baptism. The first significant tract on the subject, B. F. Snook's *The Nature, Subjects and Design of Christian Baptism*, argued that baptism was essential to salvation, that it must be preceded by true repentance and was thus not required of infants, and that immersion was the only divinely authorized form of the rite.[28] Although Snook himself soon left the church, other Adventists agreed with his arguments. As Ellen White wrote in 1876 to children raised in the church: "Heaven and immortal life are valuable treasures that cannot be obtained without an effort on your part. No matter how faultless may have been your lives, as sinners you have steps to take. You are required to repent, believe and be baptized."[29]

The Seventh-day Adventist denomination was an organization that catered to the needs of those who believed in the Second Advent and observed the seventh-day Sabbath. It could be joined by adults who underwent baptism. But it did not, as an organization, impose an identity on an amorphous religious movement. That identity already existed; the organization simply gave formal recognition to a movement whose boundaries were already defined by its distinctive theology and peculiar religious practices. Having left other churches in order to join the Adventist movement, many doubted the desirability of a formally organized church. Organization was only accepted in 1863 with a view to "securing unity and efficiency in labor and promoting the general interest of the cause."[30]

As a body, Seventh-day Adventists derived their sense of identity not from membership of a particular denomination but from a shared understanding of the significance of the Sabbath and the role of those who observed it. This was most clearly demonstrated in the development of the concept of the "remnant." The term had been used in the 1840s more for its descriptive than its theological value, when the Sabbatarian Adventists felt themselves to be the true remnant of the Millerite movement. The theological meaning of this concept was, however, soon elaborated. A reference in Revelation 12:17 suggested that the remnant could be identified by two criteria: the keeping of the commandments and the faith (or testimony) of Jesus. The latter criterion was defined, by reference to Revelation 19:10, as the spirit of prophecy. As the Sabbatarians kept all the commandments (particularly the fourth) and possessed the spirit of prophecy in the person of Ellen White, they believed they bore the identifying marks of the remnant people. The Adventist pioneers also noticed that in Revelation 14:12 the remnant are described in connection with a series of proclamations given by three angels. These proclamations, they claimed, constituted God's final call to repentance, and Adventists, as the last day remnant, were called out to present the messages to the world. Again, the Sabbath was a vital ingredient of this concept. For the messages closed with the third angel's warning of the terrible fate awaiting those who bore the "mark of the beast," which the Sabbatarians identified as Sunday observance.[31]

In 1856 Uriah Smith, editor of the Seventh-day Adventist paper, the *Review*, replied to a correspondent who wanted to know "What are you the remnant of?" by saying that Adventists were the remnant of the primitive church, "who are found in these last days keeping the Commandments of God and the Faith of Jesus." But he emphasized: "That remnant we claim to be, inasmuch as we bear their characteristics."[32] It was a claim validated by specific criteria, but it was an inclusive rather than an exclusive concept. As Smith remarked, "Show us the church besides those who profess the Third Angel's Message, who are keeping the Commandments of God *and* the Faith of Jesus, and we will go with them; for they are our people."[33] The concept of the remnant, like denominational organization itself, was thus a secondary characteristic of a movement defined by its religious practices, most particularly by the observance of the Sabbath.

This state of affairs was reflected in the high degree of contact between Seventh-day Adventists and members of the other major Sabbatarian church, the Seventh-Day Baptists. Adventists had adopted Sabbatarianism as a result of Seventh-Day Baptist influence, and early Adventist writings on the Sabbath owed much to Seventh-Day Baptist publications. The association continued. In 1876 James White was an official delegate at the General Conference session of Seventh-Day Baptists,[34] and in 1879 at a Seventh-day Adventist conference delegates resolved "that we deem them [Seventh-Day Baptists] worthy of our respect and love, and that it is for the interest of the Sabbath cause that the two bodies of Christian commandment-keepers labor to sustain friendly relations to each other."[35] James White explained the implications: "We further recommend that Seventh-day Adventists in their aggressive work avoid laboring to build up Seventh-day Adventist churches where Seventh-Day Baptist churches are already established."[36] Such cordiality was the natural result of a self-perception that concentrated primarily on the Sabbath and not on denominational affiliation. A belief that had originally defined the identity of a subgroup of Shut-Door Adventists was now seen as effectively dividing the world into two opposing camps in which non-Adventist Sabbatarians were allies but non-Sabbatarian Adventists were not.

The Seventh-day Adventist church was founded in order to overcome the practical difficulties encountered by an expanding religious movement that had no legal status. The justification was not so much that God was calling for the creation of a new denomination but rather that there was no overwhelming reason not to organize, provided this would facilitate the spread of the message. As James White put it: "All means which, according to sound judgment, will advance the cause of truth, and are not forbidden by plain Scripture declarations, should be employed."[37] Once established, however, church organization quickly came to be seen as desirable in itself. In 1873 James White asserted: "We unhesitatingly express our firm conviction that organization with us was by the direct providence of God. And to disregard our organization is an insult to God's providential dealings with us, and a sin of no small magnitude."[38] In 1880 White was able to note with satisfaction that Adventists "are said to be the most thoroughly organized Christian people known."[39] In 1911 his wife expressed sentiments similar to those of her husband. "The church," she wrote, "is God's fortress, His city of refuge, which he holds in a revolted world. Any betrayal of the church is treachery to Him."[40] James White was referring to the Adventist denomination, his wife to the church of God in history, but their ideas overlapped, for the Seventh-day Adventist church was understood to be the last manifestation of God's church in history.

This idea had been developed in the *Great Controversy*, first published in 1888. In this book Ellen White argued:

Different periods in the history of the church have each been marked by the development of some special truth, adapted to the necessities of God's people at that time. Every new truth has made its way against hatred and opposition; those who were blessed with its light were tempted and tried.[41]

When Adventists experienced rejection by the world, they could thus not only look forward to the Second Advent but also back to "Wycliffe, Huss, Luther, Tyndale, Baxter [and] Wesley," knowing that "the same trials have been experienced by men of God in ages past."[42] Adventists might be distanced from contemporary Lutherans and Methodists, but beginning in the 1880s, they started to proclaim their common heritage. At the same time, however, Adventists broke with their former allies, the Seventh-Day Baptists, by proselytizing among Baptist congregations. Thus at the very moment Adventists were looking back to their Protestant forbears, they isolated themselves from the one contemporary Protestant group with which they had had friendly relations.[43] These concurrent developments may appear contradictory. But the irony is explained if viewed in the context of a shift in Adventist self-understanding. Amity with Seventh-Day Baptists was possible if Adventist identity was based primarily on the practice of Sabbath observance but awkward if Adventist identity was understood in ecclesiological terms, for then the Seventh-Day Baptists appeared as rivals rather than friends. The Protestant heroes of previous centuries were, however, more easily accommodated by a self-perception that focused on the presence of God's guiding hand in church history.

This conception of the Adventist church as the culmination of centuries of Christian history was further developed in the twentieth century, most notably in the work of Le Roy Edwin Froom. In the four massive volumes of *The Prophetic Faith of Our Fathers* and the two volumes of *The Conditionalist Faith of Our Fathers*, Froom compiled a vast library of detailed evidence to show that Adventist views on biblical prophecy and the nonimmortality of the soul were part of an established intellectual tradition.[44] In Froom's words:

We are tied inseparably into His [God's] unbroken line of witnesses and heralds of saving truth covering the entire Christian Era. We are simply at the end of the line, with the cumulative light, and privileges, and responsibilities of the centuries shining full upon us.[45]

Combined with this idea of the Adventists as the heirs of tradition was the concept that Adventism constituted a tradition in its own right. In Froom's history of the church, *Movement of Destiny*, he presented the view that the Advent movement was an ongoing tradition in which early beliefs were perhaps only rough approximations of final truth. "The development of truth is ever progressive. Light unfolds gradually, like the dawn, and puts darkness and error to flight."[46] Froom drew out the implications of this belief still further. It was not so much the present position of the church that was significant but the direction of the journey it was taking. "History attests that God is at the helm of the ship of Zion. He guides through rock and shoal to the harbor of truth. He is leading a people on to victory."[47]

In keeping with this understanding of the church as an entity with its own history is the theological conception of the church as the "body of Christ," in other words, a living organism, with Christ as "the animating spirit," the "source of its nourishment, growth, direction and unity."[48] This model not only allows for development through time but also for diversity without division. As the Adventist academic Walter Douglas argues: "If our ecclesiology fails to reflect the notion of unity in diversity, we become guilty of what has become known as 'structural fundamentalism' which identifies the structure with fundamental or absolute truth."[49]

The enhanced appreciation of the religious significance of the church itself has had far-reaching implications for the theology of the Sabbath. The traditional belief, reiterated by the theologian M. L. Andreasen in 1942, was that the Sabbath was a separating wall between those who obey God and those who do not. Those who worship on Sunday will receive the mark of the beast and will suffer destruction at the end of time. But those who keep the Saturday Sabbath have the "seal of the living God" and will be saved.[50] For most of Adventist history, no discussion of the Sabbath was complete without consideration of "the seal" and "the mark of the beast." But although the connection is maintained in some popular writing, it is absent from recent theological studies.[51] The most comprehensive recent work, *The Sabbath in Scripture and History*, written by several Adventist scholars in 1982, relegates mention to an historical discussion and an appendix on Joseph Bates, the pioneer who had played an important part in developing the church's Sabbath theology.[52] Another Adventist writer, Samuele Bacchiocchi, subsumes discussion in his book *Divine Rest for Human Restlessness* within a chapter entitled "Good News of Belonging" that makes no mention of Adventism's prophetic understanding.[53] Another Adventist author argues that the anticipated Sabbath-Sunday controversy "will be centered . . . not merely in the issue of Sunday laws."[54] The "seal of the living God" is described with great delicacy of sentiment, if not of language, as "the constitutive norm for deciding where the demarcation line is to be found for the covenant people in its giving and receiving relationship with society."[55]

Adventism's relationship with society has reflected the changes taking place within society itself. In the face of growing secularization, Adventists, like other Christians, have placed greater weight on what divides them from the secular world than on what separates them from fellow Christians. This pattern is revealed in the reinterpretation of the theological meaning of the Sabbath. When the doctrine was introduced, it served to divide different types of Christians; it was presupposed that all would want to keep at least one day of the week holy. In the late twentieth century, it is more difficult for the Sabbath to function in the same way. The observance of Sunday as a Sabbath is now comparatively rare. Seventh-day Adventists are unusual not so much in observing Saturday as in keeping a Sabbath at all. It is unsurprising, then, that contemporary Adventist theologians such as Niels-Erik Andreasen have concentrated more on the value of the sacred understanding of the time than on the question of which segment of time is the most sacred.[56]

In the work of Samuele Bacchiocchi, who appears to have gained some of his ideas from Andreasen, the seventh day emerges as the locus of sacred opportunity: "The Sabbath . . . enables every human being to express commitment to God . . . provides a weekly opportunity to renew the baptismal covenant . . . invites the believer to express his belonging to God." More than this, the Sabbath may function as a corrective in the believer's relationship with the world. It acts as "a divine remedy" for "workaholics," "opens the door for moral reflection," "provides husbands and wives with the time and inspiration to come closer . . . to each other," "provides the opportunity to share food and friendship with the visitor," and offers "*practical opportunities* to develop . . . 'an ecological conscience.' "[57] In making these suggestions, Bacchiocchi advocates nothing previously regarded as inappropriate. What differs is his presentation: the move from obligation to opportunity—from how the Sabbath should be kept to how it might be used. The shift away from thinking of the Sabbath as an end in itself, toward viewing it as a means to other ends, is of great importance. This pragmatic theology of the seventh-day Sabbath would seem to imply that there might be other means by which the same goals could be realized. This Bacchiocchi admits:

In a country like Italy . . . where less than 10 percent of the Christian population attends church services on what they regard as their Lord's day (Saturday evening or Sunday) there is today the largest Communist party of Western Europe . . . The relationship between the two can hardly be viewed as being merely a coincidence. In other Western European nations where church attendance is even lower than in Italy, secularism, atheism, anticlericalism, immorality, and religious skepticism are rampant. It would be naive to attribute all the social and religious evils to the prevailing disregard for God's holy day, but by the same token it would be blindness to fail to see the tragic consequences resulting from the profanation of the Sabbath in society.[58]

Bacchiocchi does not distinguish between the benefits of Sunday observance and those of Saturday observance. For Adventists who, like Mrs. White, view Sunday as possessing "not one particle of sanctity," this is a radical departure.[59] Indeed, Mrs. White predicted that in the last days, Satan would persuade mankind that "men are offending God by the violation of the Sunday Sabbath" and that "this sin has brought calamities."[60] But in an address to the Lord's Day Alliance, Bacchiocchi went on to suggest that Saturday and Sunday keepers "can and should cooperate" in "redefining the theological meaning and message of the Sabbath."[61]

A striking example of such cooperation occurred in 1986 in Britain where the leaders of the Adventist church campaigned "against a general secularization of the 'British Sunday' " [62] by opposing the repeal of Sunday trading laws. A letter to Mrs. Thatcher, the Prime Minister, concluded: "our feeling as a church is that it would be better for one day each week to be retained as a day of rest and worship rather than no day at all. We would . . . request you . . . to reconsider the proposals contained in the Sunday Trading Bill."[63] The fact that prominent Seventh-day Adventists could openly recommend the observance of Sunday bespoke a significant shift in Adventist self-understanding. Adventists originally defined themselves by the development of a Sabbath theology. A church organization was created for the benefit of those who believed in the seventh-day Sabbath. The success of that organization allowed Adventists to perceive their own history as the embodiment of God's purposes. From the security provided by this understanding, church leaders have felt able to modify the theology of the Sabbath, believing that they should not be preoccupied with the boundaries of the denomination but should rather draw on the Adventist tradition for the benefit of the wider world. Thus Roy Branson, in his 1981 article "Celebrating the Adventist Experience," argues:

The besetting sin of Adventism today is preoccupation with itself. . . . But what is desperately needed are people who speak distinctively and movingly from within Adventism to the larger community; voices who, from the core of Adventist particularity, express a universal message for our time.[64]

Branson's call to universality was almost the exact inverse of Charles Fitch's cry for particularity. Fitch had pleaded with Millerites to disengage from the rest of society; Branson asked Adventists to reengage. Not only is the direction of movement different, so, too, is the context. Fitch demanded that Millerites define their identity as a group; for Branson, the Adventist identity was already determined. The result was that 140 years after Fitch's appeal to "come out of Babylon or perish," Branson's call was for Adventists to "penetrate the world around them."[65]

CHAPTER 4

The End of the World

The key to Adventist eschatology is a 2,300-day prophecy found in Daniel 8:14. The text states that at the end of the 2,300 evening-mornings, the sanctuary will be cleansed. William Miller understood the sanctuary to be the earth and thought the "cleansing" would occur at the Second Coming. Working on the assumption that one prophetic day equaled one year, he calculated that the Second Advent would take place in 1843 or 1844. His followers came up with the more precise date of October 22, 1844. Adventists accepted the validity of the date, but the Great Disappointment was the point at which Millerite and Adventist theologies diverged. Miller had focused on the imminence of Christ's return. Adventist eschatology was focused on the delay.

Adventists believe the "sanctuary" is not the earth but a sanctuary in heaven that Christ began to cleanse on October 22, 1844. The Second Advent will occur only when his work, which entails the blotting out of human sin, is finished. In the meantime, humanity is on "probation." The door of salvation is open but will close as soon as the cleansing is complete. After the end of probation, there will be a brief period prior to the Second Coming in which the fate of saints and sinners remains sealed. The Adventist pioneers developed a detailed picture of these final days that drew together many of the elements that made up the church's identity. As the custodian of the three angels' messages and the only body to bear the credentials of the remnant, the Adventist church plays a crucial part in the last struggle between good and evil. Playing opposing roles in the final conflict are the beasts of Revelation 13 and the three-fold conglomerate, Babylon, of Revelation 16:19. The United States is the two-horned beast; the Roman Catholic church is the leopard-like beast; and Babylon is made up of the papacy, Protestantism, and spiritualism. Egged on by demonic powers, the Roman and Protestant churches combine with the United States to force all men to worship on Sunday and thus bear the mark of the beast. The worldwide Sunday law, which everyone must obey on pain of death, coincides with the close of probation. Those who worship on Saturday have the "seal of God" and are miraculously protected from the fury of their opponents. During this "time of trouble," Satan has total control of the impenitent and wages ceaseless war against the saints. The general anarchy is aggravated by the outpouring of the seven last plagues of Revelation, chapter 16. Under the sixth plague, the religious and political powers assemble for the battle of Armageddon in a final effort to destroy God's people. But the battle does not begin, for Christ returns during the seventh plague. He destroys the wicked and saves his loyal subjects.

The return of Christ is not, however, the end of the Adventist eschatological scheme. The Second Coming inaugurates the millennium—a millennium Adventists believe is accompanied by three resurrections. In the first, those who have played the greatest roles on both sides of the great battle between good and evil are raised to life to witness Christ's return. The second resurrection occurs at the Second Coming and concerns the righteous only. The wicked destroyed at the appearance of Christ, including those specially resurrected to witness the event, remain in their graves, as do the wicked of previous generations. The resurrected righteous and the living righteous then reign with Christ, in heaven, for 1,000 years. This period is not spent in idleness. In fulfillment of the statement "judgment was given unto them" (Rev. 20:4), the righteous spend their time investigating the records of the wicked. But the purpose is not so much to decide the cases as to confirm the judgments of the Father so the saints can see that God is just in his dealings with men. During the millennium, the earth remains desolate, and Satan is left to roam the world, effectively "bound" because he has no one to tempt. The third resurrection then takes place, and the damned of every generation are raised to life. Satan immediately prepares the wicked to attack the Holy City in the battle of Gog and Magog, the postmillennial equivalent of Armageddon. But the wicked are stopped by the appearance of Christ, and in the final judgment, he condemns the wicked, fire falls from heaven and consumes them, and Satan, for so long a protagonist in the great controversy, is consumed in the lake of fire. With the defeat of Satan, a new heaven and a new earth are established, and the righteous reign with Christ for all eternity in a society free from sin and evil.

This unusual view of the millennium conforms to the premillennialist idea in that the Second Advent inaugurates the millennium. But it is also partly postmillennialist in that Christ returns to the earth again at the end of the 1,000-year period. Although Adventists, like dispensationalists, believe that the millennium coincides with the binding of the devil prior to his final assault on the people of God, they differ in treating the 1,000 years as a period outside of the earth's history. There are no men left alive on the desolate earth to experience the millennium. At the third resurrection, the experience of the wicked continues just as it left off 1,000 years earlier, while the saints spend the millennium not on earth but in heaven.[1]

Adventists were not, however, indifferent to history. Ellen White spent much of her life writing and rewriting her own interpretation of biblical and Christian history. The mature body of her work in this regard is found in the *Conflict of the Ages* series, particularly in the fifth volume, the *Great Controversy*. From the perspective of the great controversy, Mrs. White gave history a supernatural meaning. In effect, historical events were no more than the past battlefields of Christ's and Satan's struggle in which governments, churches, and individuals fought on either God's or Satan's side. So in the first centuries, God's soldiers are the early Christians whose persecutors are controlled by Satan. In the Middle Ages, the devil's chief agent becomes the papacy and God's representatives are groups such as the Waldenses and individuals such as Wycliffe and Huss. The Reformation era is a high point for the forces of good in the cosmic struggle in that the reformers broke the hegemony of the Catholic church, whereas the French Revolution is a darker period in which the powers of evil run riot.[2] In the critical events the Adventists expected in the future, Mrs. White thought this pattern would continue. Only this time it would be the upholders of the Sabbath who would be on God's side of the controversy, with the rest of the world under the orders of the devil.

It was clear that the prophetess believed that the great controversy was "soon to close."[3] As it reached its climax, she predicted it would become more visible to the human eye. "Fearful sights of a supernatural character will soon be revealed in the heavens in token power of miracle working demons," she wrote. "The spirits of devils will go forth to the kings of the earth ... to fasten them in deception, and urge them on to unite with Satan in his last struggle against the government of heaven."[4] The most terrible delusion would come when Satan himself would impersonate the Second Coming. It was not surprising that with all this just ahead, Mrs. White saw her times as uniquely different. In the *Great Controversy* she wrote: "We are living in the most solemn period of this world's history. The destiny of earth's teeming multitudes is about to be decided."[5] In coming to this conclusion, the prophetess claimed that the convergence of the sinister forces that would precede the Second Coming was already taking place.[6] In the context of her times, there was a sense in which this was not an implausible contention. There had been both a growing rapprochement among the churches and an upsurge in spiritualism since she first outlined the great controversy theme in 1858. These developments had also coincided with an increasing emphasis on the sanctity of Sunday, with many states upholding Sunday blue laws. Indeed, Senator H. W. Blair, chairman of the Senate Committee on Education and Labor, proposed national

Sunday legislation before Congress in 1888, the very year the *Great Controversy* was published.[7]

Ellen White's conception of the end put Adventism at the center of the world and foretold how the beliefs of the small group of Sabbath keepers would eventually triumph over all other religious and political ideologies. This was an obvious inversion of the actual state of affairs in mid-nineteeth-century America where Adventists were very much on the defensive after Christ's failure to return in 1844. By contrast, the Protestant churches were well established, the Catholic church was growing in influence, spiritualism was in tremendous vogue, and the founding of America looked as if it was going to be a lasting and successful venture. But at the end of time, it is not Adventism but the traditions of Protestantism, Catholicism, spiritualism, and American republicanism that are shown to be false.

The intriguing element in this eschatological conception was the inclusion of the American nation. Because the beliefs of the church were in conflict with those of the Catholic and Protestant churches and with spiritualists, one can understand why Adventists identified them with the dark symbols of the Apocalypse. It is less easy to see why the United States should also have been included. However, although the early Adventists recognized that the New World provided the conditions for their movement to flourish, there was a sense in which America's republican experiment posed a challenge to the Adventist world view that may explain why it also earned a place in the church's eschatology. The nature of that challenge lay in America's millennial self-understanding. From its beginnings, America has used the framework of Christian eschatology to describe itself as a nation apart, chosen by God and destined for a special purpose.[8] This was especially true in the early nineteenth century when America was "drunk on millennium" and "Americans vied with each other in producing grander and more glorious prospects for the United States."[9] But Adventists also saw themselves as marked out for a special purpose. As the nation and Adventism could not, ultimately, both be "the chosen," it is perhaps not surprising that the Adventists of the 1850s began to question the triumphalist nature of the American destiny.

In the 1851 *Review* article that first identified the United States as the two-horned beast, J. N. Andrews was clearly awed by the development of America. He wrote of its "wonderful" progress and the "wonder" of its system of government and suggested that only divine intervention could curtail the advancement of the Republic: "Mark its onward progress and tell, if it be possible, what would be its [America's] destiny, if the coming of the Just One should not check its astonishing career?"[10] Most significantly, however, Andrews felt that the postmillennial understanding America bequeathed to its people competed with the message Adventists felt they were divinely commissioned to propagate. Contrasting the two views, Andrews observed: "We look forward indeed to the time when the Lamb, who is King of Kings and Lord of Lords shall reign in person over all the earth. But with the mass this view has given place to the more congenial idea of the spiritual reign, and of temporal prosperity and triumph."[11]

With these two visions of the future thus in conflict, the United States (like other contemporary bodies that differed from the church) was transformed into an eschatological adversary that would persecute the church for its beliefs. Adventists believed that America would repudiate its libertarian values by forming a corrupt union with the churches, thereby becoming an authoritarian state. The two-horned beast was a particularly apt representation of this belief. Its lamblike horns symbolized America's twin principles of civil and religious liberty, its republicanism and its Protestantism. This lamblike appearance, however, concealed a beast that spoke like a dragon.

In 1854, another leading Adventist, J. N. Loughborough, showed an acute awareness of the powerful appeal of America's millennial vision and even suggested that, in its uncorrupted form, it eclipsed the message of Adventism. "Against the profession of Protestants, and Republicans," he wrote, "we have nothing to offer: their profession is right. *We might expect a millennium indeed*, were their profession lived out."[12] This was a significant admission. Loughborough had no doubts about the nation's real nature, or its eventual alignment with the forces of evil, but he was conscious that an American millennium would render Adventist beliefs quite meaningless. If, through the example of America, the world was brought to perfection, there would be no need for divine intervention in human history. The American dream threatened to undermine the Adventist hope. To retain hope, the Adventists transformed that dream into a nightmare, seeking out contemporary evidence of American hypocrisy. In his original article, Andrews talked about the "pretensions" of America, pointing to three million slaves and the religious intolerance shown by the churches in expelling [Millerite] believers who looked forward to Christ's imminent return.[13] Such evidence was quickly taken up by Andrews's colleagues and lent plausibility to the idea that America was—and would increasingly become—a dragon in lamb's clothing.[14]

The inclusion of the United States in Adventist eschatology has unfortunately received little attention from the church's historians. Those who have studied the question, notably Jonathan Butler, have seen the eschatological depiction of the United States as an expression of Adventist pessimism about the nation's future, prompted by the feeling that America was in decline.[15] But it is perhaps more likely that the depiction of the United States in Adventist eschatology developed from the perceived conflict between Adventist and American expectations.

What prompted the early Adventists to regard the United States as the two-horned beast was not the idea that the nation was in decline but the belief that the nation had, in fact, been a remarkable success. It was certainly the progress of the republican experiment that concerned Andrews, and it was this success that Loughborough felt might make the Adventist message redundant.

The change in America from liberal democracy to authoritarian state was, like all the other elements in Adventist eschatology, expected to occur within the pioneers' lifetimes. This conviction, which successive generations of Adventists kept alive, produced within the movement a sense of constant expectation. Adventists, while avoiding the precise date-setting of the Millerites, thus became keen discerners of "the signs of the times," producing a constant apocalyptic commentary on contemporary events. This in itself was nothing new. There was an established tradition that viewed both natural and political occurrences as portents of the end. The Lisbon earthquake of 1755 had been seen by many as the great earthquake of Revelation 6. The darkness experienced in parts of north America on May 19, 1780, was identified as the "Dark Day," and the meteoric showers of November 12 and 13, 1833, with the "falling of the stars," thus completing the three events described in the sixth seal of the Apocalypse. The Adventists took over these interpretations and added to them. A particular Adventist preoccupation was the Ottoman Empire. Uriah Smith, Adventism's leading prophetic expositor in the nineteenth century, developed the idea that the demise of Turkish power would herald the Second Advent. As a result, Adventist writers monitored the "Eastern Question" right up to the First World War. But here again Adventists simply followed a long tradition that for centuries had sought to find prophetic significance in the rise and then the apparent decline of Islam.[16]

In more general terms, Adventists, like other apocalyptically oriented groups, perceive all natural disasters and political disorder as indicative of the time of trouble. However, Adventist apocalyptic does not, in fact, flourish in crisis situations; it tends to reach a peak just before or after a crisis, when comparatively little is happening. In an actual crisis, the force of Adventist apocalyptic is deliberately muted. This is a curious phenomenon. Apocalyptic is normally expected to flourish during times of stress. A classic example of this was the growth of premillennialism in the United States during World War I. Dispensationalist journals such as *Our Hope* almost gloried in the fact that the war had shattered dreams of unending progress, and they confidently predicted that the end was near.[17] The *Review*, by contrast, was cautious and uncertain. The paper's editor, F. M. Wilcox, wrote: "We cannot predict with confidence the outcome of the present struggle. We do not know whether this war will drag along until it finally ends in Armageddon, or whether there will be for a time a cessation of hostilities."[18] Such restraint was again apparent when America itself entered the war in 1917. Commenting on an official action that counseled church workers to guard their public utterances, Wilcox wrote, "Let us not hazard our reputation . . . by making wild statements." Bible prophecies, he went on, "deal with the course of the nations in general outline. . . . They do not reveal how events will shape in reaching the final conclusion."[19]

But almost as soon as the war was over, Wilcox published a small book called *Facing the Crisis: Present World Conditions in the Light of the Scriptures.* Here, against the background of a comparatively peaceful world, Wilcox was, paradoxically, much more pessimistic about the times. Previously, he could not say whether the Great War heralded Armageddon, but now he felt confident that the "growing *agitation* in every country over *preparedness* for war is . . . a herald of the last great conflict, when the nations shall be gathered at Armageddon."[20] The irony of this situation was also evident in the pages of the Adventist evangelistic weekly, the *Signs of the Times.* In April 1914, the paper printed a front-page article that effectively said that the current war preparations would end in Armageddon. When the war duly arrived six months later, the paper promptly argued that the current conflict could not be the final eschatological battle.[21]

The outbreak of the Second World War provided another instance of Adventist caution when faced with real crisis. On September 14, 1939, the president of the church, J. L. McElhany, advised the membership in the *Review* that speculating about the outcome of the war was "unwise." A little later, F. D. Nichol, associate editor of the church paper, reiterated this view in a strongly worded editorial.[22] Yet the membership could perhaps be forgiven for being somewhat bewildered by these statements. The apocalyptic literature that had continued to pour forth from denominational publishing houses in the 1930s had, in many respects, conditioned Adventists to expect the next war to be Armageddon. As late as 1938, for example, Arthur S. Maxwell, the editor of the *Signs of the Times,* correctly anticipated the outbreak of hostilities and declared, "We are sweeping with incredible rapidity toward the final crisis of human affairs."[23] Indeed, Adventists generally dismissed the peace-making efforts of the 1930s as a delusion, so sure were they of the final conflict.[24]

Perhaps the best example of the deliberate softening of Adventist eschatology came with the election in 1960 of the Roman Catholic president, John F. Kennedy. Although the church had long warned about the union of the American nation with the Catholic church, Adventism retreated from that position when the prophecy appeared to come true in Kennedy's presidency. An editorial in the *Review* advised American Adventists to give the new president "loyal support" and, quite remarkably, urged them "to guard against imputing sinister motives to the President every time he takes a step that looks dangerous, *as viewed from the Adventist prophetic frame of reference.*"[25] Thus, Adventist apocalypticism in the twentieth century proved to be (to reverse its own symbol of America) a dragon that spoke like a lamb. In a sense, however, this was a realistic position in view of the fact that events did not turn out quite as expected. The two world wars did not produce Armageddon; the election of a Catholic president did not produce the universal Sunday law. But although the Adventist commentary on world events is sometimes strangely muted, it has never fallen completely silent. Indeed, in the twentieth century, it has moved beyond the horizons of nineteenth-century America to include new events unanticipated by Ellen White. Following her death in 1915, the Adventists who wrote about final events adapted the church's eschatology to the changed circumstances of the new century. Their apocalyptic vision extended beyond the boundaries of the United States and embraced the new order ushered in after 1914: an era of world wars and international politics and a world marked by rapid progress in science and technology.

The broadening of Adventist eschatology was no doubt facilitated by the fact that non-American Adventists were now contributing to it. One of the prominent figures to emerge in this period was the Englishman Arthur S. Maxwell, who produced a continuous stream of apocalyptic material from the 1920s to the 1960s. Maxwell epitomized the changed outlook of Adventists after the First World War. In *Christ's Glorious Return* (1924), he discussed new signs of the Second Advent: the war itself, recent tragedies such as the worldwide flu epidemic of 1918, and the shrinking world caused by increased travel and better communications. He called his era an "incomparable age," and it was clearly this age rather than the age of Mrs. White that he expected to presage the Second Coming."[26]

It was, however, the evangelist John L. Shuler who gave one of the clearest indications that the post–World War I generation expected the world to end rather differently from their nineteenth-century forebears. In *The Coming Conflict* (1929), Shuler listed nine "outstanding movements" that he claimed were "destined to be among the principal factors in the final scenes of earth's great drama." Although Shuler confidently asserted that "prophecy shows that they will all soon come to a head . . . for the final world crisis," the first four of these points would have been unrecognizable to Mrs. White or to any Adventist of her generation. The four points were: the world peace movement as embodied by the League of Nations, the development of new and deadly weapons, the rise of Japan and the nations of the Far East, and the Zionist movement, which sought to establish a Jewish state in Palestine. All four movements were, of course, very much in the news in the 1920s. Only the last five points in Shuler's list rehearsed the traditional positions of Adventist eschatology.[27]

Despite the fact that their eschatological perspective had changed in accordance with changing circumstances, Adventists still expected that the end would soon occur. They generally agreed that the momentous events of the new century amounted to *Civilization's Last Stand*, as the title of Le Roy Edwin Froom's book put it in 1928. In the book, Froom accurately summarized the Adventist attitude to the changing times: "Our vaunted civilization is honeycombed with dry rot; our golden age is soon to meet with a crash that will shake it from center to circumference; our prideful civilization is approaching a catastrophe that will involve the shipwreck of the world."[28] But perhaps the most pessimistic Adventist of this era, and the most certain of Christ's imminent return, was the evangelist Carlyle B. Haynes. Like Arthur Maxwell, Haynes produced apocalyptic material at a prodigious rate. In his numerous books, he held no hope for civilization and claimed, on more than one occasion, that his generation would witness the Second Coming.[29]

After the Second World War, expectations of an immediate Second Coming proved more difficult to sustain. However, in the 1970s Adventist eschatology showed signs of renewal once more. But it was a renewal that looked in new directions—away from the interpretation of apocalyptic signs toward an understanding of the Advent Hope itself. In part, this was a reaction to Adventism's previous obsession with specifying the political details of the time of trouble, but it was also a response to Hal Lindsey's best-selling book, *The Late Great Planet Earth*, published in 1970. Among that book's many achievements was the deep impression it made on the Adventist church. It would not be an overstatement to say that virtually all Adventist literature about final events after 1970 was written in reaction to this book or to the dispensationalism for which it stood.[30] This was particularly seen in the work of the theologian Hans K. LaRondelle, who became Adventism's foremost critic of dispensationalist thought in the 1980s.[31] In one sense, however, this was ironic, for although Adventists strongly opposed aspects of dispensationalism (particularly the rapture theory, which envisaged the saints' secret transportation to heaven), Lindsey's detailed panoramas of the end were not unlike those that characterized earlier Adventist apocalyptic.

The success of Lindsey's book, however, had the effect of making Adventists more reflective. Commenting on the power of *The Late Great Planet Earth*, Sakae Kubo notes that the book

proves how much people grasp at something that paints the future in detail. It is why . . . astrology and fortune telling are so popular. . . . To know what will happen in minutest detail before it does gives one a sense of being able to control destiny. It fascinates and attracts. Even if what one says is a little bit plausible, people will be drawn to it.[32]

It was during this moment of reflection in 1978 that Kubo himself published *God Meets Man*, which included a pioneering attempt at a theology of the Second Advent. In it he refrained from painting the future in detail. He was more concerned with the application of the Second Advent belief to Christian living. For Kubo it is the fact, not the timing, of the Second Advent that is important:

Emphasizing the nearness of the real coming in an almost time-setting way, we will continue to develop a sense of delay. . . . Disillusionment and careless living can result. But God's plans know no haste or delay. His promises are sure, and they will take place in the appointed time. We must live with that fact in mind rather than on the basis of the momentary feverish excitement of every passing crisis.[33]

These thoughts were echoed in Samuele Bacchiocchi's *The Advent Hope for Human Hopelessness*, a comprehensive theology of the Second Coming published in 1986. Significantly, the book was written partly to combat the tendency of writers who, according to Bacchiocchi, showed "more interest in formulating timetables . . . leading to and following the Second Advent than in helping believers to understand the relevance of the Advent Hope for their lives today."[34] Although Bacchiocchi is prepared to assign to the "signs of the times" slightly more importance than is Kubo, he, too, is concerned with the certainty of the Second Coming rather than its imminence.

The tendency toward greater introspection can also be seen in the way in which Adventists who retained apocalyptic interests adapted to the different situation of the 1970s and 1980s. In this period, the object of apocalyptic speculation was not a rapidly changing world but what seemed to be a rapidly changing church. The most important work in this genre was Lewis Walton's *Omega*, an Adventist best-seller published in 1981. Walton, an Adventist lawyer, revitalized an obscure Ellen White prediction concerning an "alpha-omega" heresy, which was made in the context of the pantheistic crisis that afflicted Adventism at the turn of the century.[35] "Be not deceived," she had warned the church. "Many will depart from the faith, giving heed to seducing spirits and doctrines of devils." Referring to the spread of pantheism, she said: "We have now before us the alpha of this danger. The omega will be of a most startling nature."[36] Walton invested the omega with eschatological significance. The characteristics of this latter-day heresy, he argued, included attacks on the fundamental beliefs of the church, attacks on Ellen White, attacks on the church structure and standards, and the attempt to reform the traditional message of Adventism.[37] This was in fact a description of events occurring in the church in the late 1970s. What Walton achieved in *Omega* had a familiar ring to it. He transformed new, and from his point of view, dangerous movements into eschatological enemies, just as the pioneers had done a century earlier. But for Walton, the enemies of the truth were not outside the church but within it.[38]

It is tempting to interpret the shift away from an exclusive concentration on the imminence of the Second Advent as evidence that the Adventist church has lost its early apocalyptic enthusiasm. But this would be an oversimplification. The problem of the delay of the Second Advent and the indifference generated by the delay is not new. It was the first problem that confronted the Adventists. Since then, the tide of expectation has ebbed and flowed. Following the Great Disappointment, the early Adventists faced the fact of the delay, and the growth of the church's eschatology was a part of that process. But by 1856 Mrs. White was writing that delegates at a gathering of Adventists at Battle Creek would live to see the return of Jesus. In 1868 she returned to the theme of the delay, but in 1888 the publication of *The Great Controversy* indicated that she was once more reading the times and concluding that Christ's return was very near. In 1901 she again responded to the delay, suggesting that the church's fecklessness in proclaiming the gospel was holding up Christ's return.[39] Adventist apocalyptic clearly flowered again during the interwar years, only for the postwar church to return to the question of the delay. An attempt to deal with the problem was made in the Ellen White compilation *Evangelism*, published in 1946. Several passages were collected together under the heading "The Reason for the Delay." The reasons given fell into two main categories: First Christ had not come because his people were not ready. Second, he had not come because Adventists had not preached the gospel as they had been commissioned to do. There was also a suggested solution to the delay: Christ would come just as soon as his people perfected their characters and brought the gospel to the world.[40] As Mrs. White commented in 1883: "It is true that time has continued longer than we expected in the early days of this message. . . . But has the word of the Lord failed? Never! It should be remembered that the promises and the threatenings of God are alike conditional."[41]

Within the church, the conditional nature of the timing of Christ's return became the most accepted explanation of the delay.[42] Its chief advocate in modern Adventism is the theologian Herbert E. Douglass. In a paper presented at the denomination's Bible Conference in 1974 and in his books *Why Jesus Waits* (1976) and *The End* (1979), Douglass amplified Mrs. White's theme, particularly the need to perfect Christian character. He argued that "God will wait for the maturing of Christian character in a significant number of people as the chief condition determining those events which affect the time when probation will close, and thus the time of the advent."[43] Douglass makes explicit what has always been implicit in the church's eschatology: the connection between the Adventist movement and the end of the world. It is a complex relationship. The movement owes its existence to the belief that Christ was going to return on October 22, 1844. This conviction drew men and women out of the world. The Seventh-day Adventist interpretation of the Great Disappointment ensured that at least some of the Millerites did not drift back into the mainstream of society but continued to stand apart, awaiting their eventual vindication. The elaboration of an eschatology that depicted the most prominent opponents of the church as demonic beasts perpetuated that sense of isolation. The Adventist picture of the Second Advent was of an event that made absolute the division between those who repudiated American jurisdiction and worshipped on Saturday and those who obeyed American law and observed Sunday worship. In anticipation of this final separation, Adventists have maintained the distance between themselves and the rest of the world. Thus, the Second Coming, although scheduled for some unknown time in the future, defines the shape of the present. It is retroactive, creating social divisions within the world that it will end.

Yet the timing of the Second Advent is in the control of the movement called upon to await it. The saints must be perfect in readiness for heaven; the gospel must be preached throughout the globe. The world contains the catalyst of its own destruction: the Adventist church. The Second Coming will take place only when Adventists have fulfilled the gospel commission and realized God's perfect ideals. Thus, while the end of the world is, for most non-Adventists, an external event liable to break unexpectedly into their lives, for Adventists it is an internal matter, an occurrence integral to the history of the church. The majority of humanity endures the Second Advent only long enough to register surprise and horror that it is taking place. They experience the event only as an ending. But for the Adventists, it is also a new beginning as they leave the earth to enter the divine realm.

CHAPTER 5

The Divine Realm

It took the early Christian church almost four centuries to reach agreement on the doctrine of the Trinity. During that time, there was fierce controversy about the nature of the three divine Persons, particularly the relationship of the Father and the Son. Some, following Arius, believed the Son to be the first created being, while others taught that Father and Son were of the same substance and coeternal. The latter view prevailed and has subsequently been accepted by almost all Christians, whether Catholic, Orthodox, or Protestant.

Contemporary Seventh-day Adventists are categorical in their affirmation of this traditional Christian position. The second of their fundamental beliefs asserts that "there is one God: Father, Son and Holy Spirit, a unity of three co-eternal Persons." The nature of God is further clarified as being "immortal, all-powerful, all-knowing, above all, and ever present."[1] The doctrine is now deemed to be above discussion. "A truly Christian doctrine of God is," the Adventist theologian Richard Rice argues, "unavoidably trinitarian."[2] And yet in the nineteenth century, Adventists took the opposite view. In the words of one church historian, they were "about as uniform in opposing Trinitarianism as they were in advocating belief in the Second Coming."[3] But even then, Adventists only knew what they did *not* believe; some were Arians, denying the eternity of the Son, while others were close to orthodoxy.

In the nineteenth century, this diversity of opinion was facilitated by the absence of any fixed statement of beliefs to which it was expected that members' views should conform. As long as Adventists were united on the core of their faith, there was some scope for individual opinion on other issues. It is thus difficult to know which Adventist writers are representative. The problem is compounded by the fact that Adventism's one authoritative writer, Ellen White, often appears to synthesize conflicting views. Because of this lack of uniformity, it is perhaps more helpful to examine not *what* but *how* Adventists thought, to explore the framework within major ideas developed rather than to try to disentangle every strand of opinion.

This chapter looks at the way in which nineteenth-century Adventists thought about God. Anti-Trinitarianism was one of several positions that reflected the literal understanding of the divine realm revealed by Ellen White's visions. The same literal model also provided the context for Adventist views on the nature of the atonement and the heavenly sanctuary. The doctrine of the Trinity was eventually accepted when an alternative, spiritual conception of divine activity became influential toward the end of the century. The history of ideas about God seems to follow a dialectical pattern. Two complementary models emerged after the Great Disappointment, neither of which provided the complete account of the Trinity that their eventual synthesis made possible.

Even in her first vision, which describes the saints' entry into heaven, Ellen White's description of the divine realm included elements characteristic of the early Adventist understanding of God. Although her description uses common Christian symbols, unusual emphases are also apparent. There is, for example, a marked, almost military concentration on order. The 144,000 stand in formation; they march rather than walk. Jesus welcomes those who have "stood stiffly," like soldiers, for truth. The saints are differentiated by their uniform—martyrs have a red border on their robes—and by their insignia of achievement. "Some of them had very bright crowns, others not so bright. Some crowns appeared heavy with stars while others had but a few."[4] Despite these inequalities, discipline prevails. "All," Ellen White assured her readers, "were perfectly satisfied with their crowns."[5] All, too, could have the satisfaction of seeing their salvation confirmed in writing: their names were engraved, in letters of gold, on tables of stone within the temple.[6] The New Jerusalem revealed in this vision is not a place of unrestrained luxury, still less of ill-defined piety. It is a city of organized grandeur, carefully planned, even down to the golden shelves provided in every home for the crowns of the saints.[7] Nothing has been left to chance. The sinful world is characterized by darkness and disorder; the New Earth, by decorum. As Ellen White wrote some years later, "In heaven there is perfect order, perfect obedience, perfect peace and harmony."[8]

At the apex of the heavenly formation is the Godhead, the Father and Son. Although she does not go as far as Joseph Smith who taught that God the Father had a human body, Ellen White leaves little doubt that both Father and Son are material beings. Jesus stands "head and shoulders above the saints and above the angels," with white, curly hair down to his shoulders.[9] As for God the Father, Ellen White asked Jesus "if his Father was a person and had a form like Himself." To which Jesus replied, "I am in the express *image* of My Father's *person*."[10] Jesus also shares with his Father a multitude of royal appellations. As king, monarch, sovereign, and ruler, the Godhead holds sway over the universe. Where the Father and Son are distinguished, the Father is described as the owner or proprietor of the universe, and the Son, as "a prince in the royal courts of heaven."[11]

The Godhead is brought into sharper focus in Mrs. White's account of Satan's fall. She wrote that the devil's revolt against divine law was occasioned by Satan's unwillingness to accept Jesus' position as God's coruler. Although Satan (then known as Lucifer) was "a high and exalted angel, next in honour to God's dear Son," he became jealous of the status conferred on Christ. Eventually the devil rebelled after enlisting many angels to his cause. In the ensuing battle, Jesus defeated Satan and his followers and expelled them from heaven. This mass expulsion created vacancies in the heavenly society. These vacancies, according to Mrs. White, will be filled by the saints at the Second Coming.[12]

In his capacity as the "mighty commander of the hosts of heaven," Jesus is identified, contrary to Christian tradition, as Michael the archangel.[13] Although otherwise differentiated from the angels, Christ appeared, according to Ellen White, in the form of an angel on various occasions in the Old Testament. The angels themselves are envisaged as glorious beings, possessed of intelligence a little higher than that of Adam and Eve.[14] With the departure of Satan, Gabriel now stands next in honor to the Son of God,[15] and himself conveys messages of particular importance to mankind. But the bearing of messages is just one of the angels' tasks. Some record the deeds of men; others sing in the heavenly choir; many act as guardians to men, while the cherubim and seraphim minister in the heavenly sanctuary. Some have especially demanding tasks: "The very highest angels in the heavenly courts are appointed to work out the prayers which ascend to God for the advancement of the cause of God. Each angel has his particular post of duty which he is not permitted to leave for any other place."[16] All these duties form part of "the great conflict going on between invisible agencies, the controversy between loyal and disloyal angels."[17] When not actively engaged in this struggle, the angels act as observers. At Jesus' arrest on earth, prior to his crucifixion, "many companies of holy angels, each with a tall commanding angel at their head, were sent to witness the scene."[18]

Less exalted than the angels are the inhabitants of other worlds who, unlike human beings, did not fall into sin. (Mrs. White believed that God created other beings on other planets who, unlike Adam and Eve, resisted the devil when he also tried to tempt them to disobey God.) The unfallen worlds, in contrast to the angels, enjoy only observer status in the great controversy, acting as a kind of chorus, watching and being edified by the drama of redemption. Ellen White visited one such world in an early vision and reported that "the inhabitants of the place were of all sizes; they were noble, majestic, and lovely."[19]

Rarely are all the orders of heavenly being described together. When they are, as in Ellen White's description of Christ's reception in heaven on his ascension, they constitute the full court of heaven:

There is the throne, and around it the rainbow of promise. There are cherubim and seraphim. The commanders of the angel hosts, the sons of God, the representatives of the unfallen worlds, are assembled. The heavenly council before which Lucifer had accused God and his Son, the representatives of those sinless realms over which Satan had thought to establish his dominion—all are there to welcome the Redeemer. They are eager to celebrate His triumph and to glorify their King.[20]

Ellen White described heaven as a monarchy and emphasized the similarities between the heavenly court and that of an earthly monarch. With her preference for literal language, it was easy for others to conceive of the Son as subordinate to the Father, as a prince to a king. But that conclusion might not have been drawn by her contemporaries if it had not been for the influence of spiritualism, which impelled Adventists to use literal concepts to the virtual exclusion of spiritual understanding.

The early Adventists felt an urgent need to distinguish themselves from spiritualists. Their writings are replete with vigorous denunciations of spiritualism as "the masterpiece of Satan," and they vehemently rejected allegations that they were themselves spiritualists.[21] Today the possibility of confusing the two movements seems remote, but in the 1840s and 1850s, the two groups stood back to back. There was an obvious proximity in geography. The mysterious rappings that sparked the growth of spiritualism occurred in the Fox household in Hydesville near Rochester. Between May 6, 1852, and Oct 30, 1855, the *Review* was published in Rochester, the very town from which spiritualism had emanated. Mrs. White had spoken with dead Millerites in her first vision.[22] She, of course, regarded the purported communications of the deceased as resulting from the deception of evil angels, and her own experience as different. (She had been taken in vision to the New Jerusalem; the dead had not spoken to her on earth as spirits.) But the distinction was one that could easily be missed by a casual observer.

However, it was not simply that Adventists and spiritualists lived in the same town and had superficially similar experiences. There were also "spiritualizers" within Adventism who had associations with the Shakers, a communitarian sect that had been visited by the spirits of the dead since 1837. Their practices and beliefs paralleled those of the Shakers themselves: they were highly introverted; they frequently shouted and fell on the floor during worship; some adopted the Shaker habit of crawling around on all fours; others espoused the Shaker view that Christ was a spirit.[23] Some of these practices were defended by the Whites; others, criticized. While Ellen resolutely argued in favor of ecstatic worship, both she and James firmly opposed any suggestion that the Second Advent had already taken place as a spiritual event.[24] It was specifically in order to distinguish herself from those spiritualizers who believed Christ to be a spirit that Mrs. White emphasized the material reality of Jesus' Person. James White went further, and in his eagerness to establish the literal hierarchy of heaven, he denied the doctrine of the Trinity. In a letter to the *Day Star* in January 1846, he argued that the spiritualizers came to their beliefs by "using the old unscriptural trinitarian creed, viz., that Jesus Christ is the eternal God, though they have not one passage to support it, while we have plain scripture testimony in abundance that he is the Son of the eternal God."[25] His arguments did not impress Enoch Jacobs, the editor of the paper. In the same year, he followed the example of many other Millerites in renouncing Adventism to enter a Shaker commune.[26]

Such defections only served to confirm James White's suspicions. In 1852 he again denounced "the old trinitarian absurdity that Jesus Christ is the very and Eternal God."[27] But it was Uriah Smith, White's successor as the editor of the *Review*, who became the most vigorous exponent of Arianism. In 1865 Smith commented that "an expression which signifies complete eternity, past and future," "can be applicable only to God, the Father." This language, he concluded, "is never applied to Christ."[28] Smith continued to hold an Arian or semi-Arian position for the rest of his life. He was not alone. J. H. Waggoner, editor of the denomination's *Signs of the Times*, was unequivocal in asserting that Christ was God only in a sense subordinate to the Father.[29] With Adventism's most articulate spokesmen so implacably opposed to the doctrine of the Trinity, it is unsurprising that a recent researcher was forced to conclude that he was "unable to discover any evidence that 'many were Trinitarians' before 1898, nor has there been found any Trinitarian declaration written, prior to that date, by an Adventist writer, other than Ellen G. White."[30]

Adventist resistance to Trinitarianism was grounded in an understanding of the divine realm as a hierarchical court and spurred by the need to define Jesus as a distinct person. Both of these elements were also present in the development of Adventism's distinctive doctrine of the sanctuary. The idea was originally presented by O. R. L. Crosier in the *Day Star* extra of February 7, 1846. He suggested that the appropriate referent of the "sanctuary" in Daniel 8:14 could only be the sanctuary in heaven.[31] On October 22, 1844, Jesus had simply moved from the Holy to the Most Holy apartments. This much had already been vouchsafed to Crosier's friend Hiram Edson in a vision on the morning after the Great Disappointment. The complex question that Crosier broached was that of Jesus' purpose in making this transition. He argued that Jesus entered into the Most Holy Place in order to perform two ceremonial functions. In his capacity as high priest, he entered in order to carry out an act of atonement prefigured by the

annual national rite performed by the Levitical priesthood for the blotting out of Israel's sins. In his role as bridegroom, Jesus entered to be
wedded to his bride, the New Jerusalem. Both of these ceremonies were
necessary before the Second Advent so that the saved could be brought
guiltless to heaven and the wedding formalities could be completed by
the time the saints arrived to share the feast.

Crosier's account, with its focus on the proper performance of ceremonial duties, fitted harmoniously with the thought of Ellen White.
While Crosier's article explained why Jesus had failed to return to earth
on October 22, 1844, it did not explain further delay. Neither an act
of ritual purification nor a wedding would normally be expected to
last for years. However, in the mid 1850s, J. N. Loughborough and
Uriah Smith developed an idea that easily accounted for an extended
delay.[32] This concept, known as the "investigative judgment," was expounded at length by Ellen White in the Great Controversy. The court
of the King has temporarily been transformed into a court of law. God
the Father presides as the "Ancient of Days," while Satan acts as pros-
ecutor and Jesus as counsel for the defence. The angels are interested
spectators. Commencing with "those who first lived upon the earth,"
the court deals with "each successive generation and closes with the
living. Every name is mentioned, every case closely investigated." (The
court is only concerned with professed believers. The investigation of
the wicked, as discussed in the previous chapter, takes place during the
millennium.) The procedure is methodical. All the evidence is written
in three books of heaven: a book of life in which the names of professed
Christians are registered, a book of remembrance in which their good
deeds are recorded, and a book in which "opposite each name . . . is
entered with terrible exactness every wrong word, every selfish act,
every unfulfilled duty, and every secret sin, with every artful dissem-
bling." If Jesus is able to show that the people Satan accused have
repented of their sins, the record is blotted out. If not, the name of
the sinner is blotted out from the book of life. This laborious process,
Ellen White argues, began on October 22, 1844, and is necessary so
that the saints are separated from their sins in time for the Second
Advent.[33]

The sanctuary doctrine explained the Great Disappointment, and its
emphasis on the literal details of celestial geography and personnel
provided a further bulwark against spiritualistic interpretations of the
divine realm. It dovetailed neatly with Ellen White's conception of a
spiritual struggle between opposing hierarchies of good and evil. The
investigative judgment brings the Advocate and the adversary of man
face to face. It presents the great controversy in microcosm. In so
doing, it represents God the Father as above the dispute between Christ
and Satan. It is a picture that, although not designed for the purpose,
could not but feed the Arian tendencies in Adventist Christology.

The model of heaven as a hierarchical realm bound together the doctrine of the sanctuary and anti-Trinitarianism into a system of belief that, with its delineation of the literal functions of divine persons, served as an obstacle to any reappearance of "spiritualizers" or spiritualists in Adventism. There was one further doctrinal element in the package: a unique understanding of the atonement.

In keeping with her account of the origin of sin as a rebellion against divine law, Ellen White believed that redemption could only come through a vindication of that law. As she wrote in 1858: "I saw that it was impossible for God to alter or change his law to save lost, perishing man; therefore he suffered his beloved Son to die for man's transgressions." Angels had offered to give their lives, but they lacked the status necessary for the task, for "the transgression was so great that an angel's life would not pay the debt."[34] Redemption was thus necessary because of the legal structure of divine government, but it could only be effected through the direct interaction of divine persons. Accordingly, on the day of his resurrection, Christ was not informed of his triumph by an angelic intermediary but "quickly ascended to his Father to hear from his lips that he accepted the sacrifice, and to receive all power in heaven and upon earth."[35]

However according to Mrs. White's fellow believers, the atonement had not yet begun. Christ's sacrifice was, like the sacrifices of the Israelites, not itself considered an atonement. In *A Declaration of Fundamental Principles of the Seventh-Day Adventists* published in 1872 as "a brief statement of what is, and has been, with great unanimity, held by them," it was stated that the atonement "so far from being made on the cross, which was but the offering of the sacrifice, is the very last portion of his work as priest."[36] In other words, the atonement began on October 22, 1844. This was certainly a radical departure from traditional Christianity, but it was entirely in keeping with a model of the universe in which heaven is the hub of redemptive activity and in which it is most fitting that the final obliteration of sin should be made in the same place as its origin, the court of heaven.

The picture of heaven as a royal hierarchy served as the framework within which distinctive Adventist doctrinal positions were developed. It was the dominant model for the Adventist understanding of the divine for at least forty years, but it was not the only model. There was an alternative picture of divine activity that focused on the member of the Trinity omitted from the hierarchy of heaven, the Holy Spirit. It had never been possible to exclude all spiritual ideas. Mrs. White might not encounter spirits in heaven, but she entered vision through the power of the Holy Spirit. In her first vision, she wrote that "the Holy Ghost fell upon me, and I seemed to be rising higher and higher, far above the dark world."[37] At meetings both before and after 1844, she would, along with those with whom she worshipped, be overcome with the power of God, falling to the floor, "slain by the Spirit."[38] As late as 1860, James White had similar experiences. In a letter to his wife, he related how, when visiting some believers, "I fell upon my face, and cried and groaned under the power of God. Brethren Sanborn and Ingraham felt about the same. We all lay on the floor under the power of God."[39]

Some account had to be given of the force that the Adventists experienced on these occasions. One thing was clear: the power was diffused; it affected groups as well as individuals. Ellen White describes one such occasion:

While the large family of Brother P. were engaged in prayer at their own house, the Spirit of God swept through the room and prostrated the kneeling suppliants. My father came in soon after and found them all both parents and children, helpless under the power of the Lord.[40]

The language in which these experiences were described emphasized the feeling of being submerged. "The power came down like a mighty, rushing wind, the room was filled with the glory of God, and I was swallowed up in the glory," Mrs. White wrote in 1848.[41] Three years later, she described a similar experience as having been a "deep plunge in the glory."[42]

Here then was the basis for an understanding of the divine, complementary to that of a heavenly hierarchy—an understanding that gave full weight to the collective experience of believers and emphasized the immanence, rather than the transcendence, of God. The Holy Spirit was naturally the focus of this interest. Thought of as "a mysterious influence emanating from the Father and the Son, their representative and the medium of their power,"[43] the Spirit could be seen as diffusing God's presence on a wide scale. The Spirit could be withdrawn from mankind as a whole, as it had been before the Noachian flood, or from a particular nation, as it had been from the French at the Revolution.[44] Among Christians, however, the Spirit should be omnipresent. It was, wrote Ellen White, "to animate and pervade the whole church."[45]

Just as the hierarchical model had differentiated Adventists from other former Millerites who interpreted the divine realm in spiritual terms, so the concern with the Spirit distinguished Adventists from their more formal associates who had given up the Shut-Door theology and did not enjoy ecstatic worship. In 1845 James White described how he felt sandwiched between these two groups:

While the Spiritualizers are pouring in one side, inducing some to "deny the only Lord God and our Savior Jesus Christ," on the other hand, Brethren J. and C. H. Pearson, and E. C. Clemons have given up the shut door, and are doing all they can to drag others to outer darkness.[46]

The Open-Door Adventists were viewed as "cold and formal, like the nominal churches." Ellen White warned against the "fanatics" who dabbled in mesmerism and spiritualism, but she also denounced formal worshippers who "would be as forward as the Pharisees were to have the disciples silenced." These people, who had themselves formerly "shouted aloud for joy in view of the immediate coming of the Lord," now accused Adventists of "Fanaticism." What they lacked was the Spirit, the power of God in their hearts.[47]

As ecstatic worship declined within the Adventist community, the emphasis on the Spirit shifted. Although still understood as diffusing the presence of God, the Spirit was pictured less as an ocean into which the worshipper was plunged and more as a fire that purified the individual believer of sin.[48] In this view, the practical distinction between the models of hierarchy and diffusion became apparent. In the hierarchical model, God communicates with man through a chain of command. As Ellen White wrote: "The angels of God are ever passing from earth to heaven, and from heaven to earth. . . . And it is through Christ, by the ministration of His heavenly messengers, that every blessing comes from God to us."[49] On this account, the presence of God is not communicated directly, but through a series of intermediaries. The opposite is true of the other model, in which "the Holy Spirit is Christ's representative, but divested of the personality of humanity, and independent thereof." Thus, "by the Spirit the Savior would be accessible to all."[50] Not only could the Spirit bring the believer into direct contact with the divine, it could do something that angels as distinct, individual beings could not do—enter the human soul. "The Holy Spirit," wrote Ellen White, "is the breath of spiritual life in the soul . . . the impartation of the life of Christ. It imbues the receiver with the attributes of Christ."[51]

The two models of divine activity seem to coexist quite easily within the writings of Ellen White. They did not always do so within the Adventist Church. The conflict came to a head in 1888 at an Adventist conference in Minneapolis. The emphasis on the impartation of the Spirit and the power of the in-dwelling Christ to promote a victorious life, presented by E. J. Waggoner and A. T. Jones, seemed to undermine the supremacy of God's law upheld by Uriah Smith and others. Although the debate focused on the nature of salvation rather than the nature of God, it polarized attitudes toward the divine as well. Most significant, however, was the impetus the 1888 conference gave to those who wished to interpret more radically the model of a diffused divine presence.[52]

One such extreme deviation was the Holy Flesh movement. In 1900 an Adventist evangelist in Indiana, S. S. Davies, began to teach that when Jesus passed through his agony in the Garden of Gethsemane, he was given "holy flesh" such as Adam had possessed before the fall.

The believer, Davies argued, could undergo a similar experience, the physical manifestation of which involved falling helpless to the floor. On revival, those who had undergone this experience were thought to have "holy flesh" and be unable to die until the coming of Christ.[53] This belief was an eccentric extrapolation of Mrs. White's emphasis on the purification of the soul. She had written that "through the agency of the Holy Spirit man becomes a partaker of the divine nature."[54] The Holy Flesh movement took this literally, but Ellen White deemed their interpretation fanatical. She did, however, recognize that the movement had something in common with the Adventism of the 1840s. But by 1901 her attitude toward ecstatic religion had changed. Even in the 1840s, she had been skeptical about crawling on the floor or rolling like a hoop, but now in her seventies, she had also become dubious about shouting and being felled by the Spirit in general. In the 1840s Adventists had distinguished themselves from extreme ecstatic elements not so much by the sobriety of their own worship as the development of a distinctive and literal theology of the kingdom of heaven. In 1900 the primary means of distancing the Holy Flesh movement was by insisting on calm and orderly worship. As Mrs. White now remarked, "The Holy Spirit never reveals itself in . . . a bedlam of noise."[55]

With the passing of half a century, a great deal had changed in Adventism. In 1850 Adventists had had some similarity to spiritualists in worship but held a very different theology. In 1900 their conduct was more orderly but their theology now had more in common with Spiritualism. Both Adventists and Spiritualists developed an interest in nature. The spiritualist Dr. Asaph Bemis Child had written in 1861 that "on every gigantic leaf of Nature's book, God's own finger has written in indelible lines, every word of which is unalterable Truth."[56] In 1903 Mrs. White had similar thoughts: "Upon every page of the great volume of His created works may still be traced His handwriting. Nature still speaks of her Creator."[57]

Without a strong incentive to insist on the transcendence of God, the diffused understanding of the divine presence began to develop toward pantheism. Mrs. White opposed the heresy, but once again it was only an extrapolation of ideas she herself had aired. The question of pantheism arose as a crucial one in the church's dispute with John Harvey Kellogg. Ellen White admitted that "a mysterious life pervades all nature,"[58] but Kellogg in The Living Temple went one small step further, writing, "there is present in the tree a power which creates and maintains it, a tree-maker in the tree, a flower-maker in the flower . . . an infinite divine, though invisible Presence."[59] Kellogg was not the only prominent Adventist to be inclined toward pantheism. W. W. Prescott, a leading educator, apparently at one stage considered a tree "the actual body of Christ."[60]

The roots of Adventist pantheism are not difficult to trace. It reunited two streams of thought that the divine hierarchy theology had separated fifty years before. Within the church, the source of the stream had been the experience of the Spirit in ecstatic worship, which had prompted a theology of the Spirit and a concentration on the infusion of Christ's presence into the soul. Those who had left Adventism in the 1840s believing in a spiritual Second Advent had often found their way into groups having a Swedenborgian conception of the world as a place in which the material and spiritual coexisted. It was a Swedenborgian, Warren Evens, who cofounded the New Thought movement, which held that through control of the intelligent properties in matter, disease could be overcome.[61] Although Kellogg specifically denied having read any New Thought literature, his conviction that every cell contained a divine presence was one echoed in New Thought principles.[62]

Thus, in the pantheism dispute as well, the church had returned to uncertainties of the post 1844 period. Realizing this, the Adventist leader S. N. Haskell appealed to the doctrine of the sanctuary as the chief obstacle to the wholescale acceptance of pantheistic theories.[63] Ellen White, too, was quick to recognize the appearance of old heresies. Like Haskell, she had no doubt as to which traditions of Adventism Kellogg opposed. Having explained why Kellogg could never lead the church, she gave a resounding reaffirmation of belief in the heavenly monarchy: "I write this that all may know that there is no controversy among Seventh-day Adventists over the question of leadership. The Lord God of Heaven is our King."[64] It was the old hierarchical theology that was invoked to defeat Kellogg, but it was transformed in the process. The concern with salvation that had motivated Jones and Waggoner was not entirely forgotten. The pantheistic implication of their ideas had been repudiated; their emphasis on immanence remained. But now the focus was shifted from the process of sanctification to the person of the Sanctifier. Ellen White's masterpiece, *The Desire of Ages*, published in 1898, had at last managed to convey her own Christ-centered religious experience to a wide audience. The book had taken a firm stand on the full divinity and eternity of Jesus while encouraging meditation on his earthly life.

This concentration on Christ was given more systematic treatment by W. W. Prescott in his textbook *The Doctrine of Christ*, published in 1920. His presentation exemplified the desire for consensus rather than controversy, which then motivated the church. While avoiding discussion of such potentially sensitive areas as the doctrine of the Trinity, Prescott affirmed the centrality of Christ to every part of salvation history. Urging readers to "receive him as 'the way, the truth, and the life,'" Prescott implied that if Christ was experienced "in the life, merely abstract theology" would look after itself.[65]

As it turned out, the church leadership looked after systematic theology. In 1931 the "Fundamental Beliefs of Seventh-Day Adventists" were formulated for publication in the church's yearbook. The statement of belief hardly represented a groundswell of opinion. It was formulated by four carefully chosen officials and published without consultation with the church's full governing authority.[66] For the first time, the church officially proclaimed its belief in the doctrine of the Trinity. There was no significant dissent. The two models of divine activity had been made redundant in the 1920s by the overwhelming concentration on the person of Christ in the salvation experience. Other things had changed as well. Before her death in 1915, the church had enjoyed the guidance of Ellen White. While that lasted, there was little need for creeds or formulas; the church had united around an individual rather than a set of statements.

Another factor that made the two pictures of God seem outmoded was the disappearance of the social situation that had stimulated their development. In the 1840s Adventists had been positioned between the "formal brethren" on the one side and spiritualizing fanatics on the other. The two models had served as a means of differentiating Adventist thinking from that of other groups adjacent on the religious spectrum of the time. Almost a century later, the situation had been reversed; the catalyst for theological activity was now the desire to align with fundamentalism against modernist Christianity. As the procedures followed in the adoption of the 1931 Fundamental Beliefs demonstrate, the church sought to establish a platform from which to approach the world and thus attempted to forestall internal debate.

Despite this, the hierarchical model of the divine realm did not become completely redundant. In the 1970s the theologian Graham Maxwell used it as a framework within which to develop a uniquely Adventist understanding of salvation history. Maxwell followed Ellen White in presenting evil as originating in Satan's unwillingness to accept the hierarchical social arrangements of heaven. Because Satan charged God with acting unjustly, his immediate execution would only have appeared to confirm his accusation that God was arbitrary and dictatorial: "The universe had never seen death. It was not yet apparent that death was the inevitable consequence of sin. There was danger that the universe would assume that God had executed His enemies, that onlooking beings would thus be led to obey Him out of fear."[67] To demonstrate that death was the result of sin yet not a capricious injustice, God gave up his own Son: "Christ died primarily to prove the righteousness of God in the great controversy. . . . With this supreme demonstration of God's righteousness all questions about His character and government were settled throughout the universe. God had won His case."[68]

Maxwell transformed the picture of the heavenly court. Man was not on trial, but God was: "He was inviting the universe to test even His claims and to believe only what proved to be true."[69] The jury is composed of both the unfallen and the fallen citizens of the universe. For men, a positive decision in favor of God secures salvation. Although Maxwell's picture of the universe suggested a presidential democracy in which God required popular support rather than a feudal monarchy, he stood securely within the Adventist tradition, which finds in the structure of heavenly society a means of understanding the human condition. However, in his willingness to take man out of the dock, Maxwell revealed the influence of the contemporary debate in Adventism in which the focus had shifted from heaven to earth.

CHAPTER 6

The Human Condition

In the book, *Questions on Doctrine*, church leaders published the answers they gave to the Baptist Walter Martin and the Presbyterian Donald Barnhouse, who posed questions on Adventist beliefs between 1955 and 1956. In an article on Seventh-day Adventism published in 1956, Martin considered four doctrines that Adventists were presumed to hold:

1. The atonement of Christ was not completed on the cross.
2. Salvation is the result of grace plus the works of the law.
3. The Lord Jesus Christ was a created being, not from all eternity.
4. Christ partook of man's sinful fallen nature at the incarnation.[1]

He concluded that "to charge the majority of Adventists today with holding these heretical views is *unfair, inaccurate,* and *decidedly unchristian!*"[2] On the question of the eternity of Christ, Martin's assessment was probably accurate. The issue had not been discussed in twentieth-century Adventism, and with the elimination of Arian statements from the 1944 edition of Uriah Smith's classic *Daniel and Revelation*, anti-Trinitarianism had quietly been consigned to history.[3] But on the other three topics, Martin's judgment was premature. From the publication of *Questions on Doctrine* in 1957 until the 1980s, the atonement, the incarnation, and the nature of salvation have been the subjects of constant debate within the Adventist church.[4]

That Martin misjudged the measure of agreement within Adventism is undeniable. His mistake was to accept uncritically the arguments that were later published in *Questions of Doctrine*. On the Adventist side, the dialogue with Martin and Barnhouse was viewed as an exercise in public relations. There was little attempt to give full weight to Adventist history, still less to consult the existing membership. LeRoy Edwin Froom, one of the authors of *Questions on Doctrine*, saw the meetings as "changing the impaired image of Adventism."[5] This goal was achieved but at the price of a protracted and bitter dispute within the church itself. To understand the significance of this debate, it is necessary to examine the interrelationships among several doctrinal areas. This chapter will review three decades of argument about the atonement, incarnation, and salvation in the light of the Adventist understanding of the nature of man.

The first Adventist statement of belief, the *Declaration* of 1872, denied that the atonement began on the cross. In *Questions on Doctrine*, the atonement is presented as having been completed on the cross.[6] In the intervening period, it was generally believed that the atonement began on the cross and completed in the heavenly sanctuary. Ellen White put it thus: "The intercession of Christ in man's behalf in the sanctuary above is as essential to the plan of salvation as was His death upon the cross. By His death He began that work which after His resurrection he ascended to complete in heaven."[7] For her, there was little distinction between the function of Christ's death and his heavenly ministry. He "died to make an atoning sacrifice for our sins" and is now "our interceding High Priest, making an atoning sacrifice for us."[8] In *Questions on Doctrine* this belief is reinterpreted. The authors advise that "when, therefore, one hears an Adventist say, or reads in Adventist literature—even in the writings of Ellen G. White—that Christ is making atonement now, it should be understood that we mean simply that Christ is now *making application of the benefits of the sacrificial atonement He made on the cross*."[9]

The distinction is subtle. First, the atonement is made, then its benefits are mediated. Both elements are part of the work of salvation, but only the first, according to *Questions on Doctrine*, is in itself an act of atonement. In Adventist theology, the difference was far from trivial, for the doctrine of the sanctuary had been developed by O. R. L. Crosier on the understanding that Christ "did not begin the work of making the atonement, whatever the nature of that work may be, till after his ascension, when by his own blood he entered his heavenly sanctuary for us."[10] In order to show that October 22, 1844, marked a second phase of Christ's heavenly ministry, Crosier argued that there were exact parallels between Christ's work and that of the Old Testament priesthood. *Questions on Doctrine* made the analogy a great deal less exact. For although it refers to the period since 1844 as "the antitypical day of Atonement," it scrupulously avoids reference to Christ's atoning work in the sanctuary.[11] *Questions on Doctrine* left the doctrine of the sanctuary intact, but it began to erode its foundations. What was intended to be merely a cosmetic change ended up disturbing the equilibrium of the entire Adventist theological system.

A similar pattern may be seen to have resulted from the account of the incarnation given in response to the question "What do Adventists understand by Christ's use of the title 'Son of Man'?"[12] Reassuring Martin and Barnhouse that Adventists believed in the incarnation "in common with all true Christians," the authors of *Questions on Doctrine* went on to emphasize that "in His human nature Christ was perfect and sinless," being "exempt from the inherited passions and pollutions that corrupt the natural descendants of Adam."[13]

Such statements appeared to contradict Ellen White's belief that "Jesus accepted humanity when the race had been weakened by four thousand years of sin. Like every child of Adam He accepted the results of the working of the great law of heredity. What these results were is shown in the history of His earthly ancestors."[14] In *Questions on Doctrine*, it is argued that "these weaknesses, frailties, infirmities, failings are things which we, with our sinful fallen natures, have to bear," but that "Christ bore all this vicariously, just as vicariously He bore the iniquities of us all."[15] Here again, the distinctions are subtle: the differences between the human nature of Adam before the fall and the nature of man after the fall and between the vicarious and the inherent possession of human frailty may seem relatively unimportant. But M. L. Andreasen, the veteran theologian, realized that within the context of Adventist theology, they were not. If Christ was exempt from human frailty, he could not truly be man's exemplar in keeping the law: "Only as Christ placed himself on the level of the humanity He had come to save, could He demonstrate to men how to overcome their infirmities and passions."[16]

If Christ had an unfair advantage, how could man be expected to follow his example in living a perfect life? The problem was particularly acute, as perfection had been suggested by Ellen White as the goal of the Adventist people: "While our great High Priest is making the atonement for us, we should seek to become perfect in Christ."[17] Her call to perfection was urgent: "Jesus does not change the character at His coming. The work of transformation must be done now."[18] The road to perfection could seem long and hard, all the more so if Christ was believed to have traversed it with a headstart. The feeling that there was an unbridgeable gulf between human sinfulness and the need for perfection was a source of concern to Robert Brinsmead, the Australian dissident. He describes how, when at college in the 1950s, "very few people that I questioned had any real buoyant hope of being able to pass the scrutiny of the soon-coming judgment of the living . . . most lived in real fear and dread of the judgment, having no way of knowing how to be ready except to 'try harder by God's grace' and to hope that such judgment would not come too soon."[19] Brinsmead's answer to this problem was to emphasize the miraculous infusion of perfection through the cleansing of the heavenly sanctuary. This perfection would, he believed, sustain the saints after the close of probation.[20]

Questions on Doctrine had made perfection seem a remote possibility. Brinsmead vigorously reasserted not only the possibility but the necessity of perfection. In this he concentrated on the subjective experience of salvation rather than the objective event of the cross. In contrast, the focus on the crucifixion encouraged by *Questions on Doctrine* was taken further by the Adventist theologian Edward Heppenstall. His solution to the difficulty of explaining how the sinner could reach perfection was to argue that perfection was neither necessary nor possible. "Absolute perfection and sinlessness," he maintained, "cannot be realized here and now."[21]

Heppenstall's response was, in Adventist terms, far more radical than that of Brinsmead. Heppenstall began with a thoroughgoing belief in original sin. "*Total depravity*," he wrote, "is the phrase used to describe the sinner in his lost condition."[22] All men, he believed, enter the world "in a state of separation from God."[23] Christ, alone, did not. He "was sinless, free constitutionally from every taint of sin and defilement."[24] This was necessary, for "the efficacy of Christ's sacrifice lay in his absolute sinlessness."[25] Because of the cross, God may acquit the guilty through the process of justification, in which "the righteousness of Christ is imputed or reckoned to the believer." Once justification has been imputed, sanctification may be imparted. Through sanctification the in-dwelling Christ gradually brings the believer toward a state of perfection.[26] But there are definite limits beyond which the process of sanctification cannot extend: "If Christian perfection means restoration here and now to Adam's sinless state *and complete harmony with God*, so that a man need no longer be classed as a sinner, then the Bible knows nothing of it." Heppenstall concluded that "it is spiritual maturity and stability that is possible in this life, not sinless perfection."[27] Prior to Heppenstall, no important Adventist writer had denied the possibility of perfection. Ellen White had been unequivocal: "As the Son of man was perfect in His life, so His followers are to be perfect in their life."[28] But it was Brinsmead, who had but suggested an idiosyncratic form of perfection, who became the heretic. A farmer with a genius for theological polemic, Brinsmead was impatient with the church's administration and gathered a personal following known as the Awakening movement. Heppenstall, an academic in church employment, led the attack on Brinsmead's theology. His abandonment of perfectionism could thus be construed as part of the official critique of the Awakening. Thus Brinsmead, by emphasizing an element of Adventist theology that *Questions on Doctrine* downplayed, facilitated its denial by Heppenstall, the church's most influential theologian.[29]

A further irony followed: Brinsmead's conversion to Heppenstall's position. Having given up perfectionism, Brinsmead went further than Heppenstall and dismissed sanctification altogether. In the 1970s he began to locate himself in the reformed tradition, which equated salvation with justification alone and denied that righteousness could be imparted as well as imputed. For Brinsmead, as for Calvin, all goodness is extrinsic to man. Remaining outside the denomination, but directing a constant stream of propaganda to his followers, Brinsmead remained influential. His most prominent ally in the new figuration was his fellow Australian Desmond Ford.[30]

In 1975 Mrs. Gillian Ford wrote a paper titled "The Soteriological Implications of the Human Nature of Christ" in which she argued that Christ's human nature was sinless, that perfection was impossible, and that righteousness by faith referred to justification alone.[31] She brought together the innovations of *Questions on Doctrine*, Heppenstall, and Brinsmead. It was the latter association that raised the eyebrows of conservative Adventists, for Gillian's husband, Desmond, who wrote an appendix to her paper, taught theology at Avondale College, the Adventist center for ministerial training in Australia. In 1976 a conference was called at Palmdale, California. It attempted to reconcile the views of Desmond Ford with the theology of Adventist theologians in America. The consensus statement was ambiguous, and all sides were able to claim that it supported their beliefs.[32] There were three schools of thought: that of the Fords and Brinsmead; a traditional perfectionism taught by, among others, Herbert Douglass, then associate editor of the *Review*, which argued that Christ had a sinful human nature, that righteousness involved both justification and sanctification, and that perfection was possible;[33] and an intermediate position, represented by Heppenstall and another Adventist theologian Hans LaRondelle, which denied that Christ had a sinful human nature or that perfection was possible but allowed that the process of sanctification brought the believer toward perfection.[34]

Coexistence between these groups might have been possible, but Ford went on to work out the implications of his position for belief in the doctrine of the sanctuary. The purpose of Christ's heavenly ministry is to separate the saints from their sins. Implicit in this concept is the idea that some deeds are good, others bad, and that Christ must blot out all record of the bad deeds if the saved are to enter a perfect heaven. For Ford, as for Heppenstall, sin is an ineradicable part of the human condition, no deeds are, of themselves, "good." If all sin was blotted out in the sanctuary, there would, for Ford, be no saints left to save. In short, Ford's conception of salvation made the doctrine of the sanctuary redundant.[35] On October 27, 1979, Desmond Ford publicly announced that he did not believe in the sanctuary doctrine. A year later a landmark conference was held at Glacier View, Colorado, to discuss the question, and although over a quarter of the Adventist theologians, ministers, and administrators present did not appear to believe in the sanctuary doctrine either, Desmond Ford lost his ministerial credentials and left church employment.[36]

A multitude of factors contributed to Ford's rejection of the sanctuary doctrine. A Biblical scholar with a particular interest in the book of Daniel, Ford found the traditional Adventist interpretation of certain crucial texts unsatisfactory.[37] The influence of Ellen White had been undermined by the historical research of the 1970s, with the result that Ford, himself an Ellen White enthusiast, felt able to qualify the scope of her authority in the light of her "errors" on the sanctuary question.[38] But at the root of his attack on the doctrine was his conviction that the blotting out of individual sins is no part of salvation history. Ford took the implications of *Questions on Doctrine* to their logical conclusion. If the atonement was completed on the cross, then the sanctuary can only mediate its benefits to man. If Christ did not have a sinful human nature, then there is no precedent for the perfection of man. Thus the benefits of the atonement mediated to man in the sanctuary service cannot be such as to bring man to perfection. If man is not brought to perfection, he is saved as a sinner. If man is saved as a sinner, his sins do not need to be individually eradicated. There are thus no supplementary benefits of the atonement that need be mediated to man, and the heavenly ministry of Christ becomes superfluous.

The sequence of events that leads from *Questions on Doctrine* to the dismissal of Desmond Ford is a remarkable example of the way in which a web of theological ideas can unravel once a single thread has been cut. However, it would be foolish simply to dismiss this history as revealing the unintended consequences of the church's zeal for public recognition in the 1950s. To perceive the historical and theological context of recent events in Adventism, it is necessary to examine the early development of Adventist theology in the nineteenth century—in particular the church's understanding of the nature of man.

The central element in early Adventist thought was the immediacy of the Second Advent. From this was derived a particular understanding of the nature of man, which in turn determined the Adventist understanding of salvation. D. P. Hall was the first Seventh-day Adventist to give a systematic account of the doctrine of man in the light of this apocalyptic orientation. According to Hall, "the views we entertain of man's nature will give shape and color, to a very large extent, to our views of life, death, resurrection, heaven, hell, and, in fact, all the other subjects of revelation."[39] His purpose was to attack the conventional Christian belief that "man is a compound of mortality and immortality." If this view was taken, then "three *fundamental* doctrines of holy writ are of no possible importance"—the Second Coming of Christ, the resurrection of the dead, and the Judgment.[40] His reasoning was clear. If immortal souls go to heaven or hell at death, there is no need for a cataclysmic end to the world. Therefore, there must be "no mixing up or mingling of mortality with immortality," for "*man* is a *unit*, composed of *dust*, his *mental* and *moral* nature inhering in the organized man."[41]

In his attempt to prove that the spirit is neither immortal nor separable from the body, Hall was following the conditionalism of the influential Millerite preacher George Storrs. In the conditionalist view immortality is bestowed on believers only at the Second Coming.[42] But like many other Adventists, Hall was also motivated by his opposition to spiritualism. His book, published in 1854, was entitled *Man Not Immortal: The Only Shield Against the Seductions of Modern Spiritualism*. Here, again, his thinking was simple. Spiritualism undermined one of the most attractive features of the Adventist message: the hope of being reunited with the dead. If it was only death that separated the living from their departed friends, there was no reason to wait expectantly for the Second Advent.[43]

The early Adventists followed Hall in believing that man was an indivisible being that did not possess natural immortality. The saints would be translated at the Second Coming. The righteous dead would be resurrected at the same time, while the sinful dead would have to wait until after the millennium for their resurrection and final destruction.[44] The Adventists focused on translation rather than resurrection.[45] In translation there is no break between earth and heaven. The entire man is saved, not simply his soul. At the Second Coming, the saints will be "clothed with immortality," but their complete humanity will remain, for they are about to enter a divine realm populated by beings with material bodies. Belief in the unity of man was thus the natural corollary of a concern with the Second Advent and its attendant emphasis on translation.

The Adventist answer to the question "What will be saved?" has always been "the entire man." But the answer to the supplementary question "How will men be saved?" has been formulated differently depending on how close Adventists felt the prospect of translation to be.

In early Adventist history when the Second Coming was expected at any moment, there was one crucial criterion: the saved would be those who passed the eschatological test of the Sabbath. James White was blunt: "If we violate the fourth [commandment], we shall fall in the day of slaughter."[46] This view, however, was modified when the Second Coming did not occur as many had anticipated during the seven years after 1844. If people now had to wait for translation, they needed to be adequately prepared. In Ellen White's words, "God proves His people in this world. This is the fitting-up place to appear in His presence."[47] As the character would remain unchanged at the Second Advent, it was natural for this preparation to be continued to perfection.[48] The criteria of salvation were thus elaborated to include not just correct belief and obedience to the law but also a completely self-disciplined body and character. This requirement was a corollary of the idea that at translation it was the unified body and soul that were to be taken to heaven. Eschatology demanded perfected saints and a unified human being; the two together necessitated the perfection of the whole person. For Ellen White, this meant strict control of the sexual appetite. In 1870 she argued that "salvation is not experienced by those who do not control their base passions."[49] Her counsel was specific: Meat "strengthens the animal passions,"[50] so "grains and fruits prepared free from grease, and in as natural a condition as possible, should be the food for the tables of all who claim to be preparing for translation to heaven."[51]

This emphasis on the conscious control of every habit as a means of transforming the entire human was uniquely appropriate to the Adventist understanding of human nature as a unified whole. But, like the previous emphasis on the keeping of the Sabbath, it was only capable of sustaining the spiritual life of the Adventist movement for a brief period. When the Second Advent was expected at any moment, it was appropriate that the chief criterion of salvation should be the observance of the seventh-day Sabbath. It was a habit that could be acquired within a week. As the Apocalypse gradually receded from view, the emphasis shifted to self-control. But that, too, could be practiced to apparent perfection within a relatively short time. If all that was required was modification of behavior, then the saints could soon be perfected and ready for translation. When Christ did not return as expected, Adventist soteriology underwent further modification. In the late nineteenth century, Mrs. White started to emphasize another requirement for translation: the need for spiritual perfection, achieved through Christ's presence within the believer. "Christ is waiting with longing desire for the manifestation of Himself in His church," she argued. "When the character of Christ shall be perfectly reproduced in His people, then He will come to claim them as his own."[52]

The perfection for which Christ was depicted as waiting was less easily recognized or obtained than the behavioral perfection on which the Adventists had focused earlier. One of Ellen White's earliest statements on this theme came in 1873. Never as legalistic as some of her contemporaries, Mrs. White always retained a strong appreciation of the value of spiritual experience: "The perfection of Christian character depends wholly upon the grace and strength found alone in God. . . . System and order are highly essential, but none should receive the impression that these will do the work without the grace and power of God operating upon the mind and heart."[53] Perfection understood in this way was only to be realized with difficulty. It was, she wrote in 1889, "a lifelong work, unattainable by those who are not willing to strive for it in God's appointed way, by slow and toilsome steps."[54]

Mrs. White's understanding of salvation owed something to her own Methodist background. Arminian Methodism emphasized the need for personal holiness, and the quest for perfection became the focus of the mid-nineteenth-century Holiness movement. But the prophetess's interpretation of perfection differed from that of John Wesley's followers, and she condemned "Methodist sanctification" as a "false theory."[55] Wesley perceived the "second blessing"—the moment of perfection—

to be a distinct event that took place between the time at which a person was justified and his death. Although he admitted that perfection "may be gradually wrought in some," he considered it "infinitely desirable . . . that it should be done instantaneously."[56] Mrs. White, on the other hand, made no absolute distinction between justification and sanctification and saw both as part of a single process that culminated in perfection prior to translation. Her understanding was eschatological rather than ontological.

However, the doctrine of perfection was propagated by some church members such as E. J. Waggoner, whose experience was similar to that of contemporary Americans who attended the camp meetings of the Holiness movement. Waggoner's enthusiasm was grounded in an experience he had in 1882 at a camp meeting in Healdsburg, California: "In that moment I had my first positive knowledge, which came like an overwhelming flood, that God loved me and that Christ died for me. God and I were the only beings I was conscious of in the universe. I knew then, by actual sight, that God was in Christ reconciling the world unto Himself; I was the whole world with all its sin."[57] Waggoner and A. T. Jones attempted to communicate this experience to the Adventist community at the church's Minneapolis conference of 1888. At this meeting the question of inner perfection was the subject of heated debate and the eschatological understanding of holiness was at issue. The message that Waggoner and Jones preached concerned the immanence of God in the world and the sanctifying power of Christ within the individual. As Jones proclaimed in a sermon in 1889:

If we want to be good let our faith touch him, and goodness comes to us and makes us good; if we want to be righteous, in answer to our faith, power comes to us and makes us righteous. In answer to our faith as it grows more and more of his power and goodness will come to us, and just before probation closes we shall be like him indeed, and then we shall be keeping the commandments of God in fact because there will be so much of him in us that there will be none of ourselves there.[58]

This account of salvation differed from those to which Adventists were accustomed in several ways: the emphasis was shifted from obedience to faith, from the actions of the body to the orientation of the mind; the goal of the religious life was changed from conformity to an external law to receptivity to the in-dwelling Christ. Some things did not change, notably the emphasis on perfection. Adventists could hardly reject perfectionism while they believed in the unity of man, and they were tied to their belief in the unity of man by the expectation of translation rather than death.

Salvation was now seen as a process of two stages: first, acceptance and justification and then the sanctified life. Ellen White concentrated on the second aspect; she described the process as one in which "we submit ourselves to Christ, the heart is united with His heart, the will is merged in His will, the mind becomes one with His mind, [and] the thoughts are brought unto captivity to Him." And she agreed with Jones in anticipating that this harmony could be achieved only "just before the close of probation."[59] Jones himself, and many other Adventists in the 1890s, placed greater emphasis on the first part of the process: the infusion of righteousness that accompanied the acceptance of justification. As he wrote in 1900: "While of yourself you can do nothing, God, who dwelleth in you, will work in you that which is pleasing in his sight through Jesus Christ."[60] Waggoner followed this belief through to its logical conclusion in a sermon in 1899: "[God] says that the life of Jesus should be manifested in our mortal flesh; and when that life is dwelling in our mortal flesh, mortality does not have any hold on it." The still widespread expectation of translation was evident when he was asked: "Do you ever expect to be sick?" He replied simply "No; I expect to live forever."[61]

In the Holy Flesh movement, these ideas found more dramatic expression, but they were still only the logical development of Adventism's long-standing concern for perfection in readiness for the translation of the whole man. Followers of the Holy Flesh movement believed in the divinization of the body. They contended that "the seal [of God] cannot be placed on any who are diseased, crippled or even have gray hairs."[62] It is not surprising that the views of Ellen White prevailed over those who believed in holy flesh. The credibility of any movement that asserts that its devotees are immortal is always liable to be undermined by the passage of time. Once again, the delay of the Second Advent shaped the range of options in Adventist soteriology.

In the nineteenth century, the eschatological orientation of adventism determined discussion not only of the doctrine of humanity but also of the question of salvation. During the first half of the twentieth century, Ellen White's emphasis on sanctification (developed during the 1890s and expressed most fully in her 1900 book *Christ's Object Lessons*) dominated Adventist thinking about salvation. To some degree, the balance shifted away from a concern with the in-dwelling Christ back to a preoccupation with conformity to the law. But the theological structure remained the same. "The *imputed* righteousness of Christ [was] for sins that are past, and the *imparted* righteousness of Christ for revealing the divine nature in human flesh."[63]

However, by the 1930s there had occurred a significant shift in the view of perfection. It was evident that several generations of Adventists had now died without experiencing translation. This fact prompted reassessment. Although still upheld as a goal, perfection was now generally taken to be unattainable except by the last generation on earth. This was M. L. Andreasen's particular interest. "It is," he wrote, "in the last generation of men living on the earth that God's power unto sanctification will stand fully revealed."[64] But in the next twenty years there developed an additional problem among those Adventists who still took seriously the attainment of perfection in preparation for Christ's return. The gap between the goal of perfection and the chances of its realization seemed very great. The discrepancy between what was demanded and what could be achieved manifested itself in the despondency Brinsmead found among his college contemporaries in the 1950s, and Brinsmead's own early perfectionism was, self-consciously, an attempt to cross the gap.

Brinsmead's opponents asserted that the gulf was unbridgeable. Such a view not only marked a new departure in Adventist soteriology, it also implied that the Second Coming had receded into the more distant horizons of the Adventist mind. In the late 1960s, a survey indicated that 44 percent of Adventists questioned considered that the Second Advent received less emphasis in the preaching of the church than thirty years previously, while only 15 percent thought its relative importance had increased.[65] It is perhaps in this context that Edward Heppenstall's emphasis on justification in the 1960s should be understood. Although his soteriology was a response to Brinsmead's perfectionism, which in turn was a reaction to the new soteriology of *Questions on Doctrine*, the theology of justification can be seen to compensate for a decline in belief in an imminent Second Coming. Justification enables believers to be made righteous now rather than at the end of time. It makes redundant the intrinsic perfection previously deemed necessary for translation because believers can be declared righteous without any change to their sinful state. The widespread acceptance of justification indicates that by the 1960s many Adventists were looking for a solution to the problem of how perfection was to be achieved in the present, rather than by an increasingly remote final generation of the future. It is significant that in Heppenstall's writings the prospect of translation is rarely mentioned, and the character of the last generation is never discussed. In contrast Herbert Douglass, who retains a strong belief in the nearness of the Second Advent, continually emphasizes the need for perfection of character in readiness for the harvest of the saints.[66]

Cut from their moorings in eschatology, Adventist beliefs about man and his salvation were set adrift. If most Adventists expected to die rather than be translated, then the problem of how to sanctify the body did not arise. If the Second Coming seemed distant, death seemed correspondingly near. A new set of theological problems arose, relating not to a group of people who expected to live forever but to people painfully conscious of their own mortality. As the Adventist philosopher Jean Zurcher commented: "The lugubrious but real fact of death which envelops us is of a nature to make us feel more than any other one thing the necessity of grasping the eternal life to which we are called by Jesus Christ."[67]

With death expected to intervene between human life and the immortal perfection of the redeemed, there is no continuity between mortal and eternal life. Justification changes the relationship between man and God. But it does not change the relationship between the human body and God. Original sin condemns the human body and its actions as worthless. On a spiritual level, men and women are thus separable from their bodies and their actions. Justification by faith suggests a soteriological dualism. As Heppenstall asserts: "To assume that with conversion and sanctification the Holy Spirit restores man to sinless perfection is also to assert that all the ravages of death have been eradicated. All the evidence proves otherwise."[68] This is hardly compatible with the traditional Adventist view that man is an indivisible unit and that "none of his components can exist in isolation from the others."[69] It also suggests that the properties of the mind are more essential than those of the body. D. P. Hall, in attacking those who made "the soul or spirit of man really the man proper,"[70] set the tone for generations of Adventists. But an absence of interest in translation and a concentration on justification may imply some acceptance of the theory Hall condemned.

Justification alone effects no change in the human physical condition. By driving a wedge between human activity and the act of salvation, the proponents of justification have left Adventists with the need to find a new rationale for their observance of principles previously understood to be fitting them for translation. This has been provided by the philosophy of "holism" (which Adventists often refer to as "wholism"). Although an ill-defined complex of ideas, holism was, in 1985, considered by Adventist scholars to be the church's single most important contribution to theology.[71] Its leading Adventist exponent, the bioethicist Jack Provonsha, summarizes his position as follows:

Man is a unity, a marvelously interpenetrating, interacting unity of one dimension with another. . . . This is why the health of the body is also a moral issue. What happens to a man's body is important to his entire personality and character, and thus may have eternal implications.[72]

"A Christian ethic," Provonsha argues, "becomes an ethic of health. . . . That does not mean necessarily that it is a sin to be sick, but it could mean that it would be a sin to be sicker than you need to be."[73] If the avoidance of illness is a religious duty, physical and spiritual well-being become difficult to separate. Not only does health facilitate spirituality but religious vitality promotes physical vitality. Accordingly, religious commitment may be seen to bring immediate material benefits. Thus, Adventist author Don Hawley in *Come Alive! Feel Fit—Live Longer* quotes approvingly the view that "irrespective of the future rewards of living, laying aside all discussion of future life, *it would pay any man or woman to live the Christ-life just for the mental and moral rewards it affords here in this present world.*"[74] Adventists' impressive longevity record allows Leo R. Van Dolson to develop the argument. "The better-life package God gives us contains specific laws of our being. These involve every aspect of life—physical, mental, social, and spiritual. When applied properly they enable us to enjoy life to the utmost and actually to live longer than we would if we violate them."[75]

Adventists once emphasized the fact that they expected to live forever; in the 1970s the focus switched to the possibility of living for six and a half years more than the national average. Adventists have not abandoned the hope of eternal life, but many now expect to enter it after the resurrection rather than through translation. This fundamental shift has been accompanied by changes in the understanding of salvation appropriate to a receding eschatology. The path from *Questions on Doctrine* to Glacier View can be seen as the gradual accommodation of Adventist theology to an understanding of humanity based on the premise that humans are more likely to die than to be translated. Accordingly, two new emphases developed: one that saw salvation as an external event of which humans become the beneficiary, and another that construed the transformation of the entire person as a process desirable for its this-worldly advantages.

CHAPTER 7

The Development of Adventist Theology

The most readily available literature on Seventh-day Adventism is that written by several evangelical authors in the early 1960s, each of whom concluded with the question "What, then, should be our attitude toward Adventists and Adventism?"[1] Martin hoped that "evangelical Christianity as a whole will extend the hand of fellowship to a group of sincere, earnest fellow Christians."[2] Douty disagreed, arguing that "as long as Adventism remains Adventism it must be repudiated."[3] Hoekema was more ingenuous, pleading with his "friends, the Adventists, to repudiate the cultic features and unscriptural doctrines which mar Seventh-day Adventism."[4]

Their responses may have been different, but the authors all had common presuppositions. They assumed that the version of Christianity practiced by themselves and propagated by their publishers in Grand Rapids, Michigan, was representative of, and normative for, the rest of the Christian world. In arguing that "Adventists are a truly Christian group," Martin was simply saying that Adventism bore a close resemblance to his own brand of Christianity.[5] Most people who consider themselves Christian are not, even in America, evangelicals in the Reformed tradition. The work of Martin, Douty, and Hoekema gives a view of one American minority from the perspective of another.

These evangelical commentators not only had a narrow view of the Christian world, they also ignored the diversity of the Adventist tradition. They implicitly assumed that all Adventists believed the same things and that Adventism constituted a unified body of religious doctrine. This is, and was, very far from being the case. Adventism has, as only Martin acknowledged, undergone considerable historical development. The critics were not entirely to blame for their misapprehension. The Adventist evangelist gives the impression that all Adventists hold, and always have held, the same, clearly defined set of opinions. But any new convert will quickly realize that the situation is not so straightforward. It is not just that Adventists, like everyone else, are given to individual idiosyncracies of thought. The intellectual life of the church is so structured that plurality of opinion is the almost inevitable result.

Even at the level of the local church, the opportunities for intellectual self-expression are maximized, and the means of control are minimal. Sermons are long but usually unemotional; prayers are extemporized. In Sabbath School classes, which meet before the main worship service, adults study a set of lessons prepared by the church leadership. The teacher usually has little or no theological training, but the discussion is often lively. Young people's meetings, Bible study groups, and prayer meetings provide further opportunity for lay theological expression. Although almost all Adventists have been through a sequence of Bible studies prior to baptism, their ideas are informed not only by Adventist traditions but also by whatever other Christian literature is available to them. Such lay theologizing sometimes becomes bogged down in perennial conundrums of the "Who was Cain's wife?" variety, but there is also the opportunity to develop personal philosophies free from the direct control of the church's administration.

The existence of several church publishing houses and numerous periodicals permits similar freedom on a wider scale. Although the church attempts to publish nothing that diverges significantly from the Adventist tradition, policies differ from one publishing house to the next. In the 1970s the Review and Herald Publishing Association was associated with a conservative Adventism, while the Southern Publishing Association, which later merged with the Review and Herald, printed material on the other end of the theological spectrum.[6] To the average member, however, all church publications are likely to appear equally orthodox, provided that they are distributed through authorized channels. Thus, even if Adventist sources are used, the Sabbath School teacher is likely to be drawing on a broader spectrum of opinion than might be thought.

What of the men and women who write for Adventist publishers? Many of them also teach in denominational schools and colleges and have had graduate education in secular or interdenominational institutions. A survey of religion teachers in Adventist colleges and universities conducted in 1985 revealed that most under age 55 felt themselves to be more liberal than their fellow church members and had been influenced by a wide variety of secular thinkers.[7] The publications of Adventist scholars are thus likely to convey trends in the contemporary intellectual scene to the church's membership. On the other hand, ideas can filter up as well as down. Brinsmead's popular theology succeeded in effecting a change of outlook in several of the church's intellectual leaders.[8]

Adventist thought is thus in a constant flux. Although the denomination is highly structured, centrally controlled, and administratively authoritarian, the spread of ideas cannot be effectively restrained. Adventists are encouraged to express their thoughts in many ways. The flow of information in church meetings and publications is far too great for it to be monitored successfully. It is thus difficult to know where to find Adventist theology. Is it composed of ideas articulated in Sabbath School, preached from the pulpit, published by the press, or discussed among academic colleagues? Some doctrines, such as that of the sanctuary, are officially promulgated but widely doubted by Adventist academics. Others, such as the complete inerrancy of the scriptures, are probably believed by most church members but not officially endorsed. Many elements of the church's eschatology are carefully taught to would-be converts but play no active part in the internal theological life of the church. There are, accordingly, discrepancies both between the beliefs emphasized in internal discussion and those expounded in outside evangelism, and between the ideas that circulate in various parts of the church's organization.

There is nothing mysterious or sinister about this state of affairs. The point needs to be emphasized only because it reveals the inadequacy of basing any discussion of Adventism on a single source, however highly placed its authors. (Martin and his critics made use of *Questions on Doctrine* as though it was a consensus document rather than the most controversial Adventist publication of the century.) It is impossible to gauge adequately every strand of Adventist opinion, and it would be misleading to compare data based on contemporary interviews or surveys with historical material based on published sources. Accordingly, although chapters 2 through 6 are based on published material, it should be recognized that a review of the published sources is unlikely to comprise a complete picture of Adventist thought, for this material represents the opinions of an educated elite with privileged access to the church's media.

The conclusions of Martin, Hoekema, and others were based on the assumption that Adventism stood close to conservative evangelicalism but was separated from it by the denomination's distinctive doctrinal position. One Adventist response to this accusation has been an attempt to show that even the distinctive theological positions of Adventism are drawn from sources that evangelicals claim as their own. In the four-volume work *The Prophetic Faith of Our Fathers*, Le Roy Edwin Froom traced the roots of Adventist eschatology through centuries of prophetic exegesis and in *The Conditionalist Faith of Our Fathers* compiled a comparable collection of information relating to the doctrine of the nonimmortality of the soul.[9] Adventists have also been active in excavating the lost seventh-day Sabbatarians of history, finding their own position heralded by the ancient churches of the Ethiopians, Armenians, and Celts.[10] More recently, Bryan Ball has attempted to demonstrate that the seeds of Seventh-day Adventist thought were planted by seventeenth-century English Puritans, and W. L. Emmerson has looked for precursors of Adventism in the radical wing of the Protestant Reformation.[11]

While it is true that twentieth-century Adventism differs from contemporary evangelicalism in only a few doctrines, such a doctrine-by-doctrine comparison is not altogether helpful in establishing the character and historical position of Adventist theology. Within Christianity, otherwise diverse groups may share superficially similar theological positions for entirely fortuitous reasons. There are, after all, only a limited number of options within the framework of traditional Christianity. Many of the historical studies by Adventists investigate such obscure and fortuitous parallels. The comparison of Adventist hermeneutics with those of Theodore of Mopsuestia is, for example, an intriguing but ultimately uninformative intellectual exercise.[12] Similarly, the seventh-day Sabbatarians do not constitute a continuous tradition in Christian history but rather a recurrent tendency for groups on the theological and geographical margins of Christianity to adopt or perpetuate the observance of Saturday.

Bryan Ball's *The English Connection* represents a more concerted attempt to root Seventh-day Adventism in a specific historical tradition. It is his thesis that "in its essentials Seventh-day Adventist belief traces its ancestry through the religious thought which was widespread in the British Isles during the seventeenth century, and which was epitomized in Puritanism."[13] But whatever the merits of his exposition of English Puritanism, Ball's thesis remains entirely unsubstantiated. Although he points to similarities between Puritan thought and some recent Adventist writers, he does not trace the links between seventeenth-century Puritans and nineteenth-century Adventists, and he ignores the fact that even where there is continuity, for example in the observance of Saturday by the Seventh-Day Baptists, the adoption of the doctrine by Adventists took place in the alien context of the Millerite disappointment, which transformed the content, if not the form, of the belief.

Furthermore, Ball mistakenly equates the doctrines of twentieth-century Adventism with the church's earlier beliefs. When he notes that the Puritans considered that "absolute perfection is unattainable for the believer in this life," he uncovers a similarity to late twentieth-century Adventists that reveals nothing about Adventist roots.[14] In pointing to John Owen's belief that in the Hebrew sacrificial system "sacrifice and application were both necessary" but that "the ministration of the blood by the priest adds nothing to the efficacy of the sacrifice itself," Ball implies a connection with the twentieth-century belief that the atonement was made on the cross and applied in heaven.[15] For the early Adventists, it was an article of faith that the cross was no part of the atonement.[16] In other words, Ball's view of Adventism is anachronistic, and several of the connections he establishes have more to do with the twentieth-century Adventist alignment with fundamentalism than with the existence of earlier Adventist roots in Puritanism.

A clearer impression of Adventism's historical position may be gained through an analysis of the church's origins. In the formative period of Adventist theology, the mid-nineteenth century, the founders of the church sought to distinguish themselves from their parent body on the basis of what they felt to be biblical truth. This process followed the standard pattern in which a zealous sectarian group tries to return to the purity of primitive Christianity, in contradistinction to a parent church that has become complacent and compromised.[17] The emergence of Seventh-day Adventism is unusual, not so much in the process of differentiation, but in the body from which it grew. The Millerite movement was neither complacent nor a church. It was not itself the aging product of a previous sectarian split, but a mass movement that drew its support from a variety of denominations. It had but a short history, no established traditions, little cohesion, and was united on only a single belief, which the passing of October 22, 1844, proved to be unfounded.

Seventh-day Adventism is thus not the estranged child of any mainstream American Protestant body, but the orphaned offspring of a brief liaison among several Protestant groups. There is, accordingly, no single doctrine or historical event that separates Adventists from the mainstream. There is no one mainstream group with which Adventists can forget their differences and reunite. Seventh-day Adventism's only surviving relative is the Advent Christian Church, the descendants of another former Millerite group, now much smaller than the Seventh-day Adventist church even in America.[18] In historical terms, Seventh-day Adventism is two stages removed from the Protestant mainstream. Adventist identity does not hinge on a few doctrines that deviate from those of the mainstream (as Martin and Hoekema imagined) but on a unique and isolated history. The Saturday Sabbath, for example, has never functioned solely as a dividing line between Adventists and other Christians. It was originally a dividing line between Adventists and other Millerite groups and has become a reminder of that historical marginality. The Sabbath does not turn Adventists into "outsiders"; it commemorates the fact that they are outsiders. Outsiders, however, have a remarkable capacity to become insiders. The most extreme religious dissent may, with the passing of time, be transformed into orthodoxy or incorporated into the established structures of society.[19] To what extent have Adventists moved from the margins of American life toward its center?

In his influential book *The Social Sources of Denominationalism*, Richard Niebuhr argued that the progression from sect to denomination was the inevitable result of the need to socialize a second generation into a deviant religious orientation.[20] Although many scholars have since criticized or modified Niebuhr's arguments, the thesis that deviant minorities tend to drift toward the mainstream is still widely influential. Adventist interpretations of their own theological history are broadly compatible with Niebuhr's approach. Le Roy Edwin Froom was the first to acknowledge and interpret the theological changes that have taken place within Adventism. Froom argued for a kind of progressive revelation. The church had gradually been led toward a complete understanding of the Christian gospel after a century in which the important truths, such as the Sabbath, had been accompanied by the partial incomprehension of the doctrine of Christ and his saving work. This process had, Froom argued, achieved the alignment of Adventism with evangelical Christianity.[21] Another Adventist perspective gives a different theological interpretation of the same set of data. Conservative Adventists, such as the former church president Robert Pierson, perceive the changes that have taken place within Adventism as a decline from pristine purity rather than evidence of continued divine guidance. According to this school of thought, the move from sect toward denomination has involved the dilution of the Adventist message in deference to the expectations of secular academics.[22]

Both interpretations are agreed on the basic facts. In the nineteenth century, Adventism was tied closely to its peculiar doctrines, and in the twentieth century, those links loosened as Adventism became less distinctive. However, a careful examination of adventist history warns against a straightforward equation of the nineteenth century with zeal and peculiarity, and the twentieth with laxity and accommodation. As the preceding chapters reveal, there has not been a linear progression from one orientation to another. There is rather a complex set of interconnected patterns. The Second Advent has not gradually receded from the Adventist consciousness; awareness of its imminence has ebbed and flowed with the tide of events both inside and outside the church. The Adventist understanding of the process of salvation has received different emphases according to whether translation or resurrection seems the believer's most likely fate. The doctrine of the Sabbath served as a means of distinguishing a group of ex-Millerites, but with the passage of time, this form of identification was replaced by a self-understanding that depended more on history and a sense of organic continuity. The nineteenth century saw a tension between two understandings of divine nature and activity, both of which initially served as barriers between Adventists and adjacent religious groups but which were synthesized quietly once Adventist identity had been established. In order to maintain unity and to provide a means of generating an effective response to new dilemmas, authoritative sources of guidance have been required. These have been found through using, in varying proportions, the Bible, the writings of Ellen White, and the power of human reason.

Is there any overall pattern to be discerned? At the risk of oversimplification, it could be argued that Adventist theological history falls into three, rather than two, historical divisions. The first, which might be termed Adventist radicalism, is characteristic of the period from Millerism to the death of Ellen White and the outbreak of the First World War. The second, Adventist fundamentalism, emerged in the 1880s, became dominant in the 1920s, and survives to the present day. In the 1950s, however, Adventist evangelicalism rose to prominence to the extent that it has become the official form of Adventism, while fundamentalism exists only at the margins and at a local level.

How does this overall structure clarify our understanding of the development of Adventist theology? In the nineteenth century, Adventists were in the vanguard of popular religion. They did not revere the formulations of ancient Christian councils; they took an Arian position because they felt the Bible justified no other, believed that the atonement took place not on the cross but in heaven, and placed strong emphasis on obedience to the law as the means of salvation. They put enormous intellectual effort into the explication of Biblical apocalyptic, but their worship was emotionally uninhibited. In all of these things, Adventists were not bizarre. There is no evidence to suggest that they were any further removed from the mainstream of American religion than Adventists are today. The nineteenth century was a creative and experimental period for American Christianity.[23] Adventism was not unusual in its obsession with eschatology, its doubts about the Trinity, or its emphasis on human perfectability. Nor the Adventism unique in its ability to combine seemingly divergent attitudes. A rigorous intellectual approach to doctrine often went hand in hand with an emotional approach to worship. Nineteenth-century religion rarely fits the neat dichotomies of the twentieth century. Adventists, like members of other groups, were both intellectual and enthusiastic. The one defining characteristic is radicalism, a desire to push every aspect of Christianity toward its logical conclusion, independent of tradition and indifferent to internal cohesion.[24]

In the nineteenth century, Adventists were thus not atypical religious freaks but representative of a large sector of popular religion. As such, their all-consuming problem was the need to establish their own identity in a rapidly changing religious environment. The Sabbath served as the primary means of effecting this differentiation. It was a belief upheld by the unique authority of Ellen White. Adventists had their own day of worship and their own prophet, and these two pillars of the church upheld each other while all else was in flux. At the turn of the twentieth century, Adventism underwent significant change. Ellen

White died in 1915, and the church was robbed of its chief means of authorizing innovation. The liveliness and flexibility that had characterized Adventist theological debate in the nineteenth century evaporated. The church became more cautious. The general religious climate had also changed. The groups with which Adventism had once stood shoulder to shoulder had now either disappeared or established their own identity; Adventism, too, now had more than half a century of independent history behind it. The situation was no longer one in which a multitude of religious movements were fighting for survival. The crucial issue of the First World War and the 1920s was the fundamentalist-modernist controversy. Many mainstream churches were divided, and smaller independent groups like the Adventists usually gave their support to the fundamentalist cause.[25] In the nineteenth century, the primary concern had been to find a space and stake out theological boundaries. At the dawn of the twentieth century, most religiously minded Americans felt compelled to take sides for or against evolution, biblical criticism, and secular liberalism. Adventists were no exception, and they placed themselves firmly in the fundamentalist camp. By the beginning of the twentieth century, the number of second- and third-generation Adventists was much increased. Consolidation rather than experimentation was the order of the day. The processes that Niebuhr described did indeed take place, not perhaps as the inevitable result of a second generation, but as the consequence of the need to establish order in a religious environment unusually fragmented by nineteenth-century sectarianism.

But it would be wrong to equate this stabilization with an increase in Adventist intellectualism. Quite the reverse. The intellectually disciplined theological debates that had filled the pages of the *Review* now disappeared. There were no more brilliant autodidacts like Uriah Smith and J. N. Andrews to produce scholarly justifications of the Adventist faith. Adventists had to wait over a century before any of their historians produced work on the Sabbath of comparable erudition to that of Andrews. Adventists were not, however, solely occupied in producing popular versions of their old arguments. They were also accepting new ideas, usually without arguing them out in the way their forebears would have done. Adventists, like the fundamentalists with whom they now identified themselves, quietly accepted Trinitarianism; took a stronger line on the inerrancy of the Bible; accepted, in line with the penal-substitutionary theory, that the cross was a place of atonement; and reaffirmed their belief in human perfectibility in less mystical terms than had been current in the 1890s. At the same time, they updated their eschatology with reference to the new scientific and political climate. The writings of Ellen White and the Bible now functioned not as a source of new ideas but as a compendium of truths to be expounded and memorized. Doctrines were simplified so that they could be taught effectively to the children in Adventist schools and preached in the foreign lands to which Adventists were now traveling.[26]

The changes that have taken place in Adventism since the Second World War have been far more self-conscious than those at the start of the century. In consequence, these developments have received a disproportionate amount of attention. But in fact, the changes have been less dramatic than those of the earlier period, involving a dilution rather than a transformation of Adventist belief. Theological changes may be summarized as follows: the legalistic character of Adventist soteriology has been replaced—commitment rather than performance is now the criterion of divine acceptance; the Sabbath is now seen as an expression rather than a requirement of loyalty to God; critical scholarship has been applied to the Bible and the spirit of prophecy, with a consequent diminution in the supernatural aura surrounding both. These changes have been related to both internal and external factors. To take the internal first. In the postwar world, the Second Coming has become more distant, and doctrinal modification has become necessary for believers whose expectation of translation is less vital than that of their forebears. This in turn has necessitated the reemergence of human reason as a reliable source of authority to legitimate such modifications. On the other hand, the long history of the church has facilitated a certain freedom in theological discussion, for the Adventist identity is sufficiently well established for its doctrinal boundaries to become more elastic.

Superficially, these changes resemble a return to the practices of the nineteenth century. Since the 1960s there has been lively scholarly debate within the church, as there was a century earlier. The context, however, is the reverse. In the nineteenth century, writers sought evidence to buttress the doctrinal innovations that affirmed the Adventist identity. In more recent times, scholarship has served to diminish the significance of distinctive doctrines. In the 1960s and 1970s, when organized religion appeared to be in retreat, Adventism took its stand, not against secularized Christianity, but against irreligion. Adventists identified themselves less with one set of Christians against another than with all Christians in a shared stand against a secular assault on traditional moral and religious values. In this context, the demand for doctrinal peculiarity seemed less pressing than the need to emphasize that the church offered real hope of salvation in a world of religious indifference. In the late 1970s and 1980s, Adventism, along with other Protestant groups, seemed to be affected by the general reawakening of American conservatism. But this has not led to a wholesale reaffirmation of doctrinal distinctiveness. The Adventist message is still presented in the evangelical mould as offering hope in a world of despair and morality in a culture of nihilism.[27]

A misleading picture of Adventist history can be derived from concentrating solely on the changes that have taken place since the Second World War. It can appear that the central dynamic of Adventist development has been the move away from historic certainties toward accommodation with the mainstream of American religion. But what many authors take to be historic Adventism is in fact the creation of the twentieth century—a synthesis that took place in the 1920s and remained dominant until the 1960s. It was, moreover, a synthesis that in itself represented an accommodation to the newly formed fundamentalist movement. Does this mean that one should simply back date the shift from distinctiveness to conformity? On the contrary, although Adventism's theological position in the nineteenth century was more distinctive than it is today, it was distinctive in a period in which theological diversity was the norm. Nineteenth-century Adventists were theologically peculiar and thus relatively socially normal. Adventists of the fundamentalist period became less theologically peculiar but more socially distinctive as the Adventist health message was perpetuated long after its vogue in the rest of America had passed. In the late twentieth century, Adventists have, with changing social trends, become less distinctive in their lifestyle but more isolated in historical and geographical terms, as Adventism becomes increasingly tied to ghettoes around major institutional centers.

From a theological point of view, there is little evidence to support the widely held contention that Adventists have moved from the margins of society toward the mainstream. Adventist theology has developed in parallel with that of the mainstream. It was at its most distinctive during a period of great diversity; it became fundamentalist in the era of fundamentalism; and it softened with the rise of evangelicalism. Throughout this process Adventist theology has served as a barrier between the church and its opponents. The nature of the competition has changed—from rival sects to liberal Christianity to secular humanism—and Adventist theology has been adjusted accordingly. But the changes have served to maintain the distance between Adventism and the most threatening ideological formations of the day. The clue to the central dynamic in this oppositional stance lies in the Adventist belief, examined in chapters 3 and 4, that America would one day become intolerant. Throughout all the adjustments that have been made to the church's theology, this expectation—perhaps the most striking aspect of Adventism's ideological system—has kept Adventists separated from the rest of American society. But the wider division between the church and the Republic cannot be fully appreciated without discussion of Adventism as a social system.

Part 2

THE ADVENTIST EXPERIENCE AND THE AMERICAN DREAM

CHAPTER 8

The Structure of Society

Quite apart from its distinctive theology, Adventism is a remarkable social phenomenon. In 1985 the church in North America operated 1,231 primary schools, 347 secondary schools (90 of which offered a complete secondary education), ten colleges, and two universities. This amounts to the largest Protestant school system in the United States and is second only to the educational program of the Roman Catholic church. The denomination's health care network, Adventist Health Systems (AHS), consists of fifty-three hospitals and medical centers across the continent. AHS, which admits over 300,000 patients and makes nearly two million outpatient visits every year, is the seventh-largest health system in North America. In addition there are twenty-eight Adventist nursing homes and retirement centers and a denominational health food manufacturer, Loma Linda Foods, Inc.

Two church publishing houses, the Review and Herald Publishing Association in Maryland and the Pacific Press Publishing Association in Idaho, both publish and print Adventist books. Between them, they put out nearly fifty periodicals covering a wide variety of official, professional, and minority interests. Perhaps the most important are the *Review*, the weekly organ of Seventh-day Adventism; the *Signs of the Times*, the denomination's foremost evangelistic magazine; and *Insight* (formerly the *Youth's Instructor*), the paper for the church's young people.[1] The church's large literary output is buttressed by the eleven radio stations (based at Adventist colleges and schools) that comprise the Adventist Radio Network and by the broadcasts of the Adventist Media Center in California. Three television programs, primarily of an evangelistic nature, are produced there: "Breath of Life," "Faith for Today," and "It Is Written." From the center, the church also broadcasts the long-established radio program "The Voice of Prophecy."[2]

Worldwide, the statistics of the Adventist society multiply impressively: 4,306 primary schools, 901 secondary schools, 94 colleges and universities, 152 hospitals and sanitariums, 78 nursing homes and retirement centers, 51 publishing houses, 322 periodicals, hundreds of radio stations, and 28 food companies.[3] It is clear from this that most church members' needs can be accommodated by denominational institutions. Adventists can be born in Adventist hospitals, go to Adventist schools, obtain degrees from Adventist colleges, and receive further training in Adventist universities. They can buy Adventist food, read Adventist literature, listen to Adventist radio programs, and watch Adventist television productions. They can work in Adventist institutions, and, because Adventists tend to cluster around their institutions or administrative centers (forming what are known as Adventist "ghettoes"), they can even live in an Adventist community. When they are ill, they can be treated in Adventist hospitals, and when they are old, they can live out their days in Adventist retirement centers. Adventism is an alternative social system that meets the needs of its members from the cradle to the grave.

This has not been an easy achievement. From the beginning, the cohesion of the church's social structure has been beset by two fundamental problems. The first has been caused by powerful institutions that at various times have threatened to resist administrative control. The second concerns the large debts incurred from borrowing money to finance and maintain the vast institutionalization. In 1980 the church in America lost its southern publishing house. In 1986 its timber industry, Harris Pine Mills, closed. Other Adventist enterprises, such as the Media Center, have come very close to bankruptcy.[4] Nevertheless, the creation of an alternative social system can be counted as one of Adventism's greatest successes. It has been achieved through a hierarchical administrative structure and central economic planning.

The basic unit of the Adventist hierarchy is the local church. Groups of churches form the next level of government and are known as conferences. Several conferences are administered by union conferences, and clusters of these are in turn administered by what Adventists call divisions. At conference and union levels there are also smaller administrative units called Missions. These units are not financially independent and are usually supported by their parent conference or union. The highest level of church government is known as the General Conference. The overall structure is very loosely based on geographical boundaries. In general, conferences administer the work of Adventists in regions within a country, union conferences oversee the work of an entire country (or large state or several states), and divisions coordinate Adventist work in several countries. The General Conference controls Adventism on a world scale. When the church was officially incorporated in 1863, its headquarters were located in Battle Creek, Michigan. But since 1903, the General Conference has operated from Takoma Park, Maryland, just outside Washington D.C.

The top General Conference officials are the president, secretary, and treasurer. The president's office includes four special assistants and one administrative assistant, and seven general field secretaries, who may be assigned to special projects or given other responsibilities determined by the General Conference Executive Committee. Below the office of president are five general vice-presidents who assist the president in his administrative duties and may take over the chairmanship of committees in the event of the president's absence. At this level there are ten further vice-presidents, who are responsible for the world divisions of the church. The divisions include the Africa-Indian Ocean, Eastern Africa, Euro-Africa, the Far East, Inter-America, North America, South America, the South Pacific, Southern Asia, and Trans-Europe (which includes parts of Asia and the Middle East). (The China division and the Seventh-day Adventist church in the U.S.S.R. are additional divisions of the church that are administered locally.) Next in rank are eight assistant secretaries who make up the General Conference secretariat. It is the job of the secretariat to record the proceedings of General Conference meetings and sessions and to maintain contact with Adventist leaders and personnel around the world. The secretariat has particular responsibility for the General Conference's "attached fields," that is, union missions or conferences, which for political or other reasons are run directly from Takoma Park. They include the Middle East Union Mission, the South African Union Conference, and the Southern (African) Union Mission. General Conference administrative staff also include six assistant treasurers, whose responsibility it is to receive and disburse funds and to prepare regular financial statements; a controller; the directors of the Department of Archives and Statistics; and the directors of personnel.

The president, the vice-presidential team, the secretariat, treasury, the directors of Archives and Statistics, and the directors of personnel form the denomination's central administration. But in addition, responsibilities at the General Conference are divided among seven departments that supervise areas of special interest to Adventists. The departments are Church Ministries (which includes youth and family sections), Communication, Education, Health and Temperance, Ministerial Association, Public Affairs and Religious Liberty, and Publishing. Each department has a director, several associate and assistant directors, and usually a nominal advisory board of governors and trustees. The president and other officers of the General Conference administration nearly always have a seat on these boards. There are also numerous other ancillary services and organizations that are part of the General Conference. They include the *Review*, the Adventist Media Center, Adventist Health Systems, ADRA (the denomination's disaster relief organization), the Adventist-Layman's Services and Industries (an association of privately owned Adventist institutions), and the Office of Human Relations, which oversees the interests of the church's racial minorities. The General Conference also runs Risk Management

Services, which provides insurance for Adventist institutions and interests. The Biblical Research Institute, the Geoscience Research Institute, and the Ellen G. White Estate, Inc., are other agencies of the General Conference. The former provide scholarly defenses of the faith in theology and science; the latter acts as custodian and official interpreter of Mrs. White's voluminous writings. As with the General Conference departments, the ancillary organizations have advisory boards on which the president and other officers sit.[5]

Virtually the entire membership of the General Conference administration, the departmental directors and their associates, and the directors of the ancillary organizations and their associates sit on the General Conference executive committee. The church constitution lays down that the members of the respective division administrations, all the union presidents throughout the world, the heads of the denomination's various institutions, and up to twenty laymen must also sit on the committee.[6] In theory, well over 300 people form the General Conference executive committee. In practice, however, they rarely all meet together. The committee meets weekly in Takoma Park to execute the church's business. This is made possible through other constitutional provisions that enable only fifteen members to constitute a quorum, provided they meet at church headquarters.[7] Larger meetings of the executive committee are held twice a year: at the spring meeting and the annual council. At these meetings, budgets are determined, policies are debated, and actions are voted.[8]

But by far the most important policy-making meeting is the General Conference session held every five years in a city of the officers' choosing. The General Conference session works on two levels. On one, it is a celebration, an Adventist pageant, in which glowing reports of the institutional and numerical progress of the church are presented to the membership. On the other, it is a political event in which doctrinal and constitutional changes are made and General Conference officers are elected.

Ordinary church members have no voting rights at a General Conference session. The voting constituency consists of two types of official representatives, delegates at large and regular delegates. The delegates at large consist of all the members of the vast executive committee, four delegates from each division, plus an additional delegate for every 200,000 members. The constitution also provides for an unspecified number of General Conference personnel and laypersons. The number of these representatives, however, does not exceed 25 percent of the total number of delegates at large. The regular delegates are made up of one delegate from every union (in addition to the president), one for every conference or mission within its territory, and one for every 5,000 members. The attached fields of the General Conference are similarly allowed one regular delegate and one for every 5,000 members. Both delegates at large and regular delegates are selected either by virtue of their office or through appointment by church officials.[9]

The main function of official delegates at the quinquennial session is to select the members of a nominating committee. This committee has the crucial responsibility of electing the General Conference officers, including the president. The nominating committee is dominated by representatives from the divisions. Each attached union of the General Conference also has one member, as do General Conference institutions. The divisions' share of the seats on the nominating committee used to be a specific provision, which stood at one representative per 20,000 members before the General Conference session of 1985.[10] However, constitutional amendments made at that session left the allocation distinctly unclear. Each division is now vaguely represented on the basis of its "proportion of the world membership," with the proviso that all divisions have at least eight members.[11] Again, only official delegates can serve on the nominating committee, with the exception of those General Conference and division personnel who are standing for reelection. The union presidents, who are not up for reelection, are invariably selected for the committee, forming what can be the committee's most powerful faction. This is particularly true of the North American presidents, who usually act in concert and exert wide influence.

Once the nominating committee is formed, it elects the General Conference officers, beginning with the president. For this, the committee chairman accepts the names of five to ten candidates. The names are discussed and then voted on, with each member voting for one candidate. Unless there is a clear winner on the first secret ballot, the chairman submits the two or three leading names for a second ballot. The winner is then the candidate who emerges with a simple majority. In the next stage of the process, the proposed name is brought to the floor for ratification by the official delegates. This is achieved through a vote by acclamation. The General Conference delegation cannot vote for any other individual, and it has never yet rejected the candidate of the nominating committee. The president elect then becomes an active but nonvoting member of the nominating committee, which then elects the rest of the General Conference team and the officers of the divisions.[12]

Adventist leaders insist that this administrative and electoral system is "representative." According to the *Church Manual*, the denomination's procedural bible, it is "the form of church government which recognizes that authority in the church rests in the church membership."[13] The composition of the vital Adventist committees, however, suggests that authority is in practice located in two places: the administrative structure and the church's institutions. The delegates at a General Conference are virtually all officials from these two power centers, and between them, they have total control of the denomination's electoral machinery. It was only in 1985 that constitutional provisions were made for the appointment of laypeople to the executive committee or as voting delegates at the quinquennial gathering.[14] These amendments, however, were not substantial, and a General Conference session remains, as one Adventist has observed, "a convocation of denominational employees."[15] It is far removed from the average church member, who cannot be said to participate in any direct democratic sense, either in the selection of his representatives or in the election of the leadership. What the system does represent are the various administrative groups and institutional interests that dominate Adventist society.

This is not surprising, when the development of the administrative system is considered. Adventist government was created in two main stages. The first entailed the initial organization of 1863; the second was the reorganization of 1901, at which point the church took on its modern structure. Both these developments were responses to the same problem: the question of the church's institutionalization. In the first instance, formal organization was prompted by the need to retain the denomination's first institution, the publishing house. As early as 1849, the small group of Sabbath keepers established the paper *Present Truth* (later to become the *Review*) around which they soon established a press. By the early 1860s, however, it became apparent that the church could not continue to own this institution unless it became a legal entity. Alarmed by this possibility, James White led the movement that resulted in the organization of the Seventh-day Adventist church in 1863.[16] The reorganization of 1901 was occasioned by the mushrooming of Adventist institutions in the late nineteenth century. According to one Adventist historian, twelve publishing, seventeen educational, and fourteen medical institutions came into existence between 1885 and 1901.[17] Such institutions tended to be operated independently of denominational control, and this resulted in confusion and conflict between institutions and church leaders. The 1901 General Conference session met to resolve this problem. As a result, most Adventist institutions were brought under the umbrella of the General Conference, and union structures and departments provided the framework for administering the institutions. But in return, representatives of the institutions were granted privileged positions on the church's executive and electoral committees, a situation that exists to the present day.[18]

Adventism was really an institutionalized church before it was an organized church. Indeed, the main stages of the church's organizational development can be seen as attempts by the leadership to acquire greater powers over Adventist institutions. This largely explains the authoritarian nature of Adventist government. It was not conceived to give the ordinary member a say in the running of church affairs.

Rather, the Adventist administrative system was designed to bring institutions within the legal jurisdiction of the church and then modified to resolve conflicts between institutional directors and church leaders. The Adventist form of government is one that acknowledges the power of church institutions rather than one that recognizes the authority of church members.

Scaled-down versions of the General Conference structure and electoral processes are duplicated at each level of the church. Divisions, unions, conferences, and missions are run by the officers of a centralized administration and by the directors of the church's seven departments. They all also possess their own executive committees. The officers of the divisions are elected at the General Conference session. Unions and conferences hold their own sessions every two or three years, during which time policies are determined and officers elected according to the constitutional guidelines established by the General Conference. The voting constituency of both conferences and unions consists of official delegates, of whom local ministers and institutional representatives form significant proportions. At the union level, all delegates are effectively appointed by conference or union officials. At the conference level, every local congregation appoints at least one delegate. It is at this level that Adventism is seen to be at its most democratic. But the effects of such lay participation are somewhat mitigated (at least in principle) by the automatic right of General Conference officers to be part of the official delegation. Members of the General Conference are also official delegates at union sessions. The election of conference and union personnel is achieved through a nominating committee.[19]

Even the local congregation is organized along the same basic lines. The leader is a conference-appointed pastor rather than a president, and below him are several elders, deacons, and deaconesses. In addition, members are elected to lead departments, which correspond to the departments of the General Conference. The election of church officers is conducted yearly through a nominating committee formed from the church's membership. The pastor and church officers make up the church board, which like the executive committee of higher administrative units, is the most influential committee of the local congregation.[20] It is true that in many matters, such as the receiving or disfellowshipping of members, the democratic decision of the entire membership constitutes the final authority of the local congregation. But it is also clear that the local church is modeled on the same hierarchical plan as Adventism in general.

It is strange to think that the idea of church organization filled the Adventist pioneers with horror. Adventists today are very proud of their church structure. But from 1844 to 1863, they actively resisted forming a church, fearing that if they did so they would become like the "Babylonian" churches from which they had emerged. George Storrs, the Millerite, exerted a powerful influence on the emerging Adventist community when he said in 1844 that a church became Babylon "the *moment it is organized*".[21] Opposition to forming a church persisted right up to the establishment of the denomination's constitution in 1863.

Once the decision had been taken to organize, Adventists developed a centralized, hierarchical structure. It was also a system that invested the church's top leaders with great power. In language reminiscent of the papacy, Mrs. White described the General Conference as "the highest authority that God has upon the earth."[22] She argued for the precedence of this authority over and against the claims of the individual. "When, in a General Conference, the judgment of the brethren assembled from all parts of the field is exercised, private independence and private judgment must not be stubbornly maintained, but surrendered," she wrote. "Never should a laborer regard as a virtue the persistent maintenance of his position of independence, contrary to the decision of the general body."[23]

Perhaps because of this collectivism, the individuals who become General Conference officers are rarely compelling figures. They are usually efficient bureaucrats whose chief characteristic is an ability to work within a tightly knit oligarchy. They are generally in middle or late middle age and are drawn almost exclusively from those ministers who possess proven records in the lower levels of church administration or overseas mission service. They rule the denomination conservatively and secretively. Believing that they are leading the Seventh-day Adventist Church toward inevitable triumph, church leaders are reluctant to admit failures or mistakes and prefer to withhold problems from the membership.

Among these men, the church president is first among equals. He must be a man acceptable to both the denomination's administrative and institutional groups. The president is thus likely to be a man of convenience rather than a charismatic leader. The first president, John Byington, was elected in 1863 for no better reason than, at age 65, he was the oldest Adventist pioneer and because the obvious choice, James White, declined the position. Byington had no special leadership qualities, and his election tended to confirm the idea that the creation of the system of government was more important than the individual who led it. This has, to some extent, continued to be the relationship between the president and the church hierarchy. For in Adventism, it is the collective decisions of General Conference committees that have been important in the history of the denomination, not the personal contribution of the presidents.

Of the thirteen presidents elected since Byington, few stand out as outstanding individuals or interesting personalities, apart perhaps from

White himself, president on three separate occasions, 1865–67, 1869–71 and 1874–80.[24] Another exception was Arthur G. Daniells, whose immensely strong character and liking for power led to an unusually acrimonious General Conference session in San Francisco in 1922. Having already headed the denomination since 1901—the longest period of any Adventist president—Daniells attempted to secure yet another term. However, amid bitter recriminations, he was ousted by the nominating committee, who replaced him with W. A. Spicer.[25] One other president worthy of note is Neal C. Wilson, who has led the church since 1979. An astute leader, Wilson has brought to the General Conference a professionalism that contrasts with the pietism of his immediate predecessor Robert H. Pierson. Wilson is also interesting in that he has openly used the divinely sanctioned authority of the General Conference to control dissent and to push through controversial policies.[26]

Adventism is, then, a centralized society that accords its leaders absolute authority. The church puts more value on institutions than on lay membership and regards collective responsibility as more important than individual judgment. The church's financial structure and its general attitude toward money reflect these principles. From an economic point of view, Adventist society espouses collaboration rather than competition and prefers central planning to individual or local initiative.

The basis of this economic system is the tithe. This is the 10 percent of income that the Adventist church asks from church members. Although not every member pays the tithe (the church has not made it a test of fellowship), it has proved a dependable source of income. In 1985 the worldwide tithe receipts were nearly $457 million, with North America, by far the richest section of the church, contributing more than $317 million to that total.[27] The tithe is initially collected by the local church and is channeled to the General Conference via the successive conference, union, and division administrative units. No part of the tithe is retained by the local congregation. The conference, however, retains 90 percent of the tithe it receives from constituent churches for its ministerial and administrative expenses. The remaining 10 percent is sent to the union, which likewise retains 90 percent of the money for its running costs before passing the remainder to the General Conference. The divisions, being merely sections of the General Conference, are financed primarily by church headquarters. Although there are exceptions to this financial system (for example, divisions also receive an unspecified percentage from the tithe of their constituent conferences and the conferences of the North American Division return 20 percent of the tithe to the General Conference), the basic point is that conferences and unions pay at least one-tenth of their income, which supplies the General Conference with the most important part of its funds.[28] The tithe is controlled entirely by church administrators. The local church has no say in the disbursement of funds, and it must meet its own expenses through separate offerings and contributions from its members.

Special significance is accorded to the tithe. It became an established practice within Adventism in the late 1870s and grew out of an older form of giving called "systematic benevolence" in which the pioneers encouraged adherents to give a small portion of their incomes to support the ministry.[29] The practice of giving 10 percent, however, became widespread after articles by the Adventist minister Dudley M. Canright appeared in the *Review* in 1876. On the basis of Malachi 3:8–11, he wrote that God required a tithe, or one-tenth of the earnings of church members, to support "his servants in their labors." Canright argued that the principle of tithing is rooted in the concept of God's ownership. "The Lord does not say you should *give* me a tenth," he wrote, "but he says one-tenth *is* the Lord's."[30] He saw paying the tithe as returning to God what is already his. Since Canright first introduced the idea, Adventists have justified the practice of tithing for this reason. As Ellen White later told the church: "The tithe is the Lord's; and He bids us return to Him that which is His own."[31] With this belief and the idea that the General Conference is God's highest authority on the earth, it is easy to see why it was that church officials—not ordinary members—became responsible for the Lord's funds.

The tithe was originally earmarked for the ministry. Because of the sacredness attached to it, other uses were considered inappropriate. The church has, however, always found it difficult to determine the precise use for these funds. In the late nineteenth and early twentieth centuries, it was already clear that tithe monies were being "diverted" into the church's school system, sanitarium building, and the wages of medical personnel. Ellen White strongly opposed such usage.[32] A policy document adopted by the Annual Council in 1985 indicated that the use of the tithe is (and probably always has been) quite wide. In addition to supporting the ministry, its uses include the salaries of administrators and the costs of their offices; the subsidizing of staff of elementary schools, academies, colleges, and universities; the costs of conference centers, campgrounds, or youth campsites; the church's media program; and the funding of benefits for retired denominational employees.[33] In other words, the tithe is used to finance anything the General Conference can define as having a "ministerial" function.

The portion of tithe that reaches the General Conference after the conferences and unions have taken their share makes up the bulk of the administration budget. But it is not the only source of funds. The General Conference has three other major sources of income: mission offerings, money from an annual fund-raising campaign called "ingathering," and appropriations from church institutions.

Mission offerings, like the tithes, are raised from the local churches.

Adventist leaders are constantly devising ways in which members may give more generously, with the result that new offerings are often suggested to the denomination. The various types of church offerings include the birthday offering, the thank offering, the investment offering, the annual sacrifice offering, and the missions extension offering.[34] These monies are normally donated during the Sabbath School service. The most important collections, however, are the Sabbath School offering, which is made every week, and the thirteenth Sabbath offering. This latter fund, as the name implies, is collected on the last Sabbath of every quarter, and church members are asked to make special contributions toward it. As an incentive, the General Conference determines a special project in some region of the world field, which is heavily promoted during the quarter and which the thirteenth Sabbath offering helps finance. However, only 25 percent of the total collected is set aside for the designated project. The rest is kept by the General Conference for its world mission fund.[35] So although a specific missionary project is made the incentive for the thirteenth Sabbath offering, church members are in fact mostly contributing (as is the case with all mission offerings) to the central fund of the General Conference.

The ingathering fund differs from the denomination's other forms of income in that it is raised, not from the church membership, but from the general public. For a few weeks every year, the ingathering campaign dominates the agendas of the local churches. The campaign is heavily promoted, with great emphasis placed on achieving monetary targets at every level of the denomination's administration. Ingathering is one of the few times the public encounters Seventh-day Adventists, since church members solicit funds from door to door. The focus of the campaign is always the church's extensive work in the disaster-prone areas of the Third World. The publicity handouts frequently carry evocative pictures of starving children or the isolated areas where Adventists operate medical centers or mission schools. But through the system of central funding that is characteristic of the denomination, the money is used to benefit the church as a whole. In 1985 church members raised, through ingathering, $12,641,218 for the General Conference.[36] Of the total amount collected, an undisclosed percentage is appropriated to the divisions, where disbursement is controlled by the respective executive committees.[37] It is worth noting that ingathering funds are not generally used to finance the church's disaster relief organization, ADRA, which is supported primarily by government and private agencies.[38] Although ingathering is advertised very much in terms of the church's humanitarian work in the Third World, it is, as Kenneth H. Emmerson, a former General Conference treasurer, said in 1969, "not a campaign conducted solely for our work in the foreign fields but includes the work of the church in all parts of the world."[39]

From the money received from tithing, mission offerings, ingathering, and institutions, the General Conference makes up its budget. In 1985 this budget amounted to nearly $149 million.[40] Some of this money is used in maintaining the General Conference officers and their offices. Money is also set aside in expense accounts, for church leaders are constantly traveling around the world, monitoring and assessing the progress of Seventh-day Adventism. But what also happens is that about midyear the directors of every church organization (through respective divisions) submit to the General Conference treasury an estimate of their financial needs. The treasury studies every proposal and at the Annual Council makes the final appropriations. Not all the money is spent. A proportion of the total budget (it is not clear how much) is held in reserve and invested in banks and selected companies.[41]

The financial system of Adventism is one that pools the collective resources of the church. Spending is determined by a central authority, the General Conference, which attempts to allocate funds for the benefit of all. The stronger constituencies compensate for weaker ones, and the weaker constituencies are supported by the stronger ones. For the system to work, every component must cooperate, from the humblest member to the highest church official.

The tithe is especially important in fostering this collective spirit. It puts the same obligation on all members and gives everyone the same tangible sense of cooperating with God through his appointed agency, the General Conference. The principle of God's ownership, which is the foundation of Adventist tithing, also explains the church's public fund-raising campaign, ingathering. In some respects, it is surprising that a denomination like Adventism that keeps instinctively to itself, emerges for a few weeks each year to solicit funds for its upkeep from nonmembers. The propriety of this campaign was questioned by some church members after it was introduced into Adventism by a layman, Jasper Wayne, in 1903. But Ellen White told the doubters: "The Lord has placed His goods in the hands of unbelievers as well as believers; all may return to Him His own for the doing of the work that must be done for a fallen world."[42] Adventists believe that the world's wealth is God's and therefore available to the church for its work.

Because of the structure of the Adventist economy, individual initiative must be yielded to the authority of central planners. Church members who raise almost all General Conference funds have virtually no say in how these funds are used. But the benefit, as with most total welfare systems, is that all are looked after, provided that they cooperate with the system. It is therefore not surprising to find that in their attitude toward money, Adventists early eschewed the individualistic, competitive spirit of modern capitalism. Ellen White viewed the pursuit of quick or great wealth with grave suspicion. She wrote at length about the need for Adventists to use money responsibly and to avoid capitalistic practices such as speculation in the money markets.[43] Part of the reason for this was the Adventist belief that money making in America constituted one of the signs of the end.[44] But it was also the case that the capitalist spirit did not flourish in Adventist society, which was founded on the opposite values.

A clearer understanding of this attitude can be gained by a brief look at the church's publishing industry. For over a decade after its incorporation in 1861, the Review and Herald Publishing Association was the only publishing house in the denomination. That situation changed, however, when the Pacific Press Publishing Association was founded in California in 1874. The establishment of a second publishing house upset the balance of the industry. Both houses were rivals in the same marketplace, and tensions between them inevitably grew in the late 1870s and 1880s. Given the Adventist predilection for cooperation, it was perhaps inevitable that steps would be taken to resolve this situation. In 1888 the two publishing houses signed an agreement that gave them exclusive rights to market Adventist books in—but not beyond— their respective areas. It became an established principle that church publishers would not compete against each other, so that when the church added a third publishing house in America in 1901, the Southern Publishing Association, it was made a monopoly in territories in the South.[45]

The monopolistic, uncompetitive nature of Adventist publishing is also seen in its methods of marketing. Adventist books are distributed in two main ways. In the first, books are sold directly to church members through retail outlets, known as Adventist Book Centers (ABCs). A large Adventist ghetto will normally contain an ABC from which church members can purchase their literature. Where Adventists are more widely dispersed, ABCs will travel to local churches so that members can obtain their supply of books. The other method of distribution is through sales representatives known as literature evangelists, or colporteurs. It is by this method that Adventists present their books and evangelistic literature to the general public. Adventist books are not generally sold through normal booksellers but are brought to the doors of non-Adventists by the literature evangelists. These representatives deal mostly in subscription books, as opposed to trade books, which are prepared for the Adventist public. Subscription books are normally lavish versions of standard Adventist works and are priced more highly.[46]

Both Adventist Book Centers and literature evangelists sell the books produced by the publishing house in their area, the latter through an intermediary union conference organization called the Home Health Education Service. If they want to sell a book not produced by their publisher, then they must get the institution to buy copies from the original publishing house. In this way, each press acts as a wholesaler for the other, and each can benefit from a popular book. In the event of a really successful book, all Adventist publishers eventually obtain the right to publish and market it for themselves.[47]

Despite such cooperation, the policy of having three publishing houses in one market led to severe economic problems. The Southern Publishing Association was closed in 1980 and merged with the Review and Herald, which retained the Southern printing plant. Later that year, however, the Review and Herald sold Southern's facility and moved its entire printing operation from Washington to Hagerstown, Maryland. Three years later, the Pacific Press sold its premises in California and moved to Idaho in order to avert impending bankruptcy.[48] Some church members believe it would make more economic sense to have just one publishing house, but the General Conference prefers the system of two publishers, in mutual symbiosis, that now operates in America.[49]

As well as removing competition from within, Adventist publishers have, when necessary, discouraged it from without. As a monopoly, the industry sets prices virtually unchallenged, which in the case of the subscription books, are particularly high. In the late 1970s, an Andrews University professor, Derrick Proctor, who was also a part-time dealer in Adventist books, made an individual assault on the Adventist publishing monopoly. Noting the high profit margins of Adventist books (purchasers of subscription books, for example, can pay up to four or five times the cost price), Proctor set up his own distribution network, which undercut the prices of the ABCs and the Home Health Education Service. Needless to say, the church moved swiftly to put Proctor out of business, and after a lengthy legal wrangle, the church won the right to fix prices free from competition from individual members.[50] The church demonstrated once again its preference for central planning over individual initiative, as it demanded cooperation rather than competition. The situation in Adventist publishing also holds true in other areas of the church's institutional life. Within the denomination's schools and colleges, for example, competitive sports are not encouraged, and sporting contests with other Adventist and non-Adventist institutions have not (until the mid-1980s) been countenanced.[51] Adventist schools and colleges themselves are, in America, not allowed to recruit students in areas other than those in which they are located. This is not to say that the spirit of competition does not occasionally surface among institutions in Adventist society. But the essence of the Adventist ethos is to reduce competition to a minimum.[52]

Cooperation has, however, brought its own disadvantages. Adventists have proved unusually susceptible to financiers who take advantage of the faith church members place in one another. The most important example of this was the Davenport affair, which brought the church much public embarrassment in the early 1980s. Lured by exorbitant rates of interest, Adventist leaders invested millions of dollars in the property empire of Adventist doctor Donald J. Davenport. In contravention of the General Conference's working policies, tithe monies were placed in Davenport's hands. In other instances, church leaders used their position and influence to raise capital for the Adventist doctor. When Davenport's empire collapsed in 1981, church entities lost over $20 million.[53] The Davenport scandal indicated that the church's leadership had grown accustomed to taking action without proper accountability. But it also revealed the readiness of ordinary Adventists to suspend their customary suspicion of financial speculation. Church members are accustomed to entrusting money to their coreligionists; their faith in one another applies to both tithe payments and dubious investments. In 1985 the Elmas Trading Corporation, a "commodities arbitrage" that relied heavily on Adventist investors, collapsed. The *Wall Street Journal* noted that investors remained firm believers in the company "even in the face of evidence that the enterprise could be illegal."[54]

In an Adventist setting, this response was unsurprising. The government of the church is neither monitored nor questioned by ordinary members. It is automatically assumed that an Adventist, particularly one who holds a responsible position, will act in the best interest of others. Adventists may not generally be encouraged to take economic initiatives, but if a venture gives the appearance of being endorsed by respected church members, Adventists demonstrate an uncritical willingness to cooperate with it. This is a side effect of a social system that encourages mistrust of those outside but passive acceptance of the system itself. Within Adventism, the traditional American value of self-reliance is not actively encouraged. The church's organization is hierarchical rather than democratic, and its ethos is collectivist rather than individualist. This is the consequence of specific historical circumstances. But the fact that Adventism espouses alternative values to those of American society, suggests that there may be a deeper ideological basis for this state of affairs.

The expected failure of America, the two-horned beast, probably convinced Adventists that the nation's government and institutions could not be trusted to protect minorities such as themselves or to inaugurate the millennium that was widely expected in the early nineteenth century.[55] The formation of the Adventist society can thus be seen as an attempt to insulate the church from the flawed Republic and to provide alternative institutions that would (unlike American institutions) bring about the millennium. Mrs. White wrote that one of the purposes of Adventist institutions was to prepare believers for the end.[56] Furthermore, in its hierarchical and collectivist aspects, the Adventist society is close to the heavenly society that Adventists believe will soon supersede America. The divine realm, as revealed in Mrs.

White's visions, is a hierarchy. The heavenly beings are each allotted their place. Power flows down from the Father and Son, through several tiers of angelic orders, to the inhabitants of the unfallen worlds. God's centralized, monarchical administration holds sway over the universe.[57]

Intriguing evidence of Adventists' mistrust of American ideals and their belief in the superiority of the heavenly ethos can perhaps be detected in the account of Satan's fall in the *Spirit of Prophecy*. Mrs. White's narrative bears some similarity to Book V of John Milton's *Paradise Lost*, but she introduced the novel idea that God and Satan symbolized two opposing political systems. In rebelling against the hierarchical structure of the heavenly court, Satan, according to Mrs. White, attempted "to reform the government of God." He accused the Father of taking action without consultation, and regarded Jesus' position as God's coruler as a threat to the freedom of heaven. Before a meeting of the angels, Satan declared he "no longer would submit to this invasion of his rights and theirs," and "promised them a new and better government than they then had in which all would be freedom." When the situation reached an impasse, Satan precipitated the heavenly war by arguing that the angels "must assert their liberty and gain by force the position and authority which was not willingly accorded them."[58] What is fascinating about this account is the way in which Satan appears to echo the ideals of the American revolution. He accuses the prevailing monarchy of taking unilateral action, argues for the rights of individuals, promises new and better government, and speaks of liberty and freedom. It is as though Mrs. White was giving the values of the revolutionaries diabolical expression. Through Satan, she graphically highlighted the unpredictable, alarming, and destructive consequences of individual freedom.[59]

It is therefore easy to see why Adventists—in their administrative and economic systems—show a marked preference for hierarchy and why they have rejected the assertive individualism of American society. Although Adventism ran in parallel to the Republic, its social ethic was the antithesis of the democratic ideal, which placed prime importance on the individual. The church's social structure developed into an ordered, centralized hierarchy like Mrs. White's vision of the heavenly realm. This is exactly what might be expected of a group that believed that the republican experiment would fail and would soon be surpassed by the divine government.

CHAPTER 9

The Patterns Of Growth

An appreciation of Adventism's relationship to the United States helps explain the church's development as a social system. But it does more than inform an understanding of the denomination's vast institutional structure, hierarchical government, and collectivist ethic; it also provides insights into the nature of the denomination's missionary appeal and rapid expansion. Before this phenomenon is examined in detail, it is useful to review the patterns of Adventist growth, both in America and overseas.

The preaching of William Miller and his associates was intended to warn as many people as possible of the impending Second Advent. As Miller's active ministry began only twelve years before the date of the anticipated Judgment, there was obviously little hope that every individual could be warned before the event. Although the Millerites were zealous evangelists and the movement grew to number approximately 50,000, the shortage of time meant that their missionary activity was understood as a symbolic "witness to all nations" rather than an attempt at world evangelism.[1] After the humiliation on October 22, 1844, the Adventist movement fragmented. Its Sabbatarian wing was a small minority, and in 1849 probably numbered less than one hundred. There was no real growth in the period 1844 to 1851, not only because the public was unlikely to sympathize with a group whose predictions had so recently been discredited but also because the Great Disappointment had "terminated all mission efforts of Adventists because of their general understanding that the door of mercy was closed for humanity."[2]

Despite the Shut-Door theory, converts previously unconnected with Adventism found their way into the movement. By 1852 numbers had increased to 250. This almost unwished-for expansion, combined with Ellen White's growing doubts about the theory, prompted church leaders to abandon completely the Shut-Door doctrine in 1854. Although some within the movement felt that missionary activity was useless, since "no human agency" could "stem the wickedness of the world," converts continued to be drawn, so that by 1863, when the Seventh-day Adventist Church was formed, its adherents numbered 3,500.[3] During the following decade, missionary activity continued in the United States on the assumption that the church was fulfilling its mission to preach the gospel to all peoples through its evangelism in multiethnic North America. The enthusiasm of the laity ensured that some literature was sent overseas. The leadership of the church was slow to respond to the desire for foreign missions, and the first Seventh-day Adventist missionary, a converted Catholic priest M. B. Czechowski, left for Europe in 1864 without official authorization.[4] He did not inform his European converts of his Adventist connections, but when they were discovered by accident, links were formed between Swiss Sabbath keepers and the church in America. In response to appeals from this group, J. N. Andrews, Adventism's first official overseas missionary, left for Switzerland in 1874.[5]

During the 1870s, membership nearly trebled, and by 1880 stood at 15,570. However, in the following decade the rate of growth was halved, and by 1890 membership had only advanced to 29,711. With the exception of the mission to Australia begun in 1885, new territories were entered as the result of individual lay initiative or in response to direct requests from indigenous sympathizers. Despite the success of individual missionaries, "the idea of becoming involved in this world-wide outreach was only gradually understood by the believers."[6]

In the 1890s, however, missionary work at last took on a global perspective. Membership increased by 155 percent during the decade, as Adventism became established in over thirty nations in Central and South America, Africa, and the Pacific.[7] The sudden upsurge in missionary activity was not a phenomenon unique to Adventism; the 1890s marked the zenith of general missionary outreach from the United States. But there had been important internal change as well; the 1888 General Conference marked a move, by at least some Adventists, away from an introverted legalism toward a greater emphasis on righteousness by faith and the conversion experience. The new president elected on this occasion, O. A. Olsen, was, significantly, the first to have had overseas missionary experience, having worked in Scandinavia.[8] Even if the general climate was now more favorable toward missionary activity, it was still most frequently undertaken by laymen and colporteurs. By the 1901 General Conference, with membership standing at about 80,000, it was obvious to Mrs. White and others that missionary activity could not be left entirely to local initiative. Under the presidency of A. G. Daniells, the Foreign Missions Board became directly responsible to an enlarged General Conference executive committee, which from then on supervised different aspects of its work through several departments. The reorganization was not just a move toward centralization; the formation of union conferences and missions relieved the General Conference of direct responsibility for institutions and evangelism within individual areas.[9]

This reorganization has been described as "an exemplary model of church missionary structure."[10] It was the framework within which A. G. Daniells, in the words of one, perhaps overenthusiastic, Adventist missiologist, "led out in a mission program that has not had its equal since the early Christians conquered the world."[11] Certainly, the change of official policy was dramatic: "Up to Daniells's election as president, only one or two Adventist missionaries had been sent out from North America every year. The year following his election the Seventh-day Adventist Church sent sixty new missionaries overseas, and during his whole presidency ninety new Adventist missionaries, on the average, left the shores of North America every year."[12] Despite the fact that Adventist missions now began to be established all over the world, the rate of church growth dropped to an all-time low. This may partly be attributed to internal strife within the North American church (the church's dispute with John Harvey Kellogg) but statistics indicate that the rate of growth was at least halved outside America as well. In the same period, the ratio of evangelistic workers to members rose to a level higher than any before or since. In 1910 there was one evangelistic worker for every twenty-one church members.

Although the short-term benefits of reorganization may not have been reflected in growth, the next decade was to prove more successful. In 1920 the membership stood at 185,450, a figure now almost equally divided between North America and the other divisions of the church. The First World War does not appear to have disrupted Adventist missionary expansion. In fact, Adventists may have benefited from the reduced competition of European missionary groups. The Edinburgh Conference of 1910 had marked the high-water mark of mainline Protestant mission. By the Jerusalem Conference of 1928, the effects of economic recession and growing secularization had muted Edinburgh's triumphalism.[13] Adventist missions, however, steadily expanded, entering one or more new territories every year, with membership increasing at an annual rate of 5 to 6 percent.[14] By 1940 there were half a million Adventists worldwide. This sustained growth was particularly impressive, since "during the interwar years the rate of apostasies averaged between 55 and 60 percent of conversions."[15]

The Second World War proved a greater obstacle to missionary activity than had the First, but in the aftermath of Hiroshima, according to one Adventist historian, "Adventist emphasis on eschatological prophecies suddenly appeared relevant." The church's leadership, "sensing the opportune times," issued a call in 1947 "for every Adventist minister, including those involved in departmental and institutional work, 'to actively engage in public evangelism for as much time as possible each year.'"[16] The spearhead of this campaign was high-profile evangelism in major cities, fronted by charismatic speakers like R. A. Anderson, Fordyce Detamore, and George Vandeman.[17] Church membership reached the one million mark in 1955, almost double the figure of ten years before, with growth continuing overseas at a rate twice that of the North American division. Despite the increasing employment of radio and television, the rate of growth slowed in the second half of the 1950s and early 1960s to below 5 percent per annum, only slightly more than half the rate enjoyed in the decade 1945–55.

It was during the early 1960s that Adventists started to become more self-conscious about missionary activity. The all-American style of public evangelism was questioned in some cultural contexts. The apparent inability of the church to make headway in the Middle East resulted in a series of conferences during 1961 to 1963 designed to find points of contact between Islam and Adventism.[18] A similar effort had already been made by Walter Schubert to accommodate the Adventist message to the cultural style of established Catholic nations.[19] However, neither effort was rewarded with evangelistic success (save in Latin America) or official denominational approval, and the American ethos of Adventist evangelism remained.

During the 1960s and 1970s the church enjoyed a steady 5 to 6 percent annual growth. This increase was largely the result of the rapid expansion of the church in the Third World. In 1930 North America, Europe, and Australia accounted for nearly 70 percent of world membership; by 1970 that share had dropped to 30 percent.[20] Yet although in 1970 only 20 percent of the world population was Christian, the Adventist missiologist Gottfried Oosterwal estimated that up until that time only around 5 percent of Adventists had been from non-Christian backgrounds. Although another Adventist missiologist, Borge Schantz, has challenged this assessment, a clear majority of Adventists still live in predominantly Christian countries out of contact with the two billion people ignorant of Christianity.[21] In response to this problem, the church's 1976 Autumn Council "laid aside routine business for the major part of the session, concentrating instead on methods for finishing the tasks they saw as committed to Adventists." Their conclusion was "to do all in their power to awaken the Adventist membership to the urgency of evangelism."[22] This directive bore fruit in the "1,000 Days of Reaping" in the early 1980s, a plan to harvest one thousand souls per day for one thousand days, which was successful in raising church membership to around 4.5 million in 1985.

Although by now the North American division accounted for less than one-fifth of the world's Adventist population, the United States, with over 600,000 members, was still the nation possessing the largest single membership. Furthermore, the church has, since the Second World War, achieved a growth rate matched only by the Mormons and the Assemblies of God.[23] This has been produced by the combination of conversions, biological increase (the baptism of Adventist children), and the retention of existing members. In America, where the church has a longer history than in the Third World, new recruits play a smaller role.[24] Despite this, conversions remain vital. Adventist families are smaller than the average, and the church cannot hope to retain all the second generation as members.[25] Without a steady infusion of new blood, the church would soon weaken. But it shows no sign of overall decline. From where have these converts been drawn? And what external factors are conducive to their recruitment?

A study of the background of new members of the Georgia-Cumberland Conference between 1979 and 1980 was conducted by the Institute of Church Ministry (ICM) at the denomination's Andrews University. Of those who responded to the survey, 38 percent had been raised in an Adventist home. Of the rest, 73 percent were Protestant, 6 percent Catholic, and 19 percent had no previous affiliation. The average age of those without an Adventist background was 35, and the average level of education was to about eleventh grade. Fifty-nine percent were female, 19 percent were in professional/managerial jobs, 19 percent were homemakers, 16 percent were students, 11 percent were skilled laborers, and 11 percent unskilled laborers. Fifty-four percent gave their annual family income as less than $15,000.[26]

These findings can usefully be compared with those of another ICM-sponsored project, a 1986 marketing study, which used market research techniques to profile both the existing membership and new believers. Unlike earlier studies, this was not a survey but a comprehensive, nationwide analysis that correlated addresses with census data to build up a picture of Adventist representation in forty-seven social groups—each group being defined by a cluster of socioeconomic characteristics. To some extent, this study confirmed the earlier data. New believers were drawn disproportionately from younger groups and from those with a below-average median income. But the marketing study also revealed important new information. Thirteen percent of new recruits were drawn from predominantly Hispanic groups—groups that represented only 3 percent of the general population. Eight percent were drawn from black groups, which made them marginally overrepresented as well. Of the twenty-two most geographically mobile groups, Adventists were disproportionately successful in fifteen; of the twenty-two least mobile, they were overrepresented in only five. While Adventists appeared to recruit from all sections of society, they drew few converts from the ranks of the well-educated, affluent, suburban professionals who constituted 8 percent of the population but only 4 percent of new believers.[27]

There are several conclusions to be drawn from such data. The first concerns Adventism and the disadvantaged in the United States. Although America is an autonomous nation state with sufficient economic and military power to render it almost impervious to outside influence, it is not necessarily the case that all sections of the population experience the power of the nation in the same way. To those who are fully integrated within American society, the power of the nation may seem to be something in which they share. But for those who occupy a more marginal position, national power may seem an external and possibly alien force. Some citizens may feel excluded from it. The population can thus be divided into "insiders" and "outsiders." The latter group experiences American power only passively—as something that affects their lives but over which they can exercise no control.

There are several possible indicators of a person's position within American society. Economic factors are obviously important: those with large disposable incomes are able to exert a greater degree of control over their lives than those without. They are able both to define their positions and to effect changes in their environment. Similarly, those in high-status employment have greater opportunity to set their own objectives and to influence those around them. Another indication of being an "insider" is the degree to which a person is firmly established within a particular environment. This is more likely to be true of the old than the young; it is also more likely to be true of those who have lived in the same place for a long time. Continuity and stability can contribute to a sense of belonging, even for those of only low socio-economic status. Racial differences are also important. American society has been dominated by white, Anglo-Saxon Protestants, and persons of other ethnic backgrounds have traditionally occupied more marginal roles.[28]

It is apparent that Adventists recruit heavily from among outsiders—from among those who have not established themselves and are not in a position to exercise authority. The most obvious example of this is the church's strong appeal to racial minorities. The 1986 marketing study showed that over 20 percent of new believers were drawn from black and Hispanic groups that constituted only 10 percent of the population. Adventist converts were also economically disadvantaged: 70 percent were drawn from groups with below-average income, and they were most severely underrepresented in the top income groups. Furthermore, new believers, even those of higher socioeconomic status, tended to be recruited from among the young and geographically mobile. Within America, Adventism's appeal is primarily to those who by virtue of race, poverty, age, or mobility have not yet been able to find a secure position within society. These are people who cannot take the benefits of American life for granted; for them, the American dream of autonomy and prosperity is not an everyday experience: it is, at most, an aspiration.[29]

The precarious socioeconomic position of most converts helps explain the way in which rates of growth are sensitive to fluctuations in the economy. Converts are drawn from the ranks of those least insulated from the effects of economic decline. Depression in the economy is liable to swell the numbers of outsiders and thus increase the pool of potential recruits. A clear example of this is provided by the Great Depression of the early 1930s. The Wall Street crash of 1929 triggered a general recession, the full effects of which became clear by 1931. In that year the Seventh-day Adventist Church in America baptized 10,600 new members, a 40 percent increase over the previous year. Throughout the Depression, the church enjoyed an annual net growth of between 5 and 6 percent, approximately twice that experienced during the previous decade of prosperity.[30]

The one respect in which Adventist converts do not appear to be marginal is their religious background. The Georgia-Cumberland Conference survey showed 73 percent of new recruits to be Protestant. In neither this nor other studies is there any indication that Adventists convert many members of other religious minorities.[31] On the contrary, most converts appear to be drawn from mainstream Protestantism. However, even this finding is in keeping with the general pattern of the church's evangelism. Adventists draw their recruits from the socially marginal members of the dominant religious tradition. Converts become religious outsiders as well as social and economic outsiders, bringing their religious affiliations into alignment with the rest of their experience. In this context, the theology of Adventism is particularly important. Seventy percent of new believers in the Georgia-Cumberland survey said that they were most attracted to the church by "the truth and beauty of its teaching"[32] Adventist beliefs obviously help those who espouse them to make sense of their own lives. This may, in part, be because of the way in which Adventist theology explains the position of the church relative to America. The convert's marginality to dominant structures of American society is explained and justified in theological terms. Another factor may be the conviction with which the Adventist message is expressed. Few people are attracted to churches in which theology is hedged around by qualifications. Adventism's evident ideological appeal may also be a function of the church's apparent theological certainty.[33]

People are, however, very far from being motivated solely by ideas. One of the things that came to light in the ICM studies was the importance of church institutions in both attracting and retaining converts. In the Georgia-Cumberland survey, 9 percent of new believers who did not come from an Adventist home said that they had attended one of the church's elementary schools. Still more significant is the role of the church school in bringing Adventist children to baptism. Of the Georgia-Cumberland converts from an Adventist home, 80 percent had spent at least some time at an Adventist elementary school. As the mean average age for the baptism of those from an Adventist home was barely 17, the significance of schooling is evident.[34] A survey conducted in 1950 found that the usual age for the baptism of Adventist children was twelve years. By the age of 18, 89 percent of those who became church members had already been baptized. The church school played a crucial part in bringing young people to a positive decision. The 1950 survey found that of those who had attended church schools all the way through college, 100 percent had been baptized and only 12 percent had subsequently withdrawn. In contrast, of those young people from Adventist homes who had no denominational education, only just over half were ever baptized, and of those a majority subsequently left the church.

Both the proportion and the level of denominational schooling correlated positively with church affiliation. Those with a complete Adventist education were more likely to be loyal to the church than those whose schooling had been mixed; but those who went to an Adventist academy or college after an otherwise nondenominational education were even more likely to retain their church membership than those with a complete Adventist education to the same level. Among those with a complete church education, affiliation also correlated with educational level. Of eighth-grade graduates, 48 percent were church members; of high-school graduates, 71 percent; and of college graduates, 88 percent.[35] Clearly, biological growth does not take place automatically. The church school has played a vital role in ensuring that a significant number of Adventist children retain the faith of their parents.[36] Some non-Adventists are brought into the church through denominational schooling, but the primary benefit of the system is its capacity to socialize the second and subsequent generations. The school system is thus an important adjunct to direct evangelistic outreach.

The factors involved in Adventist growth appear to include marginality to American social power, fluctuations in the economy, and institutional development. Although it is impossible to collate all relevant information on a worldwide scale, and any conclusions must remain tentative, it is possible to discern similar factors at work in the international development of the church.

In the ten years from the beginning of 1973 to the beginning of 1983, church membership increased by 72 percent, from 2.3 million to 3.9 million, with only the Islamic nations remaining impenetrable. The annual rate accelerated slightly in the second half of the decade and compares favorably with that achieved at any time since the 1950s. At the same time, the ratio of full-time evangelistic workers to church members dwindled, and in 1973 stood at about 1 to 100. In regional terms, however, rates of growth were highly uneven, ranging from virtual stagnation in Europe to a spectacular 180 percent increase during the period in Central America (see Figure 1). The result of this was

Figure 1. SDA World Growth, 1973–83

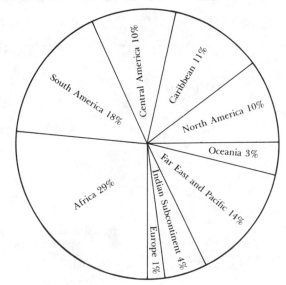

Note: Membership figures calculated on January 1 of each year

Source: Compiled from figures published in relevant editions of the *Annual Statistical Report* (Washington, D.C.: Office of Archives and Statistics, General Conference of Seventh-day Adventists).

that by 1983, half the world membership lived in Africa or Latin America.

In comparison, European Adventism looked distinctly unhealthy. All but one of the countries showing a net loss for the period (see Table 1) were located in Central or Northern Europe. (The figures for Sri Lanka are distorted by the small base and mass apostasy in 1974.) The internal problems of the Hungarian church may partially account for the setbacks there, but the situation in Germany indicated nothing but long-term decline. The total German membership (East and West) in 1983 was 35,000, exactly the same as seventy years earlier. It is worth noting that the decline is less marked in the predominantly Catholic southern part of the country, while the Lutheran northeast shares with Lutheran Scandinavia a steady erosion in numbers.

At the other end of the scale, the Adventist church in Zaire, along with other Protestant groups, has benefited from an astonishing wave of receptivity to Christianity (see Table 2).[37] The figures for the two quinquennia reveal that while the rate of growth declined slightly, Zaire remained clearly the most successful location for Adventist mission. In general, the rate of expansion increased in Africa, while decreasing in Central America. This upturn in Africa was enough to compensate for

Table 1. Countries Showing Lowest Rates of Growth

Country	Percentage Growth 1973–83
East Germany	− 14.8
Hungary	− 13.2
Denmark	− 10.4
Sweden	− 6.4
West Germany	− 2.7
Sri Lanka	− 4.7
Poland	0.3
Norway	0.7
Switzerland	2.2
Yugoslavia	2.4

Source: Compiled from figures published in relevant editions of the *Annual Statistical Report* (Washington, D.C.: Office of Archives and Statistics, General Conference of Seventh-day Adventists).

Table 2. Union Missions Showing Highest Rates of Growth

Country	Percentage Increase 1973–83	1973–78	1978–83
Zaire	244	89	82
Mexico	183	72	64
Central America	173	80	52
Angola	154	65	53
Franco-Haiti	131	60	45
West Africa	126	33	70
Antilla	120	59	39
Mozambique	117	44	51
Southern Africa (black)	116	24	75
Chile	114	56	37
Colombia/Venezuela	108	51	38
Korea	108	32	57
India[a]	102	43	42
Zambia	101	19	69
East Africa	101	42	42

[a]This represents a composite figure for the three Indian missions. (Membership figures calculated on January 1 of each year.)

Source: Compiled from figures published in relevant editions of the *Annual Statistical Report* (Washington, D.C.: Office of Archives and Statistics, General Conference of Seventh-day Adventists).

a general downward trend in the second half of the decade, when the rate of growth slowed in more than 60 percent of the union missions worldwide.

However, the changes in growth did not affect the balance of the total membership. At the beginning of 1983 the countries with the largest Adventist populations were the United States (608,290), Brazil (336,203), and the Philippines (287,288), with Mexico, Kenya, Rwanda, Jamaica, and India the other nations having a membership of more than 100,000. The size of the Adventist community is not an indication of its numerical strength relative to the rest of the population.[38] The proportion of Adventists is highest in small countries and islands like Guyana (1 to 52), Belize (1 to 26), Guadeloupe (1 to 49), the Bahamas (1 to 36), and the Solomon Islands (1 to 20). The miniscule Pitcairn Island (population 55) remains the only place with an Adventist majority, but Adventists are found in significant numbers in larger nations as well: Jamaica (1 to 20), Rwanda (1 to 45), Haiti (1 to 63), and Papua New Guinea (1 to 49).

In suggesting tentative explanations for international patterns in Adventist church growth, only external, contextual factors will be discussed. This procedure permits comparison between different areas of the world, but because in each case the intervening variables have not been exhaustively explored, the results should be interpreted with caution. It has been noted that in America, Adventists seem to attract converts during economic crises. Sociologists such as Bryan Wilson who see Adventism as a revolutionist movement might therefore expect growth to take place in times of economic deprivation.[39] These need not be periods of great poverty but may occur whenever "an individual or group may be, or feel, disadvantaged in comparison to other individuals or groups or to an internalized set of standards."[40] Such feelings are difficult to measure, but it may be possible to point to specific economic conditions that seem likely to prompt them.

A state's gross national product (GNP) per capita (usually expressed in U.S. dollars) gives no indication of the distribution of wealth within the country but often serves as an indicator of the relative wealth of nations.[41] A low relative increase in per capita GNP over a period of years will imply national economic problems. It might be also promote a sense of comparative deprivation among individuals and groups. Table 3 contrasts pairs of neighboring countries of comparable size and wealth during the late 1970s and early 1980s. In each pair, the percentage increase in GNP per capita is in inverse proportion to the percentage of the membership increase. It would be foolhardy to conclude that there must be some kind of causal connection, for it is possible to cite counterexamples (for example, Equador and Bolivia). However, it is worth noting that in several countries where there was a marked rise in the rate of growth from 1973–78 to 1978–83, there is also evidence

Table 3. Changes in GNP (per capita) and SDA Membership Increase

Country	1976 GNP (U.S.$)	1980 GNP	Percent Change	1978 Members (start)	1982 Members (end)	Percent Change
Uganda	240	280	17	13,010	20,197	55
Kenya	240	420	75	113,728	159,447	40
El Salvador	490	590	20	10,800	23,261	115
Guatemala	650	1,110	76	15,073	20,130	34
Ghana	580	420	−28	28,017	50,115	79
Nigeria	380	1,010	166	38,921	53,435	37
Peru	800	980	23	61,075	91,301[a]	50
Colombia	630	1,180	87	48,180	65,082	35

Note:
   The discrepancy in date between the two sets of GNP and membership figures allows for a time lag between the onset of sometimes barely visible ecomonic trends and the possible responses to them.

[a]But for mass apostasy in 1982, this figure would have been 9,000 higher.

Source: Figures for GNP per capita from relevant editions of John Paxton, ed., *The Stateman's Yearbook* (London: Macmillan Press). Figures for SDA membership from relevant editions of the *Annual Statistical Report* (Washington, D.C.: Office of Archives and Statistics, General Conference of Seventh-day Adventists).

of regionally atypical economic decline between 1976 and 1980. (Zambia is perhaps the best example.)

   Political crises also appear to be conducive to Adventist growth. This accords with the belief of many sociologists that millennialist movements emerge and prosper in periods of social tension. But a careful examination of Adventist membership growth in selected countries during the 1970s and 1980s yields only patchy support for this general conclusion. In countries where growth is already slow or nonexistent, a political crisis seems to have little discernable effect. Membership of the Polish Union remained completely static throughout the unstable period 1973–83. Similarly, the gradual increase of membership in Portugal showed no sign of escalating in the aftermath of the 1974 revolution. In fact, certain types of political disruption may inhibit growth. That the church suffered reverses in Ethiopia after the downfall of Haile Selassie is perhaps not surprising in view of its close association with the former monarch, but the reduction in the rate of conversions in Zimbabwe during the chaotic period following the end of white minority rule indicates that a prolonged national crisis is not the sufficient condition of increased growth. However, there are countries in South Africa where this hypothesis seems to be substantiated. The church in Angola flourished during a bitter civil war (although comparable success in Mozambique might suggest that factors other than the war were involved). Most dramatic was the burgeoning of the black South African union, the Southern Union, where the rate of growth in the tense 1978–83 period was three times that in the marginally more placid years of 1973–78.

A comparative study of Chile and Argentina may provide a clearer indicator of the precise type of political crisis that stimulates church growth (see Figures 2 and 3). In the early 1970s, both were ruled for periods of three years by what might be termed "dictatorial populist" governments. In both cases, the army put an end to instability by enforcing military rule. In Argentina the years in which Juan Péron and his widow were ascendent were also those in which the rate of Adventist growth reached its peak. In Chile during the effective years of the Marxist Allende government, the growth rate slumped to an average of 4.7 percent, down 2.2 percent from the previous two years. More striking still was the leap to 14.5 percent growth in 1974, the first full year of General Pinochet's regime, after which the annual rate averaged 9.2 percent. If any conclusions may be drawn from these figures, they would be that political instability does not in itself stimulate growth, that the church may be affected by political change, and that rightist, rather than leftist, governments provide an atmosphere more conducive to expansion.

Perhaps more significant than the precise political complexion of the regime is the extent of American involvement and influence. Allende was overthrown in an American-inspired coup, and Pinochet leaned heavily on assistance from the United States.[42] It is not altogether surprising that a switch from a Marxist to a pro-American capitalist government should be accompanied by a marked upswing in conversions to a religious movement native to America. It is generally easier for the church to operate in nations with which the United States has strong economic, political, or military ties. Furthermore, Adventism may enable people in such countries to put America's geopolitical dominance into theological context, which is perhaps analagous to the way in which Adventism in America helps outsiders come to terms with the centers of American power.

That there is some relationship between American presence and Adventist success is suggested by an analysis of the extent to which Adventism has penetrated the life of countries in the American sphere of influence. The ratio of Adventists to the rest of the population is the clearest indicator of this. As noted above, the ratio is highest in small nations where a small absolute number of church members represents a significant proportion of the total population. However, even making allowance for the small populations of nations in Central America and the Caribbean, it is interesting that almost half the countries with an Adventist penetration of more than 1 to 500 are located in this region,

Figure 2. SDA Church Growth (Argentina)

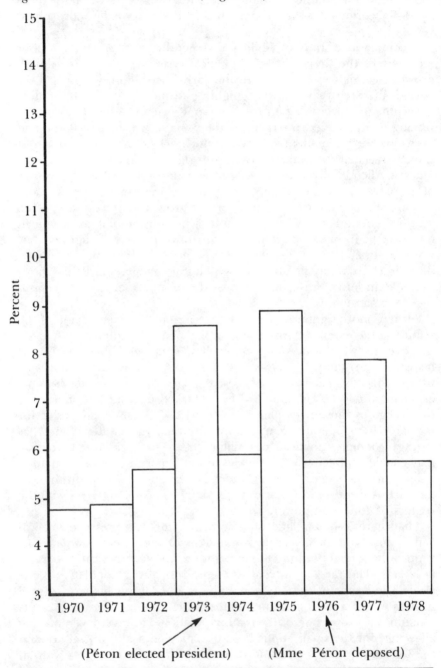

(Péron elected president)   (Mme Péron deposed)

Source: Compiled from figures published in relevant editions of the *Annual Statistical Report.*

Figure 3. SDA Church Growth (Chile)

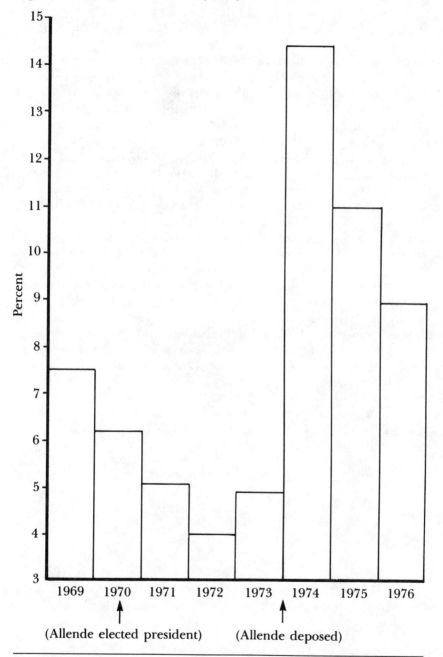

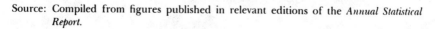

Source: Compiled from figures published in relevant editions of the *Annual Statistical Report*.

firmly within the American sphere of influence. Still more striking is the fact that of the larger nations with a significant Adventist presence—notably Brazil, the Philippines, Korea, and Mexico—almost all have close links with the United States.[43]

Another factor that emerges from this analysis is Adventism's success within the former British colonies. Central Africa, Kenya, Ghana, Tanzania, and Zambia provide the most prominent examples. Papua New Guinea, and several smaller islands where the church has progressed rapidly, are also former British colonies or protectorates, as are Australia and New Zealand. Within the British Empire, the church benefited from the grants-in-aid scheme in which government finance supported the church's schools and institutions. The denomination was thus able to build a network of institutions through which to convert and socialize the local population. In the United States, the function of church schools differs from those in the Third World, where the Adventist mission school may provide the best, and perhaps the only, available form of education and thus act as an introduction to the church itself. But the same factors may still be at work. Adventist education brings with it the benefits of all forms of education: it opens the way to higher-status occupations and increased earning capacity. These are the very things that Adventist converts most notably lack. Adventism may thus hold a dual attraction: it puts converts' low status in theological context and offers, at least for succeeding generations, the opportunity of leaving that status behind. In Adventism, "outsiders" can clothe their marginality in religious dress while simultaneously improving their socioeconomic position. Thus, the church enables outsiders to exchange one type of marginality for another: socioeconomic marginality for religious marginality. Further discussion of this process must await part three, but it may at least suggest one reason for Adventism's success at the edges of American life, both within and beyond the United States.

CHAPTER 10

The Science of Happiness

The object of Adventist evangelistic endeavor is to convert people to the doctrines of the church. But important as these doctrines are, Adventist evangelism is equally concerned to effect a change in the lifestyle of the prospective convert. As well as, say, accepting the Sabbath or being able to identify the various beasts of the Apocalypse, joining the Seventh-day Adventist church means embarking on a well-worn road to personal well-being and, it is hoped, eternal happiness.

To this end, the denomination has sought to guide its members' behavior in three important areas of human experience: health, sex, and family life. As any person who has visited an Adventist evangelistic campaign will know, the most visible of the three areas is the church's health program. In the 1980s the virtues of this program were persuasively argued in *How You Can Live Six Extra Years* (1981). The authors, Lewis Walton and the doctors Jo Ellen Walton and John Scharffenberg, had conducted workshops specifically designed to enlighten the American public about the benefits of the Adventist way of life. The book describes the main ingredients of this lifestyle. It prohibits the use of drugs, tobacco, alcohol, and many types of meat. A vegetarian diet is advocated, although it is acknowledged that many Adventists include milk and eggs. But whole grains, fruits, nuts, and vegetables are recommended as the basis of an adequate diet. It is also suggested that stimulants such as caffeine, spices, and hot condiments should be avoided.[1] The authors outline the seven principles that undergird the Adventist approach to health: pure air and water, careful nutrition, regularity, rest, exercise, and moderation in eating.[2]

What are the benefits of this lifestyle? *Six Extra Years* refers to studies suggesting that Adventists, at least in America, are far less likely than their counterparts to die from modern diseases. Only about half as many Adventists are likely to die from heart disease, strokes, diabetes, or peptic ulcers as members of the general population. Adventists suffer only 13 percent of the average number of deaths caused by cirrhosis of the liver, 20 percent of deaths from lung cancer, and 32 percent of deaths caused by emphysema. The incidence of cancer deaths among Adventists is reduced by about one-third, and in an apparent vindication of the belief that the Adventist lifestyle brings happiness and contentment, Adventists commit only 31 percent of the usual number of suicides.[3] Walton and his colleagues cite additional evidence showing that in respect to coronary thrombosis, the more Adventists conform to the church's health message, the less chance they have of suffering an untimely death. Reiterating the message that became common in the 1970s, they argue that living the Adventist way can add up to three years to your life expectancy for women and over six extra years for men.[4]

This emphasis on health is a legacy of the health reform movement, which was an important force in nineteenth-century America. In response to what one historian has called "a sick and dirty nation," a number of reformers resolved to improve the poor health of their fellow countrymen.[5] In the 1830s Sylvester Graham, a Presbyterian minister, began an extensive temperance crusade and invented one of the first health foods, the graham cracker. William A. Alcott, a doctor trained at Yale, joined with Graham to found in 1837 the American Physiological Society, the first of the health reform associations. Horace Mann inspired a campaign that culminated in 1850 in an act of the Massachusetts General Court requiring the teaching of physiology and hygiene in public schools. Other reformers included Lewis B. Coles, who elevated the principles of health reform to the level of the Ten Commandments; Drs. Joel Shew and R. T. Trall, who pioneered water cure treatments in the 1840s; and Dr. James C. Jackson, who established an influential water cure center at Dansville, New York, in 1858.[6]

These reformers shared a general distrust of existing medical practices. They believed, with some justification, that bleeding and the chemical medicines that were provided for curing disease often made matters worse. Instead, they favored natural methods such as hydrotherapy. In preventing disease, they generally advocated plenty of fresh air and water; the avoidance of tea, coffee, tobacco, and alcohol; a vegetarian diet; exercise; rest; personal hygiene; and moderation in both eating and drinking.[7]

Ellen White, who pioneered health reform among Seventh-day Adventists, learned from the reformers who preceded her. The prophetess's interest in health sprang from her own general ill health, as such interest did for so many of the people who took up the cause of reform. Mrs. White's concern with healthful living started when she received a vision on the subject in 1848, but it was not until after June 5, 1863, that she really became a committed health reformer. During that evening, at an Adventist home in Otsego, Michigan, Ellen White received a vision from God that stressed the need for health reform. The first published account of her vision reveals that there was little that previous reformers had not already said. She outlined the evils of over-indulgence, advocated a vegetarian diet, and frowned on the use of alcohol and tobacco. She also came out against the use of tea and coffee, referring to them as "slow poisons." But as well as these dietary pro-hibitions, Mrs. White stressed the deleterious effects of overwork and the importance of personal hygiene. Concerning the treatment of dis-ease, she favored water cure methods. Mrs. White had little time for conventional medicine as then currently practiced, and she thought the indiscriminate prescription of drugs a particular evil.[8]

In her account of the vision, she made a passing reference to the idea that the human body was to be regarded as the temple of God, using it to show that it was a Christian duty to keep the body as healthy as possible.[9] Based on the reference in 1 Corinthians 3:16, this belief became, in the twentieth century, an important rationale for the de-nomination's concern with healthful living. However, it played little part in the philosophy of her initial vision as a whole. If there was a philosophy underlying Mrs. White's first statement on health reform, it was the concept of the "laws of health." At the core of these laws were abstemious and temperate habits. Disease, Mrs. White maintained, only resulted when the laws of health were disobeyed or broken: "Many marvel that the human race have [sic] so degenerated, physically, men-tally, and morally. They do not understand that it is the violation . . . of the laws of health, that has produced this sad degeneracy."[10] This was the crucial point she emphasized repeatedly:

The human family have violated the laws of health, and have run to excess in almost everything. Disease has been steadily increasing. The cause has been followed by the effect. . . . Many are living in violation to the laws of health, and are ignorant of the relation their habits of eating, drinking, and working sustain to their health. . . . Multitudes remain in inexcusable ignorance in re-gard to the laws of their being. . . . I have been shown that a great amount of suffering might be saved if all would labor to prevent disease, by strictly obey-ing the laws of health.[11]

Mrs. White clearly understood the laws of health to be of divine origin. Yet her discussion of them tended to give her exposition of health reform a naturalistic rather than a supernatural basis. What is striking about the account of her vision is the general lack of scriptural justification for her message. She did supply numerous biblical ex-amples of the evils of all kinds of intemperance, but her arguments for health reform were based on the iron rigidities of natural law. "All our enjoyments or sufferings," she wrote later, "may be traced to obedience or transgression of natural law."[12]

The Otsego vision marked the point at which Seventh-day Adventists began to accept the principles of health reform in significant numbers. The founding of the Western Health Reform Institute at Battle Creek in 1866 further underlined that commitment, as did the magazine, *The Health Reformer*, which was started at the same time. Modeled on the institution at Dansville, the Adventist institute, in treating disease, used "only such means" that nature "can best use in recuperative work, such as Water, Air, Light, Heat, Food, Sleep, Rest, Recreation etc."[13] Under Horatio S. Lay, the institute was initially a success, attracting patients from all parts of the United States.[14] This did not mean, however, that all Seventh-day Adventists became diligent health reformers. On the contrary, Mrs. White had to struggle to convince many of her fellow believers to give up their former ways.[15] And at times, she herself found it difficult to live up to all the principles of health. Ronald Numbers, who examined Mrs. White's career in *Prophetess of Health*, believes that it was not until 1894 that she completely controlled her own personal liking for meat.[16]

One Adventist who apparently never wavered in his commitment to health reform was John Harvey Kellogg, the brilliant doctor who took over the Western Health Reform Institute in 1876 and renamed it the Battle Creek Sanitarium a year later. In a professional career spanning nearly seventy years, Kellogg devoted his attention to developing his own version of health reform, which he called "biologic living."[17] In this, Kellogg often seemed more interested in bringing his ideas to the wider American public than to the Adventist church. However, in the late nineteenth and early twentieth centuries, he conducted a diligent campaign against those within his own church who remained obdurately opposed to reform. Indeed, Kellogg's contempt for leaders like A. G. Daniells, who were not conscientious health reformers, was one of the factors that led to the doctor's expulsion from the church in 1907.[18]

Kellogg differed from previous health reformers in two ways. First, he did not ridicule the established medical profession as many of his predecessors had done. A product of the improving standard of medical education himself (he was trained at the University of Michigan and at New York's Bellevue Medical School), Kellogg thought it best to yoke established medicine to his goals. Second, he realized that most people found the meatless health reform diet tasteless and, in some cases, unpalatable. In one case, a patient at the sanitarium broke her dentures on the doctor's own multigrain granola cereal. Other new health products fared no better with the public. In the early 1890s, patients told Kellogg that eating the recently developed cereal, Shredded Wheat, was like "eating straw."[19]

It was partly the need to develop adequate and palatable food alternatives that fostered Kellogg's invention of a number of products that have since become standard items on the world's food tables. The most important of these were peanut butter (developed in the early 1890s, much earlier than the experiments of George Washington Carver who is still mistakenly believed to be the inventor of peanut butter), and cornflakes (originally known as Granose flakes), which Kellogg patented in 1894. In addition, Kellogg invented the first meat substitute called Nuttose, the first cereal coffee substitute, and the first artificial milk from soybeans.[20] Kellogg was slow to realize the commercial possibilities of his inventions. Consequently, his brother Wil, who had helped him produce the original flaked cereal, eventually set up his own company and marketed cornflakes on a mass scale. As Wil Kellogg was also expelled from the church in 1907, a famous American industry was lost to Adventism. John Harvey Kellogg and the church also lost the coffee substitute market—to C. W. Post, an entrepreneur who modeled his famous "Postum" on Kellogg's cereal coffee after being a patient at the Battle Creek Sanitarium.[21]

The health reform movement of which Adventists became a part and which, through Kellogg, they later led had many aspects. But perhaps the most significant was use of health reform as a means of achieving sexual control. Two recent historians of American sexual ethics, Peter Gardella and John Money, claim that the principal motivation of all the reformers from Graham to Kellogg was their disapproval of sexual activity. They believe that individuals like Graham and Kellogg formulated their dietary and health systems in order to cure sexual desire.[22] Although this argument is probably overstated, there is much evidence that supports it. Certainly, Sylvester Graham linked meat eating with the arousal of carnal or sexual passion. And sexual passion, he believed, robbed the body of its capacity to resist disease. Graham's formula of diet, exercise, and sexual abstinence as a route to health and diet as a route to sexual abstinence also found expression in the publications of many other reformers.[23] Much of Ellen White's writings on health can also be read in terms of the sexual abstinence theory. She frequently referred to the destructive physical and spiritual effects of the "base" or "animal passions," by which she almost always meant sexual passions.[24] But for Mrs. White there were additional issues at stake. She argued that Adventists could not be fitted for translation to heaven if they did not control their animal urges. Thus those who did not overcome their sexual desires could not achieve salvation.[25] In other words, the eternal happiness of Adventists depended on control of sex, which in turn depended on obedience to the laws of health.

Like Graham, the prophetess believed that sexual intercourse destroyed physical health and that health reform was a means of controlling sexual instinct. The links were made clear in her discussion of the relationship between health and sex in *An Appeal to Mothers: The Great Cause of the Physical, Mental and Moral Ruin of Many of the Children of Our Time* (1864). Mrs. White's chief concern was the practice of masturbation, or "secret vice" as it was euphemistically termed. She repeatedly emphasized the destructive effects of this form of sexual gratification, warning that in the spiritual sphere, "secret vice is the destroyer of high resolve, earnest endeavor, and strength of will to form a good religious character" and that in the moral sphere it "inflames the passions, fevers the imagination and leads to licentiousness."[26] She viewed the physical effects as equally debilitating. She saw masturbation as the cause of such handicaps as "imbecility, dwarfed forms, crippled limbs, misshapen heads and deformity of every description."[27] Like Graham, Mrs. White pointed out that one way to avoid these dreadful consequences was through the control of diet. "We should not make it a practice to place upon our tables food which would injure the health of our children. Our food should be prepared free from spices. Mince pies, cakes, preserves, and highly seasoned meats, with gravies, create a feverish condition in the system, and inflame the animal passions."[28]

If anything, John Harvey Kellogg was even more rigorous in spelling out the connection between the unreformed diet and sexual indulgence. In *Plain Facts for Old and Young* (1886), he wrote: "Flesh, condiments, eggs, tea, coffee, chocolate, and all stimulants have a powerful influence directly upon the reproductive organs. They increase the local supply of blood; and through nervous sympathy with the brain, the passions are aroused."[29] *Plain Facts*, an immensely successful early sex manual that remained in print for over forty years, advanced the view that sex was a destructive activity and was meant solely for reproductive purposes.[30] Common ailments were attributed to sexual indulgence, and Kellogg quoted with approval one medical authority who felt that "many forms of indigestion, general ill-health, hypochondriasis, etc., so often met with in adults, depend upon sexual excesses."[31] For Kellogg, the solution lay in the principles of health reform. "Nothing," he wrote, "tends so powerfully to keep the passions in abeyance as a simple diet, free from condiments, especially when coupled with a generous amount of exercise."[32]

The Adventist doctor's effect on the sexual mores of late nineteenth-century America is not be underestimated. In addition to the best-selling *Plain Facts*, he included lengthy sections on the evils of sex in his substantial works on health, *Man the Masterpiece or Plain Truths Plainly Told About Youth and Manhood* (1885) and *The Ladies Guide in Health and Disease* (1901). An earlier book, *Plain Facts About Sexual Life* (1877), which also promulgated his sexual views, is said to have sold half a million copies.[33] His influence was such that John Money believes that "wherever sex is equated with Victorianism, Kellogg's antisexual attitude continues to be felt, even though his name may not be mentioned."[34]

For Adventists, this antisexual attitude predominated even though they attached great importance to marriage and the family. On the face of it, this might seem odd, in that the family is unavoidably a sexual organization. However, for Adventists, the family was the institution to nurture sexual restraint. As Ellen White put it:

Let the Christian wife refrain, both in word and act, from exciting the animal passions of her husband. Many have no strength at all to waste in this direction. From their youth up they have weakened the brain and sapped the constitution by the gratification of animal passions. Self-denial and temperance should be the watchword in their married life; then the children born to them will not be so liable to have the moral and intellectual organs weak, and the animal strong."[35]

Her discussion of the evils of masturbation, it will be noted, was cast in an appeal to mothers. All of this may suggest one reason why, for Adventists, the family became so essential to personal well-being. Because it was seen as a means of curbing destructive sexual passions, the family, in a very direct sense, contributed to the physical health of parents and children. Certainly, Mrs. White saw (and wanted to see among Adventists) a close relationship between health reform and the family. "Healthful living must be made a family matter," she urged. "Parents should awake to their God-given responsibilities. Let them study the principles of health reform and teach their children that the path of self-denial is the only path of safety."[36] With these views it is not surprising to find an extended discussion of the home in *Ministry of Healing* (1905), Mrs. White's major book on health and disease, in which she expressed her belief that the health of the community also rested on the family. "The well-being of society, the success of the church, the prosperity of the nation, depend on home influences."[37]

The concept of the family that emerged in Mrs. White's writings conformed to the ideas of the home that developed in the nineteenth century. In contrast to the eighteenth century when the home bustled with economic activity, in the Victorian era it became distinct from the harshness of the social and economic order outside. The family home became a private place of peace and tranquility—a place to retreat from the growing secularization of the world. Various terms were used to describe the spiritual separateness of the home, among them *sanctuary*, *innerspace*, *walled garden*, and *haven*.[38] Mrs. White used the term *sacred circle* to convey the same idea.[39] She regarded "a carefully guarded Christian home" as "the surest safeguard against the corruptions of the outside world" and the family as "a place of refuge for the tempted youth."[40]

This picture of the Adventist family has remained unchanged throughout the denomination's history. What has changed is the attitude toward sex. The Adventist counselor Nancy Van Pelt wrote in 1979, "Husbands and wives should aim to be imaginative, creative, and willing lovers. God designed that sex . . . be exciting, enjoyable, and fulfilling."[41] Over the years, attitudes toward sex within the denomination have undergone a revolution. Sex is no longer considered a dangerous, functional activity but one that can bring happiness and fulfillment in its own right. The break with Kellogg's strictures had, in fact, started as early as 1931 when the staff of the College of Medical Evangelists, the denomination's medical school at Loma Linda, California, published the second edition of *The Home Physician and Guide to Health*. The authors advocated sexual restraint, mainly because they still felt that frequent sexual intercourse destroyed the health of women. But they expressed, possibly for the first time in Adventism, the idea that sex was a divine gift.[42] In contrast to Kellogg, the authors argued that the sexual act was primarily a manifestation of love and described the view that sex was only for reproductive purposes as "untenable."[43]

When the Adventist doctor Harold Shryock published *Happiness for Husbands and Wives* in 1949, he, too, was convinced of the value of sex. "Sexual expression," he wrote, "represents the culmination of all the desirable features of the family situation—the ultimate in marital happiness."[44] The appearance of Shryock's *Happiness for Husbands and Wives*, the first important Adventist discussion of sex since the *Home Physician*, did not, apparently, persuade all sections of the church of the value of his approach. Indeed, the Ellen White compilation *The Adventist Home*, which followed in 1952, was replete with warnings about the dangers of the sexual passions—warnings that were redolent of a previous age.[45] Nor did Shryocks's book immediately herald a greater willingness on the part of Adventists to discuss sexual matters when such issues were raised in a wider context. For example, when the Kinsey revelations detailing sexual behavior burst on an unsuspecting nation in the early 1950s, the *Review* took a rather dim view. "There is essentially nothing new in the Kinsey book," the church paper said, "unless it be that he has provided a statistical commentary on the words of John that the world lieth in wickedness."[46]

It was only after the change in sexual attitudes that occurred in the 1960s that Adventists, like most other people, became more willing to discuss sexual matters. In 1974 Adventism's sexologist Charles Wittschiebe published *God Invented Sex*. Unlike Kellogg, Wittschiebe was largely concerned with the question of how to improve sexual relations within marriage.[47] More books of this type followed. Among them were Nancy Van Pelt's *The Compleat Marriage* (1979) and Alberta Mazat's *That Friday in Eden* (1981). Although Adventists now celebrated human sexuality, they still strongly discouraged pre-or extra-marital sex. Not surprisingly, this position received a powerful boost when the spread of AIDS, a fatal sexually transmitted disease, reached epidemic proportions during the 1980s. The devasting effects of AIDS provided compelling new support for the Adventist view that the benefits of sex were best enjoyed within the setting of marriage and the family.[48] Thus, in contrast to the nineteenth century, where the Adventist family was an agent of sexual restraint, in the twentieth, the family became the place where sexual pleasure reached its apogee. All of which tended further to bolster the family's position within Adventism as the institution that provided ultimate happiness and a place safe from a sexually diseased society.

This continued emphasis on the family meant that the church tended to ignore the needs of members who remained single or who were homosexual. In recent years, the church has had to address the claims of groups that for differing reasons do not fit into traditional family patterns. The problem for singles was to some extent exacerbated by Adventism's strong emphasis on endogamy. The church has always advised that Adventists should marry only other Adventists.[49] If individuals failed to find a partner within the church they often remained unmarried rather than marry a non-Adventist. The problem was particularly acute for women, who by the 1970s, outnumbered male Adventists by about two to one.[50] The 1980s saw a growth in the number of seminars designed to deal with these problems. One of the first, held at the church's Andrews University in 1983, attracted forty to fifty people. David Osborne, the Adventist minister who conducted the seminar, made some pointed comments in the student newspaper. "Self-worth and fulfillment do not only come from marriage and children," he said, adding that the church "needs to accept singleness . . . build support groups, include singles in most of its functions, and most of all, it needs to quit judging."[51] By and large, the church leadership has proved sympathetic to such views. An article in the *Review* earlier that year outlined various programs the General Conference was itself conducting and the resource materials its departments were making available for the benefit of single people.[52]

The General Conference response to gay Seventh-day Adventists has been more guarded. In 1977 General Conference president Robert Pierson attacked homosexuality on the grounds that it "strikes at the very heart of family life."[53] However, homosexuality has not been unknown in the highest levels of the church's administration and in one well-publicized case, a president of Andrews University was arrested for homosexual solicitation.[54] Although the church has shown a willingness to minister to individual homosexuals, it has refused to recognize organized gay movements. Its basic position throughout the 1970s and 1980s was to regard homosexuality as a perverted state that could be changed through the power of the gospel.[55] This stand proved unacceptable to the Kinship organization, founded in the late 1970s, to cater for the needs of gay Adventists. In their statement of beliefs, the leaders of the organization boldly assert that "intimate love expressed between people of the same gender can be a positive, beautiful and healthy experience to the glory of God."[56] The assumption here, as for singles' groups, is that happiness is not solely to be found within the traditional family.

These were not the only challenges the family faced in modern Adventism. The church traditionally took a hard line against divorce and regarded adultery as grounds for automatic expulsion. It was also very difficult for divorced Adventists to remarry and retain church membership unless their estranged partners had formed adulterous relationships.[57] But these attitudes became more flexible when family life in the church was threatened by rising divorce rates in the 1970s and 1980s. A General Conference estimate in 1985 put the incidence of divorce in Adventist marriages as high as one in four.[58] An extensive survey of American Adventist families in the 1970s indicated that almost 29 percent of respondents regarded their homes as medium to low in happiness. In another question, individuals were asked to evaluate the success of their families. An average of 24 percent of the respondents judged their homes to be a failure.[59] The authors of the study, Andrews University sociologists Charles Crider and Robert Kistler, concluded that in the United States "enough family units are faltering to pose a crisis for the church as a whole."[60] The church's leadership was coming to the same conclusion. In 1975 they established a special General Conference department, the Home and Family Service, in an effort to halt the decline in family life.[61]

The problems encountered by the Adventist family were not unique; they reflected the changes taking place in wider society. But within Adventism, these changes had particular significance. Family life had once been a means of sexual control—a way of mastering the passions in readiness for translation. The family's transformation into a means of sexual fulfillment detached it from this eschatological context, for there would be no procreation in heaven. Sexuality and family life became ends in themselves, expressions of a complete humanity. As such, they became far less susceptible to regulation. When the control of the sexual impulse was considered a prerequisite of salvation, appropriate behavior was easy to define. When sexuality was seen as a divine gift, it was increasingly difficult to explain why it should be exercised only within marriage. At the same time, the new emphasis on having a happy family life for its own sake aroused expectations that were sometimes disappointed.

The disintegration of the nineteenth-century philosophy that had linked sexuality, health, and family life led Adventists in the twentieth century to give the entire message a stronger biblical foundation. But for some time after her death, Mrs. White's predominantly naturalistic philosophy exerted a strong influence. Evidence of this came in 1923 when F. M. Wilcox made a major statement on health over twelve consecutive pages of the *Review*. The thesis of this lengthy treatise was that the health message rested on naturalistic foundations. "We are to teach the principles of health reform," Wilcox argued, "upon the basis of physiological law."[62] This emphasis on natural law indicates why Adventists took a relatively long time to include health reform in their doctrinal statements. The subject was absent from the church's first statement of 1872 and again when the denomination's beliefs were revised in 1875. It was only when Adventist doctrines were reformulated in 1931 that health reform made its appearance. Adventists may not originally have regarded health reform as a scriptural belief, but by the time health was included in the 1931 statement, this position had changed. The concept of the laws of health had disappeared, and the idea of the body as the temple of the Holy Spirit was used to justify reform and the avoidance of "every body and soul defiling habit and practice."[63] Another concept that gave Adventist health reform in the twentieth century a scriptural foundation was the idea of clean and unclean meats, according to Levitical law. This was first clearly articulated within Adventism by the leader S. N. Haskell in 1903.[64] Thereafter, Adventists, whether they were meat eaters or not, were encouraged to abstain from unclean meats, particularly pork. Here again, it took time for this belief to become part of the church's fundamental beliefs. It was not included in the 1931 statement. The *Seventh-day Adventist Encyclopedia* of 1966 did mention it as an Adventist belief, but it was not until the statement of beliefs was revised in 1980 that abstinence from unclean meats became an official doctrine of the church.[65]

However, finding biblical support for Adventist health practices was not always possible. Vegetarianism was a case in point. The strongest argument in its favor had been that eating flesh would arouse the animal passions and make it impossible to exercise sexual restraint. This view, held by both Ellen White and John Harvey Kellogg, rested not on scripture but upon a particular understanding of physiology. Those twentieth-century Adventists, such as General Conference president A. G. Daniells, who did not share these scientific presuppositions failed to perceive the importance of vegetarianism. In consequence, this practice was never officially required. In 1908 Mrs. White had wanted to make it a requirement that church members abstain from meat, tea, and coffee. When she suggested to Daniells that a pledge should be circulated to this effect, the president cautiously but firmly resisted. Daniells's position evidently caused Mrs. White to reassess her thinking. At the General Conference session a year later, she said, "We are not to make the use of flesh food a test of fellowship."[66] In the 1920s, however, the meat question seems to have been quite widely debated. One church member expressed her belief to the editor of the *Review* that vegetarianism should be made a test of fellowship. In a leading article, F. M. Wilcox explained why the church felt that it should not.

Wilcox supported his position by quoting the statement in Mrs. White's General Conference address, which, had it not been for Daniells, might have been very different.[67]

Health reform evidently required another rationale to take it into the twentieth century. Divorced from the sexual abstinence theory, and with only limited explicit biblical support, healthful living now needed its own justification. The only elements of health reform to find their way into the fundamental beliefs of 1931 were prohibitions against alcohol, tobacco, and narcotics. Apart from encouraging members to regard the body as God's temple, the argument against the use of these substances appeared to be based simply on their deleterious physical and social consequences. Here the church found common ground with other temperance campaigners. The General Conference had supported the movement to ban alcohol during the prohibition era, so it naturally made the issue a test of fellowship when the opportunity arose in 1931. The specific injunctions against alcohol and drugs (but not against other elements of reform such as tea and coffee) may thus owe something to the social climate of the early twentieth century. The drinking of alcohol, in particular, seems to have been regarded as more harmful than other practices. When in 1931 a correspondent asked the *Review* editor why there should be laws against alcohol and not against smoking, drugs, or meat, he replied that alcohol was more socially destructive.[68]

But the problems with creating a hierarchy of harmfulness became increasingly evident in the 1970s and 1980s. Individual Adventists, perhaps feeling themselves able to judge the possible deleterious effects of their actions, began to indulge in practices once considered taboo. In 1982 the editors of the *Review* found the evidence of social drinking among Adventists sufficiently great to devote an entire issue to the problem. The special issue also dealt with the use of drugs and tobacco, which was also believed to be creeping into Adventism.[69] At one level, the situation seemed anomalous, for never before had the benefits of Adventist health practices been so clearly demonstrated. But the difficulty in equating particular principles with added longevity was that it probably allowed individuals to make their own calculations as to whether the loss of pleasure derived from indulgence was worth a more protracted old age. By making health its own justification, Adventists removed the absolute nature of the sanctions. Just as family life became more problematic when treated as an end in itself, so too did health reform, which, when no longer allied with the sexual abstinence theory and stripped of its eschatological significance, came to be seen as optional.

Throughout the twentieth century, health reform was gradually separated from its original partnership with sexual restraint. But while Adventists were no longer emphasizing the connection between diet and sex, people in the outside world were putting the two things back together. In time, Kellogg's cornflakes had become another refined product, no more nutritious than the average junk food. In the 1960s, however, Granola (Kellogg's first cereal experiment) was revived as a genuine health product. This time the health food revival was associated with hippies and others associated with a "back to the earth" philosophy. It was also associated with permissive, not restrictive, attitudes toward sex.[70] The modern revival of health reform encouraged a return to vegetarianism and spawned a plethora of health and fitness magazines that have since crowded the newsstands in bookshops and supermarkets around the world. In essence, all these magazines expound the same health principles as the nineteenth-century reformers but without the sexual abstinence theory. As John Money notes: "The diets and exercises that formerly were touted for their value in controlling sex now are recommended to augment sexual expression and enjoyment."[71]

In many ways, this new formula can be seen as providing a modern-day guide to Americans in their relentless quest for happiness. It was a formula, however, that owed much to the original concerns of Seventh-day Adventists. Through a philosophy that had embraced healthful living, diet, health foods, the family, and sex, the Adventist pioneers effectively created a science out of the pursuit of happiness. Church members in the twentieth century did not always view health reform in the same way as their forebears. But the pioneers' concern with health can be interpreted as a desire to give their own expression to the ideals of the founding fathers who believed the pursuit of happiness was an inalienable human right. The irony of the situation is that Adventists, who have traditionally sought happiness in the next world rather than this, have contributed to a science that both they and their fellow Americans now apply for earthly, rather than heavenly, gain.

CHAPTER 11

The Politics of Liberty

If the Adventist pursuit of happiness represented an alternative understanding of one of the key tenets of the Declaration of Independence, it perhaps provided a hint of the church's relationship to the fundamental principles of the American state. In paying great attention to individual happiness, Adventists remained close to the ideal of the nation's founders. In this context, it was surely no accident that Mrs. White saw natural law as the key to personal happiness. For in the Declaration of Independence, "the Laws of Nature and of Nature's God" provided the framework for all the rights and principles that were advanced.[1] However, Adventists believed that the key to happiness was the practice of health reform, which in the denomination's early days was deemed necessary for salvation. Adventists accepted the American right to happiness, but they interpreted it in a significantly different way from those who framed the Declaration of Independence.

It is, however, in relation to liberty, the other inalienable right enshrined in the Declaration, that Adventists have most clearly revealed the subtle difference between themselves and the founders of the nation. As with the pursuit of happiness, Adventists accepted this basic American principle. But they redefined the meaning of liberty in terms of religious liberty. As a result, Adventists have come to regard themselves as public watchdogs of the First Amendment provision separating church and state, which they have seen as vital to the maintenance of religious freedom.

The church's active involvement with religious liberty began in the 1880s. The first Adventist journal devoted to religious freedom was the *Sabbath Sentinel*, founded in 1884, which became the *American Sentinel* in 1886 and, eventually, *Liberty* in 1906. At the beginning of the twentieth century, the General Conference created a Department of Religious Liberty for the specific purpose of securing freedom of worship and belief. The church has also sponsored bodies such as the National Religious Liberty Association (1889) and the Religious Liberty

Association of America (1964) to monitor religious bills before national and state legislatures and the International Religious Liberty Association (1893) to promote religious freedom around the world.[2] In addition, Adventists have worked through the pressure group Americans United (formerly Protestants and Other Americans United) for Separation of Church and State, founded in 1948 in the wake of President Roosevelt's decision to appoint a papal envoy. The church supported this organization from the first, and in later years Adventists assumed leading roles within it. After the Second World War, Americans United became a familiar feature of the Washington lobby whenever church-state issues were debated.[3]

In practical terms, this emphasis on religious freedom affected the church's dealings with the Republic in two ways: it led the leadership to believe that the church was outside the bounds of state authority, and it prevented Adventists (apart from a handful of individuals) from participating in the political life of the nation.

As a denomination jealous of its independence, the Adventist church has never really believed that the regulations of the state should necessarily govern its affairs. This has not always come out in the open, as the church has traditionally preferred to avoid conflict with the state. However, in instances where the government has challenged their internal policies, Adventist leaders have boldly argued that the church is outside the jurisdiction of civil laws. The clearest indication of this tendentious attitude toward government authority came during the church's involvement in several legal cases in the 1970s and 1980s. In this period, women employees and federal agencies sued the church over Adventist violations of the Civil Rights Act of 1964. The background to these cases is discussed in chapter 14. It is worth noting, however, that in the legal fight to maintain its unequal pay scales, church leaders argued: "We insist that in doing its holy work, the church is free to ignore, even to flout, measures which bind all others. . . . That is what the First Amendment's Religion Clauses are all about."[4] In another brief, the church claimed "exemption from all civil laws in all of its religious institutions" and maintained that "as an organized religious denomination the Seventh-day Adventist Church insists that it is 'wholly exempt' from the cognizance of Civil Authority."[5] Similar arguments were deployed when Derrick Proctor took the denomination to court over the Adventist publishing monopoly. At issue was the Sherman Anti-Trust Act of 1890, but Adventist representatives claimed that the First Amendment placed the church outside its jurisdiction.[6]

Such radical interpretations of the First Amendment could perhaps be expected in a denomination committed to the view that religious bodies have the inalienable right to be free from state interference. For the Adventist church, the principle of the First Amendment tends to override other principles. In the legal cases of the 1970s and 1980s, the Adventist leadership believed the maintenance of church-state separation to be more important than the ethical propriety of equal pay or open business practices. In a complex world in which ethical principles may conflict with the First Amendment rule, it is the principle of church-state separation that the Adventist church tends to regard as the more important.

Adventists believed that the church had a right to be independent of the state, and they acted as if the state had a reciprocal right to be independent of the church. In general, they did not seek to influence events outside their own sphere. They preferred to avoid political and social questions on the grounds that these problems belonged to the state. The idea that church and state had separate spheres of influence guided Adventist leaders in their attitude toward politics. The *Review* pronounced in 1965 that "Seventh-day Adventists are of the firm conviction that political questions not directly involving religion or matters of conscience are strictly out of bounds for churches and church agencies."[7]

The *Review* itself made few statements on politics. The paper did, however, generally remind its readers not to participate in the quadrennial presidential campaigns. During the Garfield-Hancock election of 1880, James White urged church members to influence individuals who came within the church's realm while staying out of issues in the state's domain. He wrote: "It should be our study to adapt ourselves, as far as possible without compromising truth, to all who come within the reach of our influence and at the same time stand free from the strife and corruptions of the parties that are striving for the mastery."[8] But perhaps even more significant was the implication that the church and its mission might become endangered if it engaged in party politics. White described the work before Adventists as of "the greatest importance" from which members should not become "diverted."[9] These views were echoed by Mrs. White, who feared that active participation in politics might unnecessarily divide Adventists.[10] The church could not risk its well-being or its message over relatively unimportant issues. In 1928 an unsigned editorial in the *Review* emphasized this point. As another presidential election beckoned, the editorial commented: "God has commissioned His church with a special message to the world. . . . The message is to all men of every class. We cannot array ourselves on one side or the other of the great divisions of society that exist in the world. By so doing we shall close the door of entrance to hearts which otherwise might be reached."[11] In effect, church leaders felt that the church's liberty could be threatened by involving itself in the state's affairs. Freedom of action, freedom to proclaim its message, and the unity of members might all be adversely affected if the church entered areas where it did not belong. Adventists believed that church involvement in the state, as well as state interference in the church, had the effect of limiting religious liberty.

These conditions were evident in perhaps the most important political issue in early Adventism: the American Civil War. Most Adventists favored the abolitionist cause. The Civil War was, however, as James' White reminded them in his editorial "The Nation" in the *Review* in 1862, not their struggle. Prophecy, he argued, did not foresee the ending of slavery prior to the Second Advent. Besides, involvement in war was incompatible with the complete observance of the fourth and sixth commandments. But White did not advocate that Adventists prejudice their own safety if forced to join the army: "In the case of drafting, the government assumes the responsibility of the violation of the law of God, and it would be madness to resist."[12] The point White emphasized was that the church's liberty was currently being protected by the state. In this context, he implied that the government was the best they had and it would be wrong to jeopardize the denomination's position by taking pacifism too far. "For us to attempt to resist the laws of the best government under heaven, which is now struggling to put down the most hellish rebellion since that of Satan and his angels," would, he repeated, "be madness."[13]

White's editorial caused an outcry among the pacifists in the Adventist community. They charged him with "Sabbath-breaking and murder." But he remained unrepentant. "If any of you are drafted, and choose to have a clinch with Uncle Sam," he told his critics, "you can try it."[14] The debate continued for several weeks in the pages of the *Review*. Some members supported the Adventist leader, a few argued the pacifist case, while others advocated active involvement in the war effort. In the controversy, the dilemma that White vaguely identified—the choice between army enlistment or long-term freedom—was often submerged. But those who did see it as the heart of the problem tended to support White's position.[15] Strong support also came in a separate testimony from Mrs. White. Indeed, she condemned a group of Adventist pacifists in Iowa who "were ready to become martyrs for their faith." Their actions, she said, "only served to bring that peculiar class, Sabbath keepers, into special notice, and expose them to be crowded into difficult places by those who have no sympathy for them."[16]

In advocating compliance with the draft, it appeared that the Whites had allowed the church to clamber over the wall separating it from the state. In fact, they felt they were preserving church-state separation in the long term. There were, however, problems with "The Nation" editorial. The suggestion that the state assumed the responsibility for breaking God's law seemed illogical to many Adventists. In a letter to the *Review*, church member Henry Carver argued that White had undermined the whole basis of Adventist eschatology: "If the government can assume the responsibility now for the violation of two of these holy precepts [Ten Commandments], and we go clear, why may not the same government assume the responsibility for the violation of the Sabbath law and we go clear when the edict goes forth that all shall observe the first day of the week?"[17] Carver pinpointed a flaw in White's reasoning, and the argument was not made again. Eventually, the church's war policy was clarified into one of noncombatancy. Before the First World War, Adventists established Red Cross training schools in several Adventist colleges and sanitariums in cooperation with the surgeon general's office and the War Department. In 1936 an advanced Medical Cadet Corps Training Program was started. Church leaders regularly invited army officers to review the progress of the medical corps, and the program received many army citations for its military excellence. The founder, Everett Dick, said the program was instituted to enable an Adventist recruit "to fit into a place where he could serve God and his country conscientiously."[18] But it also enabled Adventist leaders to draw the boundaries between church and state more satisfactorily than in the Civil War. The church created its own form of military service without undesirable interference from the state. From the government's perspective, it was an acceptable way of incorporating dissidents into the military. The arrangement allowed church and state to keep within defined boundaries during the difficult circumstances of war. The arrangement could not have fitted the Adventist perspective better.

Adventist attitudes to politics and war were neatly combined in the church's policy toward another secular institution, the trade unions. In the 1930s, during the era of union strength, a labor organization put pressure on one of the church's schools to unionize its industrial department. Many other Adventists also came under pressure to join trade unions in their places of work. The church had never liked the militancy of unions or the violence associated with them. At the turn of the century, Ellen White wrote about unions in the darkest terms, regarding them as one of Satan's agents in the great controversy. Adventists, with their predominantly rural constituency, were not in immediate danger, but she warned church members "not to unite with . . . trade unions."[19] Although by the 1930s the church was ready to acknowledge the achievements of unions in securing humane hours, just wages, and improved working conditions, Adventists were still disinclined to join labor organizations. But their reasons were now derived from statements such as James White's in 1880 and the *Review*'s in 1928. The General Conference stated in 1940 that in choosing not to join trade unions, Adventists were "moved solely by the conscientious conviction that their mission in the world demands they make no discrimination between capital and labor, between employer and employee, or between social classes."[20]

Adventist leaders also tried to define the boundaries between the church and labor organizations in much the same way as they had tried to define them between church and state during war. They drew up a document, a "Basis of Agreement," to be signed by church members and their employers. The document said that Adventists would pay money into the union benevolent or welfare funds instead of paying union dues. Adventists would also abide by the rules of the shop floor and remain neutral during a strike.[21] The ethics of this latter understanding were drawn from the church's war policy. Carlyle B. Haynes, who headed the church's Council on Industrial Relations in the 1940s, wrote that in the event of a dispute "we will not fight on the side of the employer by working. We will not fight on the side of the union by picketing. As noncombatants we will withdraw altogether from the strife and await its issue."[22]

In return for these various undertakings, the Basis of Agreement asked employers to protect Adventists' working rights and to recognize their religious beliefs, particularly in regard to Sabbath observance.[23] As with the establishment of the medical cadets, it would be wrong to see the agreement primarily in terms of a compromise with secular authority. Rather, it allowed Adventist leaders to determine boundaries beyond which both the church and the union agreed not to go. The Basis of Agreement apparently worked quite well for about twenty years. According to church leaders "hundreds" of unions signed it. In the early 1960s, however, trade unions became increasingly unwilling to recognize the document, especially the provision that Adventists should pay sums of money equivalent to union dues to benevolent funds. Consequently, the document was withdrawn, although the General Conference continued its opposition to unions, helping to secure in 1980 a conscience clause within the Civil Rights Act that allowed individuals to be exempted from union membership on religious grounds.[24] Although it eventually failed, the Basis of Agreement was typical of the Adventist desire to define precisely the spheres of influence between the church and secular institutions.

This separation was not expected to apply solely to the Adventist church. General Conference leaders argued that other churches should also stay out of state affairs and avoid affiliations with secular institutions. Their traditional target has usually been the Roman Catholic church, mainly because of what Adventists consider to be Catholicism's historic advocacy of Sunday observance, its influence in the Christian world, and its close ties to the state. In the nineteenth century, Adventists generally believed the Church of Rome to be one of the world's greatest threats to religious liberty.[25] In the twentieth, they found renewed reason to suspect Rome's political aspirations when in 1939 President Roosevelt appointed Myron C. Taylor as United States representative to the Vatican. This development prompted strong Adventist protests. In a letter to Roosevelt, Adventist president J. L. McElhany said that Adventists believed the appointment contravened the separation of church and state. He thus urged the American president to withdraw the envoy to safeguard the principles of the founding fathers.[26] Forty years later, Adventists were still objecting to the ties between the United States and the Vatican when President Reagan appointed William A. Wilson as ambassador to the Holy See in 1984. B. B. Beach, who took over the General Conference Department of Public Affairs and Religious Liberty in 1980, led the Adventist protest. He appeared before Congress to remind the nation of its heritage. The Church of Rome has always had political ambitions, he told a House subcommittee. But such ambitions, he argued, run "counter to the American national spirit and heritage of separation of church and state."[27]

Adventists have also paid close attention to Rome's overtures to the Protestant world in the twentieth century. This has stemmed from the belief that the papacy would join a union of the Protestant churches and the American nation to suppress the upholders of the Saturday Sabbath.[28] Since the Catholic church improved its relations with Protestantism following the Second Vatican Council, Adventists have been particularly wary of the papacy's religious objectives. They have been equally suspicious of the breaking down of the barriers among the Protestant denominations. When the World Council of Churches (WCC) was formed in 1948, the Adventist church refused to join. In later years, the Adventist church accepted observer status at WCC meetings, but it took no active part in the organization. B. B. Beach argued in his book *Ecumenism—Boon or Bane?* that full involvement with the WCC would compromise Adventism's special mission to the world. He also implicitly criticized the organization's tendency to involve itself in political affairs.[29]

On only one political and social issue has the church blurred the boundaries between itself and the state: prohibition. This particular issue corresponded well with the church's views on healthful living. Consequently, Ellen White believed it was right for all Adventists to get involved in the debate.[30] Between 1900 and the 1930s, the *Review* frequently carried articles and editorials supporting the prohibitionist cause.[31] Adventists took part in temperance rallies in different parts of the nation and sent petitions to political representatives. Church leaders presented papers to congressional committees.[32] In 1919, when the ratification of the Eighteenth Amendment was finally completed, L. L. Caviness, associate editor of *Review*, described the event as "one of the great days in human history."[33] The church paper consistently argued that prohibition was the exception to Adventism's traditional stand on political involvement. "The Christian believer," said editor F. M. Wilcox in 1928, "has a duty . . . to place his influence decidedly on the side of temperance reform."[34] When the Adventist church incorporated the ban of alcohol into its own statement of beliefs in 1931, it provided the denomination with its own "Eighteenth Amendment," ironically just as the nation was about to repeal the controversial law.

It was, appropriately, the church's commitment to temperance that resulted in the election of the first Adventist public official. In 1882 William Gage, an ordained Adventist minister, stood for the mayorship of Battle Creek, Michigan, on a temperance platform. He won the election, much to the disapproval of G. I. Butler, General Conference president, who frowned on his involvement in electoral politics.[35] However, Gage received the support of the *Review* in an editorial on April 11, 1882.[36] His period of office was not a great success, and perhaps because of that, and because of the church's traditional attitude toward politics, very few American Adventists have since held public office. Among the exceptions are George A. Williams, who served as lieutenant governor for Nebraska between 1925–31, and Jerry L. Pettis, who was elected to the House of Representatives in 1966 for the thirty-seventh congressional district in California.[37]

As might be expected, the rare occurrence of an Adventist in public life did little to change the apolitical character of the denomination. Adventist leaders have worked hard to keep the church as neutral as possible. But the net effect was to make Adventists an anonymous people. It is not surprising that the Gallup polls of the 1970s and 1980s showed the majority of Americans to be either indifferent to or ignorant of the Adventist church. In view of the church's minimal involvement in the social and religious world, it is difficult to see what other opinions the public could have held.[38] Unlike the Mormons or the Jehovah's Witnesses, who were not afraid to impress themselves on society, Adventists chose to avoid doing anything that would bring them into "special notice." This was the motivation, for example, that lay behind Mrs. White's condemnation of the church members in Iowa who advocated pacifism in the Civil War. Those who objected to the war, she advised, should remain "very quiet."[39] The vision the prophetess had of Adventists appeared to be one of a quiet, unobtrusive people who avoided undue conflict. Perhaps the particular form of Adventist religious liberty was designed partly to nurture these very qualities. The demarcation of the boundaries between the church and the state on such issues as war and politics, and between the church and other bodies such as trade unions and the WCC, not only distanced the church from social institutions but succeeded in muting open Adventist hostility toward them. Sometimes, of course, the avoidance of conflict was not always possible, as the sex discrimination and publishing cases of the 1970s and 1980s demonstrated. But in general, the use of basic American principles turned Adventists into quiet Americans.

There were signs that in the 1970s and 1980s many Adventists were tiring of this exceptionally low public profile. Appeals were made to the church leadership to become more involved in the political and social affairs of the world.[40] Such calls bore some fruit at the General Conference session at New Orleans in 1985. Church president Neal Wilson released statements on four major issues of the 1980s: nuclear disarmament, apartheid, the family, and drugs. Wilson placed the church firmly against the arms race, which he described as "one of the most obvious obscenities of our day." He spelled out Adventist opposition to apartheid and "all forms of racism" and encouraged all family members in society to strengthen their homes. He urged "every individual and every nation to cooperate in stamping out the worldwide drug epidemic."[41] These statements appeared to herald a new readiness on the part of Adventist leaders to involve themselves in political and social issues. But it would be misleading to overemphasize the importance of these statements. Historically, the church has not expressed its views on controversial matters; it has stayed out of secular affairs and avoided conflict with the state.

The contrast between this situation and that in other countries is interesting. Lacking an American heritage, Adventism, particularly in Communist and Third World nations, has been less passive than in the United States. Owing to their Adventist beliefs, large groups of church members in the Soviet Union, China, and Hungary have revolted against Marxist totalitarianism during the twentieth century. Significantly, the American Adventist leadership has usually disassociated itself from such dissidents, either denying that they are "real" Adventists (as was the case with Russian dissidents in the 1970s) or expelling them from the church (as happened with Hungarian dissidents in 1984). Not surprisingly, the General Conference has recognized only those Adventists who did not openly protest against state authority and who conformed to the patterns of behavior Adventism has adopted in the United States.[42] In some instances, this has had unfortunate repercussions. For example, in Germany during the period of Hitler's domination, the avoidance of confrontation may have been a factor in the development of the church's open support for the Nazi party.[43] In the Third World, Adventists are far more likely to serve as public officials than in America. For example, the prime minister of Anguilla from 1967 to 1984, Ronald Webster, was a Seventh-day Adventist. Webster was the subject of international attention in 1967 when his pursuit of independence prompted a notorious British invasion.[44] Another Adventist, Dr. Samson Kisekka, became prime minister of Uganda following Yoweri Museveni's overthrow of President Obote in 1986. In the Caribbean and South Pacific, many Adventists have served successfully as government ministers.[45]

The extent of such participation may be directly related to the distance from the United States. In other countries, Adventists are far removed from, and perhaps less sensitive to, the fine balance of American Adventism. Adventists in the United States have maintained a dogged, but quiet, independence from the Republic by their use of the American Constitution—a tactic both unfamiliar and unavailable to Adventists overseas. This has helped to avert open conflict with the state. But it has also helped to overcome the practical consequences of the church's beliefs and practices, particularly the problem of observing Saturday as the Sabbath in America, where virtually everyone else observes Sunday.

It is not, in fact, difficult to see the central place of the Sabbath in the Adventist attitude toward state and secular institutions. The creation of the medical cadet force was designed partly to ameliorate the difficulties of Sabbath keeping in the military, which was a key question for Adventists during the Civil War. It was for this reason that some Adventists accused James White of Sabbath breaking when he accepted the draft. The later development of the medical corps provided an outlet for acceptable service on Saturdays. One of the aims of the trade union document, the Basis of Agreement, was to safeguard the right not to work on the Sabbath, which labor organizations found difficult to accept. The general effort to keep church and state within defined boundaries can be seen as a by-product of the belief that America would one day establish the universal Sunday law and persecute Sabbath keepers. For the same reasons, the church remained apart from the ecumenism embodied by World Council of Churches, and it objected to the links between the Roman Catholic church and the United States. For American Adventists, religious liberty was really no more than the freedom to worship on Saturday.

This explains why the church's public concern with religious liberty started in the 1880s. It was early in that decade that the clamor for effective Sunday legislation, which had been brewing for the previous twenty years, reached a climax. For the first time significant numbers of Adventists were imprisoned for Sabbath observance, which prompted the denomination's first religious liberty journals and organizations. Before the threat to Sabbath observance, Adventists were not concerned with religious liberty. Once that threat had manifested itself, religious liberty became a major Adventist preoccupation.[46]

The Sabbath, too, was the focal point of the Adventist reinterpretation of America's heritage. It was clearly when the United States established the universal Sunday law that Adventists thought the nation repudiated its values. Mrs. White saw the Sunday law and the consequent persecution of Sabbath keepers as "directly contrary to the principles of this government, to the genius of its free institutions, to the direct and solemn avowals of the Declaration of Independence, and to the Constitution."[47] Adventists made the Sabbath the test of America's fitness as the guardian of liberty. Interestingly, this was reflected in the changing name of the denomination's religious liberty journals. It was not by chance that the *Sabbath Sentinel* became the *American Sentinel* and then, simply, *Liberty*. The very titles indicated the Adventist equation of the freedom to worship on Saturday with the Declaration of Independence.

Some indication of the importance attached to the protection of Sabbath observance can be gauged by the way in which it inhibited the denomination's support of prohibition. Many temperance organizations in the late nineteenth century believed the reform of the "Lord's Day" went hand in hand with the banning of alcohol. For Adventists this was obviously undesirable, and it led them to soft-pedal their commitment to prohibition for fear of precipitating Sunday legislation. On at least one occasion, Adventists joined forces with liquor interests that opposed temperance movements that advocated Sunday observance. For this reason the church's temperance campaign was not entirely consistent. It was only in the early years of the twentieth century, when Sunday observance was detached from the temperance platform, that Adventists became fully committed to prohibition.[48]

The church opposed all Sunday legislation on the basis of the separation of church and state. The Blair bill of 1888, which proposed Sunday as a national day of rest, and the Breckenridge bill of 1890, which proposed the same thing in the District of Columbia, were defeated by lobbies in which Adventists played a vital part. Other campaigns were not as successful. Church leaders failed to prevent the Sunday closing of the World's Fair at Chicago in 1892–93, a cause célèbre in the history of religious liberty in America.[49] Adventists were also not particularly successful in preventing individual convictions in state courts. At the beginning of the 1890s, it has been estimated that about fifty Adventists had been prosecuted for breaking various Sunday laws, and thirty of them had been sentenced to prison.[50] Such prosecutions were not necessarily the result of open disregard for the sanctity of Sunday. Characteristically, Mrs. White counseled church members to avoid outright confrontation. She advised that when faced with Sunday laws, "Seventh-day Adventists were to show their wisdom by refraining from their ordinary work on that day, devoting it to missionary effort." She did not want church members to attract attention and possible adversity: "To defy the Sunday laws will but strengthen in their persecution the religious zealots who are seeking to enforce them."[51]

The man who emerged as Adventism's leading religious liberty spokesman in the 1880s and 1890s was A. T. Jones. He had spearheaded the campaigns against Blair and Breckenridge and had fought to reverse the World's Fair decision. He also took a leading role in representing Adventists convicted of Sunday violations. Jones was coeditor of the church's religious liberty journals between 1887 and 1896 and was the first president of the National Religious Liberty Association in 1889.

Drawing on his experience on the public stage, Jones published a remarkable scholarly work on the Adventist version of religious liberty in 1895. In the *Rights of the People*, he vigorously asserted the separation of church and state, argued that the "first and greatest of all the rights of men is religious right," and encouraged the idea that the freedom to worship on the Sabbath is based on "Jeffersonian, Madisonian, Washingtonian and *Lincolnian* principles."[52] Jones quoted extensively from the writings of the founding fathers, made innumerable references to the judgments of the country's courts, and presented evidence from proceedings in Congress. He demonstrated an impressive knowledge of the American Revolution and the U.S. Constitution, but this, as usual, served only to camouflage the difference in perspective between Adventists and other Americans. For Adventists, the nation was ultimately an adversary and not a reliable guarantor of religious freedom. In its continual attempts to remind the nation of its libertarian values, the church employed a rhetoric in which no Adventist could fully believe.

The importance of the Sabbath to the church's policy on religious liberty helps to clarify the nature of this paradox. Adventists have had to share the same geographical space as other Americans, but the Sabbath has caused them to maintain a different attitude toward time. While the rest of the nation observed the first day of the week, Adventists observed the seventh. The Adventist experience of America has thus been one of a common space but an anomalous sense of time. In the church's quest for religious liberty can be seen an effort to meet the problem posed by this situation—perhaps the central problem in Adventism—how to share American space without sharing American time.

CHAPTER 12

The Art of Expression

Among the early Adventists, the preferred mode of religious expression was shouting. In the 1840s they followed the practice of the "Shouting" Methodists, from whose ranks many of them were drawn, of uttering cries of spiritual exaltation. "Glory! Glory! Glory!" the phrase Ellen White repeated on falling into vision, was typical. Speaking in tongues was an unusual, but not unknown, manifestation of the same enthusiasm. In general, however, Adventists shouted out short, unconnected phrases of their own language, the vigor of enunciation making up for whatever was lacking in the sophistication of the utterance.[1]

At a contemporary white Adventist service, there is unlikely to be any comparable display of emotion. In black and Hispanic churches, there is more spontaneity: the words of the preacher may be affirmed with a chorus of "Amen," and individual worshippers may feel free to call out "Praise the Lord" or "Hallelujah." Despite this freedom, Adventist worship is generally restrained and carefully organized; and it bears no resemblance to the unstructured, ecstasy-inducing practices of modern charismatic or Pentecostal groups. It would be misleading to account for the change from an enthusiastic mode of expression to a more regulated approach solely in terms of the declining fervor and increasing respectability of the church's membership. Religious emotions are susceptible to various forms of expression: they may burst forth seemingly uncontrolled; they may be channeled into evangelistic endeavor; they may be clothed in the languages of art and music; or they may be repressed in a mute, but telling, gesture of denial. The history of Adventist self-expression is not just the familiar tale of excitement melting into indifference; it is also a story of transformation and renewal in which the peculiarity of the Adventist experience is creatively reinterpreted and reexpressed by succeeding generations.

To appreciate the richness of the Adventist tradition, it is necessary to look beyond the instrumental aspect of Adventist practices to their symbolic significance. An action or creation of the Adventist community may have both a pragmatic and an expressive function. Adventists speak in order to communicate, dress in order to keep warm, build churches in order to hold services, and so on. But the way in which they speak, dress, or build is not solely a means to an end; it also reveals, perhaps unintentionally, the aspirations and tensions that are inherent in the Adventist experience. In all that they do, church members are liable to betray something of their Adventism. The fact that they have not, on the whole, been notable for artistic achievement does not mean that Adventist culture is devoid of interest. The very absence of artistic experimentation may itself be an important aesthetic statement.

The presence of a shared set of cultural idioms is most easily discovered in Adventist churches. Members may live far from one another in homes indistinguishable from those of their neighbors; when they meet together for worship, they engage in a specifically Adventist activity in a space specially set aside for the purpose. Although it can be said that Adventism became an organized denomination in order to preserve its property, the more significant fact is that the Adventist movement was sufficiently stable to need its own buildings. Churches imply continuity of commitment. Their maintenance demands the presence of a loyal body of adherents; the merely curious, however numerous, are better accommodated in tents or hired halls. A church presupposes a community of believers.

Although in urban areas Adventists may often purchase the redundant churches of other denominations, most churches are purpose built.[2] They require few fixtures. A pulpit, a baptistry large enough to immerse adults, a communion table, and seating for the congregation are the only necessities. Of these, the pulpit is of primary importance. Communion is celebrated only four times a year, and baptisms may be infrequent, so the sermons preached from the pulpit are the natural focus of attention. The sense most vital to an appreciation of a service is hearing. There is no incense to smell, usually no bread or wine to taste, and no icons or holy water to touch. The only other sense employed is that of sight, which serves chiefly to identify the sources of sound and aid the process of hearing. To this end, the pulpit is generally located in the center of a raised platform at the end of the building opposite the entrance. Its prominence emphasizes the authority of the preacher, the centrality of the sermon, and the primacy of the word.

Potential visual distractions are kept to a minimum: ministers wear no special garb; there are usually no processions, no statues or pictures, no crosses, and no figurative stained glass. (Abstract designs in stained glass have, however, recently become a more common feature.) Congregational participation also employs the medium of sound. There are generally two or three hymns and perhaps a special musical item in the main preaching service. At the earlier service, the Sabbath School, adults listen, and perhaps contribute, to a discussion of a specially prepared and standardized Bible study provided by the General Conference. For most Adventists, Saturday morning is occupied with two or more hours of listening, singing, and speaking.

This exclusive concentration on sound is balanced only at the quarterly celebration of the Lord's Supper at which, in addition to the communion (itself purely a memorial and not a sacrament), Adventists perform the "ordinance of humility" in which, in imitation of Christ, they divide into pairs of the same sex to wash each other's feet. This practice is a legacy of the time when Adventists defined themselves by their willingness to wash each other's feet and greet each other with a holy kiss. The kiss, with its suggestion of sexual license, has disappeared, but the equally sensuous, although less obviously sensual, practice of foot washing has survived. Its intimacy serves as a reminder of the strong sense of community that binds members together, but its infrequent performance is typical of the restraint that characterizes Adventist social interaction. The exceptional nature of the rite is emphasized by the actions it requires. The congregation often leaves the church, the customary center of worship, to enter other rooms in which water, bowls, and towels have been made ready. Men and women, who customarily sit together in family groups, are separated. There may be conversation or prayer during foot washing, but it is irrelevant to the action, which is concerned not with sound but with touch. The hands, which are normally in contact with other hands, are brought down to touch another person's feet—the customary order of relationships between the parts of the body is thus disturbed. In all of these respects, the ordinance is peculiar, not only in terms of non-Adventist behavior but in an Adventist context as well. In consequence, some members feel awkward or embarrassed when performing the rite. However, the practice is not inappropriate; it can be taken to signify the Adventist estrangement from society. Men and women leave their families to enter the unfamiliar environment of Adventism into which they are initiated by another act of washing—baptism. The ordinance, anomalous in its Adventist setting, reenacts the process by which Adventists themselves have separated from the world to enter a new sphere of activity. Through its peculiarity in Adventism, the rite symbolizes Adventist peculiarity in the world.[3]

In this, the ceremony of foot washing makes explicit what is implicit in other aspects of Adventist worship. The emphasis on sound is also particularly appropriate in Adventism, because it presupposes, as does foot washing, a social context. The spoken word becomes audible only where speaker and listener are in shared space; it becomes intelligible only where there is shared language. Where worship is constituted through an exchange of sounds, as it is in Adventism, a community of speakers and listeners is assumed. In contrast, those forms of Christianity in which visual or tactile expression is more important lend themselves more easily to individual spirituality. The painter of an icon need not be in direct contact with the person who venerates it. The rosary is a solitary exercise.

The Adventists' concentration on sound belies the superficial impression that they adhere to the minimalist aesthetic of Puritanism. Unlike Quakers, Adventists are loathe to sit in silence, and music has always been a significant part of worship. Adventist churches may be architecturally uninspiring and lacking in visual interest, but the absence of decoration has more to do with a mistrust of sight than an abhorrence of superfluity. In sound, Adventists are prepared to tolerate a degree of variety and elaboration well beyond functional necessity. Churches that would never contemplate using expensive sculpture or glass are prepared to spend large sums on installing a good organ. Short items of classical instrumental music are regularly performed in church services. Adventist choirs and instrumental groups perform frequently in both religious and secular contexts. The best-known artists associated with Adventism—Prince, a songwriter who grew up in the church, the sometime church member and rock singer Little Richard, and the conductor of the San Francisco Symphony Orchestra Herbert Blomstedt—are musicians.[4]

Adventists are also encouraged to acquire rhetorical skills. In church services, members are expected to contribute to discussion of the Sabbath School lesson, announce hymns, make long extemporized prayers, and, in smaller churches, preach sermons. Obviously, all members do not engage in these functions, but many do, and children are taught to speak in public by reciting Bible texts. In Adventist schools, unusual emphasis is placed on the acquisition of skills in public speaking. Adventists, as individuals, are often unusually articulate, for speech, the organized production of sound, is their chosen, and often their exclusive, means of expression.

This concern with sound is significant, not only because it presupposes a high degree of social interaction, but also because time, rather than space, is the dimension that makes it possible. Music and speech extend through time, not space.[5] It is through the modification of tempo and frequency that variety, and thus significance, is given to sound. The Adventist preference for sound as a means of expression is indicative of particular sensitivity to the modalities of time, to beginnings and endings, speeds and rhythms. Such awareness is unsurprising. Adventist theology is primarily concerned with time—with the time of the end, the correct timing of the Sabbath, the prophetic interpretation of time.[6] To be an Adventist is to have an acute awareness of location in time. It is important to know which day of the week it is; it is vital to think of history as temporal progression punctuated by dates of prophetic significance. In particular, it is through their understanding of time that Adventists differ from the members of other Christian groups. Adventists have an unusual perception of history as a sequence of prophetically bounded time packages; they are almost alone in considering the seventh day of the weekly time cycle to be the Sabbath; and they are unique in thinking that only a Sabbath-keeping remnant will be able to move from time to eternity at the Second Coming. Adventist theology describes history in distinctive fashion, gives church members peculiar temporal obligations, and projects an extraordinary future for the church itself. Adventists use time as the dimension of expression, for it is also their primary dimension of experience.

As a corollary of this, Adventists tend to disregard the significance of all that is extended in space. As the world is soon to perish, all that it contains is an irrelevance; only that which will travel through time to eternity is important. This attitude is clearly revealed in an 1849 hymnal compiled by James White. Many of the hymns, some of Millerite origin, express this conviction:

Farewell! farewell! to all below,
My Jesus calls and I must go:
I'll launch my boat upon the sea,
This land is not the land for me.
    This world is not my home;
    This world is not my home;
    This world is all a wilderness;
    This world is not my home.[7]

The message that there is no salvation in space but only in time is perhaps most clearly expressed in a hymn reprinted from Joshua Himes's *Millennial Harp*:

Here o'er the earth as a stranger I roam,
   Here is no rest—is no rest;
Here as a pilgrim I wander alone,
   Yet I am blest—I am blest.
For I look forward to that glorious day
When sin and sorrow will vanish away,
My heart doth leap while I hear Jesus say,
   "There, there is rest—there is rest."[8]

No amount of movement in space will bring relief from the trials of life; only the passage of time and "that glorious day" offers any hope.

This perception is particularly interesting when viewed in the light of American history. The United States was founded by immigrants who crossed the Atlantic to build a new life in a strange land. The new continent may have been a wilderness, but it was one in which Christians had a mission. In the revolutionary war against Britain, the Republic was likened to "the woman in the wilderness" persecuted by the dragon.[9] The pilgrimage hymns take on additional significance when understood in this context. The words "I'll launch my boat upon the sea, / This land is not the land for me" were sung by the descendants of relatively recent immigrants. "This world is all a wilderness; / This world is not my home" is a sentiment expressed by people whose neighbors looked on the American wilderness as a sacred opportunity to realize the millennium.[10] The last verse of the hymn contains a final insult for those who took egalitarianism to be the philosophy favored by God over the antiquated, feudal institutions of Europe:

Praise be to God our hope's on high;
The angels sing and so do I:
Where seraphs bow and bend the knee,
O that's the land—the land for me.[11]

Even without this added twist, which equated heaven with hierarchical social organization, such sentiments were unorthodox. Americans felt that they could overcome their difficulties by moving through space; Adventists asserted unequivocally that this was impossible and that only temporal transition opened the prospect of eternal bliss.

This indifference to the possibilities offered in space helps to explain the Adventist preference for unadorned churches and functional buildings. That which is visible and tangible is, of its very nature, unlikely to offer anything of spiritual benefit. Adventism's unenthusiastic response to the visual arts is thus, at least in part, a reflection of the general tendency to devalue those things that are extended in space. It is an attitude that also finds expression in Adventist taboos. Ostentatious clothing signifies an undue concern with the time-bound things of this world and, as such, is discouraged. Jewelry suffers similar condemnation, as does, at least among traditional Adventists, the use of makeup. The problem with such adornment is that it draws attention to the surfaces and orifices of the body, thus emphasizing that the body is defined in space. Similarly, Ellen White objected to the use of confining garments because they were designed to create a particular shape and thus redefine the body in spatial terms. Concern with female health was the primary motivation for this stand, but it can also be seen as an effort to avoid anything that draws attention to the body as an entity extended in space.[12] For an Adventist, spatial extension was the medium of damnation; salvation was to be found in the extension of bodies through time.

Some "worldly" practices are to be avoided because they locate the church and its members in the static dimension of space and are thus liable to prevent them from moving freely through time to eternity. Such taboos are concerned with the way in which Adventists define their bodies and buildings. Another set of taboos, regarding the intake rather than the production of cultural values, derives from a different imperative: the need to prevent church members from imbibing rival understandings of the structure and significance of time. Fiction is the most obvious example.[13] Writing, like speech, depends for its effect on the ability of the reader to retain sensory impressions gained over a period of time and organize them into an intelligible sequence. Reading is unlike hearing in that it is concerned with what is visible rather than what is audible, but it shares a reliance on temporal sequence. This is true not only on the level of the sentence—where intelligibility depends on the order in which the words are read—but also on the larger scale of the book. In the novel, in which the narrative flows from a clearly defined beginning to a predetermined end and the plot develops in the shadow of its unknown but ineluctable resolution, the reader is induced into an experience of time in which impressions are manipulated to engender an awareness of duration different from that of everyday life. There is a sense of expectation supplementary to, and perhaps conflicting with, ordinary intimations of the future. In these respects, fiction performs the same function as apocalyptic, which is also concerned to reorientate perceptions of time. Adventist eschatology, with its strong apocalyptic content, offers a unique apprehension of time: enjoyment of fiction involves at least a temporary betrayal of that understanding.

Ellen White clearly perceived that Adventism was incompatible with novel reading. In *Ministry of Healing*, she compared fiction to alcohol, advising that "the only safety for the inebriate, and the only safeguard for the temperate man, is total abstinence. For the lover of fiction the same rule holds true. Total abstinence is his only safety."[14] Her objection to novels, even those of reputed quality, was that they interfered with the mind's ability to make coherent sense of the world: "Even fiction which contains no suggestion of impurity, and which may be intended to teach excellent principles, is harmful. It encourages the habit of hasty and superficial reading merely for the story. Thus it tends to destroy the power of connected and vigorous thought; it unfits the soul to contemplate the great problems of duty and destiny."[15] Novels disrupted perceptions of time: "To the active minds of children and youth the scenes pictured in imaginary revelations of the future are realities."[16] Even fairy tales "impart false views of life and beget and foster a desire for the unreal."[17] The trouble with all narrative was that it offered a sequence of perceptions to the mind that might constitute an alternative way of viewing the world. Fictional works "contain statements and highly wrought pen pictures that excite the imagination and give rise to a train of thought which is full of danger, especially to the youth. The scenes described are lived over and over again in their thoughts. Such reading unfits the mind for usefulness and disqualifies it for spiritual exercise."[18]

Along with novels, Adventists were also taught to avoid other forms of entertainment that offered an apprehension of time incompatible with that of the church's theology. The theater came in for particular condemnation, and the cinema has fallen under similar disapproval in the twentieth century. Unlike fiction, which relies solely on the organization of words in time, the cinema, the theater, and, most recently, television all involve the organization of images. As such they are manifestations of the concern with space that Adventists have long equated with worldliness. They thus embody a dual threat: not only the possibility of being seduced by a rival understanding of the world, but also the danger of being trapped in space, in the sphere of matter, in the realm of the flesh. Bodies defined by, and interacting in, space in an artificially constituted and nonapocalyptic time were free to incline toward that most spatially defined of evils—sex. Ellen White complained that in the theater "low songs, lewd gestures, expressions and attitudes deprave the imagination and debase the morals."[19] It was, she said, "the very hotbed of immorality";[20] as for dancing, it was "a school of depravity"; opera opened "the door to sensual indulgence."[21]

Adventists were well aware that their true home was in heaven and they were constantly being exhorted to emulate the devotion and obedience of the angels.[22] The corollary of this orientation toward the divine realm was the desire to be free of the limitations of this world. The angels were the representative inhabitants of heaven; the time-bound character of earth was exemplified by the animals. Humans were pictured as standing somewhere between the angels and the animals and in becoming like angels, people were expected to become as unlike animals as possible. According to Ellen White, it was the mingling of human and animal characteristics that had prompted God to destroy humanity in the Noachian flood: "But if there was one sin above another which called for the destruction of the race by the flood, it was the base crime of amalgamation of man and beast which defaced the image of God, and caused confusion everywhere."[23]

In particular, animals were associated with unbridled greed and lust. Having neither reason nor intellect, animals needed to be trained by human beings.[24] But human beings shared animal instincts and, for this reason, needed to acquire self-control. Ellen White was adamant that "the animal part of our nature should never be left to govern the moral and intellectual"[25] but should rather be kept in "rigid subjection."[26] Parents were instructed not "to degrade their bodies by beastly indulgence of the animal passions"[27] and were advised to feed their children properly lest "everything noble is sacrificed to the appetite and animal passions predominate."[28]

Food was particularly dangerous, for through eating animals, people were in danger of becoming more like them. Ellen White warned one couple that "your family have partaken largely of flesh meats, and the animal propensities have been strengthened, while the intellectual have been weakened."[29] She continued, "The use of the flesh of animals tends to cause a grossness of body, and benumbs the fine sensibilities of the mind."[30] By eating meat, people could lose those qualities of mind that distinguished them from the animal kingdom. In a sense, eating the flesh of animals was liable to effect the same confusion of the species that had existed before the flood. The amalgamation of human being and beast had "defaced the image of God." According to Ellen White, Christ died so that "the defaced image of God will be restored in humanity, and a family of believing saints will finally inherit the heavenly home."[31] Meat eating endangered this restoration: "Grains and fruit . . . should be the food for the tables of all who claim to be preparing for translation to Heaven."[32]

It was peculiarly appropriate that meat eating and the "animalism" it caused would jeopardize the reproduction of the image of God in human beings, for at the end of time, all those who were not to be saved would have the "mark of the beast" as a result of worshipping the beast of Revelation 13. The convergence of these ideas is probably fortuitous, but it is also significant, for it constitutes a coherent set of symbols. Salvation involves the repudiation of animal passions, flesh foods, and the beast and his image. For people, poised between heaven and earth, between the angels and the animals, such imagery is compelling. It reinforces the Adventist message that what is extended in space, what is purely material or animal, is to be left behind by the saints as they move into heavenly time to join the company of the angels.

In the light of this, it is especially interesting that pictures of the beasts in Daniel and Revelation are perhaps the images most characteristic of Adventist art. They were present from the beginnings of the church. When John Greenleaf Whittier attended a Millerite camp meeting, he commented on seeing "the wonders of the Apocalyptic vision— the beasts, the dragons, the scarlet woman . . . exhibited like the beasts of a traveling menagerie." One particular image caught his eye, a dragon with "hideous heads and scaly caudal extremity."[33] As evangelistic tools, pictures of the beasts proved effective. Later Adventist preachers even used three-dimensional models. Ellen White wrote warmly of one such evangelist: "Brother S. dwells especially upon the prophecies in the books of Daniel and Revelation. He has large representations of the beasts spoken of in these books. These beasts are made of papier-mâché, and by an ingenious invention, they may be brought at the proper time before the congregation. Thus he holds the attention of the people, while he preaches the truth to them."[34] Adventists devoted time and imagination to the depiction of the beasts, whose appearance could only be reconstructed from their strange description in the Bible. Uriah Smith, the great expositor of prophecy, also used his artistic skill to make woodcuts in which he depicted the beasts of Daniel 8 and Revelation 13.[35] The absence of any one authorized representation left considerable scope for individual artists to portray the beasts in ways that reflected their own preoccupations. For example, in the representations of the two-horned beast, symbolizing the United States, it is possible to perceive a gradual mellowing in the attitude of the artists' concept, from the snorting bison of 1907 to a cuddly lamb in 1947.[36]

The beasts were illustrated with regularity and ingenuity. There were obviously good pragmatic reasons for this. The biblical descriptions of the beasts were difficult to visualize, and color representations served both a didactic and a dramatic purpose. But the significance of the representations surely ran deeper. Adventists were not generally given to using visual media for religious expression. It is odd that the most striking exception to the general rule should be the pictures of the beasts. These are the visual images most likely to be referred to during a traditional Adventist religious meeting. There are no crucifixes, no representations of the nativity, no statues or icons of saints to draw the eye. The chief occasion of visual stimulus is the exposition of the prophecies in which the speaker may use charts or cloths, or in recent years, slides or videos, showing the beasts.

In assessing this practice, it must be remembered that the beasts are the adversaries of God and his remnant church. The beasts of Daniel 7 persecuted the Jews and the early Christians; the beasts of Revelation 13 are expected to persecute the Adventists. They represent dangerous and demonic powers. Could it be that Adventists, through depicting their foes on paper and in papier-mâché, are expressing both their fear and their assurance of ultimate victory? To represent such malevolent forces, to enclose them within a clearly defined space is to limit their potency; it is an act of control. The significance of this is enhanced by the fact that the Adventists who created these images were also being exhorted to control their animal passions. The beasts, with their multiple heads and monstrous deformities, exhibited the full pathology of lust. As embodiments of animality, the beasts symbolized the defacement of God's image resulting from sensual indulgence. The representation of the beasts enclosed them within space—the dimension of damnation—and distanced their creators from both their eschatological adversaries in the world and their animal appetites within.[37]

Obviously, not every act of representation has the effect of controlling and distancing its object. The peculiarity of the beasts is their appearance in the context of religious meetings in which visual imagery is largely taboo. In general, Adventists have not been encouraged to engage in the visual arts for the reason that the decoration of space is a wasteful activity. The major exception has been book illustration. Adventists, with their preference for language, have been exceptionally active in publishing and distributing books, periodicals, and tracts. As many of these are sold to the public by colporteurs, there is considerable pressure to make Adventist publications as attractive as possible. Ellen White sanctioned this practice but warned against any extravagance.[38] In consequence, Adventist publishers in the twentieth century recruited their own illustrators, some of whose work is now familiar to church members throughout the world.

The most famous of these men was Harry Anderson.[39] The son of a Swedish immigrant, he became a commercial artist doing illustrations for popular magazines. He was converted to Adventism in 1943. His first color picture for the Review and Herald Publishing Association was painted in 1945. It was called "What Happened to Your Hand?" and it established a new genre in Adventist art. It depicted Christ clad in long white robes seated in a garden with an inquisitive girl in contemporary dress on his knee and a boy holding a toy airplane at his feet. It was the first of numerous pictures in which Christ is shown in modern settings. In "Christ at the Sickbed," Jesus is depicted in a modern room at the bedside of a young girl; in "Christ of the Highway," he directs lost travelers in an open-top sports car; in "A Modern Nicodemus," he reasons with a middle-aged man in a well-appointed room; in the "Couple in a Garden," he talks to two suburbanites who have interrupted their garden chores to listen. It is a striking compositional technique, juxtaposing the eternal and temporal, the sublime and the commonplace. It was a procedure that could be reversed. In "May I Hold Him?" a group of modern children are present at the nativity in the stable in Bethlehem. In both, the figures appear united within the picture space, but the viewer can perceive the incongruity by recognizing that the figures are not united in time—one or more of them belongs to a different time or is outside of time altogether.

Another Adventist artist, Greg Constantine, a professor at Andrews University, has also explored the idea of locating Christ in a contemporary setting. Although his technique is very different, owing more to expressionism and pop art than commercial realism, Constantine's vision is essentially the same. His Christ does not inhabit suburbia but New York City. The story of the Good Samaritan becomes a mugging in Central Park. Lazarus is raised at Calvary cemetery in Queens.[40] For Constantine, picturing Christ in New York is the natural development of a series of books in which famous artists have been pictured visiting major American cities. *Van Gogh Visits New York, Leonardo Visits Los Angeles,* and *Picasso Visits Chicago* all follow a similar pattern.[41] The artist is brought out of his own time and enters the modern world, where he both adapts to contemporary culture and attempts to pursue his own projects in an unfamiliar setting. Constantine's work lacks Anderson's sentimental piety; it is urbane, witty, and depends for its effect on a detailed knowledge of art and popular culture. But Constantine's pictures of time travelers fulfill precisely the same function: they prompt reflection on the character of the alien, and they constitute an invitation to look at the world through the eyes of a stranger.

In an indirect way, these paintings may be seen to reflect the religious and social position of the artists. The time travelers of Adventist art are not distanced from their surroundings in an arbitrary fashion but in the exact manner that Adventists are separated from the rest of society. The spectator is not deceived by spatial continuities but can see that one of the protagonists owes allegiance to a different temporal framework. The viewer is placed in the position of the divine judge for whom invisible discrepancies of synchronization are manifestations of an eternal choice. But those within the picture are unable to perceive its temporal dislocation. Reassured by the apparent unity of the space they inhabit, they treat the time traveler as one of themselves. In turn, the alien seems well adapted to his new environment, at home in a world of which he is not a part. Space elides the boundaries of time.

Nothing could reflect the Adventist experience more closely. Like time travelers, Adventists share space with their fellow Americans but do not themselves belong to it. They adapt to their surroundings, for they know that their stay is only temporary. They move unnoticed. Their peculiarity is unobtrusive, their dissent silent.

CHAPTER 13

Adventism and America

In Adventist art, a dominant motif is the incongruous presence of an alien figure in familiar surroundings. The viewer realizes that the alien is displaced in time, but his interlocutors do not. The objects of everyday life are transmuted by the gaze of the stranger, who, in turn, is domesticated by the homeliness of his setting. The reassuring becomes threatening, and the startling becomes mundane. It is a vision of the world precisely aligned with Adventist eschatology in which today's newspaper is a fulfillment of yesterday's prophecy, and future salvation is an imminent reality. It accurately reflects a perspective from which American society seems foreign and Adventism is Americanized.

In early Adventist apocalyptic, the church was placed in opposition to the American nation. In the nineteenth century, many Americans believed that their country would be the vehicle through which a millennium would be realized on earth. Adventists came to believe that there would be no earthly millennium and that America would become an agent of the Antichrist before its destruction at the Second Coming. Those who survived the final cataclysm would be identified by their adherence to the seventh-day Sabbath; those who gave allegiance to the American Sunday would perish. In this scenario, the division between the saved and the damned hinges on which day of the weekly cycle is considered more important. The essential criterion of salvation is a correct apprehension of temporal sequence. Time, the least visible of divisions, is the basis for an irreversible separation of good and evil. Access to eternity is gained through synchronizing weekly routines with those of heaven and enduring the difficulties created by being out of synchronization with the rest of the world.

To appreciate fully the tensions inherent in this situation, and their precise reflection in the superficially bland productions of Adventist art, it is necessary to recapitulate. In part one it was shown that Adventist theology, although apparently a malleable cluster of beliefs, in fact constitutes a coherent ideological system in which individual elements are replaceable only within a framework that legitimates the continued independent existence of the church. Sources of authority are interchangeable; apocalyptic is renewable; identity may be defined by organic unity as well as taboo; the road to salvation may be enlarged to accommodate more travelers. But throughout these transformations, there has always been a combination of ideas sufficient to differentiate those that hold them from the rest of American society and to maintain a sense of distance between the church and the world.

In many instances, the details of Adventist theology were worked out in order to differentiate the church from other marginal groups, notably the former Millerite factions and the spiritualists. But to understand the central dynamic in Adventism, it is necessary to look beyond this jockeying for position at the sectarian margins of American religion to the larger gulf between Adventism and mainstream Protestantism. Yet Adventism has not been involved in a dialogue with any one of these groups. Despite superficial similarities, it is not an estranged off-shoot of Methodism nor a deviant Baptist group. Adventism does not define itself against individual denominations in the mainstream but against the mainstream as a united body of tradition.

That Adventism should respond to the mainstream as a single religious force is not entirely surprising. Many commentators have noted the high degree of consensus among American Protestant groups.[1] Whatever differences there may be about the correct form of church organization or the proper time for baptism, there is agreement that Protestantism is the most valid expression of Christianity and that America has provided a singular opportunity for the Christian religion to realize its full potential. The mainline denominations share a common history with the American state. The founding fathers of the nation are also the patriarchs of mainstream religion. America nurtured the Protestant impulse, and Protestantism bestowed on the state a unique role as the instrument of the divine will.

A somewhat diluted version of this religious consensus can be said to constitute a "civil religion" that "relates the citizen's role and American society's place in space, time and history to the conditions of ultimate existence and meaning."[2] As such, it loses something of its exclusively Protestant content and focuses rather on the state, investing its institutions and symbols with a sacred character. The inauguration of a president and the saluting of the flag become religious ceremonies in which citizens are reminded of God's special interest in the American nation and the consequent responsibilities placed on president and citizens alike.[3] In its stronger forms, the ideology of civil religion allots to America a vital role in the salvation of mankind. Translated into political terms, this may be expressed as a desire to save the world from the menace of Communism. In a religious context, it is found in the belief that America is the only place in which humanity is free to strive toward perfection. In the eighteenth and nineteenth centuries, this view was embedded within an eschatological framework. The colonies had justified the revolt against Britain by casting their adversary in the eschatological role of Babylon and themselves as the persecuted woman in the wilderness. Flushed with the success of the Revolution, the new nation saw itself as the stone in Daniel 2 that smashed the image of Nebuchadnezzar's dream and grew to fill the entire earth.[4] In the Second Great Awakening, revivalists called for conversion and reformation of character to achieve the perfection of society and precipitate an earthly millennium in which the American Republic would become the seat of a righteous empire.[5]

At the base of the rift between Adventism and the mainsteam is the Adventist refusal to view American society as the means of universal redemption.[6] Millerism negated the optimistic dream of progress. The world was not on the verge of perfection but at the brink of final catastrophe. In Seventh-day Adventism, the denial of contemporary orthodoxy was further refined. Not only was the world about to end, but America, according to many the instrument of the world's salvation, was actually a diabolical monster bent on the destruction of the saints. In opposition to this malevolent force, there was only the remnant, a group whose defining characteristic—the observance of the seventh-day Sabbath—made it more or less coterminus with the Seventh-day Adventist denomination. It was this group, not America, that would be the vehicle of redemption. Its members would be the sole survivors of the last judgment, the only persons for whom eternity could become continuous with the present.

For Adventists, the difference between themselves and other Americans lay in the anticipated trajectory of the two groups. Americans were participants in the somber drama of history, bounded by time and destined for destruction. But for Adventists, the world was but a temporary stage on which to rehearse the roles they were destined to play in heavenly society. Not being subjected to time, Adventists danced to a different music—harmonious with heaven but dissonant from the world—the rhythm of their lives marginally out of step with American routines. It was a lack of synchronization perfectly symbolized by the seventh-day Sabbath. Adventists joined with other Americans in putting an emphasis on one day in seven but syncopated the rhythm by emphasizing the day before everyone else's sabbath.

The Sabbath is the key to understanding the Adventist relationship with America. In its peculiarity, it makes sacred the Adventist alienation from the America way of life, but in its conformity to the American expectation that there should be one holy day in a week, it aligns Adventists with wider society. The evangelists of the Second Great Awakening had seen the proper observance of Sunday as one means of effecting the perfection of the American people. The nation's ability to

realise the earthly millennium was understood to depend upon its loyalty to the Sunday Sabbath.[7] Seventh-day Adventism denied the American dream, usurped the redemptive role of the nation, and appropriated the Sabbath as a test of collective purpose. The seventh-day
Sabbath was just the last in a series of alternatives to the ideology of
American civil religion. Adventism offered not an earthly but a heavenly millennium; it presented itself as the social vehicle of salvation;
and it enjoined the observance of a sabbath but one day earlier than
that sacred to America. Adventism did not create a new religious synthesis but an alternative form of American civil religion that provided
a divergent route to salvation.

If the development of Adventist theology can be viewed as a sustained effort to create and maintain a distinctive ideology, the history
of Adventism's organizational growth reveals the desire to reproduce
a parallel version of American society, distinguished by its alternative
ideological orientation but familiar in its internal construction.[8] It is
possible to perceive two dynamics in this process. The first is the need
to compete with America—the body against which Adventism has defined itself. The second is the need to avoid conflict. Although America
is the ultimate eschatological adversary, Adventists expect divine intervention to be the means through which they are vindicated and America is toppled. Until then, they are prepared to cohabit and to facilitate
superficial integration through the emulation of American customs
and institutions. It is essential to Adventism that its deviation from the
American way of life is expressed in the invisible dimension of time.
Deviance is both disguised and reinforced by a willingness to clothe
Adventist practices in American dress. Adventists do not so much participate as imitate. They have not been incorporated into American
society; they function as a separate organism within the larger body.

The spread of Adventism throughout the world exemplifies this relationship. The church emerged in a country that had but recently
shaken off its allegiance to Britain and whose independence was precarious. In his farewell address of 1796, George Washington counseled
the young nation not to entertain foreign influence, for it was "one of
the most baneful foes of republican government."[9] It was a suspicion
that developed easily into a thoroughgoing isolationism of which the
classic expression became the Monroe Doctrine. The early years of Adventism replicated this pattern. Having struggled away from their own
Babylon—the mainline churches—Adventists were unwilling to ally
themselves with other bodies for fear of contamination. During the
Shut-Door period, even evangelism was considered unwise. When missionary activity was eventually restarted, Adventists persuaded themselves that they could fulfil the gospel commission to "go into all the
world" by evangelizing within the boundaries of the multiracial United

States. While America was isolated from the rest of the world, Adventism, which had initially disengaged from America, only reengaged with the world within America.

When Adventist missionary activity finally began to bear fruit throughout the world in the second decade of the twentieth century, it was a world that Woodrow Wilson had pledged to make "safe for democracy" and in which America was ever more actively involved.[10] Similarly, after the Second World War when America became involved in world affairs to a hitherto unprecedented degree, Adventism's global expansion was accelerated. Countries within the American sphere of influence proved particularly receptive to the Adventist message. Interestingly, it is through American power that Adventist eschatology becomes credible. In operating as the world's policeman, the United States rehearses the very role that Adventists expect it to play in enforcing the universal Sunday law. Most converts are inspired by Adventism's apocalyptic vision of the world. Exhibitions of American economic and military strength can only serve to reinforce the Adventist message. But the fact that Adventists foresee themselves being persecuted by America suggests that Third World converts may not be wholeheartedly enthusiastic about those aspects of American power with which they are already familiar. Adventism may thus function as one means of coming to terms with America's dominating presence in the world. To become an Adventist is to join an American religion but one distanced from, and wary of, the most obvious manifestations of American power.

Adventism has appropriated and reinterpreted the central tenets of American self-understanding. "Life, liberty, and the pursuit of happiness" become, within the Adventist context, ideals of a very different character than those upheld by the signatories of the Declaration of Independence. For Adventists, the pursuit of happiness has not involved individual self-expression within a libertarian social order but the restraint of the emotions and the regulation of the appetites. Adventists have devoted more time to preparing for eternal bliss than to enjoying the fleeting moment. But they have not agreed to endure present hardship in return for future reward. Adventists do not expect to be made happy in heaven in compensation for being miserable now. For them, the pursuit of happiness means setting out on a clearly marked and unbroken path that leads from earth to heaven.[11]

The dominant Adventist conception of heaven has been of a court populated by angels. According to Ellen White, the saved would replace those angels who had fallen with Satan before the creation of the world. The heavenly court was conceived as a place of hierarchical organization and bureaucratic employment. Salvation was a continuing process by which the saints became perfectly adapted to heavenly society through acquiring the requisite characteristics on earth. Adventist perfectionism has never involved the mindless observation of a legal code: its orientation has always been toward purposive self-improvement— its objective, the reassimilation of a remnant of the human race into the divine realm. Ellen White emphasized that heaven was a place of obedience and order; to be acceptable, a person would have to acquire perfect self-control. The inhabitants of heaven, the angels, were ageless and sexless; to gain citizenship, a human being would have to become ageless and sexless, too. For Adventists, the pursuit of happiness was the quest for this transformation—a metamorphosis through which to bridge the chasm between time and eternity.

Self-control was the key. Ellen White revealed that angels lived lives of perfect order and discipline. Human activity was under angelic surveillance, and angels would be offended by any uncontrolled expression of emotion. Interaction between people should be governed by the same sense of decorum that prevailed in heaven. There was to be no accommodation of the individualism of the American frontier. The virtues to be practiced in readiness for heaven were specifically social in nature. But just as the equilibrium of social interaction might be disturbed by unrestrained emotion so, too, the balance of physical health might be endangered by uncontrolled passion.

Sex was deemed particularly injurious to the human constitution.[12] Excess, resulting either from masturbation, fornication, or marital lust, was likely to result in general debilitation and premature death. The sexual impulse, unless firmly repressed, was liable to undermine the entire Adventist program for human betterment. It was redundant in the divine realm. The angels did not marry and bear children, nor would the saints in heaven. Sexual activity was, from the perspective of eternity, dysfunctional: it devoted valuable time to a practice that would soon be disregarded; it precipitated emotional outbursts of the kind that angels shunned; it reduced the possibility of remaining alive until the Second Advent; and it caused physiological malfunction, which, as there was no disjunction between body and soul, could also result in spiritual debilitation.

To avoid any excitement that might release the sexual impulse, Adventists were instructed to abjure the use of alcohol, tobacco, meat, tea, and coffee. Dancing and novel reading were also prone to stimulate unholy passions and fell under similar disapproval. Adventists did not eschew pleasure for its own sake; they simply avoided those pleasures that might inhibit their progress toward the greater happiness given by health, holiness, and the certainty of heaven. The range of Adventist taboos prompted the creation of carefully monitored social environments. The benefits of the Adventist lifestyle could be maximized within a closed situation. In a sanitarium or a college, individuals could be freed from the distractions of the world, denied access to harmful substances and practices, and encouraged to develop a perfectly balanced way of life.

The need to disengage from America in order to establish a harmonious rapport with heaven could, and sometimes did, occasionally conflict. It is surprising, however, that Adventism, which posits the American nation as the ultimate eschatological enemy, should have enjoyed a relatively amicable relationship with the state. The source of this amity is Adventism's willingness to keep hostility in the realm of theology and to express its uncertainties about the state by replicating, rather then attacking, national institutions.[13] Thus Adventists were not primarily Sabbath breakers but keepers of an alternative Sabbath. Ellen White criticized those who thought that to keep Saturday holy required an ostentatious disregard for the sanctity of Sunday. Despite this, Adventists did encounter difficulties as a result of Sunday "blue laws." When brought to court, the church wielded the First Amendment. Liberty was, for Adventists, essentially freedom in which to promote religious deviation. Once again Adventists reappropriated the Declaration of Independence: the Revolution had sought freedom for America; Adventist wanted freedom from America. When it proved impossible for Adventists to exempt themselves from the requirements of the state, they preferred to operate under their own auspices. Rather than face the difficulties of ignoring the government war effort, Adventists established their own programs for medical cadet training. Even in their support for temperance, Adventists worked primarily through their own organization rather than with other agencies.

In order to coordinate the multifarious activities in which Adventists engaged, the church rapidly developed a hierarchical administrative structure.[14] With its widely disbursed and expanding membership, its numerous semiautonomous institutions and agencies, and its multiracial composition, the church has needed strong central government to hold it together. The absence of any significant offshoots is a testimony to the success of this arrangement. But the cohesiveness of the Adventist system is not simply imposed by the weight of bureaucratic authority; it also derives from the cooperative nature of the Adventist ethic. In anticipation of their incorporation into the divine realm, Adventists were enjoined to develop nonassertive modes of behavior. Individual initiative and expression were not particularly encouraged, but harmonious interaction with fellow believers was held to provide a foretaste of heavenly society. This emphasis on social integration combined with the need to dissociate from the Babylon of mainstream religious life meant that Adventists were, as a group, fairly easy to control. There was, of course, a constant stream of apostasies; but while an Adventist, an individual was inculcated with the virtues of passivity and mistrust for the world. Consequently, members have probably been inhibited from forming strong dissident or schismatic groups: dissent would be un-Adventist; schism might lead back into Babylon. There have been breakaway groups, but remarkably few of any importance for an international church with a 150-year history.

However, this very cohesiveness has made Adventists easy prey for fraudulent financial operators. Adventists have found it easier to cooperate with one another in the un-Adventist pursuit of quick wealth than they have to join with outsiders in the promotion of Adventist goals such as temperance. That this is so should not be taken as an indication of venality; it is rather the unintended consequence of an ideological and organizational system that has defined itself in opposition to mainstream American life and has distanced itself from national institutions by taking over many of the functions of the state for its own constituency.

The church and its institutions are the Adventists' home. America is, to some degree, a foreign land. Its institutions are familiar, but familiar through resemblance to their Adventist counterparts, not through direct contact. In its effort to exempt itself from American time (a time bounded by annihilation), while forced to share American space, Adventism has recreated America within America. It has turned the ideology of civil religion inside out to form a faith that consigns the nation to damnation and locates salvation within another social group—a group defined by the seventh-day Sabbath, inspired by ideals that reinterpret fundamental American values, and nurtured within an alternative network of institutions. It is small wonder, then, that Adventist artists have often portrayed the world around them through the eyes of a visitor from another time; Adventists in America are themselves visitors from another time, surveying a culture different from their own.

In part three the focus will shift from Adventists as a group to groups within Adventism. The purpose of this change is not only to give full weight to the diversity within Adventism but also to analyze the process by which the church produces and maintains its peculiar symbiosis with the American nation. But before turning to the internal dynamics of the Adventist subculture, it is worth making a comparison with another religious group. Is the Adventist experience of, and response to, American society a unique phenomenon? If not, with which other deviant social movement is it comparable? And how does the Adventist system differ from that of other minority religions that share a similar historical and geographical position?

The most illuminating comparison is with the Latter-day Saints. Adventists and Mormons share very little theological common ground, and Adventists stand much closer to traditional Christianity. Despite this, the public has persisted in confusing the two groups: Millerites in Britain explained repeatedly that they were not Mormons;[15] Ellen White had to make the same denial when visiting the West;[16] even in 1986, 4 percent of those who thought they knew about Adventism were actually thinking of Mormonism.[17] Such muddles are not fortuitous; the two groups emerged more or less in the same place at the same time, and both reflect the religious and social milieu from which they came.

From the early 1820s, Joseph Smith, the first leader of the Latter-day Saints, experienced visions through which he learned that all existing religions were wrong and that some golden plates covered with inscriptions contained a new revelation.[18] Smith translated the inscriptions with miraculous aid and published the *Book of Mormon* in 1830. It told the story of two Jewish tribes that had migrated to America in about 600 B.C. Despite its historical setting, the book addressed issues of contemporary relevance.[19] In particular, it dealt with America. Early in the story, the Lord tells Nephi, leader of one of the tribes that "inasmuch as ye shall keep my commandments, ye shall prosper, and shall be led to a land of promise; yea, even a land which I have prepared for you; yea, a land which is choice above all other lands."[20] Once in America, the tribes fail to live up to God's instructions, but the promise is reiterated: "Behold, this is a choice land, and whatsoever nation shall possess it shall be free from bondage, and from captivity, and from all other nations under heaven, if they will but serve the God of the land."[21] The message was clear. As Joseph Smith himself said shortly before his death in 1844: "The whole of America is Zion itself from north to south."[22]

The *Book of Mormon* rehearsed the central elements of the American myth: the flight from oppression, migration across the sea, entry into the land of promise. The early history of the Mormon people recapitulated the same events. Joseph Smith quickly attracted followers in his home region of upstate New York, but he moved to Kirtland, Ohio, in 1831 to join a communitarian group that had been converted to Mormonism. Another group of Mormons moved to Missouri. In both places the Mormons encountered fierce local opposition, so that in 1839 they relocated in Nauvoo, Illinois, where they began building a City of Zion. Eventually, when they once again fell foul of their neighbors, they moved to the uninhabited Great Salt Basin to establish their own kingdom in what is now Utah.

Each of these migrations followed the same pattern. Smith had proclaimed that "the decree hath gone forth from the Father that they shall be gathered in unto one place upon the face of this land."[23] The divine command was to "let them, therefore, who are among the Gentiles flee unto Zion."[24] Following this call, the Mormons all congregated at one center; as a result, the local population became concerned lest they be overrun by the adherents of this strange religion. Opposition mounted, persecution began, and the Mormons moved from yet another Babylon to build a new Zion.

The Mormon millennium was to be located in America and centered on the saints gathered in Zion. For the Mormons, an identifiable piece of land was the focus of their hopes. In 1837 a visitor to Kirtland complained about the crude literalism of their aspirations. The Mormons were, he said, "holding out the idea that the kingdom of Christ is to be composed of 'real estate, herds, flocks, silver, gold,' etc. as well as of human beings."[25] Whatever its theological limitations, this vision prompted geographical movement. It inspired the arduous trek from the eastern United States to the West, and it drew thousands of immigrants from among Mormon converts in Britain and Scandinavia.

In Mormonism, the sacred is located in space, not time. Its boundaries are geographical, not temporal. It can be reached by a physical journey across land and sea, not through an experiential journey through time. In this respect, Mormonism represents the mirror image of Adventism. Adventists separated themselves from other Americans by choosing as sacred their own portion of time—the Sabbath. The Mormons distanced themselves from America by moving outside the territorial boundaries of the United States and choosing for themselves a sacred place. Adventists were content to share American space, to remain dispersed throughout the continent, but were determined not to participate in American time as manifested in the observance of Sunday and the expectation of an earthly millennium. In contrast, the Mormons fought, often literally, to preserve their own space, but acknowledged the validity of Sunday and anticipated a millennium on American soil.

The Mormons explicitly identified themselves with American time, with the idea that the Pilgrim Fathers had opened a new and final chapter in the history of God's dealings with men. The Mormon vision differed only in its particularity, in its concentration on a specified location. The overall conception of the American era as the inauguration of a unique period in sacred time was accepted without question. But the Mormons did differentiate themselves from their background by their sense of time: they separated themselves not from America but from Christianity. As Jan Shipps has argued in *Mormonism*, the Latter-day Saints recapitulated the events of the Exodus, constituted themselves as a new Israel, and made a fresh start, placing themselves "once again at the beginning."[26] By identifying themselves with the Hebrew patriarchs, the Mormons bypassed Christianity, forming a new religious tradition distinct from Christian orthodoxy.

American civil religion has always involved the interpenetration of religious and political ideas. In its early nineteenth-century guise of civil millennialism, civil religion embodied the belief that the thousand-year reign of Christ was to be realized through the independence, prosperity, and moral improvement of the United States. It was a potent but uneasy fusion of ideas, suggesting that the territory and political institutions of America were peculiarly adapted to the millennium and that the religion of the majority of American Protestants was the closest available approximation to the Christian ideal. Both Adventism and Mormonism responded negatively to these ideas: Adventists questioned the first, the Mormons the second. In Adventism, the American dream is reinterpreted; in Mormonism, Christianity is reinterpreted. Adventists have become un-American in an effort to be more truly Christian. Mormons have become un-Christian in attempting to be more truly American.

Such dichotomies may oversimplify the complexities of history, but they illustrate the important contrasts between the two most important religious movements native to America. These differences are further exemplified by the disparity between the value systems of the two groups. For Adventists, the present is patterned after ancient prophecy and controlled by an apocalyptic future. For Mormons, the present is the locus of control for past and future—they baptize the dead by proxy in order to aid their progress in the afterlife. For Adventists, the present is a time of preparation; for Mormons, it is a time of action. In the nineteenth century, Adventists prepared for the kingdom of God by practicing self-control; Mormons built the kingdom through massive physical exertion. Adventists sought to restrain sexuality; Mormons advocated a plurality of wives and abundant children. In short, Adventists sought command over themselves, while Mormons took command of their environment. Unsurprisingly, Adventists have contributed more to medicine; Mormons, more to agriculture.

Such discrepancies probably owe something to the fact that the Mormon prophet was a man, and the Adventist prophet a woman.[27] Further, they may also reflect the realities of frontier America: the Mormons were the first settlers creating farmland out in the wilderness; Adventists came later at a time when secondary economic activities—trades and services—were becoming important. But such dichotomies also reveal the fundamental difference of the two religions in their perceptions of space and time. In Mormonism, spatial extension—experienced through migration, farming, building, and fecundity—is the primary dimension of experience. In Adventism, time is the primary dimension. Self-restraint engenders a heightened awareness of duration; Sabbath keeping promotes a chronometry; prophetic interpretation focuses on chronology, health reform on longevity, and the Second Advent on the hope of eternity. For a Mormon, morality is the proper use of space; for an Adventist, it is the correct use of time.

In their peculiar concentration on either space or time, Mormons and Adventists were both dissenting from an ideological consensus in which God's time was combined with American space to form the spatiotemporal unit of the American millennium. Adventism was thus not unique in responding to the dominant ideology of civil religion; Mormonism, which developed in similar circumstances, reacted to the same stimulus. But the Adventist response diverged from that of the Mormons in almost every respect. While the Mormons embarked on noisy migration across space, Adventist were setting out on a quiet pilgrimage through time.

Part 3

ADVENTIST SUBCULTURE

CHAPTER 14

Women

Seventh-day Adventism is the largest Christian denomination to have been founded by a woman. As such, it offers unique opportunities to researchers interested in female religious experience and in women's roles in social movements. Such questions fall outside the scope of this book, but the analysis of the church's relationship with America provides some indication of the ways in which Adventism exemplifies female responses to a patriarchal social order.

Within patriarchy, women are excluded from the centers of power and are confined to the margins of society. They are denied the possibility of self-definition, save in opposition to, or in imitation of, dominant male groups. Their ability to control and occupy space is limited by the boundaries established by men.[1] These characteristics apply to Adventists as well as to other marginal social groups. What is particularly interesting about Adventism is that it represents a feminine response to these conditions—feminine, that is, within the norms of modern Western culture. In other words, Adventists, like "feminine" women, have made virtues out of the limitations imposed by their social subordination. By defining themselves in the mirror image of the dominant ideology, Adventists have managed to coexist with their potential persecutors. At no stage have they willingly attempted to confront the state. They have, rather, remained quiet and malleable, not seeking to draw attention to themselves lest this provoke a hostile reaction; yet they have maintained a mute resistance to authority, refusing to participate in conflict on terms laid down by the aggressor.

Furthermore, Adventism, like traditional femininity, not only requires the avoidance of explicit sexuality and violence, it also seeks to disarm its opponents through promoting temperance, health reform, and self-control. Adventist concerns, such as health and education, are issues that have long been the prerogative of women (at least in a non-professional context). Like women, Adventists have tended to play caring, healing, and nurturing roles. Unlike the Mormons, but like many women, Adventists have not claimed the right to their own space but have defined themselves through time—not through the monthly cycle of menstruation, but by the weekly observance of the Sabbath. Even in the arts, Adventists have elected to pursue the traditional feminine accomplishment of music.

Within American society, Adventism can thus be perceived to occupy a "feminine" position. Unsurprisingly, it has attracted more women than men, and although there is a preponderance of women in most Christian denominations, the Adventist ratio of 2 to 1 is unusually high.[2] Despite this, the status of women within Adventism has been ambiguous. Women have responded positively to the Adventist message and have been eager to work for the church, but the extent of their participation has been determined by men who, from an early stage, have controlled the church's bureaucracy. Insofar as Adventist women have a history distinct from that of the church itself, it is one in which the central dynamic has been the conflict between female enthusiasm and male regulation.

This tension underlies the earliest discussions of the role of women in Adventism. In January 1850 the *Review and Herald* carried a letter by a Sister M. Ashley of Dartmouth, Massachusetts. In words that expressed the feelings of most of the *Review*'s female correspondents, she said: "I do find in my heart a love for God's precious *truth*, and I rejoice that the poor lost sheep are being gathered. Truly, God has set his hand to the work, and it will be done. . . . Glory to God, he has some precious 'jewells' [*sic*] in old Dartmouth, and they now begin to shine."[3] Letters like these filled the correspondence columns of the *Review* in its first decade. They indicate that the first Adventist women were, in general, committed believers deeply interested in the progress of the movement. Of course men also wrote to the church paper, but their letters rarely expressed the same joy of commitment as their female counterparts.

It was not just in letters to the *Review* that women kept up the morale of Adventist believers. They often made notable contributions in testimony meetings as well. An account of one such meeting in Washington, New Hampshire, in 1852 told of "a wonderful answer to prayer, in the case of Sister Huntley of Lempster, N.H." She had been badly injured after being thrown from a wagon. Her plight was announced at the meeting, and a few people then left to see her. After prayer she began to feel better, and quite soon she asked to go to the meeting "and tell what God had done for her." As the *Review* related the story: "She rode about a mile to the place of meeting, testified to the goodness of God, rested well during the night, and the next morning seemed as well as before the accident occurred."[4]

With women often featuring like this in church meetings, it was not surprising that the first question raised about Adventist women was whether, in fact, they should keep quiet in church. It was not long before an article appeared in the *Review*, headed by Paul's declaration: "Let your Women keep silence in the Churches." Some Adventists had evidently noticed the apostle's statements on women in passages like 1 Corinthians 14 and 2 Timothy 2, and were disturbed at the readiness of women to speak up at Adventist gatherings. D. Hewitt, a Battle Creek layman who wrote the article, dismissed such sentiments by a closely argued exegesis of the texts. He argued against the suggestion that Adventist women were overreaching themselves by writing that "simply praying, or singing, or speaking in meeting would not be usurping authority over the man, but edifying the man, and pleasing the Lord. . . . A sister's telling in meeting what the Lord has done for her, and what she intends to do through grace, would not be . . . usurping authority over the man."[5]

The issue, however, would not go away, and another article on the subject appeared in the *Review* in 1859.[6] In 1860 S. C. Welcome in yet another article provided concrete evidence that some Adventist churches did prevent women from speaking. He said: "Often I have been in meetings where it was contrary to the rules of the church for females to speak; and while the brethren would speak of their enjoyment, some humble sister whose heart would be overflowing with the love of God, would sit bound down by the chains of the church creed." He then went on to describe a clearly distressing example he had experienced just "a few evenings since." It involved a new convert who was barred from expressing her new found faith in church by her parents.[7]

Mrs. White herself does not seem to have engaged publicly in this debate. But the men around her were certainly willing to defend the cause of women. In 1858 James White wrote an article in the *Review* on the role of prophecy in the church. Although he did not mention his wife by name, he argued that prophecy was a work that provided equal opportunities. Quoting Joel 2:28–32 he said: "Under the influence of the Holy Spirit both sons and daughters will prophesy. Some have excluded females from a share in this work, because it says, 'Your young men shall see visions.' They seem to forget that 'man' and 'men' in the Scriptures generally means both male and female."[8] The result of this interpretation was that certain rights of equality were established for Mrs. White. This may have ensured for Adventist women some rights of church participation that might have otherwise proved harder to secure. On the other hand, the attitudes and behavior that Adventist women exhibited from the beginnings of the movement may, in turn, have provided exactly the sort of environment for Mrs. White to flourish. Whenever the prophetess sent in an encouraging article to the *Review* or testified in a meeting, she was acting in the same manner as dozens of other Adventist women.

In her book on women and Christianity, the author Sara Maitland noted that it is a characteristic of religious history that women achieve positions of leadership during times of conflict.[9] Three American sociologists in the book *Women of the Cloth* also noted that women are likely to feature at the birth of new religious movements where a new vision is advanced.[10] The observations of both Maitland and the American sociologists certainly fit the Adventist experience in its initial stages: first, in the emergence of Ellen White from the ashes of the Great Disappointment, and second, in the extent to which women participated in church meetings, despite some opposition.

The authors of *Women of the Cloth* point out that women retained a significant place in those new movements that continued to stress the importance of the "gifts of the spirit."[11] In Adventism, the emphasis on such gifts—particularly prophecy—was ensured by the presence of Ellen White. As a result, the overall status of Adventist women and their level of participation in the church did not decline when men assumed bureaucratic control following the 1863 organization. Of course, the nature of that participation was different: women could now do things other than write to the *Review* or contribute to testimony meetings. Women served as licensed ministers, Bible workers, administrative officials, and on equal terms in husband-and-wife evangelistic teams.[12] It would be a mistake to exaggerate the involvement of women in a church in which men still dominated the leadership positions. However, in the 1860s and 1870s, Adventist women made steady progress within the denomination. Indeed, the impact women made in this period is perhaps indicated by events at the 1881 General Conference session, where delegates passed a resolution advocating the ordination of women. The resolution was not adopted, however, for reasons that have still not been fully explained.[13]

At the first attempt, women failed to win ordination. Despite this, they continued to secure ministerial licenses from local conferences. Women such as Ruie Hill and Hattie Enoch served in General Conference mission areas in the United States. Ellen Lane, who had been the first Adventist woman to hold a ministerial license in 1878, conducted an effective ministry until 1889.[14] Most notably, Mrs. Lulu Wightman, another licensed minister, established nearly a dozen churches in New York State between 1896 and 1905. It was estimated in 1905 that 60 percent of all Adventist conversions in New York State were the result of the work of Mrs. Wightman and her husband. Her achievements, in the judgment of one Adventist researcher, made her "not only the . . . most outstanding evangelist in New York State during her time, but among the most successful within the denomination for any time."[15] Her experience, however, was typical of many Adventist women who have made outstanding contributions to the church. She faced prejudice, she was treated badly by her leaders, and she (or others) had to defend her right to work. In 1897 a fellow New York

State minister, S. M. Cobb, wrote to his conference president lamenting the treatment of Mrs. Wightman. "She has accomplished more . . . than any minister in this state," he said, "and yet the Conf. has held her off arms length, and refused to recognize her as a suitable person to present the truth."[16] In the end, Mrs. Wightman and her husband left the church, at least partly because of their unhappiness within the Adventist ministry.

Lulu Wightman had shown what talented Adventist women could do in evangelism. Anna Knight, a resourceful young black, demonstrated the worth of women missionaries when she went to India in the early 1900s. In education, Flora Williams became the first female principal of the denomination's Battle Creek Academy in 1907. In medicine, Drs. Phoebe Lamson and Kate Lindsay made major contributions to the church's health work. Lamson was the first woman doctor employed at the Health Reform Institute in 1866, while Lindsay initiated the denomination's first school of nursing at Battle Creek Sanitarium in 1883.[17]

By 1905 many women had advanced to church administrative positions. Research conducted in selected areas indicates that in 1910 there were around twenty women education department leaders in all conferences in the United States, over fifty Sabbath School leaders, and almost twenty conference treasurers. By 1915, the number of women treasurers had dropped to less than ten, although the figures for education and Sabbath School had increased slightly. After 1915, however, the number of women in these positions began an immediate and inexorable decline, so that by 1950 there were no women leaders in either department. The same is also true of conference treasurers, although there was a slight increase in number between 1915 and 1920. By 1950, however, all woman conference treasurers had disappeared from view.[18] This decline can be attributed to the change in the nature of the denomination. After the reorganization of 1901, Adventists placed less emphasis on the "gifts of the spirit" and more faith in a highly structured bureaucracy. In this situation, women are, as many researchers have noted, usually deprived of administrative responsibility.[19] The death of Ellen White in 1915 symbolized this change and may also have made it easier for the church's leaders to ignore the claims of female members. But the other important factor was clearly the domestication of the Adventist woman, which also occurred at this time—a development that sheds further light on the decline of women leaders in the twentieth century.

It is an interesting fact that until the late nineteenth century, Adventist women had heard surprisingly little about their role in the home. In the 1880s and 1890s, however, the church began to emphasize women's domestic duties, and the images of wife and mother were set before Adventist women as the ultimate in womanhood. Compared with other Protestants, Adventists came to this ideal relatively late. By the 1830s and 1840s, "the Protestant emphasis on the domestic virtues had blossomed into a cult of domesticity that endowed the home with . . . transcendental qualities that it was a woman's sacred mission to preserve." With this was harnessed "the cult of true womanhood" in which women, because of "their greater moral purity," were ideally placed to be "the moral inspiration of their husbands as well as the moral guardians of their children."[20]

These observations, which applied to nineteenth-century Protestantism generally, accurately portray the dominant Adventist view of women as the church moved into the twentieth century. This view was, however, largely absent from the Adventist literature of the preceding fifty years. The first articles on the family to appear in the *Review* did not differentiate between the roles of men and women. They addressed parents equally, without devolving any special responsibilities on the mother. This was well illustrated in an article that appeared in January 1851. Entitled "Duty to Our Children," it discussed the importance of teaching the commandments, without singling out the role of the mother. Articles such as this indicate that although the importance of the family was recognized in Adventist circles almost immediately, the role of women in the home was not.[21]

There may be two explanations for this state of affairs. First, the dominant women's issue in early Adventism appears to have been the question of speaking in church or, in Ellen White's case, prophesying before the brethren. The concern with these matters may have pushed other concerns, such as motherhood, to the sidelines. Second, in nineteenth-century America, the differentiation of sex roles in the family was accompanied by the separation of the family itself from the wider society. In Adventism, such differentiation may have occurred in microcosm. A clear distinction between home (which was often used for religious meetings) and church may not have occurred until the late nineteenth century, when Adventism became more organized. When the home became clearly separated from the church women's roles became clearly differentiated from those of men.[22]

What is clear is that the bulk of Ellen White's statements on motherhood, which were later collected in books such as *The Adventist Home*, came in the 1890s. She referred to the mother as "the queen of her household" who "has in her power the molding of her children's characters." She considered "the distinctive duties of woman . . . more sacred, more holy, than those of man." Ironically, the prophetess did not advise Adventist women to emulate her own dominant position. To those who looked outside the home for fulfillment, she said, "If you have the idea that some work greater and holier than this [homemaking] has been entrusted to you, you are under a deception."[23] Statements like these had a great effect on Adventism, an effect that has persisted to the present day. It is no wonder that women disappeared from church administration. The domestic ideal changed Adventist women from church leaders into homemakers. Mrs. White's views also started a preoccupation with the correct attitudes a woman should exhibit in the domestic sphere. Much less attention was devoted to the family attitudes of men. *The Adventist Home* exemplifies this. When the book came out in 1952, forty-five pages were devoted to motherhood, against seventeen to fatherhood.

But there was another side to Ellen White's writings on women. She warned about the enslaving tendencies of housework and child bearing. She felt that the mother's individuality and independence were important and argued for equality between the wife and her husband. She also stressed that women, even in their domestic situation, should develop their minds.[24] The emphasis on a woman's individuality and independence in the family was, according to feminist historians, one of the first steps in the development of feminist consciousness.[25] For example, the American feminist Margaret Fuller argued in 1843 for the equality and independence of women in the home. She spoke out against the drudgery of housework and emphasized the need for housewives to expand their capacities.[26] Eventually, of course, the home would become the enemy of the radical feminists. But in the nineteenth century, feminists were much more concerned with obtaining equality and respect in the home. In making statements of this kind, Mrs. White reflected the thought of early American feminists like Fuller. And it was that aspect of Mrs. White's writings to which some Adventist women appealed when a feminist movement emerged in the church in the 1970s.[27]

In the meantime, the church did little to foster the kind of personal development for women that Ellen White had encouraged. One exception was the formation of a women's organization at the General Conference in 1937, possibly the first recorded instance of Adventist women joining together. Formed by women office staff, the organization had as its objectives the fostering of friendly relations among women, the development of well-balanced lives, and the promotion of agreed-upon projects. The women called the organization "Keepers of the Keys," put out a monthly eight-page mimeographed paper called *Key Note*, and elected officers for one-year terms. An effusive article about Keepers of the Keys appeared in the *Review* on March 21, 1940, which provides an insight into the interests of Adventist women workers in this period. Keepers of the Keys encouraged hobbies, organized educational tours, conducted welfare work, and sponsored outdoor activities. The organization also appointed special sponsors who kept members informed about such things as the latest "worthwhile" books

and musical entertainment in Washington, D.C. Most of these endeavors were recorded in *Key Note*, which also provided news of its
members and the activities of General Conference departments.[28]

However "the cult of true womanhood" was by this time firmly established. The process was aided by able propagandists such as Mrs.
Sarepta Myrenda Irish Henry, a late convert to Adventism who had
previously established a national reputation in America as a temperance
campaigner. In the latter years of the nineteenth century, she spoke
in various parts of the United States and Canada about the importance
of women in the home.[29] Mrs. Henry's work was backed up by articles
in Adventist publications. One article that appeared in the *Review* in
1902 reflects the concentration on domestic duties. In discussing "the
model woman," the writer left little doubt that women were to serve
at the convenience of men. He believed that "nothing cools the most
ardent love of a new husband sooner than cold or indifferently or
insufficiently cooked victuals" and that even "the most doting father
soon tires of the sweetest baby when all his spare time is spent nursing
it." He also wrote that "none but bachelors enjoy sewing buttons on
outer garments, or using safety pins for want of buttons on nether
underwear."[30]

As well as placing emphasis on women's family responsibilities, Mrs.
White also wrote about female sexuality. She did not have a high opinion of women in this regard, tending to see them as sexual temptresses:
"Women are too often tempters. On one pretence or another they engage the attention of men . . . and lead them on till they transgress the
law of God." She had a particular distaste for "forward misses and bold,
forward women who have a faculty of insinuating themselves into notice, putting themselves in the company of young men, courting the
attentions" and "inviting flirtations from married or unmarried men."
Largely because of this, Ellen White advised: "Our sisters should encourage true meekness; they should not be forward, talkative and bold,
but modest and unassuming, slow to speak."[31] These general principles
were expounded by other writers in Adventist publications. From time
to time, articles appeared in which "immodest dress" was deplored and
the preoccupation with fashion and looks was dismissed. In later years,
articles discussed "outward adorning" in terms that encouraged a certain amount of attractiveness, but even in such cases, modesty and simplicity were still the major concerns.[32]

On the whole, Adventist women have been encouraged to cultivate
modesty, keeping their sexuality in check. However, the church's attitude on this has not been straightforward. From a study of the use of
women in Adventist advertising, a rather different picture emerges.
Women have always been used in the marketing of Adventist products,
probably more so than men. Part of the reason for this is that many
of the products advertised in Adventist publications are aimed at the

home. Church enterprises have obviously seen women as the natural promoters of such merchandise. Thus, images of women advertising cookery books and food products, or women with children advertising story books, abound. When products are not of this nature, however, women still seem to be the preferred sex. To take one example, in 1940 the *Review* ran four advertisements for the *Youth's Instructor*, an early Adventist young people's journal. Of these, three advertisements used women—two bright young girls and an older lady who contributed to the journal. The other advertisement used a man, but his image was a simple line drawing, unlike the women, who were photographed. The women appeared to have been employed to add to the appeal of the product.[33]

A still more striking example of this tactic is provided by the 1970 advertisement that appeared in the *Review* for the *Seventh-day Adventist Bible Commentary Reference Series*. The advertisement was headlined "spectacular offers" and displayed a large photograph of a girl. Underneath the young woman was a much smaller illustration of the Bible series. The "spectacular offers" referred to are actually for the ten-volume work, but the reader might easily imagine that it is the girl herself who is an offer.[34] The display of women in this fashion is at odds with the advice in Adventist literature, which encourages women to be modest and discreet. Ellen White's condemnation of "bold, forward women who have a faculty of insinuating themselves into notice" fits ill with an advertising strategy that uses images of women to attract male attention.[35]

The discrepancy between the advice given in books and articles and the images in advertising is one aspect of the church's ambivalence toward women. The discrepancy between the church's statements of its regard for women and its treatment of them represented another. In 1971 Robert H. Pierson, General Conference president, called for equality of treatment of men and women in the church. He promised the church would recognize a woman's eligibility to participate in "the many areas in which she is equipped to serve." He also stressed that the church must deal justly with a woman, "assuring her compensation in keeping with the responsibilities she carries." It was Pierson's desire that "our sisters join their brethren in developing the fullest potential of their talent for a finished work."[36]

Pierson's assurance that women would receive equitable compensation was soon put to the test, for the church did not, in practice, recognize a woman's right to equal remuneration. As a result of this, the church fought several equal pay lawsuits in the 1970s. The most celebrated was against Merikay Silver, a young editorial assistant at the Pacific Press. In May 1972, she had approached the manager of the press, Leonard Bohner, to ask for the same salary and benefits as a male colleague. The key problem was that her husband, Kim, had recently been laid off and had decided to go to college. This made her the breadwinner—an unusual situation in an Adventist family but a sign of the changing times. If Mrs. Silver had been a man, she would have had no difficulty in securing a special "head-of-household" allowance that was given to the family's breadwinner because of his added responsibilities. Her entitlement to the head-of-household benefit was the key element of her request. Bohner's reply, as Mrs. Silver recounted it, revealed that in his mind the justification for unequal pay was based on what he considered to be the proper sex roles: "Times may be changing," he said, "but the husband is still head of the house. *He* should be supporting you. You should be the one going to college. . . . Kim is supposed to be bringing home the bread. If you two decide that he'll return to school, why should we then have to raise your salary?"[37]

Mrs. Silver's request was refused, and in January 1973, she filed a class action suit charging the Pacific Press with violating the sex discrimination provisions of the 1964 Civil Rights Act. In August 1977, the government's Equal Employment Opportunity Commission (EEOC) filed a similar suit on behalf of Lorna Tobler, another Pacific Press employee whose help and support had been crucial to Mrs. Silver. Mrs. Silver's own action ended in a $60,000 out-of-court settlement in April 1978, but using the evidence from her case, the EEOC filed a class action suit against the press a month later. The final phases of a prolonged legal struggle came in December 1982, when the Pacific Press was ordered to pay Lorna Tobler $77,000 in lost pay and benefits, and in October 1983, when the press was ordered to pay over $600,000 in compensation to its women workers.[38]

In her book *Betrayal*, Mrs. Silver revealed that her campaign for equal pay was conducted against a background of intimidation from church officials and bitter opposition from fellow Pacific Press workers, many of them women. She paid a high personal price for her stand, as she eventually lost her job, her husband, and her church. But she won a major victory for Adventist women, whether they supported her or not. As Leona Running, an Andrews University professor, said: "Countless women employees are . . . grateful to Merikay for the size of their paychecks. Her courage and persistence have won benefits not only for her but for innumerable others."[39]

The other focus of dispute between women and the authorities of the church came over the question of the areas in which women were "equipped to serve." Ordination to the ministry was not open to women. Indeed, unlike their nineteenth-century counterparts, it was difficult for women to function in any kind of ministerial capacity. There was little opportunity for women to advance to leadership positions in the church, even though it was clear that women members outnumbered men by a large margin.[40] Pierson seems to have made his 1971 statement with one eye on the outside world. He noted that "some women seek to assure the deference and privileges they feel are due them by organizing, by demanding, by protesting." He implied that behavior of this kind was inappropriate in Adventism, where "conse-crated women . . . assure deference, privilege, and honor by . . . com-mitted service," and by "compelling Christian character."[41]

The women's movement to which Pierson alluded had been under-way since the early 1960s. Its origins are usually traced to the publi-cation of Betty Friedan's *The Feminine Mystique* in 1963, a celebrated attack on the idea of women in the home. The movement spawned by books like Friedan's had many sides. Of particular interest to Adventist women—despite the wishes of leaders like Pierson—were the general principles of equal rights and the feasibility of entering previously male-dominated occupations. Largely as a result of the women's move-ment, the number of women in occupations such as law, medicine, and church ministry rose rapidly between 1960 and 1980. The number of women clergy in all religious bodies in the United States nearly tripled in this period, growing from 4,272 to 11,130.[42] Adventist women such as Josephine Benton and Jan Daffern, who in the 1970s were among the church's first female ministers for several generations, were both influenced and encouraged by these developments. They did not re-gard themselves as radicals, but as Jan Daffern recalled; "The feminist movement helped me to decide the ministry was possible."[43]

Evidence that the women's movement was affecting Adventist women came, in fact, in the very year that Pierson made his statement. Brenda Butka, a graduate student at the University of Michigan, openly sup-ported the general principles of women's liberation in an article in *Spec-trum*.[44] A year later in another *Spectrum* article, Leona Running revealed that Adventist women were reading and were being influenced by a great variety of feminist literature.[45] There were some practical devel-opments accompanying this growing consciousness. In August 1973, Dr. Josephine Benton became the first Adventist woman minister in many years when she was appointed an associate pastor of Sligo Church, one of the largest Adventist congregations in Takoma Park, Maryland. The question of women in ministry was clearly back on the Adventist agenda, and a month after Dr. Benton's appointment, a General Conference committee met at Camp Mohaven, Ohio, to discuss this problem and the whole question of women in the church.

The meeting, which took place from September 16–29, 1973, was a high point for Adventist women of feminist persuasion. Several papers were presented that removed many of the theological cornerstones of male superiority and emphasized the equality of women with men. At around the same time, most of the church's leading theologians were unable to find any theological objections to the principle of ordaining women. Sakae Kubo argued, "It is only tradition and custom, not our doctrines . . . that have kept us from ordaining women to the ministry."[46] In its recommendations, the Camp Mohaven committee suggested a plan leading to ordination and urged greater participation of women in the leadership of the church. At the 1973 Annual Council, the committee's report was received. It was recommended that the report and selected papers be studied by General Conference divisions. The next year the divisions reported. There was no consensus on the ordination of women, and the Annual Council recommended "no move be made in the direction of ordaining women to the gospel ministry."[47] For the second time, Adventist women were denied ordination. But unlike the situation in 1881 when the reasons why the church did not proceed were shrouded in mystery, it was easy to see on this occasion why the church did not do so. In referring the issue to the divisions, church leaders made the ordination of women impossible unless the worldwide church unanimously agreed on it. With so many different cultural traditions involved, the chances of such agreement were virtually nil.

Ordination might be impossible, but women ministers continued to play a more significant role in the life of the church. In practice, women were easily accepted, once initial hostilities had been overcome. For example, a poll of the Sligo membership in 1975 indicated that Dr. Benton was being favorably received as a minister. Church members were asked if she had done a poorer job than the men on the staff. The majority of respondents, 62 percent, said no, and on the whole comments were favorable.[48] Jan Daffern, who succeeded Dr. Benton at Sligo in 1980, was of the opinion that when church members actually encountered a female minister, their attitudes tended to change. She recalled an experience as a theology student when she worked in a local church. The church elder made it clear that he would not appear on the platform if she did. He changed his mind, however, once he got to know her.[49] Experiences such as Daffern's confirm the evidence of studies conducted in the early 1980s on the impact of women ministers on lay attitudes. The results indicated that individual parishioners' and lay leaders' negative attitudes toward women pastors changed after the experience of having a female minister.[50] Jan Daffern also found attitudes at the Adventist seminary at Andrews University in need of modification. Daffern went to the Adventist seminary in 1978 with four other women. She found a world unaccustomed to dealing with women. Students interrogated her almost daily, and she felt intimidated by some of the teachers. She remembered one saying condescendingly in class; "If Jan can pass this test, anyone can pass it." Such attitudes, Daffern recalled, changed very slowly.[51]

The struggles of the 1970s made it clear to some Adventist women that a stronger organization was needed to represent women's interests in the church. In the early 1980s, the Association of Adventist Women

(AAW) came into being. In many respects, the AAW was similar to the Keepers of the Keys organization of the late 1930s and 1940s. Then, Adventist women had felt the need to unite their interests and to promote their self-development. It was the same with the AAW. The major difference, however, was that the AAW was dedicated to equal opportunities for women in the church. The organization also assumed the role of a pressure group. Through its bimonthly newspaper, *The Adventist Woman*, and through its annual national conferences, the AAW kept women's issues high on the church's agenda.[52] Yet, the ordination of women was rejected once again after a special church commission in 1985. Members of the AAW found it difficult to convince other Adventist women of the justice of their cause. A church poll conducted in preparation for the 1985 commission indicated that more women than men opposed ordination.[53] A year earlier, an anonymous group of conservative women reacted to the general ideology of the AAW, claiming that "the majority of women in the church are fulfilled and silent over the role of women issue."[54] Sometimes *The Adventist Woman* also printed individual letters of dissent. In one issue, a woman correspondent wanted to know why Adventist women felt the need to "praise and honor" themselves. She felt that in pursuing equality, Adventist women were following "the Satanic feminist movement."[55]

In some respects, such sentiments were unsurprising. If feminism is perceived as an attempt by women to gain attention and to assert themselves, it obviously appears to run counter to the Adventist ethic of self-effacement and passivity. For Adventists of both sexes, virtue has been associated with traditionally feminine attributes. Resistance to the women's movement within Adventism may thus derive not just from the feeling that women should not usurp male roles but also from the belief that male roles are, in themselves, less than desirable. The male-dominated hierarchy of the church was, after all, originally permitted only as a necessary evil. Adventism is itself a women's movement, for its takes its inspiration from a woman, is composed chiefly of women, and espouses "feminine" values. As such, it is more difficult for men to find an appropriate role. Being denied traditional forms of male expression, such as self-assertion, violence, and intemperance, Adventist men have concentrated their energies on the few channels open to them—notably the creation and perpetuation of bureaucratic and institutional structures. If women were permitted to participate fully in these areas, men might find there was almost no scope for them to play machismo roles within an Adventist context.

The conflict between the sexes in Adventism may also be perceived in a wider setting, as expressing the tension between two elements in the Adventist response to America. Adventism has both inverted the ideology of American civil religion and replicated American institutions. The first phase of this response involved the creation of a "feminine" ethic of self-restraint; the second allowed men to create structures in which to act out dominant roles. The paradoxical nature of the position of women within Adventism may thus be a reflection of the ambiguities inherent in Adventism itself.

CHAPTER 15

Blacks

Adventists have not generally been associated with dominant sexual or social groups, but with regard to race, the position has been different. Members of the church have predominantly been drawn from, and have identified with, the dominant ethnic grouping in American society—that of white Anglo-Saxons. Because of this, the black experience in Adventism has few peculiarities; rather, it follows the pattern of development in race relations in the nation as a whole and as such provides a good example of the Adventist tendency to replicate important aspects of the American experience.

If the American revolution can be interpreted in racial terms then it can be viewed, as the sociologist Van den Berghe wrote, as "a movement of political emancipation by a section of . . . white settlers against control from England."[1] Certainly, the subjugation of the native Indians and the persistence of slavery indicated that the white revolutionaries did not believe the principles of liberty applied equally to all men. Because of this, the problem of race has been, perhaps, the darkest blot on the American dream. Like the founding fathers, the Adventist pioneers were white. It is true that some blacks were connected with the Millerite movement. The black preachers Charles Bowles and John W. Lewis made notable contributions, and another black Millerite William E. Foy had visions in 1842 that were similar to those Ellen White later experienced.[2] But the Adventism that emerged after the Great Disappointment was essentially an all-white movement that embodied the prejudiced attitudes and experienced the racial problems of America as a whole.

This contrasted with the racial attitudes generally associated with the Millerite movement. Miller himself favored abolitionism, as did many of his associates until their reformist zeal was sapped by the expectation of the Second Advent.[3] Furthermore, some of the individuals who were to play important roles in the Seventh-day Adventist church were keen advocates of reform. Joseph Bates participated in the antislavery societies of the 1830s, and John Byington (the first president) and John

P. Kellogg (the father of John Harvey) are said to have offered their homes as stations on the Underground Railroad, which was set up to help fleeing slaves.[4]

It is significant, however, that individuals generally engaged in these activities either before they became Adventists or before the Adventist church became an identifiable unit. In the years after the Great Disappointment, racial attitudes amongst the Sabbath keepers underwent a subtle change. Race ceased to be an issue of social reform and became instead means of demonstrating American hypocrisy. In 1851 J. N. Andrews seized on the racist policies of the United States in order to prove his point about the lamblike beast.[5] Similarly, James White, in his notorious "Nation" editorial of 1862, linked the practice of slavery to the eschatological damnation of the nation: "For the past ten years the *Review* has taught that the United States of America were a subject of prophecy, and that slavery is pointed out in the prophetic word as the darkest and most damning sin upon this nation. It has taught that Heaven has wrath in store for the nation which it would drink to the very dregs, as due punishment for the sin of slavery."[6] To early Adventists, race was largely an abstract concept that had more to do with proving their eschatological understanding than with effecting social reform. This may be one reason why, despite their stated abhorrence of slavery, Adventists gave less-than-wholehearted support to the abolitionist cause during the American Civil War.[7]

The Adventist pioneers had very little personal contact with black people. It was not until the 1870s, when their evangelistic endeavors brought them into the South, that Adventists encountered blacks in significant numbers. They did not, however, set out to evangelize the black communities. Rather, it was blacks who found the church after turning up at Adventist meetings without being directly invited. At these meetings, Adventist ministers discovered the pattern of segregation existing in the South and to which, as northerners, they had never really been exposed. The blacks who came sat in a separate partition or outside the meeting halls. Elbert B. Lane, the first Adventist minister in the South, reported holding meetings in a Tennessee depot building with "white people occupying one room, and the colored the other."[8] This self-segregation apparently took some Adventist workers by surprise. In 1876 Dudley M. Canright described a meeting he held near Dallas, Texas. People "came from every direction," he wrote in the *Review*, "afoot, on horseback . . . with wagons, men, women and children both white and black." But then he saw "something new—the whites all seated inside the house and the colored people all outside— an invariable custom through the South."[9] There is no indication at this stage that Adventists endorsed these practices, although they did accept them as part of life in the region. The reports of Lane and Canright do show, however, that Adventists first saw blacks in the movement separated from whites or on the back seats outside the church. It was an appropriate beginning to Adventist dealings in race relations, for from that time to the present day, Adventists have never relinquished the idea that good relations between the races are best served by some kind of segregationist policy.

Racial segregation, which is still a marked feature of Adventism in the United States, was prompted first by expediency, then by choice. It was felt that blacks could not be reached without alienating whites unless mission work was divided along racial lines. Canright was one of the first to advocate this. He argued in 1876 that evangelism among the freedmen had to be a distinct mission. "A man cannot labor for them and for the whites too, as the white would not associate with him if he did," he wrote in the *Review*. "There is no objection to laboring for them and teaching them, but it must be separately."[10] This policy was adopted by other Adventist workers, including Edson White, the son of Mrs. White, who sailed down the Mississippi River in the 1890s in the riverboat *The Morning Star*. White went specifically to evangelize the black communities and took great care not to antagonize whites in doing so.[11]

Prejudiced attitudes thus dictated the Adventist approach to race relations. But soon, Adventism itself began to reflect the racial divide in America. In 1886 the first all-black Adventist church was established in Edgefield, Tennessee. It was followed by another in Louisville, Kentucky, in 1890. In 1895 Oakwood College was started for young Adventist blacks in Huntsville, Alabama. All these institutional developments were perfectly in tune with a nation whose black and white populations were becoming increasingly isolated.[12] When Jim Crow segregation became entrenched in the early 1900s, the Adventist version of it was already firmly in place.

There had, however, been a debate within Adventism about the propriety of this kind of racial segregation. Not all Adventists agreed with it, just as not all Americans—even in the South—accepted a policy of outright segregation before 1900.[13] The liberal John Harvey Kellogg did not subscribe to the principle of the "color line" and supported other Adventists who defied it. Kellogg's stand upset Edson White, who in 1899 wrote to his mother about the doctor's attitude. White felt that Kellogg and others who wanted to defy segregation would "close up the field" if their ideas gained any credence.[14] His mother, however, had more ambivalent feelings. In the 1890s she urged the integration of the Adventist church and told white Adventists they had no right to exclude blacks from their places of worship.[15] She argued that men who believed the separation of the races to be the best way of meeting the prejudice of white people "have not had the spirit of Christ."[16] But in 1908 in a pamphlet called *Proclaiming the Truth Where There Is Race Antagonism*, Mrs. White bowed to the white racism she had earlier tried to resist. "Among the white people in many places, there exists a strong prejudice against the colored race. We may desire to ignore this prejudice, but we cannot do it. If we were to act as if this prejudice did not exist, we could not get the light before the white people," she wrote. The prophetess argued for separate white and black churches "in order that the work for the white people may be carried on without serious hindrance." [17] And it was this view that determined Adventist policy as the church moved into the new century.

Before considering how Adventist race relations developed in the twentieth century, it is worth examining another interpretation of the church's early record on race. Within Adventism perhaps the most influential view is that set out in 1970 by Roy Branson in three *Review* articles. In the first, he argues that the Adventist pioneers were in the vanguard of the abolitionist movement and that they took positions that were, for the time, quite liberal. But the evidence cited is based largely on the antislavery activities of Bates, Byington, and J. P. Kellogg, even though the sources indicate that they cut their ties with the abolitionist movement once they became involved with the Adventist community. These pioneers may have had an active pre-Adventist commitment to abolition, but to transpose that commitment to Adventism itself is to exaggerate the church's interest in social reform.[18] Bates, for example, abandoned his career as a social reformer even before the Great Disappointment of 1844.[19] Evidence also suggests that even the early antislavery activity was not all that it has been claimed to be. Byington, for example, may never have used his home as a station on the Underground Railroad.[20]

In further support of his thesis, Branson cites a statement by Mrs. White in which she instructed church members to disobey the 1850 Fugitive Slave Act that required American citizens to deliver fleeing slaves to their masters.[21] Considerable doubt arises as to whether Adventists were in any way ahead of other abolitionists on this question. The law was inspired by Southern congressmen and its enactment united Northerners against it. Even people who previously had not shown much interest in the plight of the slave condemned the act. The law was generally regarded as another unwelcome attempt by the Southern states to control the affairs of the entire nation. The Fugitive Slave Act was therefore greeted immediately with widespread protests, public disavowals, and flagrant disregard. In one or two instances, individuals tried under the act were spectacularly acquitted by the courts. Thus Mrs. White brought the church into harmony with mainstream Northern opinion. Indeed, the prophetess, who made her statement in 1859, nine years after the law was enacted, took her time in protesting against what among her neighbors had long been regarded as an unjustifiable act.[22]

The point is not that Adventists were silent on racial issues; they were indeed quite vocal. But their readiness to speak out was motivated by their particular view of the end of the world, rather than by their desire to liberate Afro-Americans. Branson himself comes close to recognizing this. In his second article (devoted to the subject of slavery and prophecy) he notes: "Both Uriah Smith and James White related slavery to prophecy. . . . Oppression of blacks in America was more significant evidence that the beast in Revelation 13 was the United States." Indeed, as Branson continued: "Far from being a purely secular concern, Adventists thought race relations were intimately involved with a proper understanding of prophecy and last-day events." These judgments would seem to support the view presented earlier in this chapter that the early Adventists saw the question of race primarily as a stick with which to beat the American beast.[23]

The third article in Branson's series attempts to explain Mrs. White's early twentieth-century statements advocating separate white and black churches. He argues that the prophetess's views reflected a worsening of the nation's race relations in the 1890s. The realities of white prejudice forced Mrs. White to reconsider her stand.[24] While this explanation is plausible, it would be a mistake to imply that the advocacy of racial segregation was unrepresentative of the Adventist tradition. In an Adventist context Mrs. White's statements were not particularly anomalous. For a time she may have attempted to maintain a liberal position, but when in 1908 she finally advised segregation, she was merely repeating the ideas Canright advanced in 1876. Moreover, the priority she gave to evangelizing white people indicated that Adventism, in racial terms, had changed little during the intervening years. It was still a white movement, with a mission to a white America, and blacks were not allowed to jeopardize the evangelistic objective of the denomination.

But what began as an evangelistic expedient eventually became the denomination's preferred method of dealing with the races, especially as the black membership grew. Between 1894 and 1918, the number of black Adventists increased from 50 to 3,500.[25] As more blacks came in, the pattern of institutional segregation became more entrenched. In 1927 a Scottish Adventist, Mrs. Nellie Druillard, established Riverside Sanitarium in Nashville, Tennessee, specifically for blacks. This was followed in 1934 by the founding of the black magazine *Message*, which has since been the voice of black Adventism as well as a major tool for evangelizing American Negroes. The most important institutional development, however, was the formation of black regional conferences in 1944. The black Adventist population then stood at nearly 18,000, approximately 8.5 percent of the Adventist membership in America at that time.[26] At the behest of black leaders, the General Conference created conference structures solely for the black churches. Eight of these have so far been formed around the country. The black conferences, although administered by blacks for blacks, bear the same relationship to the union administration as other Adventist conferences.[27]

The formation of regional conferences cemented the principle of separate development, which had been implicit from the moment blacks first turned up at Adventist gatherings. In some ways, the events of 1944 put into practice the Supreme Court decision of 1896, which saw the two races, at least in theory, as "separate but equal." Given the racial climate in the nation as a whole, it might be thought that the development of black Adventist conferences was inevitable. But this is not necessarily true. Adventists shared the problem of blacks with other American sects. The Jehovah's Witnesses, however, showed a markedly greater capacity for racial integration than did the Adventists.[28] The Mormons, on the other hand, unashamedly held to a doctrine of white supremacy, barring blacks from the priesthood and avoiding contact with them.[29] It was Adventism that most closely followed national trends in that it accepted blacks into its community but adopted segregationist policies.

The Adventist church also harbored a great deal of prejudice. Regional conferences had been created in the shadow of a notorious incident of racial discrimination. In 1944 the Adventist Washington Sanitarium refused to treat a black woman after she had fallen ill while visiting the capital. Mrs. Lucy Byard, an Adventist from New York, was then rushed to another hospital in the city. But the delay was fatal. Mrs. Byard died of pneumonia before she could be properly treated. Faced by an outraged constituency, the church's black lay and administrative leadership started the campaign that resulted in the formation of black conferences.[30]

The policy of not treating blacks in the church's hospitals was only one aspect of Adventist discrimination. Blacks were barred from Adventist schools and, despite their growing numbers and increasing education, were denied equal opportunities within the general church body. These practices put black Adventists in a dilemma. Should they remain within an organization they otherwise felt to be right? Or should they leave a church whose racial policies were, to them, un-Christian? Many stayed. But some, like John M. Ragland, found racial discrimination too much to take, and left. Others like J. K. Humphrey were expelled for pursuing what they considered to be a better deal for the church's blacks.

The case of John Ragland is probably typical of many black Adventists in the first half of the twentieth century. The son of Virginian slaves, Ragland's problems began when he fell foul of the church's dislike of interracial marriages. At the denomination's Emmanuel Missionary College during 1908–9, he had what he described as "a running love affair" with a white woman named Ester Pearce.[31] In the face of opposition from school officials and Ester's brother (although not apparently from her father), the couple managed to maintain the relationship. However, one day Ragland was called into the president's office and was told he could not marry a white woman. "That night," he recalled, "I got up at one o'clock and left the dormitory and walked through the fields to the banks of the St. Joe River, just outside the little town of Berrien Springs, to commit suicide."[32] He contemplated his future for an hour before deciding not to jump into the water. Not long afterward, the college sent Ragland to work at the Review and Herald publishing house in Washington, which apparently ended his relationship with Miss Pearce.

The final straw, however, was the situation at Battle Creek Sanitarium, where Ragland went to work a few years later. He recalled that black and white workers were not allowed to eat together. This so insulted him that he decided not only to leave the Adventist church but to leave America altogether. The sanitarium was not at this time an Adventist institution, as Kellogg had maintained control after he left the denomination in 1907. However, in Ragland's mind the sanitarium was still associated with the denomination. Ragland was ninety-three when he related his story, so it is possible that his memory was faulty. But if the sanitarium he described was Kellogg's rather than the church's institution, then Ragland's experience there would cast some doubt on Kellogg's liberal reputation. It suggests that even Kellogg eventually allowed segregationist practices at his institutions.

Ragland moved to Canada but soon returned to Detroit, where he began a successful career as a public official, playing an important part in advancing the cause of blacks in different parts of the country. In the 1920s, as industrial secretary of the Louisville Urban League, he organized what he claimed was the first public housing program for blacks in the United States and saw the first Negroes onto the local police force—apparently, the first south of the Mason-Dixon line. In 1940 he became a racial consultant for Ohio's social security department, and in 1949 he received thirty-two lines in *Who's Who in America*. After a long period of estrangement, he returned to the Adventist church in the late 1960s, vowing never to leave the denomination again over the issue of race.[33]

In the end, John Ragland satisfactorily bridged the gap between his deep personal anguish and his belief in the church. J. K. Humphrey was not as lucky. Humphrey was a black Baptist minister who became an Adventist in 1902. He was a man of considerable gifts and was chosen to lead a newly formed black group in New York shortly after his conversion. Later, he founded the First Harlem Seventh-day Adventist Church, which grew rapidly under his leadership. The church, whose membership reached 600 in 1920, spawned the Second Harlem Church in 1924. It was in the 1920s that Humphrey became increasingly concerned with the status of blacks in the Adventist church. Everywhere he looked, he saw discrimination: in the church's schools, hospitals, sanitariums, and conferences. No doubt Humphrey's vision was affected by the stirring events that were then occurring on his doorstep. Harlem in the 1920s was an exciting place to be black. Marcus Garvey's black nationalist movement was in full swing. Humphrey, like Garvey, was a Jamaican, but his own solution to the problem of unyielding racism was the organization of black conferences. Along with several other black leaders, Humphrey canvassed this idea at the denomination's Spring Council meeting in 1929. The General Conference responded by setting up a commission to study the proposal.

Humphrey left the Spring Council convinced—rightly as it turned out—that the General Conference had no intention of accepting the black leadership's wishes. He therefore started work on a secret communitarian project. He called it Utopia Park. It would be situated just outside New York City and would consist of an orphanage, an old people's home, a training school, an industrial area, and health care facilities. If blacks could not go back to Africa as Garvey advocated, at least they could retreat to Utopia Park, "the fortune spot of America for colored people," as Humphrey billed it. The Adventist pastor emphasized that the park would not be just for Adventists but would be open to all blacks in the United States.

Inevitably, word of Humphrey's plans leaked out to his conference superiors. Alarmed at Humphrey's secret project, they decided to defrock him. They had, however, to reckon with the First Harlem Church. When their decision was put to the congregation on November 2, 1929, members closed ranks behind Humphrey and denounced conference leaders for their actions. At one point, the meeting became so heated that only Humphrey's intervention prevented a full-scale riot from developing. Church officials had no option but to disfellowship the church as well. The church reformed under the name United Sabbath-Day Adventist Church. In the black press, Humphrey and his members were viewed as part of the black man's struggle against white oppression. The United Sabbath-Day Adventist Church exists today, but the dream of Utopia Park eventually foundered on legal and financial difficulties. In retrospect, Humphrey's mistake seems only to have been his premature support for black conferences. He was ahead of his time in his efforts to combat racial discrimination.[34]

The extent of that discrimination pervaded even the General Conference. W. H. Green, who became the first black head of the denomination's Negro department in 1918, and his successors, G. E. Peters and F. L. Peterson, all came up against the color line that operated at church headquarters. Calvin E. Moseley, who became the fourth black to head the Negro department in 1953, recalled the situation when he arrived:

It was very uncomfortable from the very first. There were a number of southern white people in high positions in the General Conference at the time and
they brought their prejudices with them. I could not eat in the General Conference cafeteria with everyone else. Some whites would not even greet you
when they saw you in the morning. When they saw you coming, they would
look at you, look by you—there would be no greeting at all. This was largely
on the part of the womenfolk, but once in while the men would do it too.[35]

What accounted for all this prejudice? It was certainly true, as Moseley
suggests, that many Adventists simply imbibed the deep-seated attitudes of the times. But there were also some specific characteristics of
the church that made Adventists susceptible to prejudiced behavior. It
is quite likely that the desire to remain aloof from social problems may
have made the church rather insensitive to the issue of race.[36] The
policy on church and state also made white Adventists reluctant to
speak out on racial injustice. The question of race was subordinated to
what they considered to be the greater good of the church. Adventist
leaders believed it was to their advantage to accept the racial policies
that existed in America and later to adopt them for their own use. As
the Adventist A. W. Spalding explained in an unpublished history of
the black work: "Injustice and oppression are repugnant to the Christian; pride and disdain are foreign to his heart; but his Christian experience should not therefore lead him to start a crusade against customs which do not interfere with the Christian's duty."[37]

As a result of this attitude, the church did not openly support the
principle of black equality. Rather, as Abraham Lincoln had done during his senatorial debates with Stephen Douglas in 1858, Adventists
denied that blacks were equal to whites for fear of becoming unpop-
ular.[38] During his mission down the Mississippi River, Edson White and
his associate, F. R. Rogers, often met with hostile opposition from white
groups. In Yazoo City, Mississippi, the editor of the city newspaper
viciously attacked the Adventist workers for, among other things, teaching equality of the races.[39] In a letter to the paper, Rogers wrote: "Understanding the reports that have been circulated about us and our
work, I wish to state to the public, in order to right myself on these
matters, that we DO NOT believe in social equality, neither do we teach
or practise it."[40] Ellen White, too, made similar statements. She advised
that the mingling of whites and blacks in social equality was not to be
encouraged.[41] "The colored people," she wrote, "should not urge that
they be placed on an equality with white people."[42] Although not intended for the purpose, these sentiments undoubtedly helped those
within the movement who wanted to keep blacks "in their place" and
who wanted to justify discrimination against them.

The perpetuation of racial prejudice was also perhaps connected with
the changing relationship between the races in America. The Civil War
marked the point in American history when the relationship between

whites and blacks changed from a master-servant model to a competitive model. When in 1863 Abraham Lincoln emancipated slaves, he freed them to compete on an equal footing in society. But in order to maintain its position, the white majority created new forms of subordination. Blacks were segregated, disenfranchised, and denied equal opportunities on the labor market. While the master-servant relationship persisted, there was no need for this. But the white majority evidently felt it needed to maintain control of blacks by political means that were supported, through organizations like the Ku Klux Klan, by violence. It was the Emancipation Proclamation that uncorked the potent bottle of white racism.[43]

Something similar occurred in Adventism. Although the relationship between whites and blacks in the church was never one of master-servant, it was certainly one of master-pupil. In 1903 Edson White revealed to the readers of the *Review* how he saw the blacks in the South. He described them as "a world within a world," "intensely religious" but of having "no refining influence over them, because they have no associations with those who have had the opportunity for education, culture, and refinement." They were "a superstitious people," he wrote. "You could not expect anything else. When we began holding meetings on the boat [the *Morning Star*], the people who came once would always come again, and a story was started that the people who came onto the boat were 'hoodooed.' " He continued: "We need schools in the South, not only to teach these people how to read, but to teach them how to work, to teach them trades, the use of implements, and how to farm."[44] The Adventist missionary saw it as his duty to educate the uneducated Negro.

But this relationship changed as blacks became literate. The best illustration of the black membership's educational advance was Eva B. Dyke's achievement in becoming the first black woman in America—and possibly in the world—to earn a Ph.D. She completed her doctorate at Harvard in 1921.[45] Blacks lost their superstitions and began to compete with whites on an equal footing within the movement. As that competition increased, the nature of Adventist discrimination became sharper and more intense, and the white majority became more committed to denying blacks equal status in the church. Precisely when the relationship between the races moved from paternalism to competition is difficult to determine. But the formation of black conferences was the acknowledgment that it had happened.

The competitive phase of race relations helps explain why blacks often revert to a self-imposed segregation. There have always been two poles in the history of the Negro in the United States. One is the push for integration and equal rights. The other, the desire for separation and withdrawal from white society. Integration is perhaps the initial goal, but if competition becomes too fierce and the white majority proves too intransigent, blacks are likely to see separation as the best way forward. Segregation is then seen as the answer to discrimination. Certainly, in the Adventist case, blacks proposed regional conferences after they felt integration was an unobtainable goal. In the next two decades, this general pattern was continued. Black Adventists fought for equal status and participation in the church, but the 1960s ended with many of them calling for greater organizational separation. The Adventist experience was again similar to a nation that in this period produced both Martin Luther King's dream of complete integration and the militant separatism of the Black Muslims.

The Civil Rights movement of the 1960s at first heightened racial tensions in the denomination. An incident that occurred at an Adventist church in Alabama dramatically portrayed the uneasy relationship that existed between the races in the early 1960s. The church, composed mostly of white members, invited a group from Oakwood College to present a Sabbath program. Arriving at the church, the black group found a roped-off section for them to sit in. However, the section could not hold them all, so some of them attempted to find seats elsewhere in the church. As this was against the church's policies, the deacons tried, unsuccessfully, to usher the blacks out. In the midst of the confusion, an elder stood up, pulled out a gun, and declared: "I've got six bullets here and they all say nigger on them." The minister's wife started to cry. "We love you niggers," she said, "but we just don't want you to sit with us."[46]

In other cases, white Adventists linked arms outside their churches to prevent blacks from entering them.[47] Similar battles were played out in the church's schools. When a black girl was refused admission to an Adventist academy, her parents publicly attacked the denomination for what they considered to be a clear example of racial prejudice. This incident prompted a large protest at the denomination's General Conference session in San Francisco in 1962. About a thousand black Seventh-day Adventists gathered in the city in a demonstration of defiance at the church's racial policies. The event attracted considerable attention in the local press.[48]

Eventually, church leaders responded to the pressure for change. Typically, however, they distanced themselves from the campaigns inside and outside the denomination. In a 1965 editorial in the Review, F. D. Nichol implicitly criticized clergymen who took part in the freedom marches. He wrote that the Adventist church sympathized with "those underprivileged," but it did not feel that the answer lay in social protest. Revealing once again the priority given to the church's mission, he stated, "We have ever felt that we can best reveal true Christianity and thus best advance the Advent cause, by taking the more quiet and perhaps indirect approach to problems that so often arouse human passions."[49]

But throughout this period, major pillars of Adventist segregation were falling. In 1965 the *Review* carried actions of the General Conference committee that called for the ending of racial discrimination in the denomination's schools, hospitals, and churches.[50] The General Conference cafeteria had already been desegregated in the 1950s. But the integration of Adventist schools was a slow process. Southern College in Tennessee, a bastion of white Southern Adventism, admitted its first black students in 1968 after a bitter struggle, five years after the last state university, Alabama, had integrated its campus.[51] The church also appointed more blacks in leadership positions. In 1962 Frank L. Peterson became the first of several blacks to hold the position of general vice-president of the General Conference. In addition, Adventist publishing houses put out books and articles to educate the membership on racial matters. Among the most significant were Ron Graybill's *E. G. White and Church Race Relations* (1970), which presented the prophetess as a champion of racial equality, and the series of articles by Roy Branson that appeared in the same year.

Despite the moves toward integration, the black conferences remained. Indeed, the controversies of the 1960s convinced many black leaders that only through the creation of black unions, the next level of government in Adventism, could parity be reached with whites. The question, for the black Adventist E. E. Cleveland, was one of power. He saw that union presidents were decisive figures in church administration but that blacks had very little hope of reaching such positions. He thus supported black unions because it was "imperative that black men have someone at Union Conference level to speak for them".[52] However, Calvin Rock, another black leader, later argued for black unions on the grounds of the genuine cultural differences that exist between the races.[53] He also had in his support the fact that the separation of the black work had apparently led to a spectacular increase in the black membership. Between 1944 and 1970, the number of black Adventists rose from around 18,000 to just under 74,000, or 18 percent of the total American membership. Throughout the 1970s, black unions were debated. The proposal was rejected several times during the decade by General Conference committees.[54] But the black constituency received some consolation when a black man, Charles Bradford, was appointed president of the North American Division in 1979.

In addition to the calls for greater separation, black leaders also raised the level of black consciousness in the 1970s. This was not dissimilar to the "black is beautiful" movement of the 1960s. The roots of this in Adventism, however, went back to 1934, when Frank L. Peterson published *The Hope of the Race*. It contained the traditional Adventist themes, but it differed from all Adventist books before it in the attention it paid to black history. Its pages were sprinkled with photographs of black heroes such as Booker T. Washington and the singer

Roland Hayes. The book celebrated the black experience almost as much as the Adventist message.[55] E. E. Cleveland wrote a similar book in 1970 called *Free at Last*. The inside cover contained a collage of famous black figures from Jesse Owens to George Washington Carver. The book was dedicated to the black man's hopes and, like Peterson's work, was clearly a black interpretation of Adventism.[56]

Because they have sought to establish a black identity as well as an Adventist identity, black Adventists have drawn inspiration from black role models outside the Adventist community. Conversely, prominent blacks who emerged from Adventism, such as the writer Richard Wright, strongly asserted black pride. Wright's most famous novel, *Native Son* (1940), revolves around a black character who finally discovers a meaning for his existence when he accidentally kills his white employer's daughter.[57] Little Richard is also noted for his black consciousness. When the rock singer retired in the late 1950s, he attended the black Adventist institution Oakwood College, where he particularly enjoyed classes in black history. Although he resumed his musical career in the early 1960s, he again turned to religion in the 1970s, when he established an independent ministry aimed at Afro-Americans that drew inspiration from, among others, the black Adventist leader, E. E. Cleveland.[58] The black identity of Prince, the other world-famous singer with an Adventist background, is also marked. Prince's Adventist heritage reveals itself in the strongly apocalyptic content of many of his songs.[59] In contrast, the black musicians produced by the Jehovah's Witnesses, such as Michael Jackson and George Benson, draw little on their racial or religious heritage.[60] It would appear that the black artists who emerge from Adventism have a stronger and more aggressive sense of racial identity than do their counterparts from the Jehovah's Witnesses—a sect with a better record of racial integration.

In a famous study of race relations, Robert Park and Ernest Burgess argued in 1921 that blacks would eventually be assimilated into American society.[61] In the equally famous 1944 analysis *An American Dilemma: The Negro Problem and Modern Democracy*, Gunnar Myrdal made the same assumptions. He believed that not only did blacks want to be assimilated but that this was the only viable option.[62] With the early emergence of individuals such as W. E. B. Dubois, Marcus Garvey, and even Booker T. Washington, it is doubtful if black leaders have seen integration as their only objective. But it was the black nationalist movement of the later 1960s that forced sociologists to recognize the separatist, as well as the integrationist, impulse in black history.[63]

The paradox of race, observed the writer Joel Williamson, "is that black people have to get out of white society in order to get into it, and they have to get into it in order to get out. They have to get into the society to get a minimum of those palpable things that people need in order simply to survive—material goods, education, government, a minimum of justice. . . . Yet because white people are prejudiced and have the power to manifest their prejudices in a multitude of ways, they have to get out . . . to maintain a sense of worth and self-esteem."[64] In their own experience of race relations, Adventists have provided a small illustration of this aspect of American society. The separation of races in the church witnesses to the continuing tensions between them, and Williamson's paradox appear to apply to the Adventist black, who, although perhaps loved by his white brothers, has never been totally convinced that they want him to sit with them.

CHAPTER 16

Ministers

Disharmony among church members can, of course, be occasioned by many issues in addition to that of race. Denominational leaders generally try to maintain unity and order even, as has been the case in race relations, at the price of ethical compromise. Their agents in this difficult task are the ordained ministers of the church. They are expected to lead exemplary lives while at the same time giving priority to their professional responsibilities. This chapter examines the tensions inherent in the position of those called on to be model individuals and to be committed to sustaining the efficiency of a complex social organization.

Among the major sects that emerged in nineteenth-century America, the Seventh-day Adventist church was the only one that developed a professional ministry. The Mormons did not do so, nor did the Jehovah's Witnesses or the Christian Scientists. Adventists, however, had ministers from the start. This was largely due to the church's distinctive origins. The Millerites had converted many established ministers, some of whom later became Sabbatarians. One example was Frederick Wheeler, who was effectively the first Adventist minister. Wheeler was an ordained clergyman of the Methodist Episcopal church when he became impressed with Millerite views around 1842. Two years later, he accepted the Sabbath and thereafter led what was essentially the first Seventh-day Adventist congregation in Washington, New Hampshire. Another example was James White, ordained in 1843 by an obscure denomination called the Christian Connection. Wheeler, White, and others like them provided the burgeoning church with a ready-made ministry.

As Adventism gradually expanded throughout America after the Shut-Door era, more ministers were appointed. Often, as in the pre-1844 period, they were clergymen previously ordained in other denominations. M. B. Czechowski, the church's first unofficial missionary, is an example. Czechowski was a Catholic priest and then a Baptist minister before being converted to Adventism in 1857. Other individuals who joined the Adventist ministry usually had farming backgrounds. Elbert B. Lane, the evangelist who pioneered the Adventist work in the Southern states, was among many people in the Midwest who ran a farm before beginning a ministerial career in the 1860s. A third type of ministerial recruit was the very young convert who demonstrated particular ability or commitment and who subsequently rose rapidly in the Adventist hierarchy. Among those who fell into this category were J. N. Andrews, J. N. Loughborough, and Uriah Smith. All were in their early twenties when they were ordained.[1]

By 1876, the Adventist Church possessed 166 working ministers (96 of whom were ordained) who supervised 398 churches in America.[2] According to the Adventist historian A. W. Spalding, individuals without previous ministerial training were educated during evangelistic tent meetings. "A young man aiming at the ministry," he wrote, "was taken into company with an evangelist, and acted as his tent master." The prospective pastor had to erect and maintain the tent, advertise and promote meetings, lead out in congregational singing and, "on some fateful evening to try his callow wings at preaching."[3] It was not long, however, before the denomination's leaders decided that pastors needed more formal academic training. In 1874, the church founded its first college in Battle Creek, Michigan. Planned in part as a ministerial training center, the college gave Adventism's increasing number of home-grown ministers the opportunity to obtain formal qualifications.

Additionally, the General Conference devised rigorous reading programs for the edification and improvement of Adventist pastors. For example, in 1881 church officials recommended for Adventist ministers a six-year reading course that was remarkable for its breadth. In addition to denominational publications, Ellen White books, and works of practical ministry, church pastors were expected to read Rollin's entire multivolume *Ancient History*, Gibbon's *Decline and Fall*, and D'Aubigne's *History of the Reformation*. They were to study standard histories of England and the United States and were expected to be fully conversant with authors as varied as Josephus, Eusebius, and Hagenbach.[4]

However, these attempts to improve the Adventist ministry seem to have failed. Because the need for workers was so great, it appears that few ministerial students actually finished the course at Battle Creek before taking up pastoral responsibilities. Nor did the prescribed reading courses improve the competence of Adventist pastors. Toward the end of the nineteenth century General Conference President O. A. Olsen lamented the "exceedingly weak" condition of the Adventist clergy. This situation shortchanged local members who were, Olsen reported, "in many things ahead of the ministry."[5] Such criticism spurred on the professionalization of the clergy. Significant steps included the creation in 1922 of the General Conference's Ministerial

Association, an organization designed to cater to the interests of Adventist clergy, and the founding in 1928 of *Ministry* magazine, which provided a forum for the exchange of ideas.

But the most important development was the establishment in 1937 of the Seventh-day Adventist Theological Seminary in Takoma Park, Maryland. The seminary soon became the premier center for ministerial training, although preparatory theology courses continued to be offered at the denomination's colleges. Within a decade, the seminary had developed full master of arts and bachelor of divinity degrees (the master of divinity replaced the bachelor of divinity in 1972) and had founded departments of archaeology and history of antiquity, Bible and systematic theology, biblical languages, church history, and practical theology. In 1959, the institution moved to Berrien Springs in Michigan to become part of Andrews University. In the 1970s the seminary inaugurated its first doctoral programs and received accreditation from the American Association of Theological Schools.[6]

Some indication of the type of ministry the seminary helped to create is revealed in the definitive 1980s study *Ministry in America*.

Researchers of the Association of Theological Schools in the United States and Canada and of the research agency Search Institute identified four different models of ministry in contemporary North America. They are (1) the spiritual emphasis model practiced by various Baptist groups, (2) the sacramental-liturgical model favored by the Roman Catholic and Orthodox churches, (3) the social action model of Jewish and Unitarian groups, and (4) the model of combined emphases which incorporates different features of the first three models. Lutherans, Methodists, and Presbyterians are the chief exponents of this type of ministry.[7]

Along with several other bodies (the Church of God, the Church of the Nazarene, Swedenborgians, the Evangelical Congregational Church, the General Conference Churches of God, and the Evangelical Covenant Church of America), Seventh-day Adventists were found to conform, in general, to the spiritual emphasis model of ministry. In this, the Bible and the person of God are given primary place in preaching, teaching, and worship. A conservative biblical faith is generally espoused, and evangelism is considered of great importance. Emphasis is also placed on religious piety, God's forgiveness, sanctification, and born-again Christianity. A secular lifestyle, which is viewed as detrimental to Christian development, is discouraged, and theological counseling and the resources of faith are emphasized in helping members cope with their personal problems.[8]

The researchers noted that in the spiritually oriented ministry, great emphasis is placed on the personal conduct and behavior of the minister. The pastor is expected to set an unimpeachable Christian example, and if he does not, his ministry is likely to be called into question. In the other models of ministry, the personal example of the minister is not considered as essential to effective pastoral work, not even in the liturgically oriented churches where the clergy are otherwise deeply committed. Indeed, it was discovered that some denominations do not want their clergy to appear too pious. For denominations that emphasize a spiritual ministry, this is seldom a serious concern. Any hint of a lack of piety or of a secular lifestyle will normally hinder the pastor's ministry to his congregation.[9]

In the case of Seventh-day Adventists, the *Ministry in America* study was certainly correct. Adventist ministers have long been warned that their personal lifestyle has a vital effect on their pastoral performance. "An unsanctified minister," Ellen White wrote, 'can do incalculable harm. While professing to be the ambassador of Christ, his example will be copied by others; and if he lacks the true characteristics of a Christian, his faults and deficiencies will be reproduced in them."[10] Mrs. White wrote a great deal on the type of ministers she felt were fit to lead Adventist congregations. Her counsels seemed to cover everything from their dress (which should be of dark color) to their platform manner (which should be cultured and dignified).[11] She envisaged only holy men in the Adventist pulpit: "The minister of Christ should possess sobriety, meekness, love, long-suffering, forbearance, pity and courtesy. He should be circumspect, elevated in thought and conversation, and of blameless deportment."[12]

A great deal has always been expected of Adventist ministers. What sort of contemporary individuals decide to bear these heavy responsibilities? In general, it can be said that the people who become Adventist ministers possess a strong sense of God's calling. The call to the ministry is strongly emphasized within Adventism and is an important force in motivating young men to consider a pastoral career. On the other hand, some Adventist ministers do admit to having "rationalized" calls after career plans did not work out as they had hoped. Even in these cases, however, there is still evidence of a serious desire to discover God's will: failed career plans are interpreted as signs of God's leading toward the denominational pulpit. This indicates that the person who decides to become an Adventist pastor possesses a high degree of Christian commitment, probably higher than the average church member. The individual who chooses the ministry may previously have been an active church member, a leader in his church's youth department. Similarly, the prospective Adventist minister is often a new convert. Joining the church's ministerial work force tends to be seen by converts as the most natural way to demonstrate further their deep commitment to the church—a tradition that seems to date back to the days of Andrews, Loughborough, and Smith. While it would be unwise to make too much of this fact, it is clear that a significant proportion of students studying theology in the denomination's colleges in any given year have been members of the church for only two years or less.

As a group, the church's ministers tend to be slightly unusual. Using the 16PF character test, Andrews University's Institute of Church Ministry (ICM) found in 1982 that in many personality traits, the Adventist minister is likely to be significantly different from an ordinary member of the population. His composite personality is revealed as more outgoing, intelligent, conscientious, and venturesome than average. He is also more tender minded and imaginative and possesses a greater capacity for shrewdness, self-sufficiency, and self-discipline. On the 16PF scale, however, the Adventist pastor is less happy-go-lucky, less suspicious, and less apprehensive than the normal individual. Being rather conservative, he is also, the ICM found, less inclined to experiment.[13]

The Institute of Church Ministry discovered that Adventist pastors possess an above-average school achievement potential.[14] This is not at all surprising, for the young man who embarks on theological training cannot expect to enter the Adventist ministry until he has completed at least five years of undergraduate and postgraduate study. This period can rise to seven years if he takes the recommended masters of divinity (M. Div.) course at the theological seminary. Unless the ministerial candidate does possess high academic potential—and the ability to endure many years of study—he is unlikely to realize his ambitions to join the church's ministerial work force. For these reasons, many do not.

In addition to possessing academic ability and the personal spiritual qualities that Mrs. White described, the modern Adventist minister also needs to master a wide variety of other skills. As one Adventist clergyman wrote in 1966: "To fulfill his responsibilities today a pastor must be an administrator, an organizer, a promoter, a salesman, a businessman, a financier, a fund raiser, a builder, a public relations expert, a personnel director, and a counselor on marriage and family relations in addition to his calling as a preacher, shepherd and soul winner."[15]

As a consequence of the multifaceted nature of the Adventist ministry, there is no unanimity among the denomination's pastors as to exactly what the pastor's role should be. In sorting out their priorities, they have basically three considerations to take into account: the expectations of their church members, the expectations of their conference administrators, and their own inclinations. Left to themselves, Adventist ministers (according to a 1981 ICM study on pastoral morale) derive by far the most satisfaction from preaching and personal evangelism or from giving Bible studies. Next in their priorities are visiting people, public evangelism, and counseling.[16] The area of ministry Adventist ministers most dislike is motivating church members to fulfill their various responsibilities.[17] The difficulties here may be related to the personality characteristics of the church's clergymen. Adventist ministers do not appear to be comfortable in an aggressive leadership role. They are not always sure when they should lead or when they should follow their congregations. The 1982 ICM study discovered that the majority of the church's pastors (nearly 78 percent) possess only a moderate leadership capability and are less dominant than the average person.[18] In general, Adventist ministers tend to be rather submissive, which may explain why they dislike exerting pressure on their members. In addition, administrative work, dealing with members' problems, and the time consumed by attending various church committees and business meetings are also significant causes of frustration to the Adventist pastor.[19]

In some cases, the preferences of Adventist pastors would seem to correspond with those of their parishioners. The *Ministry in America* study showed that of all the surveyed churches, the laity of the denominational family that included Adventists (along with the Christian Disciples and United Methodists) attached the highest importance to competent preaching and worship leading. This group also recorded very high scores for evangelism, with only the laity of another evangelical grouping, the Southern Baptist and Christian (non-Disciples) churches, scoring higher.[20] The apparent agreement between the preferences of church pastors and the expectations of their members does not imply, however, that the Adventist laity is always satisfied with the actual performance of its clergymen. Preaching is an important case in point. In 1973 the Adventist youth magazine *Insight* found that many young people who had left the church often blamed what they considered to be the poor quality of Adventist preaching.[21] There would also appear to be some areas of genuine disagreement between the inclinations of the church's ministers and the wishes of the membership. Administrative work, for example, was ranked as the second greatest cause of frustration and disappointment in the ministry. But although the Adventist clergy dislike this aspect of their calling, their members seem to expect it. The *Ministry in America* survey found that more than any other church group, the laity of the Adventist family of churches regard the effective administration of church affairs as important.[22] Similarly, even though dealing with members' problems was the third-ranking cause of dissatisfaction among Adventist ministers, the *Ministry in America* study found that the laity of the Adventist grouping attached the highest importance to the "caring availability" of the pastor. More than the laity of most other denominations, Adventist church members desire their clergy to be ready and available to help them through crisis situations.[23]

It would be unwise to draw too many definite conclusions from the juxtaposition of the results of the ICM survey on pastoral morale and the *Ministry in America* study. The surveys were made in different contexts and, in the case of *Ministry in America* encompassed more than just the Adventist church. Nevertheless, it would appear that in certain areas the expectations of the membership are a source of frustration for Adventist ministers. In some cases, therefore, there may be a discrepancy between lay and clerical perceptions of the ministerial role.

The other main cause of dissatisfaction among Adventist ministers appear to result from the expectations of their conference superiors. The ICM survey of 1981 found that the joint fifth-ranked area of frustration was the promotion of the annual ingathering campaign, and the joint sixth-ranked problem concerned the promotion of Conference programs in general. The eighth-ranked problem was listed simply as "conference administration." Moreover, when ministers were given the opportunity in the ICM questionnaire to suggest changes to the pattern of the Adventist ministry, four of their first ten suggestions advocated less intrusion but more understanding from conference officers. What the surveyed pastors wanted was less promotion of conference programs, less administrative direction, more understanding and sensitivity from the conference, and more input from ministers in setting conference goals.[24]

In the survey, some ministers also indicated that they would like their conferences to provide them with longer tenures.[25] As pastors are appointed to local congregations by conference administrators, they are seldom allowed to stay at one church for more than a few years. The church's ministerial workers are treated rather like a government's diplomatic corps: they are moved on every few years and are expected to promote the interests of their superiors wherever they are stationed. If, for example, funds are needed to build a radio station in a corner of the Third World, or a new, special offering needs to be brought to the attention of the membership, then the minister is the one to undertake these tasks. Such ambassadorial functions ensure that the minister's loyalties stay with the conference administration rather than the local congregation, just as an ambassador's loyalties reside with the home government rather than with the assigned country. But this kind of function evidently interferes with the minister's own self-perception of his role, which he sees primarily in terms of preaching, evangelism, visiting, and counseling. In the hierarchy of the church's government, the minister has the unenviable task of providing the link between the conference administration and the local church. As such, he is expected to represent the interests of the conference to his congregation, but he must also represent the interests of the local church to the conference. In the case of obtaining denominational funds for a new church building, for example, the minister and congregation are usually united in their representations to the conference. But the process can work the other way around. In the promotion of evangelism, the conference and the minister are sometimes allies against idle congregations.

Generally, however, Adventist minsiters feel they do not receive enough support from their conference leaders, especially during personal crises in the ministers' own lives. The ICM survey on pastoral morale quoted one minister who had undergone a painful divorce. "I felt totally unhelped by the conference leadership," he said. "I got more help from a Pentecostal pastor and counselor than from our people. Sad but true. Even though I was not at fault . . . I lost my job."[26] Significantly, "more understanding and sensitivity from the conference" came high on the list for change in the Adventist ministry. Furthermore, 34 percent of the surveyed pastors were concerned about not meeting the approval of their respective conference officials. In the isolated nature of church ministry (58 percent of the surveyed ministers admitted to feelings of loneliness and isolation in the job), many pastors would be grateful of more help from their superiors.[27] The Adventist pastor, in general, has no one to turn to. As one of them said in the ICM survey: "Being a pastor is the loneliest job in the world. You are not really a conference official, so you feel fully accepted there; you are not really a church member, so they cannot fully accept you. You have no one who is your minister, no one you can fully trust."[28]

It may be thought that Adventist pastors receive some support from their peers. But strangely, there does not appear to be a great deal of solidarity among the church's ministers. This is partly because the nature of their work means that they seldom have time to see their ministerial friends. But it is also partly due to a subtle competition that Adventist pastors say exists among them, especially in evangelism. Such competition, and the petty jealousies that can result, may be a function of conference pressures. Ministers are not particularly happy with this situation. "More opportunities for interrelationships with other Adventist pastors" was one of the fifth-ranked suggestions for change in the Adventist ministry. Some bemoaned the jealousies among church ministers; others wanted to see "real genuine collegiality" among the denomination's pastors.[29]

In addition to dealing with loneliness and isolation, the Adventist minister must also cope with receiving little recognition for the work he faithfully performs year after year. Although 94 percent of the surveyed ministers said they enjoyed being a pastor and 87 percent believed they were successful in their work, Adventist pastors have few tangible indicators of success, except perhaps the number of people they are baptizing and the number of apostasies they are preventing.[30] There are also very few promotion prospects within the profession. The normal pattern of development is from intern to licensed minister (a status that confers the authority to preside in all but certain reserved ordinances) to ordained minister. The next step is usually up to the conference level, in some administrative or departmental capacity, or perhaps sideways into full-time evangelism. The administrative officer and the working evangelist are the prestige ministerial positions in Adventism, but the opportunities in either area are very limited. Another possible option, but again with limited possibilities, is to progress to the pastorship of one of the denomination's large institutional churches such as those based at Andrews University, Loma Linda University, and at Sligo (near General Conference headquarters) where the membership can be as many as three thousand people. The pastor with academic potential may transfer to the theology department of an Adventist school or college, but here again it is not always easy to do so.

A good prospect can easily become an ordained minister within five years of the commencement of his ministerial career. If by the time he is forty he has not been appointed to a conference office or become a notable evangelist, he may grow increasingly restless. Significantly, 21 percent of the respondents in the ICM survey on pastoral morale were hoping they would soon be called to a conference or teaching position.[31] Some ministers believe that there is a possible connection between the lack of career development after ordination and the problems that often afflict Adventist clergymen. Certainly, many ministers do seem to reach a crisis point a few year after they are ordained. This manifests itself in a variety of ways. A theological problem may develop, as may a problem with the congregation. Problems in the minister's marriage and family may become acute. To alleviate the stress caused by midcareer crisis, some ministers believe that the conference should provide some kind of recognition of senior status—some means, as in the military, of obtaining another stripe.

In addition to the expectations of church members and conference officials, there is one other external factor that has a vital bearing on the Adventist pastor's ministry—his family. The 1981 ICM survey showed quite clearly that the greater the pastor's family problems, the more frustrated he is likely to be in his ministry—a conclusion that only confirms what Mrs. White and others believed about the importance of the minister's wife and home.[32] Seventy-eight percent of the surveyed pastors said that they regularly take time to spend with their wives and children.[33] However, when ministers' wives were themselves studied by the Institute of Church Ministry in 1981, they generally felt they took second place in their husband's priorities and complained that their husbands rarely took time off for recreation or to be with the family.[34]

The minister's vocation puts peculiar strains on his wife and family. Because important aspects of his work—visiting, prayer meetings, evangelistic meetings, and so on—all take place in the evenings, it may be difficult for the Adventist minister to see his family. In addition to the feelings of neglect experienced by the minister's wife, she also has to cope with the exacting expectations of her husband, as well as those of church members and conference officials. In the survey on ministers' wives, these expectations were listed as the chief source of frustration.[35] Similar problems are experienced by ministers' children, who face the daunting prospect of growing up under the critical eye of the congregation. Again, it would be wrong to paint too pessimistic a picture. As with Adventist pastors themselves, the majority of ministers' wives enjoy their position, believe they are successful, and do not feel that ministers' children experience more problems than other children.[36] Nevertheless, the study noted that the nature of the pastor's work exacted a high price from ministerial families. As was true throughout the church as a whole, it was becoming clear by the 1980s that the rate of divorce among the church's ministers was rising at an "alarming rate."[37] Thus, the Adventist pastor is sometimes a victim of the emphasis placed on two vital Adventist institutions: the ministry and the family.

Precisely why the ministry has assumed such importance within Adventism is worth some consideration. Once the Shut-Door era passed, the importance of the ministry grew as it became linked with the evangelistic mission of the denomination. In a series of articles in the *Review* in 1865, James White appeared to lay the theoretical foundations of the Adventist ministry, basing the importance of the ministry on the commission to "go ye into all the world, and preach the gospel." In the first article, he argued that the behavior, spirituality, intellect, and ability of the minister needed to be cultivated, because the preaching of the gospel commission affected man's eternal destiny.[38] Allied to these considerations was another conception of the minister that White developed in his second article. In this instance, he viewed the minister as a sort of watchman—the keeper of the eternal interests of the congregation. The minister is thus the guardian who warns the members of impending dangers. It is his duty to prevent sin from entering the gates. It is also his duty to "watch for the salvation of men."[39] The idea of the minister as the keeper of the gates became a favorite theme of Mrs. White's, and it provided an appropriate framework for her stress on the vital personal qualities required in those who must remain vigilant at their isolated outposts.[40]

Depicting ministers as watchmen is also perhaps an appropriate concept given the church's attitude toward society. Adventists constantly watch looked for evidence of society's malevolent character in anticipation of the day when it will turn its wrath upon them. Viewed in this light the idea of the minister as watchman takes on a symbolic importance. Ministers stand at the gate between the church and an implicitly hostile culture. They keep a watchful eye on the monster that lurks outside the wall that separates Adventism from the rest of America and at the first signs of danger, they act as a sort of early warning system for the Adventist community. This almost military image of the ministry is plainly revealed in the language Mrs. White chose to describe their functions. Ministers, she wrote, "are to stand as watchmen on the walls of Zion, to sound the note of alarm at the approach of the enemy."[41] Elsewhere, the prophetess described Adventist pastors as "sentinels" who must remain constantly "on duty."[42] The importance of the minister in a denomination isolated from the surrounding culture can perhaps also be seen in the way in which ministers are expected to maintain the ideological and structural foundations of Adventism's alternative society. According to Mrs. White, the pastor was to be a "correct exponent"[43] of Adventist doctrine and an upholder of the church's organization.

The strategic importance of the clergy was a major reason why they quickly achieved a position of dominance within the Adventist community. Effectively, the Adventist clergyman was set above the ordinary church member. In many respects, Adventism reverted to a pre-Reformation ethic in its attitude toward God's calling. Martin Luther had taught that all legitimate occupations were of equal worth in the sight of God. Adventists, however, held that the minister's calling was more sacred than others. But in the 1890s the minister's supremacy within Adventism was challenged. At that time, John Harvey Kellogg began to be more open about his deep contempt for Adventist pastors. He considered the men who comprised the Adventist ministry to be uneducated, ignorant, second-rate individuals. He believed that the standing of the doctor was at least as high as the minister. During the 1890s, Kellogg, in the words of those who knew him, "ran down the ministry in every way that he could."[44]

During this period, Mrs. White felt obliged to defend the position of the church's ministers. She had written earlier that physicians had responsibilities greater than those of ministers.[45] Now she argued that "no enterprise should be so conducted as to cause the ministry of the word to be looked upon as an inferior matter.... The highest of all work is ministry in its various lines, and it should be kept before the youth that there is no work more blessed of God than that of the gospel minister." In a reference that seemed particularly aimed at Kellogg (although she did not mention him by name), she went on: "Let not our young men be deterred from entering the ministry. There is a danger that through glowing representations some will be drawn away from the path where God bids them walk. Some have been encouraged to take a course of study in medical lines who ought to be preparing themselves to enter the ministry. The Lord calls for more ministers to labor in His vineyard."[46]

Mrs. White's clear support for the church's ministers provided a suitable foundation for the professionalization of the Adventist ministry that took place later in the twentieth century. But her comments also brought into focus a deep conflict between the church's ministers and doctors—a conflict that was not just about the relative status of these two groups, but one that also embodied fundamental differences about the nature of Adventism. Insofar as they were called upon to insulate the congregation from a hostile world and to sustain the ideological and structural bases of the church's alternative society, ministers personified the Adventist response to the American nation. Adventist doctors, on the other hand, symbolized a new tradition. They were the first group to mount an effective challenge to the authority of the clergy, and to attempt to modify the church's attitude toward the world around it.

CHAPTER 17

Doctors

It was not anticipated that the church's ministers and doctors would come to represent alternative interpretations of the Adventist tradition. The two groups were to work in tandem. Like harnessed horses, they were to pull the Adventist carriage at the same speed, along the same route. Perhaps for a time they did. Until the 1890s, Mrs. White did not find it necessary to discuss the relative status of ministers and doctors. They were both equally vital in disseminating the church's message, which, on the one hand, concerned a distinctive theology and, on the other, an unusual emphasis on health. But ever since Dr. Kellogg had taken over the Battle Creek Sanitarium in 1876, he had slowly been redefining the nature of Adventism. He presented a reinterpretation that challenged both the church's internal management and the way in which Adventism related to American society. Mrs. White's implicit rebuke of Kellogg was not simply an attempt to put the Adventist doctor in his place. It can also be seen as an effort to stem a form of Adventism that, by the 1890s, threatened to upset the balance of the church's relationship with the Republic.

Kellogg's Adventism revolved around an almost fanatical devotion to health reform. He used the Battle Creek Sanitarium as a platform to promote "biologic living"—a system of human perfection that could be reached through obedience to natural law and the strict control of diet. Kellogg was one of the few Adventists to take seriously Mrs. White's views on health. The church's ministers in the nineteenth century did not regard health as central to the Adventist message. As a medical practitioner, Kellogg found this difficult to understand. He viewed Adventism from the perspective of health reform rather than the other way round. He arrived at deviant theological positions as a direct result of his adherence to biologic living. In a letter to Mrs. White in 1898, he argued that those saved at the Second Coming would be those who had overcome the power of disease—a condition that could only be reached through obedience to health reform. On this basis, he questioned the church's traditional understanding of the seal of God (Sabbath keeping) and the mark of the beast (Sunday worship). He argued that these concepts had less to do with adherence to different days of the week than with obedience to the laws of health. He wrote: "It seems to me our people have been wrong in regarding Sunday observance as the sole mark of the beast. . . . [It] is simply the change of character and body which comes from the surrender of the will to Satan."[1]

This erosion of the church's theological foundations was accompanied by a diminution of Adventist distinctiveness. This is best seen in the development of Battle Creek Sanitarium. When Kellogg was appointed superintendent, he aimed to make the institution a force in the community. Local residents were invited to attend sanitarium functions, and the institution advertised extensively throughout the country. Into its wards flowed a constant stream of famous visitors and patients. It is true that many of them came because Kellogg offered special rates, but his success in creating an institution attractive to the world's elite was remarkable.[2]

A key element in this success was Kellogg's rejection of Adventist peculiarity. In 1897 he declared, much to the consternation of Adventist leaders, that the work of the sanitarium was "of an undenominational, unsectarian, humanitarian and philanthropic nature."[3] When he stated that the sanitarium was not in the business "of presenting anything that is peculiarly Seventh-day Adventist in doctrine," Kellogg placed the sanitarium on a path that diverged from traditional Adventism.[4] The institution met the outside world on medical and humanitarian grounds rather than on a specifically Adventist basis. What mattered was one's state of health, not one's theology. Kellogg's belief that disease constituted the mark of the beast and that those sealed at the end were those who overcame it appeared to render doctrine superfluous. The important thing—and this was the essence of biologic living—was making sick people well and keeping them well when they attained good health. This was the key to salvation. Mrs. White had also considered health reform to be a vital element of the salvation process, but for her it was an adjunct to, rather than the foundation of, the Adventist message. Kellogg went a step further. For him the practice of health reform was more important than commitment to theological ideas. He determined to keep the sanitarium free from Adventist practice, not so much because he wished to annoy church leaders, but because in his system, doctrinal issues really were irrelevant.

Perhaps the most important casualty was Sabbath observance. Kellogg did not enforce strict Sabbath keeping at Battle Creek Sanitarium—something that concerned Adventist leaders. In 1886 G. I. Butler, the church president, wrote to Ellen White about the lax attitude toward the Sabbath that prevailed at the sanitarium.[5] Such behavior was not surprising given Kellogg's feelings about the Sabbath theology and his desire to create an "unsectarian" institution. But the loss of interest in the Sabbath may also have been a consequence of the special Sabbath privileges granted to Adventist medical personnel. Unlike other workers, Adventist doctors were exempted from strict Sabbath observance once the denomination established medical institutions. This was granted only after due consideration and some hesitation. Nevertheless, Mrs. White concluded it was right for medical staff to work on the Sabbath "for the relief of suffering humanity."[6] The doctor's special status in this respect may have contributed to the looser attitude toward the Sabbath that existed at Kellogg's sanitarium.

There were other ways in which Kellogg's version of Adventism differed from the mainstream. Kellogg advocated a social gospel "without sectarian trammels."[7] He conceived of the church as a benevolent organization and argued that it was "more important for a man to be a good Samaritan than to be a good theologian."[8] He wanted to "rescue lost souls, not to teach theology," and he believed that humanitarian work would win more converts to the Adventist cause than all the church's ministers combined.[9] In the Judgment, Kellogg argued, the great question would not be what a person preached, but what he had done to help someone in need.[10] To promote these goals, the Adventist doctor not only founded other sanitariums around the country, but he also established the denomination's first orphanage in 1891 and developed the church's burgeoning work in American cities with the founding of the Chicago Medical Mission in 1893. In that same year, he became the first director of the Seventh-day Adventist Medical Missionary and Benevolent Association (MMBA), which controlled all the denomination's humanitarian endeavors. Through this organization, Kellogg ministered to society's disadvantaged, the poor, and the unemployed.[11]

Another factor in Kellogg's revisionism was the introduction of recognized, professional education in the church. As early as 1878, he opened a School of Hygiene at the Battle Creek Sanitarium. In 1883 a nursing school was added to the sanitarium, with a woman doctor, Kate Lindsay, playing a prominent role in its formation. The most important development, however, was the establishment of the denomination's American Medical Missionary College (AMMC) in 1895. The AMMC's graduates were recognized by various state examining boards. Recognition even came from the London Medical Council, which Kellogg called the "highest examining body in the world."[12] Such public acceptance was highly significant. Up to this point, Adventists had considered accreditation from outside bodies as a potentially corrupting influence on their institutions. Kellogg was the first to break with this tradition, and the AMMC produced the first Adventist professionals acknowledged by society at large.

What precisely motivated the doctor's reworking of Adventism? Kellogg was clearly a new phenomenon in the church. He was a second-generation Adventist, one of the first to make his presence felt within the denomination. He knew nothing of the collective experience of the Great Disappointment and was born at a time when the denomination was emerging from the Shut-Door period. He received his education in secular institutions and had chosen a vocation with professional status. All of this made Kellogg different from the Adventist pioneers, most of whom were farmers or poorly educated individuals. As able as they were, J. N. Andrews, Uriah Smith, and James and Ellen White had not received much formal higher education. Even among his own generation, Kellogg stood head and shoulders above most other workers in terms of educational achievement. He was well respected among his peers, having invented several influential fitness machines, made genuine contributions to medical science, and won a reputation as one of America's leading surgeons. He was a member of several medical associations. He mixed with non-Adventists to a greater extent than other church members. Through his invention of cornflakes and influential books on sex, he achieved a measure of fame unprecedented in the denomination.

All of this enabled Kellogg to relate to society on a level different from that of other Adventists. The average member, minister, or leader generally viewed the rest of the community from the standpoint of church affiliation and related to non-Adventists primarily in order to warn them to separate themselves from America, the two horned beast. But Kellogg could approach the world as a medical professional, with a mission to heal—not damn—other Americans. This was probably an important factor in his distaste for sectarianism. With his superior education, his fame, and his brilliant, if wayward mind, it was perhaps inevitable that Kellogg would bring a new perspective to the church. That perspective took the form of a commitment to health reform and an Adventism untrammeled by sectarianism. He stood for a social, benevolent Adventism that was virtually devoid of theological content. It embodied a looser attitude to Sabbath keeping, included institutions approved by society, accorded a distinguished position to doctors, and fostered a spirit of medical innovation.

At the turn of the century, it was apparent that Kellogg's version of the Adventist dream was in the ascendancy. Battle Creek Sanitarium eclipsed all other church institutions in terms of influence; the MMBA employed more workers than the General Conference and conducted more effective missionary work than the church's Foreign Missions Board.[13] The great question in Adventism at the time was whether the church would follow Kellogg or whether it would remain a clerically dominated organization.

In the ensuing conflict, Kellogg set the medical network against the church hierarchy. He opposed the General Conference administration and declared the medical work independent of denominational control.

He even managed to keep the medical work free from the administration's grasp following the reorganization of 1901. On the other hand, he ensured that a disproportionate number of MMBA representatives (six out of twenty-five) were elected to the enlarged General Conference executive committee. Both sides appealed for support from the church membership. Kellogg wanted the church's brightest young people to go into medicine. Mrs. White urged them to go into the ministry. The prophetess allied herself with the church leaders, who in 1901 elected as president A. G. Daniells, a man capable of matching the imperious doctor. In 1907 Kellogg was finally banished, but he took the Battle Creek Sanitarium and the American Medical Missionary College with him.[14]

Although Kellogg's expulsion was a turning point in the history of the denomination, the event was not decisive. The clerical leadership did maintain control of the church, but it was unable to eradicate the form of Adventism Kellogg advocated. Adventist doctors continued to enjoy a special status within the church, continued to practice an "undenominational" Adventism, and maintained the tradition of medical innovation. Kellogg was the archetypal Adventist doctor, and since his time, many of the church's doctors have, in one way or another, caught some of his spirit. A good example was Percy Tilson Magan. He was himself a Kellogg sympathizer who nevertheless remained within the denomination following the doctor's dismissal. Magan was not originally a doctor but an educator who had helped establish an alternative form of Adventist education in the early 1900s.[15] He received his M.D. degree at the age of 46 from the University of Tennessee in 1914. He arrived at the church's College of Medical Evangelists (CME) as dean in 1915 and was president of the institution between 1928 and 1942. Magan probably did more than any other person to build the medical school that became incorporated into Loma Linda University in 1961.[16]

Like Kellogg, Magan desired society's recognition. When he became dean at CME, the institution had been established for a decade. The new college made tentative steps toward accreditation, and it received a C rating from the American Medical Association in 1911. Since this meant that graduates could not take recognized examinations, Magan described the rating as "utterly worthless." He thus set himself the task of obtaining the coveted A rating, which, after Herculean efforts, was eventually granted in 1922.[17] Thus, within fifteen years of Kellogg's dismissal, Adventism possessed another accredited medical institution that combined the prestige of the Battle Creek Sanitarium and the recognition of the AMMC.

Following accreditation, the CME began to feed the church's sanitariums with qualified, recognized doctors. These sanitariums expanded rapidly, became more professional, and during the 1920s won an excellent reputation for their standard of health care. Glendale Sanitarium in California and the Washington and New England facilities on the East Coast made impressive progress. Many of the sanitariums also added nursing schools, which produced an increasing number of Adventist nurses to support the growing community of doctors.[18]

It was not long before the prosperity of the medical institutions and the power of the doctors who ran them once again began to threaten the church. Adventist leaders felt that the sanitariums were consuming money that could be spent on foreign missions. They particularly criticized the cost of rebuilding the Glendale Sanitarium in 1924. At the Annual Council of that year, they called a halt to all further sanitarium expansion during 1925.[19] In particular, church leaders were concerned about the type of Adventism symbolized by the sanitariums. The medical flagship, CME, seems to have been different in this respect, but, in general, church leaders felt that the medical work was drifting into worldliness. This was because of the spirit of professionalism and "universititus" (as leaders called it) that Adventist medicine engendered and because the popularity of the health institutions brought about an alien and unwelcome rapport with the world.[20]

All of this served to underline the fundamental differences between the Adventist doctor and the Adventist minister or administrator. There was no Kellogg, yet by 1930 medical work had developed in exactly the same way as it had before 1900. The sanitariums espoused the same unsectarian Adventism, and this caused the same problems. The type of Adventism associated with Kellogg was not unique to him. Adventist physicians were governed by their own traditions and those of the profession. Like the needle of a compass, they naturally pointed in their own direction, which always seemed to differ from that of the church's administration.

In the subsequent development of Adventist medicine, this divergence became clearer. One reason for this was the gradual disappearance of the old sanitarium ideal. In the beginning, Adventist doctors practiced in institutions in which patients were taught the principles of healthful living. Patients were seldom acutely ill and could be expected to stay for relatively long periods of time. Around the midcentury, however, the nature of health care in Adventist institutions began to change. Because of rising costs, patients stayed only as long as was necessary. They were normally seriously ill and were interested only in getting well, not in the long-term principles of health reform. These developments helped accelerate the changes in medical personnel and institutions. Doctors became practitioners of scientific medicine; sanitariums were transformed into hospitals. These changes were also the result of new demographic trends. At first, Adventist sanitariums were located in the country, well outside metropolitan areas. As time passed, however, they became caught in the net of urban development. Whole suburbs grew up around them, and they had to become community hospitals, with an emphasis on acute care, in order to remain viable institutions.[21] A good example is the Washington Sanitarium. When it was founded in 1907, it was located in the peaceful environs of Takoma Park, Maryland. By the 1960s it was surrounded by Greater Washington. Its changing name reflected the evolution of Adventist health care. Originally known as the Washington Sanitarium, it was renamed the Washington Adventist Hospital in 1973.[22]

This change in medical practice was not, of course, confined to Adventism. Doctors and medical establishments elsewhere underwent similar transformations. The change within Adventism, however, drove an even bigger wedge between Adventist health care and the rest of the church. Divorced from health reform, the church's doctors and the hospitals in which they practiced became virtually identical to their counterparts in the outside world. This fact did not escape church leaders. In 1963 F. D. Nichol, editor of the *Review*, urged the church to curtail the growth of acute care hospitals and develop institutions to teach people the laws of health. In support of his case, Nichol produced a brochure that described the philosophy of the kind of institution he had in mind:

This institution is unique and seeks to fill a distinct need. . . . Here you will receive both restful and tonic treatments—hydrotherapy and related types of physical medicine. . . . Here you may listen to medical specialists give lectures on how to follow rules to improve your health and to ward off sickness. . . . This is a place with all the advantages of a quiet vacation spot. . . . Why not come and enjoy a new kind of vacation that may help you live to enjoy many more in the future? . . . Not operated for the acutely ill or regular medical or surgical patients.[23]

One hundred years after Mrs. White's Otsego vision, Nichol was trying to recreate a medical practitioner and an institution that had all but disappeared. The editor's imaginary brochure highlighted the changes that had occurred in Adventist medicine. Adventist doctors now saw patients for an average of seven days, according to Nichol, not for the weeks and months that had been common in the nineteenth century.[24] They used the latest scientific techniques, not natural methods. And they worked in hospitals that were concerned to provide the best in modern health care while remaining financially viable institutions. By the end of the 1960s, it was evident that the numerous Adventist hospitals had more in common with each other in furthering these interests than with the general church body. It was therefore not surprising that the directors of the medical institutions should seek their own organization.

In the 1970s five regional corporations of Adventist health institutions were created: Eastern and Middle America, North, Loma Linda, Sunbelt, and West. These corporations comprised the beginnings of the Adventist health system. In 1982 a national organization, Adventist Health Systems/United States (AHS/US), was formed to oversee the medical work as a whole, although the regional subdivisions remained.[25] The health institutions are thus the only segment of the church to form an alternative administrative and economic structure to the system of conferences and unions. Ironically, the formation of the national organization represented, to some degree, the final realization of John Harvey Kellogg's goals. For although AHS/US was created by an act of the Annual Council and it retains a majority of General Conference personnel on its board, it remains largely independent of clerical control. Its headquarters are in Texas, not Washington, D.C., and it is largely self-financing. Its employees are paid at higher rates than other church workers, the hospitals having broken free of the denominational wage scale in 1979. It holds the power to acquire or close down hospitals. It functions much like the General Conference in that it provides central direction and pools the resources of its constituent institutions, so that stronger hospitals support weaker ones.[26] As the seventh-largest system in America, AHS/US enables Adventist health care to compete with other national corporations. The Adventist system was not left behind, for example, when American health care underwent another revolution in the 1980s, signified by the move from inpatient to outpatient treatment. As a result of the changes in health insurance introduced by President Reagan's administration, patients found it more economical to be treated in outpatient departments for a few hours than to be admitted as an inpatient in hospital. Adventist hospitals adjusted accordingly.[27] It meant, among other things, that the interaction between the doctor and patient became much less than the seven days about which F. D. Nichol complained in the 1960s.

AHS/US provides an alternative Adventism to that practiced in the rest of the church. To visit the hospitals of the system today is to see an Adventism that is "of an undenominational, unsectarian, humanitarian and philanthropic nature." The hospital administrators emphasize that they seek to preserve a "Christian" rather than a specifically "Adventist" atmosphere.[28] Meat is sometimes served in the hospitals— something not countenanced in other Adventist institutions. Looser attitudes toward the Sabbath generally prevail. The unsectarian nature of Adventist hospitals is epitomized by the fact that at least half the medical and nursing staff are usually non-Adventist. For example, in 1985 at Florida Hospital, a prosperous Adventist institution in the SunBelt, 66 percent of all employees were not members of the church.[29] The Sabbath is probably the key factor in this state of affairs. The combination of downplaying the Sabbath's importance and granting special Sabbath privileges to Adventist medical personnel undoubtedly facilitated the influx of non-Adventist doctors and nurses because they were not required to make sacrifices in regard to Sabbath observance.

The administration of church hospitals is still overwhelmingly Adventist, but it is not impossible to find a nonmember in the position of public relations officer. This is not insignificant: virtually anyone can speak for the work of an Adventist hospital.[30]

Within this setting, Adventist doctors have flourished. Their independence and professionalism have allowed them to constitute themselves as the elite segment of the church and to advance medical practice in the world beyond Adventism. The College of Medical Evangelists became part of Loma Linda University in 1961 and changed its name to the Loma Linda Medical School. In the years that followed, several of the institution's staff made significant medical breakthroughs. Between 1960 and 1964, for example, Edward H. Hon developed methods to monitor the condition of the fetus. Later, he moved to Yale and established there the world's first fetal intensive care unit in 1969. His techniques proved successful in increasing the safety of childbirth and have been widely influential. In 1969 *Life* magazine, in a feature on the Loma Linda graduate, reported that Hon's system reduced the number of Caesarean sections by three-quarters and the incidence of infant injuries by half.[31]

All of this was preparatory to Loma Linda's Baby Fae operation in 1984. Dr. Leonard Bailey's controversial transplant of a baboon's heart into the body of a baby girl startled the outside world. But it was not surprising to anyone acquainted with the tradition of the church's doctors. Dr. Bailey was merely the latest in a long line of innovative Adventist physicians. The Baby Fae transplant in many ways typified the history of Adventist doctors and the role they have played within the denomination. An advance was made, worldwide publicity was attracted, and Loma Linda confirmed its place as the best-known Adventist institution. But this was achieved at the expense of long-standing Adventist traditions. Dr. Bailey and his associates had effectively brought about an "amalgamation of man and beast," which Mrs. White had viewed as an abomination.[32] She referred to the sexual union of different species; the Baby Fae operation concerned the transposition of organs. Nevertheless, some Adventist members perceived the operation to have effected an amalgamation not intended by God between human and animal kingdoms. Once again, the pursuit of scientific medicine was seen to be undermining the church's religious principles.[33]

Throughout the history of Adventist medicine, the church's medical professionals have rarely been free of the charge that they are subverting the theology and discipline of the denomination. The underlying causes of this phenomenon are not difficult to discover. The church is a clerically dominated organization, and Adventist doctors constitute the only group with sufficient authority and independence to challenge clerical control. Ministers sometimes view doctors with suspicion. Doctors perceive ministers in equally negative terms. A survey of Loma Linda medical students in 1969 revealed that only 22 percent rated ministers positively, while 42 percent rated them negatively, considering them to be poorly educated, insincere, and incompetent.[34] This rather condescending attitude is probably rooted in the superior status society accords to the medical profession. Ministers justify their actions in terms of Adventism's distinctive theology; doctors can draw on the wider consensus of scientific opinion to back up their decisions. For this reason the church's leadership sometimes defers to medical authority, particularly on ethical matters. The issue of abortion is a good example. In 1971, in the only statement they have made on the matter, General Conference officers did not make any attempt to resolve the ethical difficulties and did not draw on the Adventist theological tradition in formulating their guidelines. Instead, they deferred to the judgment of the church's doctors for, they argued, "the performing of abortions" is "the proper business of responsible staffs of hospitals." There were plenty of Adventist theologians and ministers who, on the basis of their interpretation of Adventist theology, were prepared to make a stand *against* abortion. But, officially, it was doctors' concerns and the realities of their work in the public sphere that took precedence in determining the church's open, noncommittal, position.[35]

Adventist doctors have, however, not been happy to rely solely on their own professional prestige. Since the 1960s, they have been involved in decisions with significant ethical and theological implications. The moral dilemmas posed by such issues as abortion, euthanasia, artificial insemination, and interspecies transplants inspired the foundation of a center for ethics at Loma Linda University in 1984. Its director, Jack Provonsha, himself a physician, defended the Baby Fae operation against its critics within and without the denomination. The philosophy espoused by Provonsha makes no absolute distinction between those factors that produce physical health and those that promote spiritual growth.[36] This holistic approach has the effect of giving a religious sanction to health promotion, for that which effects physical well-being is also likely to facilitate spiritual development, and vice versa. Holism provides an ideology that validates the activities of health professionals in Adventist theological language. As such, it plays a similar function to Kellogg's biologic living. Just as Kellogg wanted to see the mark of the beast as general spiritual and physical illness, so contemporary holism diminishes the significance of traditional doctrines in favor of an approach that interweaves medical and theological objectives.

There is some indication that holism may become increasingly influential outside of Adventist medical circles. In 1985 a survey indicated that religion teachers considered holism to be the church's most important contribution to theology.[37] If this health-related philosophy becomes a significant element in Adventist teaching, it will not be the first time that Adventist medicine has altered the direction of denominational education. In the 1930s, medicine brought about a shift not in the content but in the status of the church's education. The accreditation of the medical school was a significant event in twentieth-century Adventism. Full accreditation meant that the College of Medical Evangelists could only accept students from recognized institutions and that Adventist colleges had to become accredited in order to send students to the medical school. This duly occurred in the 1930s, as each college, in turn, gained recognition. As the church's colleges now had to meet the requirements of the state, it meant that they could never again be completely under denominational control.[38]

Church leaders watched this development with rising alarm. They knew it represented a fundamental and irreversible shift in the nature of Adventism. They were, however, powerless to do anything about it. They had bowed to the accreditation of the medical school because the U.S. Army had ordered that unless it had an A rating, Adventist students would be drafted. They did try to halt the accreditation trend in the mid 1930s, but by then it was too late. All the colleges wanted to prepare students for a medical career, which was rapidly becoming the most favored profession among Adventist young people. This, too, worried the General Conference, as it had disturbed church leaders of the Kellogg era. Several appeals were issued in the *Review* in the 1920s and 1930s urging young men to choose the ministry instead of medicine. On one occasion, General Conference president W. A. Spicer actually described the interest in the medical profession as "the pull of the world."[39]

But the process of accreditation was a clear demonstration of the special status of the Adventist doctor. The direction of Adventist education was changed because Dr. Magan wanted full recognition of his school. Modern Adventist education was thus the result of the precedence accorded to medical training and the by-product of the Adventist doctor's accommodation to the world. The full implications of this will be explored in the next chapter.

CHAPTER 18

Educators

The accreditation movement of the 1930s was a turning point in Adventist education. Thereafter, church schools and colleges were primarily concerned with preparing students for professional careers, and Adventist educators, particularly those in higher education, became increasingly preoccupied with their professional standing as academics and researchers. This bred a skeptical spirit toward the Adventist tradition, which, in its own way, paralleled that of the church's doctors.

In assessing the effects of this, it is tempting to believe that the Adventist educator has always been in tension with other sections of the church. But the relationship between Adventist teachers and, for example, church leaders has not been quite so simple. For most of the denomination's history, educators and leaders have shared the same presuppositions about Adventist education and have been equally responsible for the development of the church's vast school system. When disagreements have broken out, it has normally been over the teaching community's desire to take the denomination's commitment to academic endeavor to its logical conclusion and the leadership's unwillingness to accept the consequences of policies they have themselves instituted.

The establishment of the denomination's first school at Battle Creek in 1872 reveals several assumptions that were prevalent in early Adventism. One of these was the pioneers' acceptance of the academic ideal. Intellectual development was important because, as James White believed, "a well disciplined and informed mind can best receive and cherish the sublime truths of the Second Advent."[1] Another reason for the foundation of the school was the perceived need to train ministerial workers—again a major concern of James White.[2] A third factor was the distrust of the public school system exhibited by the believers in general. This had, in fact, led to the establishment of several short-lived church schools in the 1850s and 1860s, before the emergence of the Battle Creek School.[3] In other words, the pioneers' tendency to distance themselves from society by replicating its institutions can be seen in the creation of Adventist schools. Adventists revealed their distrust of American education by establishing an independent system of their own. But this was not the result of adherence to a specifically Adventist educational philosophy (there was initially no philosophy); rather, it was a function of the church's drive toward institutional independence.[4]

It was in keeping with this understanding that the church encouraged two educated converts to run the first school. Adventist leaders did not appoint an established pioneer—something that might have been expected if Adventist education had been founded simply to inculcate the church's worldview. The chosen educators were Goodloe Harper Bell and Sidney Brownsberger. As teachers who had been educated in secular institutions and taught in public schools, they brought to the denomination the weight of their professional expertise. They were qualified to operate schools based on secular models, not on sectarian ideals. Bell founded the Battle Creek School. He started with twelve students at the old print shop of the *Review*. He had become an Adventist after being treated at the Western Health Reform Institute in the late 1860s. He was noted for his mechanical teaching methods, his incessant drilling, his strict discipline, and a desire "to inspire his pupils with a spirit of cheerful, voluntary industry in study." Bell was a grammarian who frequently used poets like Longfellow and Coleridge to illustrate his exercises, and he later published several successful books on the English language.[5]

Sidney Brownsberger arrived as head of the school in 1873, which left Bell free to concentrate on teaching. Brownsberger was studying classics at the University of Michigan in the 1860s when he became convinced of the Adventist message. He wanted to curtail his studies and enter the church's ministry, but, as he recalled, James White "wrote me suggesting that it might be my duty . . . to pursue my college course as there were but few comparatively that had so favorable an opportunity as myself."[6] Brownsberger was probably more of an educational thinker than was Bell, and he retained his enthusiasm for the classics. His basic academic outlook is evident in the subtle twist he gave to the Adventist hope: "When the Lord comes, Adventists expect to leave their farms, their business, and their homes, and take their brains with them."[7] Accordingly, he introduced a rigorous five-year degree in the classics as the core program, when the school evolved into a college in 1874. The college also offered degrees in science and English and diplomas in business, ministry, and teaching. It was a measure of the secular nature of the college that Bible courses were not made compulsory and, in an early echo of the Adventism Kellogg later developed, the catalog of 1876 stated that "nothing in the regular course of study" was "in the least denominational or sectarian."[8]

The college continued to operate under a classically dominated curriculum for the rest of the decade. Brownsberger resigned in 1881 and was succeeded by Alexander McLearn, another recent convert. He knew very little about the church but was recommended to the college presidency by James White, who regarded McLearn as "a highly educated Christian gentleman."[9] McLearn's tenure was disastrous—not so much because of his tenuous Adventist links but because of certain aspects of his personality. He was not a disciplinarian, and he liked to interfere in the running of college departments. Disagreements with Bell precipitated the latter's resignation in April 1882. A few months later, owing to the General Conference's perception that the "policy of the school has been gradually changing, becoming more and more like that of the worldly schools around it," the college was shut down by the Adventist leadership.[10]

The closure of Battle Creek College marked the end of the first phase of Adventist education. Because of the glaring lack of an "Adventist" content in the school, it is usually viewed as a puzzling episode in denominational history. Adventist writers tend to dismiss the period as a false start, as the product of un-Adventist educators who somehow slipped through the denominational net.[11] But far from being an accident, the development of independent education was in keeping with the nature of early Adventism, which emphasized the autonomy rather than the philosophical peculiarity of church institutions. In keeping with this, secular authors were studied, traditional curriculum practices adopted, and educators with flimsy denominational ties were placed in positions of authority. These developments accorded perfectly with the attitudes of James White, who seemed content for Adventist education to replicate the public school system. The progress of Adventist education from Bell to McLearn was underpinned by, and made possible through, the attitudes of the Adventist leadership. Thus, the idea that the college was closed because it had become like worldly schools appears to have been misplaced. The practices of the college had scarcely altered since its foundation. The change was rather to be found in the attitudes of Adventist leaders after the death of James White in 1881. The resignations of Bell and Brownsberger coincided with a new desire in the church to make the curriculum more distinctive. The closure of the college signified that church leaders had changed their minds about denominational education. The college had not become more worldly; the Adventist community had become more sectarian.

It was Ellen White who inspired the revision of educational policy. At first, this involved criticizing the methods of the college's principal teachers. In 1880 she accused Bell of making "grammar his idol."[12] He had made it "the one all-important study . . . and some had left college with only half an education."[13] In a speech read in the college hall in December 1881, she implicitly held Brownsberger responsible for taking the college to "a position that God does not approve."[14] It was in this speech that Mrs. White advocated change. She stated that "the study of the scriptures should have the first place in our system of education," for "as an educating power the Bible is without a rival." She also argued that agriculture and practical trades should be introduced "to instruct the students in the various departments of physical labor." In advocating a biblically based education, Mrs. White rejected the classical curriculum of the church's pioneer educators. She broke, too, with her husband's emphasis on intellectual development. She urged a practical, sectarian education that was better adapted for ministerial training.[15]

Although she had made some earlier observations on Adventist schools, Mrs. White's educational philosophy developed in reaction to the college at Battle Creek.[16] The early educators did not depart from a blueprint laid down by Ellen White; she rejected the principles established by them. But it was not for another twenty years, until she published her classic work *Education*, that all her ideas came to fruition. The book brought together a number of themes she had emphasized repeatedly in the late nineteenth century: the centrality of the Bible; the benefit of manual labor; the importance of character; and the necessity of firm, but not mindless, discipline. Mrs. White argued that education must produce balanced, Godlike individuals for both earthly and heavenly existence. In a much quoted passage, she wrote:

True education means more than the pursual of a certain course of study. It means more than a preparation for the life that now is. It has to do with the whole being, and with the whole period of existence possible to man. It is the harmonious development of the physical, the mental and the spiritual powers. It prepares the students for the joy of service in this world and for the higher joy of wider service in the world to come.[17]

The prophetess presented this philosophy in a religious context. "In the highest sense," she wrote, "the work of education and the work of redemption are one."[18]

Despite the force of Mrs. White's arguments, they did not permanently change the attitudes of Adventist educators. Like the church's doctors, most denominational teachers were governed by their sense of professionalism and found it either difficult or undesirable to reverse the course they had set for the school system. Brownsberger, for example, founded another institution at Healdsburg, California, in 1882, which later became Pacific Union College. According to one Adventist historian, he established there "an almost exact replica of the academic program of Battle Creek College."[19] Even Battle Creek, when it reopened under Wolcott Littlejohn in the 1883–84 school year, continued to offer a classical course.[20] While later presidents such as W. W. Prescott established a more biblically based curriculum and others, such as E. A. Sutherland, attempted a practical and labor-oriented program, mainstream Adventist educators cannot be said ever to have followed Mrs. White's philosophy completely.[21] Sutherland's reforms were short lived and controversial. So, too, was his plan, which other Adventist colleges followed for a time, to dispense with academic degrees. He did, however, succeed in moving the college from Battle Creek to a more rural location in Berrien Springs, Michigan, and his reformist inclinations were to some extent reflected in the institution's change of name to Emmanuel Missionary College in 1901.[22]

At the turn of the century, the Adventist church also possessed a wide and expanding elementary school system. The teachers at these institutions were supplied primarily by Battle Creek College, which had assumed the role of a teacher training institution. Elementary school teachers appeared to have faithfully put into practice Mrs. White's ideas.[23] But any hope that their counterparts in higher education would follow her philosophy in the years after the publication of *Education* foundered in the accreditation process. By 1930 there were six Adventist colleges: Emmanuel Missionary and Union in the central states; Atlantic Union and Washington Missionary (later Columbia Union College) in the East; and Pacific Union and Walla Walla in the West. By 1942 all six had been recognized as senior colleges by American accrediting associations.[24] Thereafter, Adventist colleges developed within the liberal arts tradition.

The liberal arts concept of education was undergoing a revival in America in the 1930s.[25] It was in keeping with this trend that Adventist colleges were accredited and began offering—as they still do—a broad-based training in the sciences and humanities. Students were prepared for professional careers, and Mrs. White's redemptive ambitions for the church's education were pushed into the background. At first, the most important of the professions was medicine, but in time, Adventist institutions offered options in other fields. In 1937 M. E. Kern founded the Adventist Theological Seminary, which meant that Adventist ministers could obtain training comparable to that of the church's growing group of professionals.[26]

The 1930s accreditation process fundamentally altered the concerns of Adventist educators. In the three decades following Mrs. White's speech at Battle Creek, teachers had conducted a lively debate about the education system. After the prophetess died, this debate was continued by Frederick Griggs. Chairman of the General Conference Education Department in the early part of the century and president of Emmanuel Missionary College between 1918 and 1924, Griggs advocated a philosophy that mediated between traditional education and Mrs. White's reforms.[27] After accreditation, however, Adventist educators ceased to think creatively about educational philosophy. Their new concerns were survival, consolidation, and the maintenance of the colleges' hard-won recognition. Financial considerations, enrollment levels, and the quality of degrees became the prime indicators of success. In other words, it was the problem of having, rather than forming, an educational system that now preoccupied Adventist educators.

Another possible reason for the lack of attention to educational theory was the development within the church of a concept of scholarship. Again, this was a direct consequence of accreditation. In order to obtain recognition, Adventist colleges sent staff to acquire doctoral degrees at outside universities. The individuals who undertook such studies became increasingly enamored with their status as professional scholars and researchers, with the result that the energy once expended on defining the role of Adventist education was now largely spent on defining their own role within Adventism. After the General Conference established Andrews University (an amalgamation of Emmanuel Missionary College and the Theological Seminary) in 1959 and Loma Linda University (which joined the College of Medical Evangelists with the church's La Sierra College) in 1961, it was inevitable that these institutions would prove fertile breeding grounds for the independent Adventist scholar.[28] The concerns of this new type of teacher were reflected in the pages of the denomination's *Journal of True Education* in the 1960s. Discussions of hitherto unexplored concepts, such as academic freedom, became common and revealed the interests of those in the denomination for whom academic respectability was fast becoming an article of faith.[29]

Eventually, then, Adventist college teachers came to see themselves as scholars rather than educators. This change was not envisaged by Ellen White, and it did not conform to her sectarian educational philosophy—even though she did write, as the liberal Adventist professor never failed to point out, that an object of Adventist education is to produce individuals who are "thinkers, and not mere reflectors of other men's thought."[30] The modern Adventist professor was largely a creation of church leaders. Whatever their initial reservations, they accepted accreditation, nurtured liberal arts colleges, and made the decisions that provided the resources for the denomination's universities. They supported the expansion of graduate education, encouraged talented individuals to secure Ph.D. degrees, and employed only those teachers with the best academic qualifications. It was clear, once the dust of accreditation settled, that the General Conference wanted an educational system that compared with the best in outside society. What they found difficult to accept were the consequences of their own policies.

The most important result of the formation of a community of scholars within the denomination was the establishment of an academic organization, the Association of Adventist Forums (AAF), in 1968. The association was largely the brainchild of Roy Branson, an ethicist at the Theological Seminary. The church's doctors, who through the accreditation movement had sparked the growth of Adventist scholarship, also helped to foster this new development. A physician, Molleurus Couperus, was appointed as the first editor of the AAF quarterly journal *Spectrum*, and the medical community gave generous financial support to the organization.[31] But the AAF might not have succeeded if General Conference officers had not supported the organization and the aims and objectives of its constitution. The General Conference approved the existence of an independent, academic organization in the denomination.[32] It is difficult to know exactly what the church hierarchy expected, but the founders of the AAF were determined to carry out the obligation "to examine . . . freely ideas and issues relevant to the church in all its aspects."[33] The contributors to the AAF's quarterly, *Spectrum*, faithfully followed the journal's objective "to look without prejudice at all sides of a subject."[34] The effects were far reaching. The AAF gave Adventist academics the opportunity to turn their scholarly expertise on the Adventist tradition, sometimes to devastating effect. Professors from the denomination's colleges, universities, and seminary published in *Spectrum* critical articles on Adventist theology and history. This provided the educated Adventist, and other members who cared to look, with a new view of the church and its development. *Spectrum* became a meeting place for those in the church who believed in the benefits of academic freedom. Donald McAdams, an academic who took a leading role in the demythologizing of Ellen White in the 1970s, summed up the position of Adventist scholars: "We have no choice but to be honest at heart, acknowledge facts, and seek the truth." To McAdams "the search for truth is, after all, the basic premise upon which Adventism is founded."[35]

The other effect of the publication of *Spectrum* was on the denomination's media. Initially, the journal was an academic publication, which specialized in scholarly debate. But toward the end of the 1970s, *Spectrum* began hiring trained journalists to report objectively the affairs of the church. It was a form of journalism of which the denomination had relatively little experience. *Spectrum* took on the role of an independent press. As a result, General Conference leaders were unable to control the publication of information in the same way their predecessors had done. The AAF journal did not immediately affect the *Review*, which under Kenneth Wood (editor from 1966–82) continued to present an uncritical view of the Adventist church. In this respect, Wood did not depart from the tradition of *Review*'s two most powerful editors in the twentieth century, F. M. Wilcox and F. D. Nichol. But when William Johnsson took over the editorship in 1982, he realized the *Review* would cease to be credible if readers had to go to elsewhere in order to find accurate information about the church. Johnsson thus began reporting more openly the issues and problems that faced Adventism.[36] In a similar way, the denomination's clerical paper, *Ministry*, took to reporting doctrinal debates in the manner that *Spectrum* had pioneered. The AAF's journal also created the climate for other, more radical publications to appear. In 1983 an independent magazine, *Adventist Currents*, was founded, which styled itself as "an unauthorized free press supplement to official Seventh-Day Adventist publications." In these ways, *Spectrum* opened up a closed society to a freer circulation of information.

For the most part, church leaders kept to themselves whatever reservations they had about the activities of Adventist scholars. Indeed, throughout the 1970s, they continued to serve as advisers both to the AAF and *Spectrum*. However, there was one preoccupation of the academic community that proved more sensitive than others. This was its dissatisfaction with the denomination's hierarchical structure. Articles advocating the reform of Adventist government appeared at regular intervals in *Spectrum*.[37] In 1982 the AAF commissioned a special task force to work out proposals for an alternative administrative system. After two years, the task force reported in *Spectrum*, calling for a democratic church, open elections, freedom of information, and the end of the General Conference oligarchy.[38] Adventist leaders were not slow to perceive this threat, and later in the year, the church president Neal Wilson finally ostracized the organization. He rejected the notion that "*Spectrum* is the most authentic source of information regarding church affairs" and attacked "the AAF and *Spectrum*" for "actively urging what appears to us to be irresponsible concepts of, and changes in, denominational administration, operations, structure and organization."[39] That Wilson was the individual who made this statement was particularly ironic. In the late 1960s, as president of the North American division, he was heavily involved in setting up the AAF. In the mid 1980s, he attempted to close a Pandora's Box that he himself had opened.

It did not, however, prove easy to silence the AAF. Historically, the organization was the product of an increasingly well-educated community that the provision of Adventist graduate education had created. The close connection between the AAF and the educational system was one of the sources of its strength. The organization's members were drawn from the colleges, and the colleges often provided the location for meetings of chapters of the AAF. It would be wrong to conclude from this that all church academics were equally critical of the Adventist tradition. Within the faculties of the colleges, universities, and theological seminary, professors held different positions. Adventism's scholarly community was not entirely homogenous. The criticism generally reserved for the church's beliefs could be turned on the work of fellow academics, with equally effective results. For example, the impact of Ronald Numbers's *Prophetess of Health* (1976), the book that first undermined the authority of Mrs. White, was dented by the skepticism of colleagues whom Numbers might have expected to be more sympathetic. This undoubtedly aided church officials in their efforts to counter the damage to the Adventist prophetess.[40] Similarly, Desmond Ford's challenge to the sanctuary doctrine in 1980 was blunted by the lack of unequivocal support from the church's theologians, even though surveys indicated that many shared the same doubts. A united stand at Glacier View might have achieved a major revision of belief. As it turned out, the uncertainties of the theologians left the doctrine virtually intact and provided church officials with the opportunity to fire the troublesome professor. The theologians complained about this afterward, but in fact they did not act with Ford. As Donald McAdams has observed, Adventist college faculty members "do not make good followers."[41] This is one reason why the General Conference is usually able to contain the potential threat of highly educated academics. When it matters, the Adventist academic community is rarely a cohesive force. The outrage expressed by church scholars following Glacier View perhaps had less to do with the conviction that Ford was treated unfairly than it did with the realization that they had been outmaneuvered by the administration that had used them to discredit the Australian theologian.[42]

Nevertheless, the removal of Ford marked the end of an era. The spirit of open enquiry that had burned brightly with the founding of the AAF in 1968 was quenched by the events of 1980. Glacier View defined the limits of academic freedom in the modern church and left Adventist scholars defeated on the sidelines. All sections of Adventism now took advantage of the academic community's weakened position. At two colleges, Pacific Union in California and Southern Missionary in Tennessee, church members conducted a successful campaign against individuals whom they considered to be heretical teachers. The campaign resulted in the resignations in 1983 of the respective presidents, John Cassell and Frank Knittel.[43] The grass-roots movement at these colleges appears to have been inspired by the *Review*. In an unusually sharp editorial in 1980, Kenneth Wood attacked "the strange winds of doctrine that blow on some campuses" and backed parents who wanted to send their children to church schools that taught "historic Adventism."[44] Church officials themselves either sacked or forced the resignations of dissident academics. When the opportunity arose, they installed acceptable personnel. The best example of this latter process was the appointment, against the staff's wishes, of the hard-line traditionalist Gerhard Hasel as the dean of the Theological Seminary in 1981.[45] In the view of many professors, Hasel's deanship, which lasted until 1988, badly damaged the seminary's academic reputation.[46] All of these developments were connected with Glacier View. Church leaders, recognizing the opportunity, took the initiative from Adventist scholars, who had for twelve years led the denomination into strange, uncharted territory.

The church's academics went through a difficult time following Glacier View. They made an attempt to reassert the principle of academic freedom in the Atlanta Affirmation, a seven-point charter signed by seventeen college professors in 1981.[47] They also met with denominational leaders in several "consultation" meetings in 1980–81 that were designed to rebuild the bridges between them.[48] But the period was one in which Adventist scholars were in retreat. The professors realized this better than anyone and reportedly gathered on Adventist campuses to sing bitter parodies of well-known hymns against the church president, Neal Wilson. In one hymn, Rust and Obey (a parody of Trust and Obey) they sang:

When we work for the church
We'll be left in the lurch
If we choose Wilson's creed not to sign.
While we do Wilson's will, work abides with us still
And with all who will rust and obey.
Rust and obey, for there's no other way
To avoid unemployment than to rust and obey.[49]

Such hymns revealed the problem in Adventist education that had been present from the day that Goodloe Harper Bell founded the first school. Adventist teachers are both denominational employees and professionals who work in institutions modeled on secular equivalents. As such, they are expected to adhere to the church's beliefs as defined by their employers. At the same time they must attain the standing and adopt the attitudes demanded by the profession. The dilemma is perfectly illustrated by the history of another set of educators, the church's scientists. Adventism has never possessed a scientific community as such, but Adventist scientists have, like other academics, argued among themselves, challenged the church's traditions, and run into bitter conflict with General Conference leaders. An examination of Adventist science is also important in view of the contribution it has made to American creationism.

Adventism's best-known creationist was George McCready Price. He promoted antievolutionism in the first half of the twentieth century, deriving his views from Ellen White and interpreting them in the light of Baconian principles. Price believed in a literal six-day creation and in an earth that was no more than 6,000 years old. In the 1920s, his trenchant attack on evolution brought him to the attention of the public outside Adventism, and he became, in the view of one critic, fundamentalism's leading creationist apologist.[50] Price wrote his first book in 1902, a work published at his own expense, called *Outlines of Modern*

Science and Modern Christianity. In the next twenty-five years, there followed over twenty other books. His magnum opus was *The New Geology*, published in 1923, which represented a monumental effort to correlate geological data with the Genesis flood. It was this book that secured his reputation. At the famous Tennessee evolution trial of 1925, Price's work was cited by the prosecution's main witness, William Jennings Bryan.[51]

Most of Price's theories denied the principles of geological science. He did not recognize progressive order in the geological column or the concept of thrust faults (or overthrusts) by which geologists explained instances of out-of-order sequence in stratified rocks. He refused to believe in the validity of index fossils as geological dating devices or in the occurrence of continental glaciation. To explain the layering in the geological column, he invented a "law of conformable stratigraphic sequence," which proposed that "any kind of fossiliferous rock . . . may be found conformably on any other kind of fossiliferous rock." In this way, he held that the arrangement of the column was arbitrary.[52] Like Mrs. White before him, he believed the Genesis flood accounted for the geological record.[53]

Price's influence waned in the middle of the century, but two years before his death in 1963, his views were rehabilitated with great success by the non-Adventists John Whitcomb and Henry Morris in the book *The Genesis Flood.* This book marked the rebirth of the creationist movement in the United States, and Morris went on to become the leading creationist of the next two and a half decades, founding the influential Institute for Creation Research in 1972. Many observers noted, correctly, that this new movement was little more than a revival of the philosophy of Price's *New Geology.*[54] The Seventh-day Adventist geologist was the founding father of the creationist movement that became such a marked feature of American life in the 1970s and early 1980s.

Ironically, Price's theories were most effectively challenged by other scientists in his own church. Harold Clark, a biology teacher, used the *New Geology* in his classes at Pacific Union College until his fieldwork in 1938 led him to conclude that the geological column "seemed to have a definite order which could not be denied."[55] Clark also studied the question of glaciation, index fossils, and thrust faults. They all appeared to be valid geological concepts. The only problem was how to explain the data in a way consistent with a short chronology and a worldwide flood. Clark solved this with an ingenious "ecological zonation" theory. He postulated that the natural world was arranged in distinct zones. When the flood came, it simply buried organisms in this orderly arrangement. The geological column therefore represented "not ages of time, but stages of flood action—the burial of the zones or habitats of the antediluvian world."[56] Clark published his findings in *The New Diluvialism* in 1946, a milestone in the church's creationist literature. Price was so shocked by the acceptance of the geological column that he suggested Clark's explanation was "a theory of Satanic origin."[57] But it was Clark's views that eventually prevailed and became the church's accepted position.[58]

A little over a decade after the publication of *The New Diluvialism*, the General Conference made a contribution to the debate by establishing the Geoscience Research Institute (GRI). In keeping with the pursuit of academic respectability that had resulted in the establishment of Andrews and Loma Linda Universities, the institute was founded in 1958 so that church scientists could conduct research in geology and biology.[59] As with the universities, the General Conference wanted a center of academic excellence and encouraged promising individuals to gain the necessary scientific qualifications to make the institute credible. Again, it was not clear precisely what the General Conference envisaged, but like the Association of Adventist Forums, the institute was soon busily undermining Adventist traditions.

It is important to note that several GRI staff were very conservative. The institute's first director was Frank L. Marsh, whose books, *Evolution, Creation, Science* (1947) and *Studies in Creationism* (1950), strongly defended Ellen White's creationist framework. Later, GRI scientists Harold Coffin and Ariel Roth saw themselves as keepers of the church's faith. Nevertheless, in much the same way as the denomination's colleges, the institute became a breeding ground for the independent Adventist scientist. The experiments of Peter Hare, the research of Richard Ritland, and the work of Harold James and Ed Lugenbeal cast what appeared to be serious doubts on a 6,000-year chronology and on the efficacy of the Genesis flood. These conclusions derived from the discovery that radioactive dating was apparently much more reliable than Adventist scientists had previously supposed, that the layered fossil forests at Nova Scotia and Yellowstone Park suggested an earth of great age, and that the distribution of animals and plants in the geological record suggested some kind of evolutionary development. On this basis, the liberal scientists at GRI rejected the explanations of Harold Clark just as he had rejected the ideas of McCready Price.[60]

The views of Hare, Ritland, James, and Lugenbeal dominated the institute in the 1960s. It seemed possible that these scientists would change the church's understanding of the earth's origins until the Geoscience Field Conference in 1968. At this meeting of church leaders and Adventist scientists, several speakers seriously questioned traditional creationism. Adventist officials became so alarmed that they started to abort the proceedings. This was not necessary, however, because the scientists proved to be divided among themselves—Coffin and Roth defended the 6,000-year chronology and the Genesis flood. As would be the case at Glacier View, the way was now open for the

General Conference to take control. The church president Robert Pierson issued a resolution instructing GRI personnel to refrain from raising problems in public and exerted pressure on the institute to abandon its open-ended approach. The institute's liberal scientists were then placed in a situation where they felt they had no option but to resign.[61]

The dramatic events of the 1968 Geoscience Field Conference remained hidden from the general membership. However, to the perceptive eye, the polarization that had occurred among Adventist scientists could be detected in two books published in 1969 and 1970. The first, *Creation—Accident or Design?* by Harold Coffin, supported the two traditional answers to the evolutionary theory: the young earth and the Genesis flood as the main cause of the geological record. Significantly, Coffin cited Ellen White as a scientific authority on over seventy occasions.[62] In the second book, *A Search for Meaning in Nature*, Richard Ritland did not repeat established Adventist views. He maintained a discreet silence about the age of the earth, questioned the influence of the flood, and made only one passing reference to Ellen White.[63] While Coffin addressed himself "to the task of helping God's remnant people to preserve an intelligent faith," Ritland argued that accepted explanations "very often . . . impair or repress inquiry prematurely." It was, therefore, "continually essential to re-examine and test the validity of theories and basic assumptions."[64]

In the 1970s, the Geoscience Research Institute was governed by Coffin's traditional, rather than Ritland's open-minded, philosophy. Ritland resigned as director of the institute in 1971. Thereafter, the institute's staff became increasingly estranged from their liberal colleagues and, ironically, found more in common with fundamentalist creationists such as Henry Morris. At the beginning of the 1980s, GRI personnel became involved in the public debate about the teaching of evolution and creation in American schools. Coffin, Roth, and another Adventist creationist, Robert Gentry, testified for creation legislation in Arkansas at the highly publicized court case of 1981.[65]

At the very moment that GRI scientists were presenting creationism to the nation, support for evolutionary theory was growing within the church. A survey in 1980 showed that 39 percent of Adventist scientists believed the earth to be around 4.5 billion years old.[66] In 1983 an editorial in the *Review* acknowledged that Adventist creationism was "under fire," and in 1984 Peter Hare, one of the original members of the Geoscience Research Institute, argued that the strict creationist view was an extreme position that should only be taught in an historical context. He believed that creation and evolution might be a false dichotomy and actually advocated the teaching of evolution "as a working model."[67]

These developments should be kept in perspective. A group that is coming to terms with evolution more than a century after Darwin is hardly in the vanguard of intellectual progress. As Donald McAdams wryly observed: "by the standards of American academia, Adventist academics are, as a whole, just to the left of Atilla the Hun."[68] It is not so much the individual intellectual enterprise of Adventist scholars that has aligned Adventist education with secular thought as the institutional framework within which they operate. The spread of evolutionary ideas would not have been so rapid if the Geoscience Research Institute had not been set up in 1958. Like the church's other educational institutions, it became a center that eroded Adventist beliefs. The church's colleges, universities, seminary, and institutes were all manifestations of the Adventist proclivity to replicate secular institutions. They were designed to insulate Adventists from the rest of society. But in the field of education, this replication proved self-defeating. It produced a community of academics and scientists who narrowed the gap between the church and the world.

CHAPTER 19

The Self-Supporting Movement

It is often difficult to tell if an institution is owned and operated by the Seventh-day Adventist church. In the hospitals run by Adventist Health Systems, the majority of the staff are often non-Adventist, and the type of patient care is determined by the latest developments in medical science and the everpressing need to balance the budget, rather than the natural principles espoused by Ellen White. In Adventist schools and colleges, the primary focus is usually on obtaining the grades required to follow a professional career. Teachers generally use the same books and advance the same arguments as their secular colleagues. In both colleges and hospitals, the most urgent concern is the need to remain economically viable in a competitive market. The views on education and health that Ellen White propounded in the closing years of the nineteenth century may inform the long-term objectives of these institutions, but there is little evidence that they have any influence on short-term planning.

The same cannot generally be said of the hospitals and schools operated by Adventist laypeople independent of denominational control. There are numerous such institutions, including hospitals, colleges, academies, health food restaurants, small industries, and farms.[1] These are, however, not just ventures that happen to be owned by Adventist persons but self-conscious attempts to realize the Adventist ideal outside the structure of the church. Although affiliated to a denominational organization, Adventist-Laymen's Services and Industries (or ASI), the self-supporting institutions represent an implicit criticism of what is considered to be the church's willingness to compromise its distinctive beliefs and practices. Despite their diversity, most self-supporting institutions follow a similar pattern.[2] Usually in a rural area and located on agricultural land, the Adventist community operates a small health care facility, a school, and various basic industries. There may also be a vegetarian restaurant or health center in a nearby town.

Many of those who work in the town will commute to and from the rural base. All employees, whatever their titular role, will probably perform some kind of manual labor. The wages paid to everyone are extremely low, and the wage differential between a physician and a gardener is marginal.

The best-known institution of this type is Wildwood Sanitarium, located in Georgia, close to Chattanooga, Tennessee. The small hospital is run on the principles advanced by Ellen White and pioneered by Kellogg. Although staffed by qualified physicians, the medical facilities are limited, and the sanitarium specializes in postoperative care, "no-hope" cancer victims, and lifestyle readjustment for those with cardiac problems. The regimen is based on natural remedies: daily water treatment, a diet free of animal products, moderate exercise, and fresh air in delightful surroundings. At the Weimar Institute in northern California, Ellen White's educational principles are put into practice, and the students work for fifteen hours a week alongside their teachers in one of the campus industries. The college, which offers bachelor's degrees in religion, health, and agriculture, is unaccredited by either Adventist or government bodies, as it is feared that this would require some modification in a curriculum that does not separate educational and spiritual concerns.

The difference between the self-supporting approach to education and that of denominational and secular schools is perhaps clearest at the elementary level. Children do not take part in competitive sports but may spend part of each day gardening. Dress may also be unusual. Girls do not wear trousers or sleeveless dresses, and boys do not wear shorts. Incipient male-female relationships are discouraged, and the focus of all teaching is on a religious understanding of the world. Grading is not competitive. Schools run by the denomination are regarded as "worldly." The result of this refusal to conform to contemporary secular expectations is that students may experience some difficulty in rejoining mainstream education. In addition to whatever social and psychological difficulties may be encountered in moving from a school run on the plans of late nineteenth-century educational reformers, there is the added difficulty, at college level, of gaining acceptance for credits earned at a nonaccredited institution. However, unlike other Adventists, those at self-supporting institutions do not encourage the view that professional education is an ultimately desirable end. The dignity of manual labor is emphasized, and the merits of agricultural work are particularly extolled. It is the spiritual and not the material welfare of the individual that is considered to be of primary importance, and employees of self-supporting institutions take seriously the belief that true spirituality may necessitate material sacrifice.

In theology, the employees of self-supporting institutions retain their allegiance to fundamentalist Adventism, emphasizing the human nature of Christ, the work of sanctification, and the need for moral perfection. They place great trust in supernatural intervention in everyday life and perceive God's direct involvement in the development of self-supporting work. They regard the changes that have taken place within Adventist theology since *Questions on Doctrine* with undisguised suspicion.[3]

There is considerable tension between the conservative Adventists associated with independent institutions and the educational and administrative authorities of the church. Places like Wildwood are the bases from which conservative leaders call for revival in the church and a return to traditional values. Notable in this regard has been Colin Standish, an Australian educator, formerly dean of Weimar and subsequently president of another self-supporting enterprise, the Hartland Institute in Virginia. In conjunction with his twin brother, Russell, he has written numerous books upholding traditional Adventist views on theology and education and criticizing the church's leadership for its openness to secular influence.[4] In return, church leaders, particularly those in denominational colleges, complain bitterly about what they perceive to be the disruptive effects of conservative polemic.[5] The debate is carried on by both sides with a fair amount of *odium theologicum*. The conservatives consider that the church has been hijacked by a minority of liberal intellectuals, while their opponents argue that the self-supporting ideal represents a narrow-minded and anachronistic response to contemporary problems.

The fissures that underlie these disputes are difficult to trace. Conservative Adventism is an important and complex phenomenon that has been unduly neglected by the church's scholars, many of whom wish that it would simply disappear. As a result, any analysis must remain tentative, for it is not immediately clear that theological traditionalists, health enthusiasts, educational conservatives, and self-supporting workers form a united group. In what follows, it is argued that there is a sufficient degree of historical continuity, doctrinal similarity, and institutional overlap to indicate that there is an identifiable movement that, although it contains several currents of opinion, represents a particular kind of response to mainstream Adventism.[6]

The movement was formed in two stages. The first was the development of an alternative type of Adventist institution in the form of Madison Sanitarium, Tennessee, founded in 1904. The second was the return to the ideals of Ellen White by those displeased with trends in Adventism since the Second World War. The first stage represented the emergence of a separate tradition within the church; the second embodied a reaction to a church that was perceived to be changing beyond recognition.

Madison was the creation of two senior educators who had the enthusiastic support of Ellen White.[7] At the turn of the century, E. A.

Sutherland was president of the denominational college at Battle Creek. Along with the dean, Percy Magan, he attempted reorganization. The transfer of Battle Creek College to Berrien Springs, Michigan, and its redesignation as Emmanuel Missionary College represented a success for Sutherland's vision of missionary education in a rural setting. But the victory was achieved at a cost. The church's membership lost confidence in the college, enrollment plummeted, and, amid bitter criticism, Sutherland and Magan resigned. But as one experiment failed, the opportunity to start another emerged.

Edson White's independent work for blacks in the South had suggested to his mother that an agriculturally based program might benefit poor southern whites. Accordingly, Sutherland and Magan moved to Tennessee, where a farm was purchased and a school established. Ellen White was particularly excited about the project; in 1908 she penned "An Appeal for the Madison School." She remained on the school board (the only occasion she ever held such a position) until her death, and she recommended that "every possible means should be devised to establish schools of the Madison order in various parts of the South."[8] Her interest continued, and while at Madison on a picnic arranged in her honor, she suggested that a sanitarium might be built.[9]

Her advice on both counts was soon heeded. A sanitarium was established, and Sutherland and Magan, both in middle age, qualified as physicians. In 1924 the Layman Foundation was organized. It was designed to foster the growth of rural self-supporting units that were offshoots of the mother institution. In the years before the Second World War, about forty such units were established. One unit sometimes spawned another. Thus, in 1924 the Layman Foundation purchased a farm near Knoxville, Tennessee, which became the basis for the Little Creek Sanitarium and Academy, and in 1950 a teacher went from Little Creek to establish Laurelbrook School on a farm near Dayton.[10] Of the one thousand Madison graduates, over one-quarter went on to work in self-supporting institutions—far more than were employed by the denomination itself.[11] Thus, a network was created that provided an alternative to the system offered by official church institutions.

Although some of its progeny survive, Madison itself was closed in 1964, one year after being transferred to denominational control. Its failure was precipitated by the state's requirement that the hospital be rebuilt to higher standards, but the underlying causes of decline lay in the postwar prosperity of the young, who no longer needed to work in order to be able to study, and the declining commitment of the staff for whom Madison was no longer a pioneering institution. The closure did not herald the demise of the self-supporting work, for a major new center had emerged at Wildwood.[12] Although influenced by Madison, Wildwood was not an offshoot. Rather it represented a return to the

vision of Ellen White by the members of a younger generation, notably
W. D. Frazee, who were inspired by the ideal of rural Adventist communities as centers of health evangelism. Although it was initially difficult to find medical staff committed to natural remedies, the sanitarium gradually succeeded in developing a favorable local reputation.
The subsequent development of a vegetarian restaurant in Chattanooga set the pattern for several of Wildwood's numerous daughter
institutions, which operate successful restaurants in major cities such
as New York and London.

Wildwood appears to have taken on Madison's role as the inspiration
for a wider movement. But the differences are instructive. Madison
was founded by the church's leading educators, at the direct behest of
Ellen White, with a view to its being an integral part of the denomination's work in the South. The initiative that resulted in the formation
of Wildwood did not come from the church's established leadership,
nor did it represent any currently authorized policy; it derived from
the spontaneous recommitment of private individuals to an earlier set
of ideals. The oppositional stance implicit in the development of Wildwood and its offshoots is clearer still in the foundation of the Weimar
Institute in 1977.[13]

The Hewitt Research Foundation, a consultancy designed to foster
traditional Adventist health and education programs, was organized in
1969, funded by a gift from a wealthy Loma Linda couple. In 1976 its
director, Raymond Moore, published a book, *Adventist Education at the
Crossroads*, that argued that denominational education had grown increasingly ineffective because of its failure to create a balanced work-
study schedule grounded in agriculture and oriented toward religion.[14]
These ideas were viewed sympathetically by a group of Adventists in
California, and the Weimar Institute was set up, specifically in order
to realize the goals that other church schools had not achieved. Despite
protests that the institute's work is not "in opposition to, or in competition with, the program and institutions of the church,"[15] the very
existence of an alternative college, inspired by criticism of established
practices and competing for students in a shrinking market, reveals the
inherent conflict between mainstream Adventism and its conservative
wing.

However, the two stages in the development of the self-supporting
movement do not necessarily represent a significant shift in orientation. The movement is both an alternative tradition within Adventism
and a reactionary response to contemporary change; it has a distinct
but continuous history and yet also provides a current critique of the
mainstream church. This dual function is facilitated by two factors.
First, the expansion of self-supporting work and its ability to absorb its
own graduates may exacerbate any initial tension by developing an independent way of life parallel to that of the mainstream. Second, the

tradition itself was formulated in conscious opposition to Adventist educational practices of the nineteenth century. In responding critically
to the mainstream, the self-supporting movement remains true to its
own origins.

This alternative philosophy was most clearly articulated by E. A.
Sutherland in his book *Living Fountains or Broken Cisterns*, published in
1900.[16] It traces the history of education from the Garden of Eden
through the Israelite schools of the prophets and follows the development of medieval universities to the current condition of church and
state education in America. The central argument is that contemporary
American education is heavily reliant on papal procedures propagated
by the Jesuits. The granting of degrees, the rote learning of classical
languages, and the method of Socratic doubt are all cited as examples.
In contrast, the study of nature is suggested as a bulwark against doubt,
and the development of practical skills is advised to counteract the ill
effects of rote learning. Sutherland believed that all education—even
mathematics—should have a religious content. In 1901 he published a
book entitled *Mental Arithmetic* in which the required calculations involved puzzling out the chronology of the Hebrew kings and comput-
ing tithe payments.[17]

Sutherland's arguments were of peculiar relevance to his Adventist
audience, for they neatly synthesized the reformist educational views
of Ellen White with her great controversy theme. For Sutherland and
his followers, educational philosophy became a major issue in the dispute between Christ and Satan, but it was a dispute in which mainstream Adventism appeared to be firmly located on the wrong side.
Prior to Sutherland's reforms, Battle Creek College offered a B.A. degree that could be earned only through an extended study of Greek
and Latin literature. Adventist education embodied precisely those
characteristics Sutherland abhorred.

According to Sutherland's successors, Adventist schools continue to
exemplify the failings of contemporary education. In a recent study
authored by the Standish brothers, many of Sutherland's themes are
reiterated, but there is also a subtle shift of emphasis. Sutherland had
argued that "a failure to make the development of thought—independent thinking, in fact—the main object in instruction stamps any
method of teaching as papal."[18] For the Standishes, the issue is no
longer the thoughtless repetition of classical grammar but the view that
"academic freedom is necessary for the pursuit of truth."[19] Their response is that "the freedom cries are based upon the fundamental error
that freedom will lead to truth, while Christ clearly declares that it is
the reverse—truth will lead to freedom."[20]

The context in which Sutherland wrote was different. He was pro-
posing radical ideas in opposition to the educational traditionalists of
his day. His followers are writing against moral relativism rather than

intellectual dogmatism and in the modern world appear conservative.[21] It is, however, the prevailing intellectual climate rather than the self-supporting philosophy that has changed. Its central tenet remains the view that education is best undertaken through direct involvement with nature. The Standishes repeat Ellen White's statement that "study in agricultural lines should be the A, B and C of the education given in our schools"[22] and conclude that "true Christian education will offer every opportunity for students to gain an education in the pursuits of the soil."[23] Such activities will, the authors argue, help to develop patience, responsibility, self-discipline, and obedience to rules. It is an approach that reflects Sutherland's idea that God's laws are embedded in nature and the belief that man can learn them through contact with the natural environment. As Sutherland put it: "At his work of dressing the garden, Adam learned truths which only work could reveal. As the tree of life gave food to the flesh, and reminded constantly of the mental and spiritual food necessary, so manual training added light to the mental discipline."[24]

A comparable discrepancy exists between the philosophies of the self-supporting health facilities and those of the Adventist health system. W. D. Frazee distinguished "genuine medical missionary work" from other medical work by its ability to meet three criteria. According to Frazee, a medical missionary should ask himself

1. Is my work done wholly from love—unselfish, self-sacrificing love?
2. Am I more concerned with leading people to obedience of nature's laws than I am in relieving symptoms? And are the methods I am using accomplishing that result?
3. Is my great goal in all my work the winning of souls for Christ and his message? And is the program I am following, the work I am doing, producing souls that I can present to Jesus at his coming?[25]

In practice, these principles are interpreted to mean that health professionals should receive much less than the customary remuneration, that symptom relieving drugs should be avoided, and that distinctive Adventist beliefs should be presented to patients. This is the basis on which Wildwood and similar sanitariums are run. Other Adventist hospitals charge and pay commercial rates; make extensive use of drugs; and emphasize that a Christian, rather than a specifically Adventist, atmosphere prevails. In health care, too, denominational institutions define themselves primarily by professional and commercial standards, while independent institutions are operated on specifically Adventist guidelines.

Self-supporting ventures thus not only have a long history independent of the denomination but also have an independent philosophy, which gives full weight to Ellen White's reformist ideals in a way that denominationally operated institutions have never done. It would thus be a mistake to imagine that self-supporting centers preserve the ethos and ideals of earlier generations of mainstream Adventists. Even the first Adventist institutions, Battle Creek College and the Western Health Reform Institute, did not realize these principles. On the contrary, the ideals of health and education that Ellen White advanced were formulated as a criticism not so much of existing secular practices but of contemporary Adventist practice. Adventist institutions predated Ellen White's ideals for them. They did not depart from those ideals; they never changed enough to realize them. Self-supporting institutions represent an implicit criticism of the denominational system because they are founded on Ellen White's explicit criticism of that system. They have an independent ancestry that goes back to Ellen White's writings; denominational institutions were founded, not on the basis of a written program but in emulation of similar secular institutions. Self-supporting and denominational institutions do not share a common origin.

This conclusion points to the fact that among self-supporting workers there exists a form of Adventism that is not so much deviant or anachronistic as it is alternative. It is true, however, that the self-supporting philosophy was formulated in the 1890s and that the theology of the movement preserves the beliefs and concerns of the turn of the century—the transitional period between Adventist radicalism and Adventist fundamentalism. But the movement was born at a time when mainstream Adventism was divided. In the crisis of 1900–1905, Adventist radicalism, in the form of Kellogg and his associates, was forced outside the denomination. The new fundamentalism downplayed health, harmony with nature, and social service in favor of revivalist evangelism and clearer boundaries between the sacred and the secular. The self-supporting movement, however, represented an alternative response to the crisis based on a synthesis of radical and fundamentalist ideas. Sutherland and Magan, who were suspected of being Kellogg sympathizers, retained his devotion to nature, natural remedies, and understanding of life in which there was little division between sacred and secular. Unlike Kellogg, they went a step further by sacralizing almost every activity. They rejected modernism and retained an unswerving loyalty to Ellen White.[26]

The self-supporting movement may be viewed in historical terms as an alternative form of Adventism that developed from a synthesis of conflicting trends at the turn of the century. But what of the contemporary position of the movement and its interrelationship with the mainstream of the church? The most prominent self-supporting institutions have some ties with the church. At Weimar, for example, both students and faculty may spend only a limited period at the institute before returning to denominational employment or education. The leadership is drawn from the upper echelons of the church itself. Before becoming dean, Colin Standish was president of the church's Columbia Union College in Maryland; his successor, Herbert Douglass, was previously an associate editor of the *Review*.[27] Within mainstream Adventist education, such people are rather isolated individuals. In the context of the self-supporting movement, they are at the center of a network that propagates their ideas.

Members of this network who are not attached to any particular center keep in touch through a constant interchange of magazines, manuscripts, and tapes. One publication that acts as a forum for this exchange is *The Layworker*, a quarterly magazine published in California.[28] Ironically, the journal originally supported the early perfectionism of Brinsmead but failed to move with him when he changed his position.[29] It now advertises tapes by contemporary opponents of Brinsmead, such as the Standish brothers. Although leading figures in the self-supporting movement do not write for *The Layworker*, the magazine provides a meeting place for many of the Adventist church's other conservative critics. The editor recommends the work of William Grotheer, a former Bible teacher at the Madison school who publishes a newsletter entitled *Watchman, What of the Night?*[30] Another bulletin, *Pilgrim's Waymarks*, produced by Vance Ferrell of the Pilgrim's Rest organization, receives similar commendation.[31] Both publications are devoted to monitoring denominational compromises with the secular world, but neither is as hostile to the Adventist mainstream as the newsletter of the Hoehn Research Library, written by Hermann Hoehn, a contributor to *The Layworker*.[32] Hoehn, who specializes in producing unflattering cartoon representations of the General Conference president, is not a figure with whom the more sober leaders of conservative Adventism wish to identify. But he operates within the same Adventist subculture. The individuals who write in *The Layworker* and similar publications sometimes espouse ideas eccentric to Adventism, but in the main, they are faithful to the traditional emphases maintained in the self-supporting movement. The letters reveal that efforts are being made to put the movement's philosophy into practice by persons isolated from self-supporting centers:

For the last six weeks, I have been developing our ten acres. I have my land all paid for. I have had tractor clearing and septic tank put in, a garden spot and clearing for a garden. I have spring water running on the garden and a permit for my mobile home. The garden is planted now, so I am preparing for the crises. My wife is dragging her feet. I haven't lost interest in mission work, but I feel its time to get out of the city. So I am preparing to set a mobile home on my land. At present I have a travel trailer there and developing [*sic*].[33]

As such correspondence demonstrates, the ideals of the movement are shared and expressed by conservative Adventists who sometimes single-handedly attempt to realize its objectives. Thus, although the movement's constituency extends beyond institutional boundaries, there remain common goals, acknowledged theological leaders, and established channels of communication. The self-supporting movement is not an organized sect with uniform beliefs and established hierarchies, but an interlaced network of people, places, and publications that share certain ideals and have a common heritage. Within this context, any one center is best understood not as an institution but as a community, for the primary purpose of a self-supporting unit is not to provide any one service or facility but to create an integrated program of industries and services that will minimize the center's reliance on external support.

Frazee suggests an eschatological justification for this. In *Another Ark to Build*, he argues that just as Noah built an ark in an age of confusion and wickedness, so in the last days, the saints will need oases of safety. "The 'ark,' " he states, "is a complete little program that God gave our people to establish outside every city; a farm, a school on that farm, a little sanitarium connected with it, [and] an evangelistic center."[34] Frazee envisages that these communities will cater to refugees from the cities and be able to provide home-grown food to Sabbath keepers unable to purchase supplies because of the final Sunday law. In other words, these centers aim to be socially and economically self-contained. Although a great deal is purchased from outside, a well-developed, self-supporting community will be able to provide its members with employment, food, basic supplies, education for children, and health care for the sick. Life can thus be lived with little direct contact with the outside world. Contact is, however, often made, chiefly for purposes of evangelism and health promotion. But the boundaries between the community and the world are emphasized through geographical distance and the community's mildly distinctive forms of dress and behavior.

The self-supporting community is able to realize the ideal of self-sufficiency far more effectively than the man who wrote to *The Layworker* describing his efforts to set up a mobile home on ten acres. Individual survivalists may share the same objectives as a self-supporting community, but their goals can only be fully attained within a social framework. In this respect the movement functions as an accelerated version of mainstream Adventism, which also takes people out of the world and places them within a largely self-contained social environment.

Self-supporting institutions may thus be seen to realize the communitarian impulse within Adventism—the desire to separate from the world and to live according to God's plan without compromise or interference. Mainstream Adventism has fulfilled the first of these objectives, but not the second. The self-supporting movement is not the first attempt to deal with the problem. From the days of Millerism, Adventists have shown marked interest in communitarian experiments. Many former Millerites joined the Shakers,[35] while others founded communities of their own. The Celesta community in Pennsylvania was founded in 1852, and the Adonai-Shomo group, which observed a seventh-day Sabbath, in 1861.[36] Neither of these experiments directly involved Seventh-day Adventists, but both reveal the openness of other Adventists to regulated forms of social grouping. For white Seventh-day Adventists, institutional growth has largely satisfied the need for community. Significantly, it was a black minister, J. K. Humphrey, who in his dream of Utopia Park envisaged Adventism's most remarkable dissident community project.[37] (Blacks had benefited little from the expansion of medical and educational work.) Similarly, the self-supporting movement may create an opportunity for marginal whites to become socially integrated into an exclusively Adventist environment. Madison was founded to help the poor rural whites of the South, and self-supporting centers continue to provide employment and training for the unskilled. Most denominational institutions have a heavy concentration of skilled and professional jobs. For new converts who are more likely than their fellow church members to be of low socioeconomic status, the self-supporting movement may provide more opportunities than the mainstream church. It is not, therefore, altogether surprising that at the self-supporting Oak Haven center in Michigan, 80 percent of the work force were reported, in the early 1980s, to be new converts.[38]

At a time when the mainstream church finds it difficult to inspire commitment among white Americans, the self-supporting movement is one of the few areas of growth. It seems primarily to attract whites, both from within and without the church. As the racial balance of the American church shifts toward blacks and Hispanics, the self-supporting movement may become a more significant element in white Adventist experience. It is even conceivable that with the passing of time it may become defined less by its alternative philosophy than by its racial constituency. In the meantime, the movement is differentiated from the rest of the church by its greater distance from contemporary American customs.

But the self-supporting movement also represents the antithesis of mainstream Adventism for a totally different set of reasons. It has grown through the individual initiative of laymen rather than the bureaucratic procedures of the church. In particular, it has allowed wealthy individuals, both Adventist and non-Adventist, the opportunity to promote a dissident form of religious expression. The Adventist church's economic base has always been the systematic, small-scale generosity of a high percentage of its membership. The self-supporting movement has been financed by a few rich individuals and maintained by the sacrifice of its members. In other words, the self-supporting movement, which represents the ideal of egalitarian cooperation, has been promoted through the power of individual capital concentration, while mainstream Adventism, which espouses a set of values a little closer to the American ethos, is founded on bureaucratically controlled schemes of funding.

The paradox should not be overstressed. For in its reliance on individual benefactors, the self-supporting movement is following in a long-established tradition in which the wealthy finance organized forms of self-denial. Monasticism is but one example; others may be found in the communitarian experiments of eighteenth- and nineteenth-century America. F. D. Nichol was the first to compare the self-supporting movement to a monastic order. He suggested that just as the various orders within Catholicism contributed to the vitality of the church despite their diversity, so in Adventism the ASI was an independent but positive force.[39] Nichol's point is valid. Like monasticism, the self-supporting movement represents a rigorous interpretation of the ideals of the church, combined with a strong reaction against the laxity with which these ideals are usually enforced. Although the movement, like Catholic monasticism, embodies an implicit criticism of the church's worldliness and is a base for rigorist revivalists, it also provides an outlet for zealous individuals whose enthusiasm might otherwise lead them outside the church and attracts those for whom the church might otherwise have little to offer. The movement permits adherence to the Adventist denomination through partial opposition to it. In this it may be seen to function in relation to Adventism in precisely the same way that Adventism functions in relation to the mainstream of American life. As an intensification of the Adventist experience, the self-supporting movement replicates that experience in microcosm.

CHAPTER 20

Conclusion: The Revolving Door

Some religious organizations are impossible to join. Others are almost impossible to leave. Most fall between the extremes of exclusivity and inclusivity. They have boundaries that can be crossed in both directions. This is certainly true of American Protestantism. Only about 60 percent of people remain within the denomination in which they are brought up.[1] But one church's loss is usually another's gain.[2] Some denominations maintain a steady total membership that disguises a high turnover. A growing church combines numerous gains with few losses. In decline, the ratio is reversed. A denomination may thus be characterized by the flow of people through its entrances and exits. Its relationship to other groups can be clarified by the source of its gains and the destination of its losses. Churches appear to be static bodies continuous through time. But those with a shifting constituency can be seen not as discrete entities but as processes through which a constant stream of individuals may pass. This final chapter looks at Adventism as a process. It seeks to account both for the diversity within the church and for the position of Adventism within American society.

For about the first seven years of its existence, Adventism was a movement that was impossible to join. The door of mercy was deemed to be shut, and so entrance to the movement was also barred. Adventists were so estranged from the surrounding culture that they did not even recruit from it.[3] When the entrance was opened in the 1850s, converts came through, at first in a trickle, later in a flood. Who were these people? And where did they come from? A study of the accounts of the *Review and Herald* for 1869 provides an answer to these questions. The subscribers, who could have been drawn to the movement only during the previous decade, were remarkably homogenous. Seventy-eight percent of those in Michigan were farmers or farm operators, a state in which farmers numbered 38 percent of the population as a whole. A mere 5 percent of subscribers were unskilled laborers, compared to 31 percent of the general population. In 1860 the people entering Adventism were relatively affluent members of isolated rural communities.[4]

What happened to them and their descendants? It is difficult to answer that question directly, but a survey conducted in California in the 1930s provides a clue. Adventists were still disproportionately involved in agriculture, but they were also overrepresented in clerical and technical occupations.[5] How did the change come about? A national survey conducted in 1950 revealed that although the number of Adventist farmers was now about average, the proportion in the older generation was almost twice as high as that in the younger age group. Of farmers' children, only 26 percent still worked in agriculture, while over 55 percent had become technical, clerical, or skilled workers. The occupations in which Adventists were now overrepresented were of a professional/technical or craft nature.[6]

What was to be the fate of the next generation? The 1950 survey pointed to the probability that they would move into the professions. Twenty-nine percent of the employed children of those in clerical/sales occupations, 26 percent of the children of craftsmen, and 28 percent of the children of managers had already moved into the professional/technical field. Of those whose parents were professionals, 47 percent had taken up similar employment. In 1950, 31 percent of Adventists were in professional/technical occupations, a figure four times higher than the national average.[7] If the marked tendency of Adventist youth to embark on professional careers continued, one would anticipate that, thirty years later, Adventists would be massively overrepresented in the professional classes.

In 1986 the Institute of Church Ministry, in association with Donnelley Marketing Information Services, used marketing research techniques to profile the Adventist membership in the United States. In this project, the population was divided into forty-seven clusters of economic and lifestyle characteristics, which were combined into ten multifactor cluster groups. Although Adventist members were drawn from higher status groups than were Adventist converts, they were found to be markedly underrepresented in the first group, the group with the highest proportion of professionals, and underrepresented to a lesser degree in all of the top four groups.[8] The everenlarging body of Adventist professionals indicated by the 1950 survey seemed to have disappeared. At midcentury, Adventists already had four times the average number of professionals in their ranks, and were moving into the professions in large numbers. Just over a generation later, most of these people seemed to have vanished. Where had they gone? The absence of data precludes the possibility of any conclusive answer to this question, but there is enough evidence to draw some tentative conclusions. To do this it is necessary to review the process by which the convert enters more fully into the Adventist experience.

In the nineteenth and early twentieth centuries, Adventists recruited heavily from among the farmers of the western states. A successful farmer was often an affluent man, and Adventists were rarely the poorest members of the community. But life was hard. Farmers and their families were unlikely to have received more than a rudimentary education. They were self-sufficient, but their manners were coarse and their social skills limited. Adventism sought to remedy these deficiencies. Converts were exhorted to exercise self-restraint in every area of life and to develop the ability to work harmoniously with their fellow believers. Ministers were the agents appointed to effect this transformation. They were expected to improve their congregations, both through the model decorum of their own behavior and by maintaining religious and social discipline.[9]

When the church started offering education for the children of its members, the school became the chief means of socialization. Just how important church schooling was in effecting the integration of the young into Adventist society was revealed in the 1950 survey "Seventh-Day Adventist Youth at the Mid-century." There was, it appeared, a direct correlation between the amount of Adventist education a young person received and the likelihood of his or her becoming and remaining a member of the church. Most children educated outside the denomination, or with only eight grades of Adventist schooling, had left the church.[10]

Here, then, was a contrast. For the first-generation Adventist, the convert, the primary point of contact with the denomination was the local congregation. Through the work of the minister, church elders, deacons, and Sabbath School teachers, the convert was brought to a fuller understanding of the principles of the church. For the second-generation member, these values were mediated by another institution—the school. While their parents probably attended church on only one day a week, Adventist children (especially after the initial phase of denominational education) were likely to receive some form of religious instruction on five subsequent days. In the school, behavior compatible with Adventist values was encouraged, along with academic excellence.

However, the 1950 survey indicated that while Adventist schooling encouraged children to maintain the religion of their parents, it was liable to discourage them from following the same occupation. The convert, traditionally a farmer or skilled worker, was generally pursuing a career that required little formal education. The successful completion of an Adventist education provided new opportunities unavailable to the previous generation. The education that facilitated continued church involvement also enabled the second generation to change their social and occupational status. At this point, another element of the Adventist experience emerges—church employment.

Converts, unless young, were likely to have preexisting economic ties. Where employment was incompatible with Sabbath observance, converts might change jobs or become self-employed. But they were unlikely to become full-time employees of the church. Their skills, as farmers and craftsmen, were not those in high demand in Adventism. For the second generation, the situation was different. One of the functions of Adventist education was to train workers for the cause. The net result of this was that the successful completion of an Adventist college education not only confirmed students in their faith and distanced them from the occupational roles of their parents, but also equipped them to engage full-time in the work of the organization. To complete an Adventist education was to be fully trained as a potential church employee.

In the 1950 survey, 11 percent of employed Adventists worked for the church. Of these, a clear majority of both men and women were engaged in professional/technical occupations.[11] The range of activities covered by this designation was probably wide. The Adventist church needed ministers and administrators. It also required teachers for denominational schools, doctors and nurses for hospitals and clinics, plus all the personnel to teach these professions. For the second-generation Adventist, or the young male convert, the ministry was often the most accessible and appealing of these careers. It combined very directly the goals of religious and educational improvement and, for the convert, offered a unique opportunity to pass on his experience to others. For most second-generation Adventists, however, the other professions might have seemed more attractive. For women, teaching and nursing appeared as the two main options. For both sexes, but predominantly for men, medicine was an alluring career.

At midcentury, those in church employment accounted for a significant proportion of the total number of Adventist professionals. These people were, it is safe to assume, usually the products of Adventist education. Once again, it is worth contrasting their position with that of the previous generation. For the mature convert, association with Adventism began and ended with church membership. For a successful member of the second generation, the Adventist church might also have provided education and employment. Affiliation to the church was thus a more complex affair, involving loyalty to an employer and respect for values received in education as well as allegiance to a particular congregation.

The 1950 survey indicated that the role toward which Adventist youth seemed most inclined to move was that of the denominationally employed professional. Thus, the question arises: What happened to the children of the second generation? The survey showed that almost half the children of those in professional/technical occupations had obtained employment in the same sphere. A fair proportion of these young people must have been not second-, but third-generation Adventists, for whom denominational education and employment was not a novelty but a recapitulation of their parents' careers. Unfortunately, the 1950 survey did not differentiate between different types of professional career. But impressionistic evidence suggests that for those whose parents were already in professional/technical employment, the most attractive careers were in the health professions. The church's medical school, intended to train staff for denominational hospitals in the United States and overseas, for a long time constituted the only form of recognized professional education available within the church. As such, it was the best means for second- and particularly third-generation Adventists to move beyond the educational level of their parents while staying within the Adventist system.

Becoming a doctor, dentist, or nurse was, and to some degree remains, the natural culmination of the Adventist experience. The physician is, in Ellen White's words, "God's nobleman," someone with a work above that even of the ordained ministry.[12] The status of the profession is enhanced by the long years of training necessary to qualify. In a system where good students are usually good Adventists, a career open only to the best students is naturally accorded a certain reverence. In Adventism, the authority of doctors extends well beyond mere professional competence, for they are individuals who are assumed to have realized the shared ambitions of the church community. Doctors complete twenty years of education, most of it probably in denominational schools, and are acknowledged experts on health—a major Adventist preoccupation. One further factor adds to doctors' status: their professional position is recognized not only by Adventists themselves but also by non-Adventists. Despite having been trained within Adventism, denominationally educated physicians have a qualification equally acceptable outside the church.

This is significant. Adventist ministers or institutional employees have generally gained their positions by virtue of their allegiance to the church. They are unlikely to have qualifications that would secure them a comparable post outside the denomination, and non-Adventists, whatever their qualifications, would be considered unsuitable replacements. In the health professions, the situation has long been the reverse. The majority of Adventist physicians do not work for the church, and the majority of doctors and nurses employed by the denomination in the United States are non-Adventists. Adventist health professionals are interchangeable with their secular counterparts in a way that other denominational personnel are not. Their role is perceived in a fundamentally different way. They are not primarily Adventists but members of a particular profession. Their religious affiliation takes on secondary importance.[13]

The health professions thus have a dual function. They are both a culmination and a negation of the Adventist experience. Throughout the process by which professional status has been attained, the most significant distinctions have been between Adventists and non-Adventists, church schools and public schools, sacred and secular. Once professional status has been reached, these divisions become irrelevant. Physicians are presumed to be doing God's work by virtue of their profession, rather than their denominational allegiance. No suspicion attaches to Adventist doctors in secular employment, but professors employed in non-Adventist colleges are often presumed to hold deviant opinions. Doctors and nurses enjoy the freedom to work on the Sabbath. Their work is presumed to be, and probably often is, essential to save lives. But Adventists are not encouraged to join, and are rarely to be found in, other equally essential occupations, to which such liberty is not accorded. Only medical professionals are allowed to disregard the practices that otherwise regulate and define the Adventist identity.

There is, then, a sense in which physicians have transcended the Adventist experience. Adventism, with its mistrust of American society, has traditionally drawn converts from that society, encouraged them to send their children to Adventist schools, ad provided opportunities for the second generation to work for the church. Throughout this process, the rationale for movement (movement out of "the world" and into church schools and employment) is that American society is doomed and that involvement with it may lead to a share in its damnation. The health professions provide a means of reengaging with the world in a fashion that is taken to be nonpolluting. The physician is in a position to dictate rather than to be dictated to. He can go beyond the Adventist injunction to exercise self-control, for he can control the lives of others who do not share his religious opinions. Medical practitioners do not need to escape the authority of American society, for they can wield authority in that society. Because of their professional status, doctors may reenter society without compromising their Adventism.[14]

The health professions have thus become the terminus ad quem of the Adventist experience, the last stage in a prolonged and often multigenerational process in which Adventists change their relationship with other Americans. Potential persecutors are transformed into patients, as isolated farmers become respected physicians. This process is characterized by rapid socioeconomic advance. Within Adventism, upward mobility occurs naturally and easily. Self-restraint and hard work are religious duties, and education is strongly encouraged. These are characteristics Adventism shares with many other minority religious groups. Adventism's unusual capacity to promote upward mobility derives from two further factors. First, Adventists as a group appear to be particularly mobile, because those who are not leave the church. A 1981 Institute of Church Ministry survey found strong positive correlations between church growth and the educational and economic level of the congregation.[15] This is unsurprising. If the patterns discovered by the midcentury survey have continued, a majority of the Adventists whose education terminates at eighth grade are destined to exit. These are the people whose limited education is unlikely to facilitate upward mobility; they are also the people who leave. Among those that remain in education, the ones most likely to stay in the church are those with college education.[16] Adventism does not automatically produce upward mobility; it retains those most likely to achieve it. The second factor is related. Adventism promotes mobility not so much within wider society as within Adventism: the unusually high numbers of high school and college graduates are the products of Adventist institutions; a substantial minority of Adventist professionals are, or at least were in 1950, employed by the church itself. Upward mobility is easier within the church than it is outside. Education at Adventist colleges is generally of a high standard relative to the low admission requirements. The church's heavy institutionalization creates far more professional posts than would normally be available to a similar number of potential employees. Adventism's alternative society is one in which upward social mobility is more readily achieved than it is outside. Those who make an exit from the Adventist system appear to be the people who either fail to progress within it or who cannot progress further.

This conclusion suggests two explanations for the absence of Adventist professionals in the 1986 ICM study. First, the study may easily have underestimated the number of Adventist professionals because of their geographical concentration. A large number live in the immediate vicinity of Adventist institutions. These so-called ghettoes are often located in areas not otherwise characterized by the high socioeconomic status of their inhabitants. Adventist colleges are frequently in rural locations, and hospitals are often in lower-class urban areas, not in professional, suburban neighborhoods. Accordingly, the Adventist professional may have been invisible in a study, the basic unit of which was not the individual household but the local neighborhood.

The second explanation—which is complementary rather than alternative—is simpler. The total number of Adventist professionals is smaller than one would anticipate from church members' marked upward social mobility, owing to the fact that some professionals and many of their children leave the church. Although graduate education in architecture and business is now offered at Andrews University and the church's membership also includes an increasing number of lawyers, for most of the century, the health professions were the only ones open within the Adventist system. Those who wished to pursue other professional careers had to move outside to find education and employment, and in the course of this, many became separated from the church. Even some of those who might have worked for the denomination became estranged. When their status increased, they abandoned their religious heritage. As one commentator noted, in the 1960s "many . . . second, third, and fourth generation Adventists began leaving the church because their questions and needs were not being addressed."[17] Adventism could, and often did, seem irrelevant to those whose social and intellectual experience was radically different from that of their forefathers.

The composition of the Seventh-day Adventist church is thus defined by three factors: the nature of its recruits, the process by which they enter more deeply into the life of the church, and the identity of those who exit. Putting these elements together, it is possible to sketch a tentative model of the Adventist experience that takes into account both the separation of Adventists from American society and the diversity that exists within the movement. The model also provides a framework through which it is possible to understand and assess the nature of the changes that have taken place within the church.

Adventism is a process that draws people out of American society and embeds them in a subculture subtly at variance with it. It is also a process that projects people back into the outside world. Both the entrances and the exits to the movement are open. The best way to conceive of the process is as a revolving door, with a continuous flow of people both entering and leaving. The process can be subdivided into three distinct stages, corresponding, perhaps, to individual segments in a revolving door. In the entrance segment, converts embrace the Adventist message and strive to leave the world behind. In the second, believers are already established within the church and seek to progress within it. In the third, the exit segment, Adventists move to reexplore the world. In the first phase, Adventists aspire to realize the church's ideals; in the second they attempt to sustain those ideals; and in the third, they seek to transform the ideals.

Each segment in the revolving door is positioned as shown in Figure 4 (see page 264).

In moving through this process, Adventists are first drawn quickly away from societal norms into a deviant social and religious position; they then maintain a constant level of deviance while experiencing accelerated upward mobility. As Figure 4 makes clear, there is an inverse relationship between deviance and socioeconomic status: the rate at which the level of deviance changes is inversely proportional to the speed at which socioeconomic status is increased. This relationship may be seen as one of exchange. On the way into Adventism, socioeconomic marginality is exchanged for religious marginality. On the way out of

Figure 4. The Revolving Door

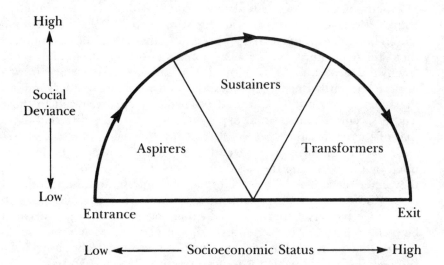

Adventism, religious marginality is exchanged for socioeconomic centrality.

This, it must be emphasized, is a model designed to interpret a wide variety of evidence about who Adventists are and what they believe and do. As such, it has no claims to prescriptive accuracy. It is also inapplicable to the many people who are Adventists for only a short period of time. Numerous converts and their children leave the church while still in the first segment of the revolving door. They exit the way they came in, without ever moving through the full range of the Adventist experience. These people neither enjoy upward social mobility nor participate fully, or for long, in the life of the church. But for those that remain, Adventism offers a long and varied religious career, each phase of which has its own distinctive character.

At the point of entry, converts, who are usually persons of limited education and low status, are inspired by an apocalyptic vision of the world. They are eager to separate themselves from a society bound for destruction and to ally themselves with a body of believers bound for heaven. They are, however, still embedded within American society. Their friends, neighbors, and workmates are unlikely to share their convictions. Their contact with Adventism is chiefly a religious matter, for they do not have an Adventist education, have but limited social ties, and are unlikely to be employed by the church. They are enthusiastic about their new faith and eager to convert others. But they may encounter problems. The very literalism of their beliefs may lead to some unorthodoxy on questions of eschatology or the divine nature. Although keen to adopt the Adventist lifestyle, they may find it difficult to conquer established habits and follow Adventist health principles to the letter.

For the next generation, or for converts young enough to alter fundamentally the direction of their lives, the situation is different. They will probably have at least some Adventist education and are likely to be attracted by the idea of working for the church. The minister may prove a particularly attractive role model. Failing that, "sustainers" may opt for other denominational employment. Even if their work is secular, they are likely to be leading figures in the local congregation, perhaps as church elders or Sabbath school teachers. For people in this phase of the Adventist experience, there is little need to shun the world, for its temptations are distant. They are fully socialized into an Adventist milieu in which they are bound to the church by economic, educational, and social ties. The objectives of those in this segment are to maintain the Adventist system and advance within it. They usually accept Adventist beliefs and lifestyle without question and are able to find new justifications for any doctrines that seem unattractive.

In the final phase of the Adventist experience, "transformers" have a long personal and family history of church involvement. Adventist values do not need to be maintained, still less aspired to, for they are taken for granted. Socialization into Adventism has been so complete that at the start of the third phase, Adventists are quite unlikely to know intimately anyone who is not an Adventist. Their parents, relatives, friends, and schoolmates are all likely to be church members. Their education will probably have been completely within denominational schools and colleges, but they may hold some qualifications that give them professional status outside Adventism as well. This provides a means of reaching out into a world about which transformers are understandably curious. They will make professional contact with non-Adventists, perhaps adopt some elements of non-Adventist lifestyle, and seek to reconcile Adventist beliefs with the philosophical presuppositions of their profession. As many Adventist professionals are medically orientated, this synthesis is usually expressed as holism, which perceives Adventism as a superior lifestyle package that maximizes physical and psychological health. The concerns of the transformers are primarily individual. For them, Adventism is malleable, waiting to be shaped to their personal requirements. They have little contact with or sympathy for the literalism of the aspirer and perceive the activities of the sustainer to be inimical to their self-fulfillment. This quest for self-realization may lead transformers outside of the church as a religious organization, although they may maintain social contacts with its members. It is certainly unlikely to provide a framework within which a further generation of Adventists can be successfully reared. The differences between each phase of the Adventist experience is summarized in Table 4.

Table 4. Different Phases in Adventist Experience

	Phase One: Entrance	Phase Two: Transition	Phase Three: Exit
	Aspirers	Sustainers	Transformers
Historical archetype	Farmer	Minister	Physician
Occupations	Skilled worker	White-collar worker	Professional
Generation	First	Second	Third
Primary modes of SDA affiliation	Religious, becoming social	Religious, social, educational, economic	Educational, social
Contact with the "world"	Unavoidable, undesired	Avoidable, undesired	Avoidable, desired
Deviance	Increasing	Static	Decreasing
Church involvement	Becoming active	Active	Becoming passive
Religious orientation	Apocalyptic	Pastoral	Holistic
Beliefs	Literal, somewhat unorthodox	Spiritual, orthodox	Spiritual, unorthodox
Religious type	Sectarian	Denominational	Mystical

The differences between the various phases of the Adventist experience have been evident for a long time. In 1950 the American sociologist James T. Borhek studied an Adventist congregation in California and identified three groups—the doctrine oriented, the group oriented, and the community oriented—that broadly correspond to the three phases in the model above. Borhek investigated a single congregation for only a limited period of time and thus failed to emphasize both the transformational power of the Adventist experience and the potential for losses among the community-oriented group.[18] A social anthropologist, Gary Schwartz, studied another Adventist congregation just over a decade later. He observed the strong drive toward upward mobility in Adventism but, perhaps because his sample was limited to a single urban, ethnic congregation, he did not perceive the diversity that already existed within the church.[19]

The model of the revolving door is designed not only to describe the diversity within Adventism but also to emphasize the relationship between continuity and change. As the door turns, those in the exit segment move out; the sustainers become transformers, the converts become sustainers, and a new generation of converts enters the process. While the door continues to revolve and the final products of the process make an exit, there is no reason why the internal composition of

Adventism should alter. Each stage in the process is equally vital. If there is a relatively constant flow through both entrance and exit, the door continues to revolve. There is thus no reason to believe that Adventism is a sect in the course of transformation into a denomination. Only in the first phase are Adventists sectarian; the orientation of the sustainers is denominational and that of the transformers almost mystical.[20]

The maintenance of this process has depended on three factors. The first, discussed in chapter 7, is the maintenance of ideological difference, which legitimates the separation of Adventism from the mainstream of society. The second, discussed at length in part two, is the creation of strategies and institutions that allow the church to work within, but remain distinct from, the American state. The third, discussed above, is the provision of a variety of roles that permit Adventist converts and their descendants to reenter American society at a higher level than that from which they came. There is a close relationship between the maintenance of deviance, the resistance to incorporation, the provision of internal social opportunities, and the flow of people through the Adventist system. A diminution of Adventist distinctiveness delegitimates the church's institutions. If converts cannot be persuaded to enter those institutions, they are less likely to experience upward mobility. If converts do not experience mobility, they are more likely to leave the church after a relatively brief involvement. The equilibrium of the Adventist system is thus delicately balanced. It can be disturbed by any changes in the speed of social and religious transformation within the church. The position of Adventism in society depends on the maintenance of its internal processes. The speed at which the revolving door turns may either be slowed or accelerated. In either case, the character of the Adventist experience may be modified.

Adventism is a movement at variance with the mainstream of American society. It recruits from mainline Protestant denominations. Adventists who exit from the third phase are liable to become unchurched or to rejoin the mainline. Between entrance and exit, Adventists pass through a range of experiences similar in structure to those of any other American undergoing rapid upward social mobility. They advance in education and obtain qualifications and professional employment. In the course of this rise, their orientation is comparable to that of their secular counterparts. They first aspire to what they do not possess, then attempt to uphold what they have achieved, and finally shake off the memories of their own rise. What is unusual in Adventism is not the process itself but the fact that it takes place almost entirely within an alternative society at odds with American culture.

Because this transformation occurs largely within the Adventist system, it is outside the view of the American observer. This fact explains the peculiarly unbalanced perceptions of Adventism recorded in chapter 1. Adventists have been perceived either as apocalyptic fanatics or as philanthropic physicians. These images, it will now be apparent, correspond to the first and third phases of the Adventist experience. Adventists fall within the public gaze as they leave American society to enter the church, inspired by visions of impending catastrophe. They reemerge as public-spirited professionals prepared to guide the nation toward better health. The public perceives only entrances and exits. It sees William Miller going in and John Harvey Kellogg coming out. Hidden from view is the internal process—the second phase of Adventism characterized by Ellen White. It is that process that takes men and women out of American time, places them within heavenly time, and accelerates their progress in human society. For those who undergo this experience, Adventism is the place where one social identity is exchanged for another. During that exchange, Adventists have a religious identity but little social identity, for they have moved outside American society.

In chapter 13 it was argued that Adventism had defined itself as a negation of the American dream of unlimited material and spiritual progress. The millennium would not take place on American soil, for the nation was in league with the devil, and its achievements were doomed to destruction. The way to salvation and the experience of a heavenly millennium was to seek a sanctuary among the band of Sabbath keepers who were moving toward perfection. From the first, Adventism presented itself as a more effective means of realizing the spiritual objectives for which the rest of society was striving. Interestingly enough, Adventism has also proved to be an effective means of gaining the material and social benefits for which most Americans yearn. But the accelerated upward mobility that Adventists achieve depends on their deviation from the mainstream. It is precisely because Adventism has developed an alternative network of schools and institutions that it is possible to rise so rapidly within it. Adventism's deviant ideology has provided a justification for the replication of state institutions. This, in turn, has provided a way to realize more rapidly the goal of material prosperity. Through negating the American dream, Adventism has made it into a reality.

Abbreviations

Ellen G. White

EGW   Ellen G. White

Ellen G. White Books and Manuscripts with Dates of Publication.

AA   *The Acts of the Apostles* (1911)
AH   *The Adventist Home* (1952)
ChS   *Christian Service* (1925)
COL   *Christ's Object Lessons* (1900)
CS   *Counsels on Stewardship* (1940)
CSW   *Counsels on Sabbath School Work* (1938)
CT   *Counsels to Parents, Teachers, and Students* (1913)
CW   *Counsels to Writers and Editors* (1946)
DA   *The Desire of Ages* (1898)
Ed   *Education* (1903)
Ev   *Evangelism* (1946)
EW   *Early Writings* (1882)
FE   *Fundamentals of Christian Education* (1923)
GC   *The Great Controversy* (1888)
GW   *Gospel Workers* (1892)
LS   *Life Sketches of Ellen G. White* (1915)
MH   *The Ministry of Healing* (1905)
MM   *Medical Ministry* (1932)
MS-1   *Manuscript-1 (MS-2*, and so on, accompanied by revelant date of release)
MYP   *Messages to Young People* (1930)
PK   *Prophets and Kings* (1917)
PP   *Patriarchs and Prophets* (1890)
1SG   *Spiritual Gifts,* vol. 1 (1858)
2SG   *Spiritual Gifts,* vol. 2 (1860)
3SG   *Spiritual Gifts,* vol. 3 (1864)
4SG-a   *Spiritual Gifts,* vol. 4, pt. 1 (1864)
4SG-b   *Spiritual Gifts,* vol. 4, pt. 2 (1864)

1SP   *Spirit of Prophecy*, vol. 1 (2*SP*, and so on for vols. 2–4, 1870–84)
1SM   *Selected Messages*, bk. 1 (1958)
2SM   *Selected Messages*, bk. 2 (1958)
SW   *The Southern Work* (1966)
1T   *Testimonies*, vol. 1 (2*T*, and so on, for vols. 2–9, 1885–1909)
TM   *Testimonies to Ministers and Gospel Workers* (1923)

All Ellen White books are published either by the Review and Herald Publishing Association, the Pacific Press Publishing Association, or the Southern Publishing Association.

Works of Reference

1BC   *The Seventh-day Adventist Bible Commentary*, vol. 1 (2*BC*, and so on, for vols. 2–7) All references are to the 1976–80 revised edition except where otherwise indicated.
SDA Encyclopedia   *The Seventh-day Adventist Encyclopedia.* All references are to the 1976 revised edition except where otherwise indicated.
SDA Yearbook   *The Seventh-day Adventist Yearbook*

Publishing Houses

PPPA   Pacific Press Publishing Association
RHPA   Review and Herald Publishing Association
SPA   Southern Publishing Association

Church Paper

The *Review* refers to Adventism's general church paper, which has changed its name on three occasions. Originally the *Advent Review and Sabbath Herald*, it became the *Review and Herald*, and is currently known as the *Adventist Review*.

Notes

1. Introduction: Public Images

1. "U.S. Public's Awareness of, and Attitudes Toward, the Seventh-day Adventist Church." (Princeton, N.J.: The Gallup Organization, Inc., 1986).
2. "The Public's Attitudes Toward the Seventh-day Adventist Church." (Princeton, N.J.: Gallup International, 1970).
3. *Religion in America 1977–1978*. The Gallup Opinion Index. (Princeton, N.J.: The Gallup Organization, Inc., 1978).
4. J. M. Rieder, "A Study of the Attitude of Non-Seventh-day Adventists Toward Seventh-day Adventists in Lawrence and Berrien Springs, Michigan, and a Comparison of Each" (unpublished paper, Andrews University, 1981).
5. See F. D. Nichol, *The Midnight Cry* (Washington D.C.: RHPA, 1944); and Ronald L. Numbers and Jonathan M. Butler, eds., *The Disappointed: Millerism and Millenarianism in the Nineteenth Century* (Bloomington: Indiana University Press, 1987).
6. See Ruth Alden Doan, "Millerism and Evangelical Culture," in Numbers and Butler, eds., *The Disappointed*, 118–35.
7. John Greenleaf Whittier, *The Writings of John Greenleaf Whittier*, vol. 5 (London: Macmillan, 1889), 420.
8. Ibid., 423.
9. See David I. Rowe, *Thunder and Trumpets: Millerites and Dissenting Religion in Upstate New York, 1800–1850* (Chico, Calif.: Scholars Press, 1985), 135ff.
10. See Whittier, *Writings*, vol. 5, 424.
11. Nichol, *Midnight Cry*, 335–36.
12. *Portland Bulletin* (Maine), Mar. 14, 1843; quoted in Nichol, *Midnight Cry*, 377. (Italics in original.)
13. Quoted in *Midnight Cry* (Millerite paper), March 10, 1843, p. 45; quoted in Nichol, *Midnight Cry*, 375.
14. Ibid.
15. Quoted in *Midnight Cry*, Apr. 7, 1843, p. 106; quoted in Nichol, *Midnight Cry*, p. 382.
16. Nichol, *Midnight Cry*, 386.
17. Ibid., 321–34.
18. *Philadelphia Spirit of the Times*, Oct. 24, 1844; quoted in Nichol, *Midnight Cry*, 323.
19. *Pennsylvania Inquirer*, Oct. 24, 1844; quoted in Nichol, *Midnight Cry*, 329.
20. *United States Saturday Post* (Philadelphia), Oct. 26, 1844; quoted in Nichol, *Midnight Cry*, 323.
21. J. Thomas Scharf and Thompson Westcott, *History of Philadelphia 1609–1884*, vol. 2 (Philadelphia: L. H. Everts, 1884), 1448.
22. Nichol, *Midnight Cry*, 377–79.
23. Ibid., 336.
24. See Gary Scharnhorst, "Images of the Millerites in American Literature," *American Quarterly* 32 (1980): 19–36, on which this review is based.

25. Nathaniel Hawthorne, *Centenary Edition of the Works of Nathaniel Hawthorne*, vol. 10 (Columbus: Ohio State University Press, 1974), 247–62; quoted in Scharnhorst, "Images of the Millerites," 22–23.
26. See Scharnhorst, "Images of the Millerites," 24.
27. Ibid., 23.
28. Ibid., 28. Henry Wadsworth Longfellow, *Kavanagh: A Tale*, ed. J. Downey (New Haven: College and University Press, 1965).
29. Edward Eggleston, *The End of the World: A Love Story* (London: George Routledge and Sons, 1872). (English ed.)
30. Ibid., 39.
31. Ibid., 205.
32. Ibid., 220.
33. Scharnhorst, "Images of the Millerites," 22. J. A. Harrison, ed. *Complete Works of Edgar Allan Poe*, vol. 16 (New York: Crowell, 1902), 193.
34. See Malcolm Bull, "The Seventh-day Adventists: Heretics of American Civil Religion," *Sociological Analysis*, 50:2 (1989): 177–87.
35. See P. Gerard Damsteegt, *Foundations of the Seventh-day Adventist Message and Mission* (Grand Rapids, Mich.: William B. Eerdmans, 1977), 161, 285.
36. See Gary Land, "The Literary Image of Seventh-day Adventists," *Spectrum* 5:1 (1973): 50–61, which provides the basis for this review.
37. Sinclair Lewis, *Elmer Gantry* (New York: Harcourt, Brace, 1927), 34; quoted in Land, "Literary Image," 51.
38. Jerome Charyn, *On the Darkening Green* (New York: McGraw-Hill, 1965), 242–43; quoted in Land, "Literary Image," 52.
39. Lawrence Durrell, *Balthazar* (New York: Dutton, 1961), 29.
40. Richard Wright, *Black Boy: A Record of Childhood and Youth* (London: Longman, 1970), 88.
41. Ibid.
42. Ibid., 110.
43. See Lowell Tarling, "Who Killed Azaria: Adventists on Trial in Australia," *Spectrum* 15:2 (1984), 14–22, and 15:3, 42–59.
44. John Bryson, *Evil Angels* (Ringwood, Victoria: Viking, 1985), 3–6.
45. See Malcolm Bull, "Infanticide and Religious Marginality," forthcoming.
46. *Riverside Press Enterprise*, (California) Oct. 12, 1979, sec. B, pp. 1,2.
47. "U.S. Public's Awareness."
48. On Kellogg, see Richard W. Schwarz, "John Harvey Kellogg: American Health Reformer" (Ph.D. dissertation, University of Michigan, 1964).
49. Ibid., 207.
50. Ibid., 170.
51. Ibid., 194ff.
52. Ibid., 236.
53. See John Money, *The Destroying Angel: Sex, Fitness, and Food in the Legacy of Degeneracy Theory* (New York: Prometheus Books, 1985), 83ff. See also ch. 10.
54. Schwarz, "John Harvey Kellogg," 135.
55. George Wharton James, "Spiritual Life of Great Men: Dr. John Harvey Kellogg," *New York Magazine of Mysteries*, Aug. (1906). See cutting in Scrapbook 2, Kellogg Papers, Michigan Historical Collections, University of Michigan, Ann Arbor.
56. Kellogg to S. N. Haskell, Feb. 6, 1906; quoted in Richard W. Schwarz, "Adventism's Social Gospel Advocate: John Harvey Kellogg," *Spectrum* 1:2 (1969), 16.
57. President Nixon's Speech at Loma Linda University, 1971 document file, Loma Linda University, La Sierra campus, Riverside, Calif.
58. Booton Herndon, *The Seventh Day* (New York: McGraw-Hill, 1960), 99.
59. Ibid., 1,2.
60. See Lewis R. Walton, Jo Ellen Walton, and John A. Scharffenberg, *How You Can Live Six Extra Years* (Santa Barbara, Calif.: Woodbridge Press, 1981).

61. John Cook, "A Church Whose Members Have Less Cancer," *Saturday Evening Post*, Mar. 1984, pp. 42, 108.
62. Lawrence K. Altman, "Baboon's Heart Implanted in Infant on Coast," *New York Times* Oct. 28, 1984, p. 1.
63. Kit Konolige, "A Change of Heart," *Philadelphia Daily News*, Nov. 5, 1984, p. 5.
64. Jan-Christina Sears, "Surgeon Is Called a 'Visionary'." *San Bernardino Sun*, Nov. 4, 1984, p. B–1.
65. See Ellen Robinson-Haynes, "Why Transplant?" and Diane Divoky, "Transplant Center Churns out Highest Number of M.D.s," *Sacramento Bee*, Oct. 30, 1984, pp. A–1 and A–12 respectively.
66. Lawrence K. Altman, "Confusion Surrounds Baby Fae," *New York Times*, Nov. 6, 1984, pp. C1, C11.
67. Stephen Cook, "Baby Fae's Legacy," *San Francisco Examiner*, Nov. 16, 1984, p. 1.
68. Christine Russell and Boyce Rensberger, "Baby Fae Case Leaves Tremors," *Washington Post*, Nov. 17, 1984, p. A–4.
69. Loretta McLaughlin, "Turf War Emerging Over Heart Research," *Boston Globe*, Dec. 3, 1984, p. 7.
70. See for example, Dudley Canright, *Seventh-day Adventism Renounced*, 4th ed. (Chicago: Fleming H. Revell, 1889); and Walter Rea, *The White Lie* (Turlock, Calif.: M & R Publications, 1982).
71. See Nichol, *Midnight Cry*.
72. Martin and Barnhouse established Adventism's evangelical credentials in a series of controversial articles that appeared in the Christian magazine *Eternity* between September 1956 and January 1957. See the discussion in T. E. Unruh, "The Seventh-day Adventist Evangelical Conferences of 1955–1956," *Adventist Heritage* 4:2 (1977): 35–46.
73. Gary Schwartz, *Sect Ideologies and Social Status* (Chicago: University of Chicago Press, 1970).
74. Robin Theobald, "The Seventh-day Adventist Movement: A Sociological Study" (Ph.D. dissertation, London University, 1979).
75. Bryan Wilson, "Sect or Denomination: Can Adventism Maintain Its Identity?" *Spectrum* 7:1 (1975), 34–43.

2. Authority

1. There is no adequate biography of Ellen White, but for a critical review of her life, see Ronald L. Numbers, *Prophetess of Health: A Study of Ellen G. White* (New York: Harper & Row, 1976).
2. EGW, *EW*, 12. The classic exposition of the dark night of the soul is given by St. John of the Cross, *The Complete Works*, vol. 1, trans. and ed. E. Allison Peers (London: Burns Oates and Washborne, Ltd., 1948), especially p. 10. See also Ingemar Linden, *The Last Trump: An Historico-Genetical Study of Some Important Chapters in the Making and Development of the Seventh-day Adventist Church* (Frankfurt, West Germany: Peter Lang, 1978), 153–62.
3. EGW, *EW*, 79–81. See St. Teresa of Jesus, *The Complete Works*, vol. 1, trans. and ed. E. Allison Peers (London: Sheed and Ward, 1946), 170.
4. EGW, *EW*, 12; and St. Teresa, *Complete Works*, vol. 1, 193.
5. J. N. Loughborough, *The Great Second Advent Movement: Its Rise and Progress* (Nashville: SPA, 1905), 203–11, for a collection of eyewitness testimonies. Numbers, *Prophetess*, p. 18, uncharitably uses the term *indignities*. See also James White, *Life Incidents in Connection with the Great Advent Movement* (Battle Creek, Mich.: Steam Press, 1898), 272–73.
6. See Ronald L. Numbers and Janet S. Numbers, "The Psychological World of Ellen G. White," *Spectrum* 14:1 (1983): 25.
7. EGW, *EW*, 20.

8. Ibid., 33.

9. EGW, 1*T*, 119.

10. For a description of the spread of print in mid-nineteenth-century America, see Carl Bode, *The Anatomy of American Popular Culture, 1840–1861* (Berkeley: University of California Press, 1960), 109–16.

11. EGW, 1–4*SG* and 1–4*SP*. The *Conflict of the Ages* series comprises *GC, PP, DA, AA,* and *PK*.

12. See Bode, *Anatomy*, 145–48.

13. EGW, 1*SG*, 20, and 1*SP*, 33.

14. EGW, 1*SG*, 21, and 1*SP*, 38.

15. EGW, 1*SP*, 35, and *PP*, 53.

16. Ibid.

17. See, for example, Daniel March, *Night Scenes in the Bible* (Philadelphia: Zeigler and McCurdy, 1868–1807) and *Walks and Homes of Jesus* (Philadelphia: Presbyterian Publishing Committee, 1856); Alfred Edersheim, *Bible History: Old Testaments*, 4 vols. (1876–1880; reprint ed., Grand Rapids, Mich.: William B. Eerdmans, 1949); William Hanna, *The Life of Christ* (New York: American Tract Society, 1863); John Harris, *The Great Teacher*, 17th ed. (Boston: Gould and Lincoln, 1870); W. J. Conybeare and J. S. Howson, *The Life and Epistles of the Apostle Paul* (New York: Crowell, 1852); J. H. Merle D'Aubigné, *History of the Reformation*, vol. 4, bk. 9 (Glasgow, Scotland: Collins, 1841); J. W. Wylie, *History of the Waldenses* (London: Cassell, Pelter and Galpin, n.d.). Comparisons of these and other sources with Ellen White's writings may be found in Rea, *White Lie*. For a review of the literature on Mrs. White's borrowing, see Donald McAdams, "Shifting Views of Inspiration: Ellen White Studies in the 1970s," *Spectrum* 10:4 (1980), 27–41.

18. Ann Douglas, *The Feminization of American Culture* (New York: Knopf, 1977), 83.

19. EGW, *Ed*, 134.

20. "Address to the Public," *Midnight Cry*, Nov. 21, 1844, p. 166.

21. Sylvester Bliss, *Memoirs of William Miller* (Boston: Joshua V. Himes, 1853), 66–67, 68. For an account of Miller's deist phase, see pp. 24–26.

22. On Scottish realism and American religion, see Theodore Dwight Bozeman, *Protestants in an Age of Science: The Baconian Ideal and Antebellum American Religious Thought* (Chapel Hill: University of North Carolina Press, 1977), especially pp. 3–31 and 132–59. See also Herbert Hovenkamp, *Science and Religion in America 1800–1860* (Philadelphia: University of Pennsylvania Press, 1978); and Sydney E. Ahlstrom, "The Scottish Philosophy and American Theology," *Church History* 24 (1955): 257–72. For the importance of Baconianism to dispensationalism, see George Marsden, *Fundamentalism and American Culture: The Shaping of Twentieth-Century Evangelicalism: 1870–1925* (New York: Oxford University Press, 1980), 55–62.

23. Robert Frederick West, *Alexander Campbell and Natural Religion* (New Haven, Conn.: Yale University Press, 1948), 91. On the disciples and Bacon, see David Edwin Harrell, Jr., *Quest for a Christian America: The Disciples of Christ and American Society to 1866* (Nashville, Tenn.: Disciples of Christ Historical Society, 1966), 28.

24. David T. Arthur, "Joshua V. Himes and the Cause of Adventism, 1839–1845" (M.A. thesis, University of Chicago, 1961), 12.

25. Bliss, *Memoirs*, 13.

26. Ibid., 69.

27. See Richard Hofstadter, *Anti-Intellectualism in American Life* (New York: Knopf, 1963), 92–95; and David Arnold Dean, "Echoes of the Midnight Cry: The Millerite Heritage in the Apologetics of the Advent Christian Denomination, 1860–1960" (Th.D. dissertation, Westminster Theological Seminary, 1976), 171–77.

28. Alexander Campbell, in the *Millennial Harbinger*, 1843; quoted in Bliss, *Memoirs*, 240.

29. For a discussion of the psychological consequences of the Great Disappointment, see Leon Festinger, Henry W. Riecken, and Stanley Schachter, *When Prophecy Fails* (Minneapolis: University of Minnesota Press, 1956), 12–28.

30. Ronald Graybill, "The Power of Prophecy: Ellen G. White and the Women Religious

Founders of the Nineteenth Century" (Ph.D. dissertation, Johns Hopkins University, 1983), 88–90.

31. See Hovenkamp, *Science and Religion,* 52, on the Scottish realist understanding of language; cf. EGW, *EW,* 211–12.

32. George I. Butler, *Review* supplement, Aug. 14, 1883, p. 12.

33. Bliss, *Memoirs,* 70.

34. EGW, *1SM,* 206.

35. EGW, *2SG,* 97–98 and *1SM,* 206.

36. EGW, *1SM,* 207.

37. EGW, *2SG,* 98–99.

38. EGW, *2T,* 605.

39. A. G. Daniells, quoted in "The Use of the Spirit of Prophecy in Our Teaching of Bible and History," transcript of the 1919 Bible Conference, July 30, 1919, in *Spectrum* 10:1 (1979): 30, 31.

40. W. W. Prescott, quoted in ibid., 39.

41. See Steven G. Daily, "How Readest Thou: The Higher Criticism Debate in Prophetic America and Its Relationship to Seventh-day Adventism and the Writings of Ellen White, 1885–1925" (M.A. thesis, Loma Linda University, 1982). See also Marsden, *Fundamentalism and American Culture,* especially pp. 141–70; and Ernest Sandeen, *The Rise of Fundamentalism: British and American Millenarianism 1800–1930* (Chicago: University of Chicago Press, 1970), 233–69.

42. William G. Wirth, *The Battle of the Churches: Modernism or Fundamentalism, Which?* (Mountain View, Calif.: PPPA, 1924), 5.

43. Carlyle B. Haynes, *Christianity at the Crossroads* (Nashville, Tenn.: SPA, 1924).

44. George McCready Price, *The Fundamentals of Geology* (Mountain View, Calif.: PPPA, 1913), 240.

45. See ch. 18.

46. William Jennings Bryan, quoted in Hofstadter, *Anti-Intellectualism in American Life,* 125.

47. Raymond F. Cottrell, "The Untold Story of the Bible Commentary," *Spectrum* 16:3 (1985): 44.

48. *Seventh-day Adventists Answer Questions on Doctrine: An Explanation of Certain Major Aspects of Seventh-day Adventist Belief* (Washington, D.C.: RHPA, 1957), 89–98.

49. See M. L. Andreasen, *Letters to the Churches* (1959; reprint ed., Payson, Ariz.: Leaves-of-Autumn Books, 1980), 35–50.

50. See, for example, the discussion in General Conference Defense Literature Committee, *The History and Teaching of Robert Brinsmead* (Washington, D.C.: RHPA, 1961). See also ch. 6.

51. Roy Branson and Harold Weiss, "Ellen White: A Subject of Adventist Scholarship," *Spectrum* 2:4 (1970): 30–33.

52. See McAdams, "Shifting Views," 27–41.

53. Desmond Ford, "Daniel 8:14, The Day of Atonement, and the Investigative Judgment," (unpublished manuscript, n.d.). See also ch. 6.

54. Harold Weiss, "Formative Authority, Yes; Canonization, No," *Spectrum* 16:3 (1985): 10.

55. See, for example, Terry Eagleton, *Literary Theory: An Introduction* (Oxford: Basil Blackwell, 1983), 47–50, 106ff.

56. F. D. Nichol, *The Answer to Modern Religious Thinking* (Washington, D.C.: RHPA, 1936), 228.

57. Siegfried Horn, *The Spade Confirms the Book* (Washington, D.C.: RHPA, 1957). An Adventist, Leona G. Running cowrote with David N. Freedman Albright's biography: *William Foxwell Albright: A Twentieth Century Genius* (New York: Two Continent Publishing Group, 1975).

58. The progress of the Heshbon excavation was reported regularly from 1969 to 1980 in *Andrews University Seminary Studies,* (1969–1980), vols. 7–18, Andrews University.

59. Raoul Dederen, "Revelation, Inspiration and Hermeneutics," in Gordon M. Hyde,

ed., *A Symposium of Biblical Hermeneutics* (Washington, D.C.: RHPA, 1974), 4–5 and 10–11.

60. For example, see Edward Thiele, *The Mysterious Number of Hebrew Kings* (Chicago: Chicago University Press, 1951); and Steven Thompson, *The Apocalypse and Semitic Syntax* (Cambridge: Cambridge University Press, 1985). Thompson's arguments have been developed by another Adventist, Kenneth G. C. Newport, in "Semitic Influence on Some of the Prepositions in the Book of Revelation," *The Bible Translator* 37 (1986): 328–34.

61. Gerhard Hasel, *Understanding the Living Word of God* (Mountain View, Calif.: PPPA, 1980), 36.

62. Gerhard Hasel, "General Principles of Interpretation," in Hyde, ed., *Symposium on Biblical Hermeneutics*, 165.

63. Harold Weiss, "Revelation and the Bible Beyond Verbal Inspiration," *Spectrum* 7:3 (1975): 53.

64. *SDA Encyclopedia*, 1966 ed., 428–29.

65. Jerry Gladson, "The Bible Is Inspired," *College People* 5 (1985): 18–20.

66. See Brother Waldorf's comment in "The Use of the Spirit of Prophecy," 42.

67. EGW, *4T*, 211.

68. See EGW, *CSW*, 34.

3. Identity

1. Everett N. Dick, "The Adventist Crisis of 1843–44" (Ph.D. dissertation, University of Wisconsin, Madison, 1930), 232.

2. EGW, *LS*, 50–53.

3. Charles Fitch, " 'Come Out of Her, My People'—A Sermon" (Rochester, N.Y.: J. V. Himes, 1843), 15.

4. Ibid., 17.

5. Ibid., 23.

6. Ibid., 24.

7. See Festinger et al., *When Prophecy Fails.*

8. William Miller, letter dated Nov. 18, 1844, in the *Advent Herald*, Dec. 11, 1844, p. 142. (Italics in original.)

9. S. S. Snow and B. Matthias, editorial in the *Jubilee Standard* 1:1 (1845), quoted in *Morning Watch*, Mar. 20, 1845, p. 94.

10. On post-Disappointment splintering, see David T. Arthur, " 'Come Out of Babylon': A study of Millerite Separatism and Denominationalism, 1840–1865" (Ph.D. dissertation, University of Rochester, 1970), 85–145.

11. Eli Curtis, letter in the *Day Star*, Dec. 6, 1845, p. 37. (Italics in original.)

12. Benjamin Spaulding, letter in the *Hope of Israel*, April 11, 1845 quoted in the *Morning Watch*, May 1, 1845, p. 141. (Italics in original.)

13. Editorial comment on the above; ibid. (Italics in original.)

14. Sister Minor, letter quoted in Sister Cook's letter in the *Day-Star*, Jan. 3, 1846, p. 9.

15. James L. Boyd, letter published in the *Day-Star*, Nov. 22, 1845, p. 25. (Italics in original.)

16. EGW, *EW*, 15.

17. Ibid., 33.

18. EGW, letter to Brother and Sister Howland, Nov. 12, 1851.

19. "Mutual Conference of Adventists at Albany," *Morning Watch*, May 8, 1845, p. 151. (Italics in original.)

20. H. S. Gurney's hymn "The Seal," printed in Joseph Bates, *The Seal of the Living God* (New Bedford: Press of Benjamin Lindsey, 1849), 70. (Italics in original.)

21. EGW, *1SG*, 111.

22. Ibid.

23. J. N. Andrews, *History of the Sabbath and First Day of the Week* (Battle Creek, Mich.: Steam Press of the Review and Herald Office, 1859), 93.

24. EGW, *5T*, 712.
25. Ibid.
26. EGW, *EW*, 42.
27. For the development of Adventist ideas on the timing of the Sabbath see *SDA Encyclopedia*, 1251. For the manner of Sabbath observance see *SDA Encyclopedia*, 1253–54. An independent account of Sabbath keeping in Adventism can be found in Joan Craven, "The Wall of Adventism," *Christianity Today*, Oct. 19, pp. 20–25.
28. See B. F. Snook, *The Nature, Subjects, and Design of Christian Baptism* (Battle Creek, Mich.: Steam Press of the Review and Herald Office, 1861).
29. EGW, *4T*, 40.
30. "Report of General Conference of Seventh-day Adventists," *Review*, May 26, 1863, p. 204.
31. See Revelation 14:9–11. For the development of Adventist ideas on the remnant and the three angels' messages see *SDA Encyclopedia*, 1200–01 and 1483–84.
32. Uriah Smith, "Who Are the Remnant?" *Review*, Feb. 28, 1856, p. 176.
33. Ibid. (Italics in original.)
34. See R. J. Thomsen, *Seventh-day Baptists—Their Legacy to Adventists* (Mountain View, Calif.: PPPA, 1971), 53.
35. Quoted in R. J. Thomsen, *Seventh-day Baptists*, 50.
36. Ibid., 53.
37. James S. White, "Making Us a Name," *Review*, Apr. 26, 1860, p. 180.
38. James White, "Organization," *Review*, Aug. 5, 1873, p. 60.
39. James White, "Organization," *Review*, June 24, 1880, p. 8.
40. EGW, *AA*, 11.
41. EGW, *GC*, 609.
42. Ibid.
43. See Seventh-day Baptist General Conference, *Seventh-day Baptists in Europe and America*, vol. 2 (Plainfield, N.J.: American Sabbath Tract Society, 1910), 856, 858.
44. LeRoy Edwin Froom, *The Prophetic Faith of Our Fathers*, 4 vols. (Washington, D.C.: RHPA, 1954), and *The Conditionalist Faith of Our Fathers*, 2 vols. (Washington, D.C.: RHPA, 1965–66).
45. Froom, *Movement of Destiny*, 38.
46. Ibid., 33.
47. Ibid.
48. R. Dederen, "Nature of the Church," supplement to *Ministry*, Feb. 1978, pp. 24B, 24D.
49. Walter B. T. Douglas, "The Church: Its Nature and Function," in R. E. Firth, ed., *Servants for Christ: The Adventist Church Facing the 80s* (Berrien Springs, Mich.: Andrews University Press, 1980), 74.
50. M. L. Andreasen, *The Sabbath: Which Day and Why* (Washington, DC: RHPA, 1942), especially 233–50, 271–73 and 301–04. (The authors have come across two printings of this book, both dated 1942, one containing 312 pages, the other 255 pages. The references here are to the 312 page book.)
51. See M. S. Nigri, "The Sabbath a Landmark," *Review*, Jan. 3, 1980, pp. 4–7, for a restatement of the traditional position.
52. See Raymond F. Cottrell, "The Sabbath in the New World," and C. Mervyn Maxwell, "Joseph Bates and Seventh-day Adventist Sabbath Theology," in K. Strand, ed., *The Sabbath in Scripture and History* (Washington, D.C.: RHPA, 1982), 256–59 and 356–61.
53. Samuele Bacchiocchi, *Divine Rest for Human Restlessness*, (Rome: privately published, 1980), 109–30. This change was not lost on reviewers; see *Christianity Today*, Oct. 2, 1981, p. 102.
54. V. N. Olsen, "Theological Aspects of the Seventh-day Sabbath," *Spectrum* 4:3 (1972): 17.
55. Ibid.

56. See, for example, Niels-Erik Andreasen, *The Christian Use of Time* (Nashville, Tenn.: Abingdon, 1978).
57. Bacchiocchi, *Divine Rest*, 129, 130, 95, 198, 206, 207, 214. (Italics in original.)
58. Ibid., 113.
59. See EGW, quoted in 7 *BC*, 981.
60. EGW, *GC*, 590.
61. The address was reprinted in Samuele Bacchiocchi, "The Lord's Day Alliance Hears Sabbath Scholar," *Ministry*, July 1979, pp. 10, 11.
62. W. J. Arthur, vice-president, British Union Conference of Seventh-day Adventists, to C. Calver, general secretary, Evangelical Alliance, Feb. 27, 1986.
63. W. J. Arthur, letter to Mrs. M. Thatcher, Mar. 27, 1986.
64. Roy Branson, "Celebrating the Adventist Experience," *Spectrum* 12:1 (1981): 5.
65. Ibid.

4. The End of the World

1. This outline of Adventist eschatology has made little attempt to include all the scriptural passages Adventists use to justify the scheme. For a more detailed summary, see Raymond F. Cottrell, "The Eschaton: A Seventh-day Adventist Perspective of the Second Coming," *Spectrum* 5:1 (1973): 7–31. For a less detailed summary with a brief discussion of contemporary Adventist attitudes to the eschatology, see Richard Rice, *The Reign of God: An Introduction to Christian Theology from a Seventh-day Adventist Perspective* (Berrien Springs, Mich,: Andrews University Press, 1985), 330–36. For more details on the Adventist view of the first resurrection, see EGW, *GC*, 637, and *SDA Encyclopedia*, 1204.
2. See EGW, *GC*, ch. 2–15.
3. Ibid., 518.
4. Ibid., 624.
5. Ibid., 601.
6. Ibid., 579, 580, 588.
7. The context of the *Great Controversy* is discussed in Jonathan Butler, "The World of E. G. White and the End of the World," *Spectrum* 10:2 (1979): 2–13.
8. Numerous studies have been devoted to this feature of American culture, including H. Richard Neibuhr, *The Kingdom of God in America* (New York: Harper & Row, 1937); Ernest L. Tuveson, *Redeemer Nation: The Idea of America's Millennial Role* (Chicago: University of Chicago Press, 1968); and Nathan Orr Hatch, *The Sacred Cause of Liberty: Republican Thought and the Millennium in Revolutionary New England* (New Haven: Yale University Press, 1977).
9. Sandeen, *Roots of Fundamentalism*, 42, 43.
10. J. N. Andrews, "Thoughts on Revelation XIII and XIV," *Review*, May 19, 1851, pp. 83, 84.
11. Ibid., 84.
12. J. N. Loughborough, "The Two-Horned Beast," *Review*, Mar. 21, 1854, p. 66. (Emphasis added.)
13. Andrews, "Thoughts on Revelation," 84.
14. Loughborough, for example, repeated Andrews's arguments in "The Two-Horned Beast," 66–67.
15. See Jonathan M. Butler, "Adventism and the American Experience," in Edwin S. Gaustad, ed., *The Rise of Adventism: Religion and Society in Mid-nineteenth-century America* (New York: Harper & Row, 1974), 181–82.
16. On Smith's preoccupation with the Ottoman Empire see Eugene F. Durand, *Yours in the Blessed Hope, Uriah Smith* (Washington, D.C.: RHPA, 1980), 207, 211. For a discussion of the Adventist preoccupation with Turkey during the war, see Gary Land, "The Perils of Prophecying: Seventh-day Adventists Interpret World War I," *Adventist Heritage* 1:1 (1974): 28–33, 55–56. Researchers interested in the back-

ground of Adventist prophetic interpretation should consult Durand, *Yours in the Blessed Hope*, 202–06 and Froom, *Prophetic Faith*.

17. See Marsden, *Fundamentalism and American Culture*, 141–53, especially pp. 143, 144.
18. F. M. Wilcox, "Vain Assumptions and Idle Speculations," *Review*, Sept. 10, 1914, p. 9.
19. F. M. Wilcox, "Public Utterances by Writers and Speakers," *Review*, May 24, 1917, p. 3.
20. F. M. Wilcox, *Facing the Crisis: Present World Conditions in the Light of the Scriptures* (Washington, D.C.: RHPA, 1920), 23. (Emphasis added.)
21. See "The Mad Rush of War Preparations," *Signs of the Times*, Apr. 14, 1914, p. 210, and compare "Is Europe's War Armageddon?" *Signs of the Times*, Aug. 18, 1914, p. 503. Adventist uncertainty during the war is also well documented in Land, "Perils of Prophecying," 28–33, 55–56.
22. See J. L. McElhany, "The Present Crisis," *Review*, Sept. 14, 1939, p. 24; and F. D. Nichol, "What We Don't Know about the War—and What We Do," *Review*, Nov. 2, 1939, pp. 10–11. Nichol was one Adventist who consistently opposed apocalyptic speculation. See his *Behold, He Cometh* (Washington, D.C.: RHPA, 1938), 137–43.
23. Arthur S. Maxwell, *These Tremendous Times* (Washington, D.C.; RHPA, 1938), 50. Another Adventist book that foretold the imminence of Armageddon was Gynne Dalrymple's *The Hour of Destiny* (Mountain View, Calif.: PPPA, 1937), 13.
24. An example of this attitude is found in Alonzo L. Baker et al., *Our Changing World: Wither Bound?* (Mountain View, Calif.: PPPA, 1933), 16–21.
25. Kenneth H. Wood, "The President-elect," *Review*, Dec. 8, 1960, p. 3.
26. Arthur S. Maxwell, *Christ's Glorious Return* (Watford, Herts, Britain: The Stanborough Press, Ltd., 1924), especially pp. 11–12.
27. John L. Shuler, *The Coming Conflict* (Nashville: SPA, 1929), 12–13.
28. LeRoy E. Froom, *Civilization's Last Stand* (Mountain View, Calif.: PPPA, 1928), 10.
29. See, for example, Carlyle B. Haynes, *On the Eve of Armageddon* (Washington, D.C.: RHPA, 1924), 7; *Our Times and Their Meaning* (Nashville, Tenn.: SPA, 1929), 37; and *The Blackout of Civilization and Beyond* (Nashville, Tenn.: SPA, 1941), 9, 14.
30. A possible exception to this general rule is the collection of essays by Adventist academics in Roy Branson, ed., *Pilgrimage of Hope* (Takoma Park, Md: Association of Adventist Forums, 1986). These essays, many of which first appeared in the 1970s in *Spectrum*, examine the relevance of the Second Advent in the context of the late twentieth century.
31. See Hans K. LaRondelle's series on dispensationalism, which ran in *Ministry* in 1981 in May (pp. 4–6), July (pp. 12–14), Sept. (pp. 17–19), and Nov. (pp. 16–18). His attack on dispensationalist eschatology culminated in the book, *The Israel of God in Prophecy: Principles of Prophetic Interpretation* (Berrien Springs, Mich.: Andrews University Press, 1983).
32. Sakae Kubo, *The Open Rapture* (Nashville, Tenn.: SPA, 1978), 26.
33. Sakae Kubo, *God Meets Man: A Theology of the Sabbath and Second Advent* (Nashville, Tenn.: SPA, 1978), 103.
34. Samuele Bacchiocchi, *The Advent Hope for Human Hopelessness* (Berrien Springs, Mich.: Biblical Perspectives, 1986), 13.
35. See ch. 5.
36. EGW, 1*SM*, 197; quoted in Lewis R. Walton, *Omega* (Washington, D.C.: RHPA, 1981), 50.
37. Walton, *Omega*, 77–86.
38. See also Robert Johnston's discussion in "Omega: A Theological View," *Spectrum* 12:2 (1981): 53–4.
39. See EGW, 2*SG*, 208; 2*T*, 194; *GC*, 518; "A Message for Today," *Review*, June 18, 1901, p. 1.
40. EGW, *Ev*, 694–97.
41. Ibid., 695.

42. See the General Conference book, *Problems in Bible Translation* (Washington, D.C.: RHPA, 1954), 102–5.
43. Herbert E. Douglass, *The End: Unique Voice of Adventists about the Return of Jesus* (Mountain View, Calif.: PPPA, 1979), 65.

5. The Divine Realm

1. *SDA Yearbook 1986*, 5.
2. Rice, *The Reign of God*, 88.
3. C. Mervyn Maxwell, "Sanctuary and Atonement in SDA Theology: An Historical Survey," in A. V. Wallenkampf and W. R. Lesher, eds., *The Sanctuary and the Atonement: Biblical Historical and Theological Studies* (Washington, D.C.: General Conference of Seventh-day Adventists, 1981), 530.
4. EGW, *EW*, 18–19, 16.
5. Ibid., 16.
6. Ibid., 19.
7. Ibid., 18.
8. EGW, *4T*, 429.
9. EGW, *EW*, 288, 16.
10. Ibid., 77. (Italics in original.)
11. See EGW, *CT*, 273 and *4T*, 219.
12. See EGW, *1SP*, 17–24 and EGW quoted in *7BC*, 949.
13. See EGW, *1T* 296 and *DA*, 99, *4SG*-a, 58.
14. EGW, *PP*, 50.
15. EGW, *DA*, 99.
16. Quoted in *4BC*, 1173.
17. Ibid.
18. EGW, *EW*, 168.
19. Ibid., 40.
20. EGW, *DA*, 834.
21. EGW, *EW*, 77.
22. Ibid., 17.
23. On the Shakers, see Edward Deming Andrews, *The People Called Shakers* (New York: Dover, 1963). For crawling Adventists, see EGW, *LS*, 85–86. On the relationship between the groups, see Lawrence Foster, "Had Prophecy Failed? Contrasting Perspectives of the Millerites and Shakers," in Numbers and Butler, eds., *The Disappointed*, 173–88.
24. EGW, *EW*, 107–10; and EGW, *2SM*, 34.
25. James White, letter to Enoch Jacobs Jan. 8, 1845 [sic]. Published in the *Day Star*, Jan. 24, 1846, p. 25.
26. Andrews, *People Called Shakers*, 223.
27. James White, "The Faith of Jesus," *Review*, Aug. 5, 1852, p. 52.
28. Uriah Smith, *Thoughts, Critical and Practical, on the Book of Revelation* (Battle Creek, Mich.: Steam Press, 1865), 14.
29. For information on Waggoner and a survey of Adventist Arianism, see Froom, *Movement of Destiny*, 148–87.
30. Erwin R. Gane, "The Arian or Anti-Trinitarian Views Presented in Seventh-day Adventist Literature and the Ellen G. White Answer" (M.A. thesis, Andrews University, 1963). 65.
31. O. R. L. Crosier, "The Law of Moses," in the *Day Star*, extra ed., Feb. 7, 1846, pp. 37–44.
32. *SDA Encyclopedia*, 671–72.
33. EGW, *GC*, 480–84.
34. EGW, *EW*, 152.
35. Ibid., 187.

36. Quoted in Froom, *Movement of Destiny*, 159ff.
37. EGW, *EW*, 14.
38. James and Ellen White's participation in ecstatic Adventist worship services is perhaps most clearly indicated by the eyewitness testimonies given in the Dammon trial of 1845. Israel Dammon, an early Adventist leader, was sentenced to ten days in prison for holding ecstasy-inducing meetings, although he does not appear to have served his sentence. See the court transcript in "Trial of Elder I. Dammon, Reported for the *Piscataquis Farmer*," *Spectrum* 17:5 (1987): 29–36.
39. James White, letter to EGW, Nov. 6, 1860.
40. EGW, 1*T*, 47.
41. EGW, letter to Brother Hastings, portion written June 1, 1848.
42. EGW to Brother and Sister Howland, Nov. 12, 1851.
43. Uriah Smith, quoted in *SDA Encyclopedia*, 590.
44. EGW, *EW*, 45, n. 1 and *GC*, 265.
45. EGW, 9*T*, 20.
46. James White, letter to Brother Jacobs, Oct. 11, 1845.
47. EGW, *EW*, 107–10.
48. EGW, *DA*, 107.
49. Ibid., 143.
50. Ibid., 669.
51. Ibid., 805.
52. See also ch. 6 for further discussion of the 1888 conference.
53. See Ella M. Robinson, *S. N. Haskell: Man of Action* (Washington, D.C.: RHPA, 1967), 168–76.
54. EGW, *DA*, 675.
55. EGW, 2*SM*, 36.
56. Dr. A. B. Child, *Whatever Is, Is Right* (Boston: Berry, Colby, 1861), 4; quoted in Laurence Moore, "Spiritualism" in Gaustad, ed., the *Rise of Adventism*, 88.
57. EGW, *Ed*, 17.
58. Ibid., 99.
59. J. H. Kellogg, *The Living Temple* (Battle Creek, Mich.: Good Health Publishing Company, 1903), 29.
60. J. H. Kellogg to G. I. Butler, June 1, 1904; quoted in Schwarz, "John Harvey Kellogg," 387.
61. On New Thought, see Charles S. Braden, *Spirits in Rebellion: The Rise and Development of New Thought* (Dallas: Southern Methodist University Press, 1970).
62. Schwarz, "John Harvey Kellogg," 388.
63. Ibid., 386, n. 110.
64. EGW, 8*T*, 237–38.
65. W. W. Prescott, *The Doctrine of Christ*. (Washington, D.C.: RHPA, 1920), 3.
66. Froom, *Movement of Destiny*, 414.
67. A. Graham Maxwell, *Can God Be Trusted?* (Nashville, Tenn.: SPA, 1977), 82.
68. Ibid., 88.
69. Ibid., 42.

6. The Human Condition

1. Walter R. Martin, "Seventh-day Adventism Today," *Our Hope*, Nov. 1956, p. 275.
2. Ibid.
3. Froom, *Movement of Destiny*, 465.
4. See, for example, Geoffrey J. Paxton, *The Shaking of Adventism* (Grand Rapids, Mich.: Baker Book House, 1977); or Colin D. Standish and Russell R. Standish, *Adventism Challenged*, 2 vols. (Rapidan, Va.: Historic Truth Publications, n.d.).
5. Froom, *Movement of Destiny*, 465.
6. *Questions on Doctrine*, 349, 369. For the 1872 statement on the atonement see Froom, *Movement of Destiny*, 160–61.

7. EGW, *GC*, 489.
8. EGW, *MS*-29, (1906); and *FE*, 370.
9. *Questions on Doctrine*, 354–55. (Italics in original.)
10. Crosier, "Law of Moses," 41.
11. *Questions on Doctrine*, 444.
12. Ibid., 50.
13. Ibid., 50, 55, 383.
14. EGW, *DA*, 49.
15. *Questions on Doctrine*, 59–60.
16. Andreasen, *Letters to the Churches*, 11.
17. EGW, *GC*, 623.
18. EGW, *AH*, 16.
19. Robert D. Brinsmead, *A Review of the Awakening Message*, pt. 1 (Fallbrook, Calif.: Present Truth, 1972), 4.
20. Ibid.
21. Edward Heppenstall, "Is Perfection Possible?," *Signs of the Times*, Dec. 1963, pp. 10–11, 30.
22. Edward Heppenstall, *Salvation Unlimited* (Washington, D.C.: RHPA, 1974), 15. (Italics in original.)
23. Edward Heppenstall, "Let Us Go on to Perfection," in H. Douglass, ed., *Perfection: The Impossible Possibility*, (Nashville, Tenn.: SPA, 1975), 64.
24. Heppenstall, *Salvation Unlimited*, 142.
25. Edward Heppenstall, *The Man Who Is God* (Washington, D.C.: RHPA, 1977), 140, 141.
26. Heppenstall, *Salvation Unlimited*, 57, 144ff.
27. Heppenstall, "Let Us Go on to Perfection," 61, 67. (Italics in original.)
28. EGW, *DA*, 311.
29. M. Bull and K. Lockhart, "The Intellectual World of Adventist Theologians," *Spectrum* 18:1 (1987): 33, 34.
30. For a conservative response to this alliance, see A. John Clifford and Russell R. Standish, "Conflicting Concepts of Righteousness by Faith in the Seventh-day Adventist Church: Australasian Division" (Victoria, Australia; circulated by the authors, 1976).
31. Gillian Ford, "The Soteriological Implications of the Human Nature of Christ," (unpublished paper, Avondale College, Cooranbong, Australia, 1975.)
32. The statement "Christ Our Righteousness" was published in the *Review*, May 27, 1976, pp. 4–7.
33. Herbert Douglass, "Men of Faith—The Showcase of God's Grace," in Douglass, ed., *Perfection: The Impossible Possibility*, 13–56. See also Eric C. Webster, *Crosscurrents in Adventist Christology* (Frankfurt, West Germany, and New York: Peter Lang, 1984) on Douglass and Heppenstall.
34. Hans K. LaRondelle, "The Biblical Idea of Perfection," in Douglass, ed., *Perfection: The Impossible Possibility*, 93–136. See also Hans K. LaRondelle, *Perfection and Perfectionism: A Dogmatico-Ethical Study of Biblical Perfection and Phenomenal Perfectionism* (Berrien Springs, Mich.: Andrews University Press, 1971).
35. See Ford, "Daniel 8:14," 214–16, 222–24, 260–61, A56–61 and A63.
36. For an extended discussion of Glacier View, see the articles in *Spectrum* 11:2 (1980).
37. Ford, "Daniel 8:14," 346–53 and 470–78.
38. Ibid., 583–86.
39. D. P. Hall, *Man Not Immortal: The Only Shield Against the Seductions of Modern Spiritualism* (Battle Creek, Mich.: Steam Press, 1854), 3.
40. Ibid., 6, 24–25. (Italics in original.)
41. Ibid., 65, 85. (Italics in original.)
42. Ibid., 85.
43. Ellen White had similar fears, see EGW, *EW*, 262–66.

44. The Millerite George Storrs had advocated conditionalism, but the Seventh-day Adventists disagreed with his followers in the Advent Christian Church on this point.
45. EGW, 1*T*, 132.
46. James White, "Repairing the Breach in the Law of God," in *The Present Truth* 1:4 (1849), p. 29.
47. EGW, 1*T*, 188.
48. EGW, 2*T*, 355–56.
49. Ibid., 453.
50. Ibid., 63.
51. Ibid., 352.
52. EGW, *COL*, 69.
53. EGW, 3*T*, 188.
54. EGW, 5*T*, 500.
55. EGW, 1*T*, 334, 335. On the Holiness movement, see Melvin Easterday Dieter, *The Holiness Revival of the Nineteenth Century* (Metuchen, N.J.: Scarecrow Press, 1980).
56. John Wesley, *Works*, vol. 5, 3d ed. (London: John Mason, 1829), 53.
57. E. J. Waggoner, *Confession of Faith* (n.p., 1916), 5.
58. A. T. Jones, "Five Sermons on Righteousness," presented at Ottawa, Kansas, Institute and Camp Meeting, May 1889 (duplicated typescript, General Conference Archives, Washington, D.C.), 8.
59. EGW, *COL*, 312.
60. Quoted in Bert Haloviak, "From Righteousness to Holy Flesh: Disunity and Perversion of the 1888 Message" (unpublished paper, General Conference Archive, Washington D.C., 1983), 27.
61. Ibid., 14.
62. Ibid., 17.
63. A. G. Daniells, *Christ Our Righteousness* (Washington D.C.: RHPA, 1941), 6. (Italics in original.)
64. M. L. Andreasen, *The Sanctuary Service* (Washington D.C.: RHPA, 1937), 282.
65. C. M. Maxwell, "Trends in Second-Coming Emphasis and Interpretation Among Seventh-day Adventists" (unpublished paper, Andrews University, early 1970s).
66. Herbert Douglass, *Why Jesus Waits* (Washington D.C.: RHPA, 1976), especially 65–82.
67. Jean Zurcher, *The Nature and Destiny of Man*, trans. Mabel Bartlett (New York: Philosophical Library, 1969), 171.
68. Heppenstall, "Let Us Go on to Perfection," 70.
69. Rice, *Reign of God*, 131.
70. Hall, *Man Not Immortal*, 6.
71. See Bull and Lockhart, "Intellectual World," 33, 36. For a definition of holism see Frank B. Minirth and Paul D. Meier, *Counseling and the Nature of Man* (Grand Rapids, Mich.: Baker Book House, 1982), 13.
72. Jack W. Provonsha, *God Is With Us* (Washington D.C.: RHPA, 1974), 45.
73. Jack W. Provonsha, "The Health of the Whole Person" (cassette tape, Loma Linda University, March 1985).
74. Don Hawley, *Come Alive! Feel Fit—Live Longer* (Washington D.C.: RHPA, 1975), 144. (Italics in original.)
75. Leo R. Van Dolson, *The Golden Eight: Eight Dynamic Rules That Lead to Total Health* (Washington D.C.: RHPA, 1977), 94.

7. The Development of Adventist Theology

1. Norman F. Douty, *Another Look at Seventh-day Adventism* (Grand Rapids, Mich.: Baker Book House, 1962), 182.
2. Walter R. Martin, *Truth about Seventh-day Adventism* (Grand Rapids, Mich.: Zondervan, 1960) 236–37.

3. Douty, *Another Look at Seventh-day Adventism*, 189.
4. Anthony A. Hoekema, *The Four Major Cults* (Grand Rapids, Mich.: William B. Eerdmans, 1963), 403.
5. Martin, *Truth about Seventh-day Adventism*, 7.
6. For example, Desmond Ford, *Daniel* (Nashville, Tenn.: SPA, 1978).
7. See Bull and Lockhart, "Intellectual World."
8. See ch. 6.
9. See Froom's *Prophetic Faith* and *Conditionalist Faith*.
10. See Strand, ed., *Sabbath in Scripture and History*, pt. 2.
11. See Bryan Ball, *The English Connection: The Puritan Roots of Seventh-day Adventist Belief* (Cambridge: James Clarke, 1981); and W. L. Emmerson, *The Reformation and the Advent Movement*, (Washington D.C.: RHPA, 1983).
12. See Royal Sage, "Does Seventh-day Adventist Theology Owe a Debt to Theodore of Mopsuestia?" *Andrews University Seminary Studies* (1963), pp. 81–90.
13. Ball, *English Connection*, 14.
14. See ibid., 78; compare with ch. 6 on Adventist perfectionism.
15. Ball, *English Connection*, 113.
16. See ch. 5 on the early Adventist view of the atonement.
17. See Rodney Stark and William Sims Bainbridge, *The Future of Religion: Secularization, Revival and Cult Formation*, (Berkeley: University of California Press, 1985), ch. 2.
18. On the origin of this group, see Clyde E. Hewitt, *Midnight and Morning: An Account of the Adventist Awakening and the Founding of the Advent Christian Denomination 1831–60* (Charlotte, N.C.: Venture Books, 1983).
19. See R. Lawrence Moore, *Religious Outsiders and the Making of Americans* (New York: Oxford University Press, 1986).
20. H. Richard Niebuhr, *The Social Sources of Denominationalism* (New York: Henry Holt, 1929).
21. Froom, *Movement of Destiny*, 465ff.
22. See Robert H. Pierson, "An Earnest Appeal from the Retiring President of the General Conference," *Review*, Nov. 26, 1978, pp. 10–11; and Standish and Standish, *Adventism Challenged*.
23. See, for example, Whitney R. Cross, *The Burned-Over District: The Social and Intellectual History of Enthusiastic Religion in Western New York 1800–1850* (Ithaca, N.Y.: Cornell University Press, 1950).
24. Compare Cross's account of "ultraism," ibid., 173.
25. See ch. 2.
26. On the background to the period, see Marsden, *Fundamentalism and American Culture*.
27. On evangelicalism, see Richard Quebedeaux, *The Worldly Evangelicals* (San Francisco: Harper & Row, 1978), and *The Young Evangelicals* (New York: Harper & Row, 1974).

8. The Structure of Society

1. Statistics from *123rd Annual Statistical Report, 1985* (Washington, D.C.: Office of Archives and Statistics, General Conference of Seventh-day Adventists, 1985), 19 (primary schools), 28 (secondary schools), 31–32, 33 (health institutions and retirement centers), 30 (food manufacturers), 35 (publishing). (Note that figures relate to North America.)
2. Brief notes on these institutions can be obtained from the *SDA Yearbook 1986*, 19, 541–43.
3. *123rd Annual Statistical Report, 1985*, 25, 29, 34, 35, 30. (Radio stations or studios are not listed systematically, but most Adventist conferences and unions run at least one.)
4. Details of these problems can be obtained from Bruce M. Wickwire, "SPA and Review Join Their Operations," *Review*, Apr. 3, 1980, p. 23; "Harris Pine Mills Board Votes to Shut Down Operations," *Review*, Dec. 18, 1986, p. 6; Neal C. Wilson, "The Loss of Harris Pine Mills," *Review*, Jan. 1, 1987, pp. 6–8; and Bonnie Dwyer, "Soul Search-

ing at the Adventist Media Center: A Multimillion Dollar Debate," *Spectrum* 13:1 (1982): 26–35.

5. The entire list of General Conference personnel and organizations is found in *SDA Yearbook, 1986*, 15–16. Their functions are described in "The Constitution and By-laws of the General Conference of Seventh-day Adventists" in the 1986 *Yearbook*, 9–14.

6. Ibid.; see constitution, Art. V and VI, in "Constitution and Bylaws," 10.

7. Ibid.; see bylaws, Art. XIII, Sec. 4 and 5, in "Constitution and Bylaws," 13.

8. Ibid.; see bylaws, Art. XIII, Sec. 2(a) and (b), in "Constitution and Bylaws," 13.

9. Ibid.; see constitution, Art. III, in "Constitution and Bylaws," 9.

10. See bylaws, Art. II, Sec. 2 (a)(1), in "Constitution and Bylaws," *SDA Yearbook, 1985*, 11.

11. See bylaws, Art. II, Sec. 2 (a)(1), in "Constitution and Bylaws," *SDA Yearbook, 1986*, 11.

12. A clear account of the election procedure (although with dated figures) can be found in Alvin L. Kwiram, "How the General Conference Election Works," *Spectrum* 7:1 (1975): 17–21.

13. *Seventh-day Adventist Church Manual*, rev. ed. (Washington D.C.: General Conference of Seventh-day Adventists, 1981), 53.

14. See constitution, Art . III, Sec. 3 (b), and Art. V, Sec. 1 (b), in "Constitution and Bylaws," *SDA Yearbook, 1986*, 9, 10. These provisions are absent from previous church constitutions.

15. Kwiram, "How the General Conference Election Works," 20.

16. For more details on Adventism's initial organization, see R.W. Schwarz, *Light Bearers to the Remnant* (Mountain View, Calif.: PPPA, 1979), 86–98.

17. See Gary Land, "Where Did Adventist Organizational Structure Come From?" *Spectrum* 7:1 (1975): 24.

18. More details on the 1901 reorganization can be obtained from Schwarz, *Light Bearers*, 267–81.

19. A general idea of how unions and conferences work can be obtained from the model conference constitution in *General Conference Working Policy* (Washington D.C.: RHPA, 1985–86), 78–82.

20. Local Adventist church organization is fully described in the *Seventh-day Adventist Church Manual*.

21. Quoted in Schwarz, *Light Bearers*, 86. (Italics in original.)

22. EGW, 3T, 492.

23. EGW, 9T, 260.

24. See Daniel A. Ochs and Grace Lillian Ochs, *The Past and the Presidents: Biographies of the General Conference Presidents* (Nashville, Tenn.: SPA, 1974), 17–34.

25. Eugene F. Durand, "Reporting the Big Event: Adventist and Non-Adventist Perspectives on Selected General Conference Sessions," *Adventist Heritage* 10:1 (1985): 32–35.

26. A brief appraisal of Wilson can be found in George W. Read et al., "Meet the Presidents: Historical Vignettes," *Adventist Heritage* 10:1 (1985): 55. An example of Wilson's readiness to enlist divine authority occurred in his success in strengthening the position of the General Conference at the Annual Council of 1984. See Neal Wilson, "The Rationale for a Special Relationship," in Bonnie Dwyer, "Right Turn on the Road to General Conference," *Spectrum* 15:4 (1984): 22, 24.

27. *123rd Annual Statistical Report, 1985*, 24.

28. This financial system is described in *General Conference Working Policy*, pp. 406–7. For general discussion on division financing, see pp. 382–83.

29. For more details on systematic benevolence see Schwarz, *Light Bearers*, 89.

30. Dudley M. Canright, "Systematic Benevolence or the Bible Plan of Supporting the Ministry," *Review*, Feb. 17, 1876, p. 50. (Italics in original.) Canright's series on tithe ran between February and April. A history of tithing in the church can be found

in Brian E. Strayer, "Adventist Tithepaying—The Untold Story," *Spectrum* 17:1 (1986): 39–52.

31. EGW, *Ed*, 139.
32. See Bert Haloviak's discussion on the diversion of tithe funds in "Ellen White and Tithe 1895–1905: Focusing upon the Last Warning Message" (unpublished paper, 1984).
33. Details of the tithe document were given in "Actions of General Interest from the Annual Council," *Review*, Dec. 12, 1985, pp. 17–18.
34. See *General Conference Working Policy*, 413–15.
35. Ibid., 414.
36. *123rd Annual Statistical Report, 1985*, 4.
37. See *General Conference Working Policy*, 418.
38. Ibid., 186.
39. Kenneth H. Emmerson, "Financing a World Church" (Washington, D.C.: General Conference of Seventh-day Adventists, 1969), 20.
40. Figures from Lance L. Butler, "Much for Which to Be Thankful" (report of the General Conference treasurer), *Review*, June 30, 1985, p. 29.
41. See *General Conference Working Policy*, 352–61. For policy on appropriations, see p. 348.
42. EGW, *ChS*, 168.
43. See, for example, EGW, *MYP*, 299–303, and *CS*, 231–44. It should be noted, however, that when the first Adventist college was founded in 1874 its curriculum included business studies. It appears that Adventist colleges have continued to offer business courses since this time.
44. EGW, *9T*, 13–14.
45. An excellent account of the early history of adventist publishing is found in Donald McAdams, "Pacific Press Versus Review and Herald: The Rise of Territorial Monopolies," *Spectrum* 8:4 (1977): 11–21. (It should be noted that both the PPPA and the RHPA were known by other names in their early years.)
46. A critical study of the industry's publishing and distribution methods was undertaken by Wilfred M. Hillock in "Why We Should Use Nondenominational Printers and Bookstores," *Spectrum* 8:4 (1977): 6–10. See also George Colvin, "A Short History of Adventist Colportering," *Spectrum* 14:1 (1983): 8–9.
47. See McAdams, "Pacific Press Versus Review and Herald," 11.
48. For details of these events, see Wickwire, "SPA and Review Join Their Operations"; "Review to Move to New Site," *Review*, Oct. 30, 1980, p. 24; Lowell Bock, "Pacific Press to Relocate and Still Print," *Review*, June 30, 1983, p. 32. The church paper dealt with the upheavals in the industry in Jocelyn R. Fay, "The Publishing Work: Facing Changing Times," *Review*, Jan. 20, 1983, pp. 3–8, and "The Publishing Work: North American View," *Review*, Feb. 10, 1983, pp. 4–7.
49. Some idea of the internal debate concerning Adventist publishing can be gained from Dort F. Tikker, "The Case for Consolidating the Publishing Houses," *Spectrum* 8:4 (1977): 2–5; and Richard C. Osborn "Why the *Review* Voted to Leave Washington," *Spectrum* 11:3 (1981): 52–59.
50. The Proctor case was initially reported in Sheree Strom, "Attorney General Studying SDA Literature Policies," *Student Movement* (Andrews University student newspaper), May 27, 1981, p. 1. See also George Colvin, "Sad Tidings: Adventist Publishing in North America," *Spectrum* 14:1 (1983): 10–12. The verdict was recorded and discussed in Lorna Tobler, "Where Has the Proctor Case Taken Us?" *Spectrum* 17:4 (1987): 26–32.
51. For Adventism's traditional attitude toward sports see "Sports in Seventh-day Adventist Academies and Colleges: A Statement Prepared by Arthur L. White" (Washington D.C.: Ellen G. White Publications, Dec. 1967). The growth of Adventist intercollegiate competition in the 1980s is chronicled in Bonnie Dwyer, "Play Has Already Begun," *Spectrum* 19:1 (1988): 19–22. The question of sport and the church's educational institutions was the subject of heated debate at the 1988 Annual

Council. However, the General Conference made few concessions to those who advocated relaxing the traditional line that opposed participation in league competition. See Carlos Medley, "Annual Council Brings Excitement to Nairobi," *Review*, Oct. 27, 1988, pp. 6–7.

52. A rare incidence of open intercollege rivalry was reported in the early 1980s. At a time when enrollments were dwindling, Columbia Union College in Maryland and Southern College in Tennessee were found poaching each other's students. See Maurice Miller, "Northern Industry vs Southern Comfort," *Student Movement*, Apr. 27, 1983, p. 7.

53. The Davenport affair was well chronicled. See, for example, Tom Dybdahl, "Bad Business: The Davenport Fiasco," *Spectrum* 12:1 (1981): 50–61, and "The Davenport Bankruptcy and Recent Litigation," *Spectrum* 12:3 (1982): 49–54; and "The Church of Liberal Borrowings," *Time*, Aug. 2, 1982, p. 39.

54. Brenton R. Schlender, "Religion and Loyal Investors Play Big Role in Alleged Trading Fraud," the *Wall Street Journal*, Sept. 20, 1985, sec. 2, p. 17.

55. See ch. 4.

56. EGW, *Ev*, 20.

57. See ch. 5.

58. See EGW, 1*SP*, 18, 19, 20, 21, 22–23.

59. This is discussed in Malcolm Bull, "Eshatology and Manners in Seventh-day Adventism," *Archive de Sciences Sociales des Religions* 65:1 (1988): 155–56.

9. The Patterns of Growth

1. Damsteegt, *Foundations of Seventh-day Adventist Message and Mission*, 56.

2. Ibid., 163.

3. Uriah Smith, quoted in Borge Schantz, "The Development of Seventh-day Adventist Missionary Thought: A Contemporary Appraisal" (Ph.D. dissertation, Fuller Theological Seminary, 1983), 232. Church statistics in this chapter are compiled from the relevant editions of the *Annual Statistical Report* unless otherwise stated.

4. See R. L. Dabrowski and B. B. Beach, eds., *Michael Belina Czechowski 1818–1876* (Warsaw, Poland: Znaki Czasu, 1979).

5. See H. Leonard, ed., *J. N. Andrews: The Man and the Mission* (Berrien Springs, Mich.: Andrews University Press, 1985).

6. Schantz, "Development of Seventh-day Adventist Missionary Thought," 316.

7. Ibid., 766–67.

8. See Ochs and Ochs, *Past and the Presidents*, 75–87.

9. Schwarz, *Light Bearers*, 276–79.

10. Gottfried Oosterwal, *Mission Possible* (Nashville, Tenn.: SPA, 1972), 29.

11. Ibid., 30.

12. Ibid.

13. Stephen Neill, *A History of Christian Missions* (London: Hodder and Stoughton, 1965), 395–96, 455–56.

14. Schantz, "Development of Seventh-day Adventist Missionary Thought," 768.

15. Schwarz, *Light Bearers*, 344.

16. Ibid., 579.

17. See Howard B. Weeks, *Adventist Evangelism in the Twentieth Century* (Washington D.C.: RHPA, 1969), ch. 14.

18. Schantz, "Development of Seventh-day Adventist Missionary Thought," 405–7. See also Baldur Ed Pfeiffer, *The European SDA Mission in the Middle East* (Frankfurt, Germany: Peter Lang, 1981).

19. See Walter Murray, "A Biographical Sketch of Part of the Life of Elder Walter Schubert" (unpublished paper, Andrews University, n.d.).

20. Oosterwal, *Mission Possible*, 44. (Figure 1.)

21. See Gottfried Oosterwal, "Seventh-day Adventist Mission in the Seventies," *Spectrum*

2:2 (1970): 7; and Schantz's discussion in "Development of Seventh-day Adventist Missionary Thought," 412–19.

22. Schwarz, *Light Bearers*, 596.

23. See Dean R. Hoge, "A Test of Theories of Denominational Growth and Decline," in Dean Hoge and David Roozen, eds., *Understanding Church Growth and Decline 1950–1978* (New York: Pilgrim Press, 1979), 179–97.

24. The Andrews University Institute of Church Ministry conducted growth surveys in the Oregon, Ohio, Washington, Atlanta-Georgia, and Texas Conferences in the early 1980s. In all of these, at least 50 percent of the predominantly white respondents had had at least one Adventist parent during the first twelve years of life.

25. See *Seventh-day Adventist Youth at the Mid-Century* (Washington D.C.: RHPA, 1951).

26. "The Background and Experience of New Members in the Georgia-Cumberland Conference of Seventh-day Adventist 1979–80," Institute of Church Ministry, Andrews University, n.d.

27. Statistics from the North American Division Marketing Program, Institute of Church Ministry, Andrews University, 1986.

28. See Charles F. Marden and Gladys Meyer, *Minorities in American Society*, 4th ed. (New York: Van Nostrand, 1973).

29. See North American Division Marketing Program.

30. See Weeks, *Adventist Evangelism*, 152.

31. "Background and Experience of New Members." See also Gottfried Oosterwal, *Patterns of SDA Church Growth in North America* (Berrien Springs, Mich.: Andrews University Press, 1976), 50.

32. "Background and Experience of New Members," 20.

33. See Dean M. Kelley, *Why Conservative Churches Are Growing* (New York: Harper & Row, 1972).

34. "Background and Experiences of New Members."

35. *Seventh-day Adventist Youth at Mid-Century.*

36. "A Study of Factors Relating to Church Growth in the North American Division of Seventh-day Adventists," Institute of Church Ministry, Andrews University, 1981.

37. See Donald McGavran and Norman Riddle, *Zaire: Midday for Missions* (Valley Forge, Pa.: Judson Press, 1979).

38. Population figures derived from *The World Almanac and Book of Facts* (1984). (New York: Newspaper Enterprise Association, 1983).

39. See Bryan R. Wilson, *Religion in Secular Society: A Sociological Comment* (London: C. A. Watts, 1966), 196.

40. Charles Y. Glock and Rodney Stark, *Religion and Society in Tension* (Chicago: Rand McNally, 1965), 246.

41. Figures for GNP per capita from John Paxton, ed., *The Statesman's Yearbook* (London: Macmillan Press, 1978 and 1984).

42. See Arturo Valenzuela, *The Breakdown of Democratic Regimes: Chile* (Baltimore: Johns Hopkins University Press, 1978), 56, 57, for discussion of the cutback in American economic and military aid during Allende's presidency.

43. See Gordon Connell-Smith, *The United States and Latin America: An Historical Analysis of Inter-American Relations* (London: Heinemann, 1974).

10. The Science of Happiness

1. Walton, et al., *How You Can Live Six Extra Years*, 69.

2. Ibid., 68.

3. Ibid., 4–5.

4. Ibid., 5–7. For the theological implications of this, see ch. 6.

5. Numbers, *Prophetess of Health*, 48–49.

6. Ibid., 48–76.

7. Ibid., 48–49. See also George W. Reid, *A Sound of Trumpets; Americans, Adventists, and*

Health Reform (Washington, D.C.: RHPA, 1982), 28–31. The methods of the health reformers are detailed in Numbers, *Prophetess* 48–76. It should also be noted that proper dress was another important element of health reform that Ellen White later stressed. See Numbers, *Prophetess*, 129–50.

8. The first published account of Mrs. White's Otsego vision is in 4SG-a, 120–51.
9. Ibid., 148.
10. Ibid., 124.
11. Ibid., 120, 134, 137, 140.
12. EGW, "Moral and Physical Law," *The Health Reformer*, 7:10 (1872): 314. George Reid also discusses the importance of natural law in Mrs. White's thinking in *Sound of Trumpets*, 120–21.
13. "The Western Health Reform Institute," *Review*, Aug. 7, 1866, p. 78.
14. See Dores E. Robinson, *The Story of Our Health Message: The Origin, Character, and Development of Health Education in the Seventh-day Adventist Church* (Nashville, Tenn.: SPA, 1943), 133. See also Numbers, *Prophetess*, 107.
15. Numbers, *Prophetess*, 169–70.
16. Ibid., 172.
17. See Schwarz, "John Harvey Kellogg," 114.
18. Ibid., 347–48, 395.
19. Ibid., 277–79.
20. Ibid., 283–88.
21. Ibid., 276–77, 286–87.
22. See Peter Gardella, *Innocent Ecstasy: How Christianity Gave America an Ethic of Sexual Pleasure* (New York: Oxford University Press, 1985), 44–56, and Money, *Destroying Angel*, 17–27.
23. See Numbers, *Prophetess*, 150–59. For a general discussion of Graham and sex, see Stephen Nissenbaum, *Sex, Diet and Debility in Jacksonian America: Sylvester Graham and Health Reform* (Westport, Conn.: Greenwood Press, 1980), 105–24.
24. See, for example, her reference in the account of her health vision in 4SG-a, 124.
25. EGW, 2T, 453. See also ch. 6.
26. EGW, *An Appeal to Mothers: The Great Cause of the Physical, Mental and Moral Ruin of Many of the Children of Our Time* (Battle Creek, Mich.: SDA Publishing Association, 1864), 9.
27. Ibid., 17.
28. Ibid., 19–20.
29. J. H. Kellogg, *Plain Facts for Old and Young: Embracing the Natural History and Hygiene of Organic Life* (Burlington, Iowa: I. F. Segner, 1886), 178.
30. Ibid., 119, 462.
31. Ibid., 467.
32. Ibid., 179.
33. See Schwarz, "John Harvey Kellogg," 233.
34. Money, *Destroying Angel*, 24.
35. EGW, 2T, 477–78.
36. EGW, 6T, 370.
37. EGW, *MH*, 349.
38. For a good discussion of the nature of the Victorian home, see Maxine Van de Wetering, "The Popular Concept of 'Home' in Nineteenth-Century America" *Journal of American Studies* 18:1 (1984), especially pp. 13–19. See also Olive Banks, who discusses the Victorian home from a feminist perspective in *Faces of Feminism: A Study of Feminism as a Social Movement* (Oxford: Martin Robertson and Company, Ltd., 1981), 85–86.
39. EGW, *AH*, 177.
40. Ibid., 19, and EGW, *MH*, 354.
41. Nancy Van Pelt, *The Compleat Marriage* (Nashville, Tenn.: SPA, 1979), 143.
42. *The Home Physician and Guide to Health*, rev. ed. (Washington D.C.: RHPA, 1931), 669.
43. Ibid., 676.

44. Harold Shryock, *Happiness for Husbands and Wives* (Washington, D.C.: RHPA, 1949), 173.
45. EGW, *AH*, 121–28.
46. F. D. Nichol, "Comments on the Recent Kinsey Furor," *Review*, Dec. 10, 1953, p. 11.
47. See Charles Wittschiebe, *God Invented Sex* (Nashville, Tenn.: SPA, 1974), 11–14.
48. For example, see Harvey A. Elder, Joyce W. Hopp, and John E. Lewis, "Adventists and AIDS: How We Should Relate to this Modern Scourge," *Review*, Oct. 6, 1988, p. 21. For a general report on how Adventists coped and related to AIDS see "AIDS Comes to Adventism," *Spectrum* 18:1 (1987).
49. For example see EGW, *MYP*, 439–42; 453–54.
50. For a discussion of Adventist sex ratios see ch. 14.
51. See Cheri Richardson, "Singles' Seminar a Big Success," *Student Movement*, Apr. 20, 1983, p. 3.
52. Jocelyn R. Fay, "Singles: What Is the Church Doing?" *Review*, Jan. 27, 1983, pp. 11–12.
53. General Conference statement, June 24, 1977. Quoted in Michael Pearson, "Seventh-day Adventist Responses to Some Contemporary Ethical Problems" (D. Phil. thesis, Oxford University, 1986), 304.
54. Details of this and other cases can be found in Pearson, "Seventh-day Adventist Responses," p. 327, n. 128.
55. Ibid., 298, 304, 311.
56. Seventh-day Adventist Kinship International, Inc., "Objectives, Purposes and Beliefs"; quoted in Pearson "Seventh-day Adventist Responses," 320.
57. For a detailed historical and sociological account of the Adventist attitude toward divorce and remarriage, see Pearson, "Seventh-day Adventist Responses," 219–76.
58. Ibid., 266.
59. Charles C. Crider and Robert C. Kistler, *The Seventh-day Adventist Family: An Empirical Study* (Berrien Springs, Mich.: Andrews University Press, 1979), 76–77, 223–25.
60. Ibid., 247.
61. See Pearson, "Seventh-day Adventist Responses," 265.
62. F. M. Wilcox, "Healthful Living: Physical Habits and Their Relation to Spiritual Life," *Review*, 25, 1923, p. 12.
63. See 1872 and 1875 statements in *SDA Tracts*, vol. 1 (n.p., n.d.), pp. 297–310, and *SDA Miscellany*, vol. 3 (n.p., n.d.), pp. 577–87; and compare with no. 17 of the "Fundamental Beliefs of Seventh-day Adventists," *Review*, Feb. 19, 1931, p. 7.
64. See Ron Graybill, "The Development of Adventist Thinking on Clean and Unclean Meats," (E. G. White estate pamphlet), June 10, 1981, p. 5.
65. See *SDA Encyclopedia*, 1966 ed., 342, and no. 21 of the revised statement of beliefs in the *Review*, May 1, 1980, p. 26.
66. This episode is related in Numbers, *Prophetess*, 173–74. Mrs. White's General Conference address of 1909 was reprinted in *9T*, 153–166; quote from p. 159.
67. See F. M. Wilcox, "The Diet Question," *Review*, Mar. 15, 1923, p. 3.
68. F. D. Nichol, "Liquor Laws, Tobacco Laws, Meat Laws: An Inquirer's Questions Examined," *Review* Jan. 22, 1931, pp. 22–23. Adventist involvement in prohibition is discussed in ch. 11.
69. See the introduction to the special temperance issue, *Review* 159:8 (n.d.): 2.
70. Money, *Destroying Angel*, 26.
71. Ibid., 15.

11. The Politics of Liberty

1. *Declaration of Independence*, preamble.
2. Details of Adventist religious liberty magazines and organizations can be obtained from the *SDA Encyclopedia*, pp. 1264–65, 1320, 785, 1199–1200 and 1158–64, respectively.

3. For Adventist support of Americans United see F. D. Nichol, "Protestants Organize Against Catholic Legislative Campaign," *Review*, Apr. 1, 1948. p. 3–4, and "A New Organization Favors Religious Liberty," *Liberty*, 43:2 (1948): 34–35. Adventist involvement in Americans United is discussed in Mary F. Beasley, "Pressure Group Persuasion: Protestants and Other Americans United for Separation of Church and State, 1947–1968" (Ph.D. dissertation, Purdue University, 1970). Americans United is also discussed in James L. Adams, *The Growing Church Lobby in Washington* (Grand Rapids, Mich.: William B. Eerdmans, 1970), 96–97, 163, 165.

4. Quoted in Douglas Welebir, "Is the Church Above the Law? God and Caesar in the California Lawsuits," *Spectrum* 9:2 (1978): 7.

5. Ibid.

6. See Tobler, "Where Has the Proctor Case Taken Us?" 28–29.

7. Raymond F. Cottrell, "Churches Meddling in Politics," *Review*, July 29, 1965, p. 12.

8. James White, "The Political Campaign," *Review*, Mar. 11, 1880, p. 176.

9. Ibid.

10. See EGW, *FE*, 475.

11. "The Question of Politics," *Review*, Jan. 19, 1928, p. 10.

12. James White, "The Nation," *Review*, Aug. 12, 1862, p. 84.

13. Ibid.

14. James White, "The Nation," *Review*, Aug. 26, 1862, p. 100.

15. See, for example, J. H. Waggoner, "Our Duty and the Nation," *Review*, Sep. 23, 1862, pp. 132–33; and D. T. Bourdeau, "The Present War," *Review*, Oct. 14, 1862, p. 154–55.

16. EGW, 1*T*, 357.

17. Henry E. Carver, "The War," *Review*, Oct. 21, 1862, p. 166.

18. Everett N. Dick, "The Adventist Medical Cadet Corps," *Adventist Heritage* 1:2 (1974): 19.

19. EGW, 7*T*, 84.

20. See appendix A, "Statement by the General Conference Committee, 1940," in Robert C. Kistler, *Adventists and Labor Unions in the United States* (Washington D.C.: RHPA, 1984), 111.

21. See appendix C, "Basis of Agreement Council on Industrial Relations of the Seventh-day Adventist Church," in Kistler, *Adventists and Labor Unions, 116–17*.

22. Carlyle B. Haynes, "Adventists and Strikes," *Review*, Apr. 18, 1946, p. 23.

23. "Basis of Agreement," in Kistler, *Adventists and Labor Unions, 116–17*.

24. On the failure of the Basis of Agreement see M. E. Loewen, "Seventh-day Adventists and Labor Unions," *Review*, Mar. 15, 1962, pp. 1, 9. On the 1980 law see Gordon Egen, "U.S. Congress Enacts Consience Clause," *Review*, May 7, 1981, pp. 4–8.

25. See, for example, A. T. Jones *The Two Republics or Rome and the United States of America* (Battle Creek, Mich.: Review and Herald Publishing Company, 1891).

26. See J. L. McElhany's letter of Dec. 29, 1939, in *Review*, Jan. 11, 1940, pp. 4–5.

27. See B. B. Beach's presentation in *Review*, Apr. 5, 1984, p. 4.

28. See ch. 4.

29. For the Adventist position on the ecumenical movement and the World Council of Churches, see B. B. Beach, *Ecumenism: Boon or Bane?* (Washington D.C.: RHPA, 1974), especially pp. 283–84, 230–35, 275–77. On the Roman Catholic involvement, see B. B. Beach, "Ecumenism," *Review* Dec. 31, 1964, pp. 4–6, and *Vatican II: Bridging the Abyss* (Washington D.C.: RHPA, 1968).

30. EGW, *GW*, 387–88.

31. For example, "Note and Comment," *Review*, Nov. 12, 1903, p. 7; L. L. Caviness, "Prohibition Advances," Feb. 22, 1917, p. 2; G. B. Thompson, "Prohibition," Apr. 26, 1923, pp. 6–7; E. H. Cherrington, "The Benefits of Prohibition," Sept. 18, 1930, pp. 9–10.

32. See Butler, "Adventism and the American Experience," 198–99.

33. L. L. Caviness, "A Great Day," *Review*, Jan. 30, 1919, p. 5.

34. F. M. Wilcox, "Politics and Prohibition," *Review*, Sept. 27, 1928, p. 3.

35. Accounts of the political career of William Gage can be found in John Kearnes, "Ethical Politics: Adventism and the Case of William Gage," *Adventist Heritage* 5:1 (1978): 3–15; and Yvonne D. Anderson, "The Bible, the Bottle, and the Ballot: Seventh-day Adventist Political Activism: 1850–1900," *Adventist Heritage*, 7:2 (1982): 44–49. Butler's disapproval of Gage is found in his article, "Politics and Temperance," *Review*, Apr. 11, 1882, p. 234.

36. Uriah Smith, "The Temperance Cause in Battle Creek: An Explanation," *Review*, Apr. 11, 1882, p. 232.

37. For more details on these two Adventist politicians, see William G. White, Jr., "Lieutenant Governor George A. Williams: An Adventist in Politics," *Adventist Heritage* 5:1 (1978): 25–38; and Miriam Wood, *Congressman Jerry L. Pettis: His Story* (Mountain View, Calif.: PPPA, 1977).

38. For a discussion of the Gallup polls, see chapter 1. For the concern they caused within the Adventist leadership, see William G. Johnsson, "What the Gallup Survey Reveals," *Review*, July 3, 1986, p. 5.

39. EGW, 1T, 357.

40. For example, see Tom Dybdahl, "We SHOULD Be Involved in Politics," *Spectrum* 8:3 (1977): 33–37.

41. See "GC President Issues Statements on Racism, Peace, Home and Family, and Drugs," *Review*, June 30, 1985, pp. 2–3.

42. For the story of church members who revolted in the U.S.S.R. see Marite Sapiets, "Shelkov and the True and Free Adventists," *Spectrum* 11:4 (1981): 24–32. Roland R. Hegstad, associate director of the General Conference Public Affairs and Religious Liberty Department, distanced the denomination from the True and Free Adventists in "The Church in the U.S.S.R.: A Conversation with Hegstad," *Spectrum* 11:4 (1981): 42–43. The split in the Chinese Adventist Church is recorded in S. J. Lee, "Adventism in China: The Communist Takeover," *Spectrum* 7:3 (1975): 18. The expulsion of the Hungarian dissidents was reported in the *Review* on Nov. 22, 1984, p. 6, and in "A Visit to Hungary," *Pilgrim's Rest*, Tracts WM 105, 106, n.d.

43. See Jack M. Patt, "Living in a Time of Trouble: German Adventists under Nazi Rule"; and Erwin Sicher, "Seventh-day Adventist Publications and the Nazi Temptation," *Spectrum* 8:3 (1977): 2–10 and 11–24 respectively.

44. See *Keesing's Contemporary Archives—Weekly Diary of Important World Events* vol. 26 (London: Keesing's Publications, Ltd., 1967–68), 222622–23.

45. The career of Kisekka is reviewed from an Adventist viewpoint in D. D. N. Nsereko, "Adventist Revolutionary Leads Uganda," *Spectrum* 17:4 (1987): 5–12. Other examples of Third World Adventist politicians can be found in Dion E. Phillips and Glen O. Phillips, "Preacher-Politician in the Caribbean," *Spectrum* 16:2 (1985): 14–17.

46. See Eric Syme, *A History of SDA Church-State Relations in the United States* (Mountain View, Calif.: PPPA, 1973), 28, and Butler, "Adventism and the American Experience," 196.

47. EGW, *GC*, 442.

48. See Syme, *A History of SDA Church-State Relations*, 26–27, 28, 44–45, 49–68.

49. For an account of the denomination's early campaigns against Sunday legislators, see Syme, *A History of SDA Church-State Relations*, 20–48. A useful discussion of Adventists and the World's Fair can be found in Ben McArthur, "The 1893 Chicago World's Fair: An Early Test for Adventist Religious Liberty," *Adventist Heritage* 2:2 (1975): 11–21.

50. Butler, "Adventism and the American Experience," 197.

51. EGW, 9T, 232.

52. See A. T. Jones, *The Rights of the People or Civil Government and Religion* (Oakland, Calif.: Pacific Press, 1895), 9–47, 82, 264. (Italics in original.)

12. The Art of Expression

1. See Graybill, "Power of Prophecy", ch. 4.
2. For a discussion of Adventist church architecture, see Walter O. Comm, "A Study of the Spiritual Influence of the Arts on Christian Liturgy with Special Emphasis on the Impact of Architecture on Seventh-day Adventist Worship Practice" (unpublished D. Min. project, Andrews University, 1976).
3. On the use of symbolic reversal to enhance community self-awareness, see, for example, Clifford Geertz, "Deep Play: Notes on the Balinese Cock-Fight," in *The Interpretation of Cultures: Selected Essays by Clifford Geertz* (London: Hutchinson, 1975), 412–53.
4. On Little Richard see Charles White, *The Life and Times of Little Richard: The Quasar of Rock* (London: Pan Books Ltd., 1985). Curiously, White does not mention Seventh-day Adventism explicitly, but the rock singer's Adventist background is revealed by Little Richard's references to Ellen White (p. 93), his conversion through the denomination's "Voice of Prophecy" correspondence course (p. 98), his subsequent attendance at the black Adventist college, Oakwood, in the late 1950s (pp. 98–101), and his admiration of the Adventist preachers H. M. S. Richards, George Vandeman, and E. E. Cleveland (p. 189). On Prince's Adventist upbringing see Barney Hoskins, *Prince: Imp of the Perverse* (London: Virgin, 1988), 17, and Dave Hill, *Prince: A Pop Life* (London: Faber and Faber, 1989), 67. Little Richard and Prince are discussed further in chapter 15. On Blomstedt see "Herbert Blomstedt: Peak Performance," *Review*, July 5, 1984, pp. 5–8.
5. On music's links with, and possible effects on, perceptions of time, see Robert Newell, "Music and the Temporal Dilemma," *British Journal of Aesthetics* 18:4 (1978): 356–67.
6. The discussion of time in Bull, "Eschatology and Manners," p. 153, needs some clarification. Adventists are unusual among millenarian groups in that the timing of the end has not, since the 1840s, been a dominant preoccupation. The Adventist concern with time focuses on the coexistence of sacred and secular time, rather than the ending of secular time.
7. Hymn no. 15. Reproduced with commentary in Lyell Vernon Heise, "The 1849 Hymnal: A Theological Study" (unpublished paper, Andrews University, 1974), 31. See also Ronald D. Graybill, "Singing and Society: The Hymns of the Saturday-Keeping Adventists, 1849–1863" (unpublished paper, Andrews University, n.d.).
8. Hymn no. 23, ibid., 42.
9. See Hatch, *Sacred Cause of Liberty*, 61.
10. See Perry Miller, *Errand into the Wilderness* (Cambridge: Harvard University Press, 1956).
11. Hymn no. 15, in Heise, "1849 Hymnal," 31.
12. See Numbers, *Prophetess*, pp. 129–50.
13. See Frank Kermode, *The Sense of an Ending: Studies in the Theory of Fiction* (New York: Oxford University Press, 1967) ch. 2.
14. EGW, *MH* 446.
15. Ibid., 445–46.
16. Ibid., 444–45.
17. Ibid., 447.
18. Ibid., 445.
19. EGW, *4T*, 653.
20. Ibid.
21. EGW, *AH*, 516, 515.
22. EGW, *4T*, 71–72, and *1T*, 216. See also Bull, "Eschatology and Manners," 150–51.
23. EGW, *3SG*, 64.
24. EGW, *3T*, 132.
25. EGW, *2T*, 364.
26. EGW, *4T*, 244.

27. EGW, 2T, 391.
28. EGW, 4SG-a, 132.
29. EGW, 2T, 60–61.
30. Ibid., 63.
31. EGW, DA, 625.
32. EGW, 2T, 352.
33. Whittier, Writings vol. 5, 425.
34. EGW, Ev, 204.
35. J. Paul Stauffer, "Uriah Smith: Wood Engraver," Adventist Heritage 3:1 (1976): 17–21.
36. Ronald Graybill, "America: The Magic Dragon," Insight, Nov. 30, 1971, pp. 6–12.
37. The pittura infamante fulfilled a similar function in Renaissance Florence. See Samuel Y. Edgerton, Jr., Pictures and Punishment: Art and Criminal Prosecution During the Florentine Renaissance (Ithaca, N.Y.: Cornell University Press, 1985), 71 ff.
38. EGW, CW, 169.
39. See Raymond H. Woolsey and Ruth Anderson, Harry Anderson: The Man Behind the Paintings (Washington D.C.: RHPA, 1976), in which all the following paintings are reproduced.
40. See Constantine's paintings "Central Park Mugging" and "Lazarus and Friend in Calvary Cemetery."
41. Greg Constantine, Vincent Van Gogh Visits New York (New York: Knopf, 1982), and Leonardo Visits Los Angeles (New York: Knopf, 1985).

13. Adventism and America

1. See, for example, Will Herberg, Protestant—Catholic—Jew: An Essay in American Religious Sociology, rev. ed. (New York: Doubleday, 1960), 99–135.
2. Gail Gehrig, "The American Civil Religion Debate: A Source for Theory Construction," Journal for the Scientific Study of Religion 20:1 (1981): 52.
3. See Robert N. Bellah, "Civil Religion in America," Daedalus: Journal of the American Academy of Arts and Sciences 96:1 (1967): 1–21. See Gail Gehrig, American Civil Religion: An Assessment, SSSR monograph series, no. 3 (1979), for a review of the literature.
4. See Hatch, Sacred Cause of Liberty; and Ruth Bloch, Visionary Republic (Cambridge: Cambridge University Press, 1985).
5. See Paul E. Johnson, A Shopkeeper's Millennium: Society and Revivals in Rochester, New York, 1815–1837 (New York: Hill and Wang, 1978).
6. An extended presentation of this argument can be found in Bull, "Seventh-day Adventists."
7. See Roy Z. Chalee, "The Sabbath Crusade: 1810–1920" (Ph.D. dissertation, George Washington University, 1968).
8. This situation bears some similarity to the pillarization of the state in the Netherlands and Belgium. See John Coleman, The Evolution of Dutch Catholicism 1958–1974 (Berkeley: University of California Press, 1978); and Karel Dobbelaere, "Professionalization and Secularization in the Catholic Pillar," Japanese Journal of Religious Studies 61 (1979): 39–64.
9. Quoted in Daniel J. Boorstin, ed., An American Primer, vol. 1 (Chicago: University of Chicago Press, 1966), 205.
10. See ch. 9.
11. For an extended presentation of this argument, see Bull, "Eschatology and Manners."
12. See ch. 10.
13. See ch. 11.
14. See ch. 8.
15. See Hugh I. Dunton, "The Millerite Adventists and Other Millenarian Groups in Great Britain 1830–1860" (Ph.D. dissertation, University of London, 1984), 218.
16. EGW, 2SG, iv.

17. See ch. 1.
18. On Joseph Smith and Mormonism, see Leonard J. Arrington and Davis Bitton, *The Mormon Experience: A History of the Latter-day Saints* (New York: Knopf, 1979).
19. See Thomas F. O'Dea, *The Mormons* (Chicago: Phoenix Books, 1964), 22–40.
20. *The Book of Mormon*, 1 Nephi 2:20.
21. Ibid., Ether 2:12.
22. Quoted in O'Dea, *The Mormons*, 171.
23. Quoted in Arrington and Bitton, *Mormon Experience*, 127.
24. Ibid., 128.
25. Ibid., 37.
26. Jan Shipps, *Mormonism: The Story of a New Religious Tradition* (Urbana: University of Illinois Press, 1985), 122.
27. This is not to suggest any essential discrepancy between the world view of the two sexes, but rather reflects the rigid sex stereotyping of nineteenth-century America.

14. Women

1. See Shirley Ardener, "Ground Rules and Social Maps for Women: An Introduction," in Shirley Ardener, ed., *Women and Space* (London: Croom Helm, 1981), 11–32.
2. See Gordon Hyde, "A Summary-Report to the Biblical Research Institute Administrative Committee (BRIAD) on the Roles of Women in the Seventh-day Adventist Church" (unpublished paper, General Conference of Seventh-day Adventists, Washington D.C., 1977), 1–2. It should be noted that Hyde also estimated that the proportion of women rose to between 75 and 90 percent of the membership in many local Adventist congregations.
3. Sister M. Ashley, letter, *Review*, Jan. 1851, p. 39. (Italics in original.)
4. "Eastern Tour," *Review*, Oct. 14, 1852, p. 96.
5. D. Hewitt, "Let Your Women Keep Silence in the Churches," *Review*, Oct. 15, 1857, p. 190.
6. See B. F. Robbins, "To the Female Disciples in the Third Angel's Message," *Review*, Dec. 8, 1859, pp. 21–22.
7. S. C. Welcome, "Shall Women Keep Silence in the Churches?" *Review*, Feb. 23, 1860, pp. 109–110.
8. James White, "Unity and Gifts of the Church," *Review*, Jan. 7, 1858, p. 69.
9. Sara Maitland, *A Map of the New Country: Women and Christianity* (London: Routledge & Kegan Paul, 1983), 9.
10. Jackson W. Carroll, Barbara Hargrove, and Adair Lummis, *Women of the Cloth: A New Opportunity for the Churches* (San Francisco: Harper & Row, 1981), 20, 21.
11. Ibid., 21.
12. For a list of various women who served in these capacities, see Bert Haloviak, "Route to the Ordination of Women in the Seventh-day Adventist Church: Two Paths" (unpublished paper, General Conference Archive, Washington, D.C., Mar. 18, 1985), pp. 3–6; Rosalie Haffner Lee, "A Brief History of the Role of Women in the Church" (unpublished paper, n.d.), 3–4; Ives McCarthur Roberts et al., "Women in the Seventh-day Adventist Church: A Report Prepared for the Office of Human Relations General Conference of Seventh-day Adventists" (unpublished paper, Institute of Church Ministry, Andrews University, Feb. 1982), 4–5.
13. See *The Adventist Woman*, Nov. 1984, p. 2.
14. Haloviak, "Route to the Ordination," 5, 8.
15. Ibid., 10.
16. S. M. Cobb, letter to A. E. Place, Aug. 6, 1897. Quoted in Haloviak, "Route to the Ordination," 11.
17. Information on these individuals is from John G. Beach, *Notable Women of Spirit: The Historical Role of Women in the Seventh-day Adventist Church* (Nashville, Tenn.: SPA, 1976), 65–66, 81–82, 102. It should be noted, however, that Flora Williams was not a principal of Battle Creek College, as Beach appears to imply.

18. Bertha Dasher, "Leadership Positions: A Declining Opportunity?" *Spectrum* 15:4 (1984): 35–37.
19. See, for example, the fate of women within the Separate Baptist and Pentecostal churches in Carroll et al., *Women of the Cloth*, 22–23; and the fate of women within the Methodist church in Maitland, *Map of the New Country*, 10.
20. Banks, *Faces of Feminism*, 85, 86.
21. Joseph Bates, "Duty to Our Children," *Review*, Jan. 1851, (1:5) pp. 39–40. For examples of other early *Review* articles that dealt with the family but not the roles of women within it, see Elias Goodwin, "Duty of Parents to Their Children," Aug. 5, 1852, p. 53; "Hints to Promote Harmony in a Family," Jan. 20, 1853, p. 139; "Family Worship," Sept. 18, 1855, pp. 46–47; "Rules for Governing Children," Jan. 24, 1856, p. 131; "Family Devotion," Aug. 21, 1856, p. 123; "Family Worship," June 18, 1857, p. 51; "Teach Your Children," Feb. 11, 1858, p. 109; "What Family Government Is," Apr. 1, 1858, p. 155; "Rules for Home Education," Apr. 15, 1858, p. 175.
22. For a general discussion of the differentiation of the family from society, see Van de Wetering, "Popular Concept of 'Home,' " 5–18, especially p. 15. See also, Banks, *Faces of Feminism*, 85–86.
23. EGW, *AH*, 231, 245.
24. EGW, *2SM*, 431; *AH*, 231; *2T*, 187–88.
25. See Banks, *Faces of Feminism*, 86. See also John Charvet, *Feminism* (London: J. M. Dent & Sons, Ltd., 1982), 20, 28.
26. See Charvet, *Feminism*, 28.
27. See for example Kitt Watts, "The Role of Women in the Seventh-day Adventist Church" (unpublished paper presented to the Biblical Research Institute Committee of the General Conference of the Seventh-day Adventist Church, Washington D.C., Feb. 1972), 20–46.
28. "Keepers of the Keys," *Review*, Mar. 21, 1940, pp. 14–15, 17.
29. Beach, *Notable Women of Spirit*, 87–94.
30. J. H. Egbert, "The Model Woman," *Review*, Nov. 11, 1902, pp. 11–12.
31. EGW, *AH*, 333, 334.
32. See, for example, "Immodest Dress," *Review*, Aug. 25, 1910, pp. 7–8; Ammy W. Welch, "Simplicity in Dress," *Review*, Aug. 19, 1920, p. 21; Pearl L. Rees, "That Outward Adorning," *Review* Sept. 12 and 19, 1940, pp. 16–17 and pp. 16–17, respectively.
33. See the 1940 advertisements of the two girls, the older woman, and the man in the *Review*, July 25, p. 30, October 31, p. 29, Aug. 22, p. 23, and Sept. 26, p. 28, respectively.
34. See the *Review*, May 7, 1970, p. 27.
35. For other examples, see the advertisement inducing young people to sell the church publication *Life and Health* to raise funds for their college education in the *Review*, June 27, 1940, p. 25; and the advertisement for the Adventist book *Happiness and Health* in the *Review*, Aug. 24, 1950, p. 29. The black Adventist magazine *Message* was not above this kind of advertising either. See the *Review*, Mar. 24, 1960, p. 29.
36. Robert H. Pierson, "True Christian Woman Power," *Review*, Feb. 4, 1971, p. 2.
37. Merikay McLeod, *Betrayal: The Shattering Sex Discrimination Case of Silver vs. Pacific Press Publishing Association* (Loma Linda, Calif.: Mars Hill Publications, 1985), 52.
38. Ibid., 338–39
39. Ibid., back cover.
40. Hyde, "A Summary-Report to BRIAD," 1–2.
41. Pierson, "True Christian Woman Power," 2.
42. Figures from Carroll et al., *Women of the Cloth*, 3–4.
43. Authors' interview, Takoma Park, Md. Sept. 10, 1985.
44. Brenda Butka, "Women's Liberation," *Spectrum* 3:4 (1971), 22–28.
45. Leona Running, "The Status and Role of Women in the Adventist Church," *Spectrum* 4:3 (1972): 61 (n. 1).

46. Sakae Kubo, "An Exegesis of 1 Timothy 2:11–15 and Its Implications." (Unpublished paper, Andrews University, Mar. 1976), 14.

47. "Actions of General Interest from the 1974 Annual Council," *Review*, Nov. 28, 1974, p. 19.

48. See *Sligoscope*, church paper of the Sligo Adventist Church, Feb. 1975.

49. Authors' interview, Takoma Park, Md., Sept. 10, 1985.

50. Carroll et al., *Women of the Cloth*, 152–53, 159.

51. Authors' interview, Takoma Park, Md., Sept. 10, 1985.

52. A statement of belief by the Association of Adventist Women can be found in *The Adventist Woman*, Nov. 1984, p. 4.

53. See *The Adventist Woman*, May–June 1985, p. 4. An account of the 1985 meeting can be found in Debra Gainer Nelson, "Commission Postpones Decision on Ordination of Women," *Spectrum* 16:2 (1985): 32–38.

54. Quoted in *The Adventist Woman*, Nov. 1984, p. 4.

55. Mary K. McLaughlin, letter, *The Adventist Woman*, May–June, 1985, p. 7.

15. Blacks

1. Pierre L. Van den Berghe, *Race and Racism: A Comparative Perspective* (New York: Wiley, 1967), 77.

2. See Jacob Justiss, "A Remarkable Century of Progress," *The North American Informant: A Bimonthly Report of the North American Regional Department*, Nov.–Dec. (1971): 1.

3. See Nichol, *Midnight Cry*, 54, 175–78, 301; also Ronald D. Graybill, "The Abolitionist-Millerite Connection," in Numbers and Butler, eds., *The Disappointed*, 139–52.

4. On Bates, see Nichol, *Midnight Cry*, 180–84; on Byington, see Ochs and Ochs, *The Past and the Presidents*, 10; and on J. P. Kellogg, see Schwarz, "John Harvey Kellogg," 5. See also *SDA Encyclopedia*, 1192.

5. See ch. 4.

6. James White, "The Nation," Aug. 12, 1862, p. 84.

7. See ch. 11.

8. Elbert B. Lane, "Tennessee," *Review*, May 2, 1871, p. 158.

9. Dudley M. Canright, "Texas," *Review*, May 25, 1876, p. 166.

10. Ibid.

11. See Ronald D. Graybill, *E. G. White and Church Race Relations* (Washington D.C.: RHPA, 1970), 53–87. A general account of Edson White's work on the Mississippi is also provided by Graybill's *Mission to Black America* (Mountain View, Calif.: PPPA, 1971).

12. See Joel Williamson, *The Crucible of Race: Black-White Relations in the American South Since Emancipation* (New York: Oxford University Press, 1984), 50–52.

13. This point has been well made for the American South by C. Vann Woodword in *The Strange Career of Jim Crow* (New York: Oxford University Press, 1974), 31–65.

14. The episode is related in Graybill, *E. G. White and Church Race Relations*, 61–64.

15. Quoted in EGW, *SW*, 15.

16. Ibid., 19.

17. See EGW, "Proclaiming the Truth Where There Is Race Antagonism, in *Ellen G. White Pamphlets in the Concordance*, vol. 2 (Payson, Ariz.: Leaves of Autumn Books, 1983), 121, 123. This pamphlet was also reproduced in 9T, 204–12.

18. Roy Branson, "Ellen G. White: Racist or Champion of Equality?" *Review*, Apr. 9, 1970, p. 3.

19. See Graybill, "The Abolitionist-Millerite Connection," 143.

20. See John O. Waller, "John Byington of Bucks Bridge: The Pre-Adventist Years," *Adventist Heritage* 1:2 (1974): 10–11.

21. Branson, "Ellen G. White: Racist or Champion of Equality?" p. 3.

22. See Merton L. Dillon, *The Abolitionist: The Growth of a Dissenting Minority* (New York: W. W. Norton & Co., 1979), 175–79 and 184–86. Mrs. White's statement on the Fugitive Slave Act can be found in 1T, 202.

23. Roy Branson, "Slavery and Prophecy," *Review*, Apr. 16, 1970, p. 8.
24. Roy Branson, "The Crisis of the Nineties," *Review*, Apr. 23, 1970, pp. 4–6.
25. Figures are from the *SDA Encyclopedia*, 1195.
26. These and subsequent figures are obtained from the relevant editions of the *Annual Statistical Reports* of the North American Office of Regional Affairs and of the General Conference Archives and Statistics Department.
27. For details of the original conference proposals, see the General Conference officers' minutes, Apr. 10, 1944, General Conference Archives, Washington, D.C.
28. See James M. Penton, *Apocalypse Delayed: The Story of Jehovah's Witnesses* (Toronto: University of Toronto Press, 1985), 284–87.
29. Mormon racial attitudes are chronicled by Newell G. Bringhurst in *Saints, Slaves, and Blacks: The Changing Place of Black People Within Mormonism* (Westport, Conn.: Greenwood Press, 1981). A more sympathetic account is given by Arrington and Bitton, *Mormon Experience*, 321–25.
30. See Jonathan Butler, "Race Relations in the Church," 4, *Insight*, Feb. 20, 1979, pp. 9–10.
31. Quoted in Philip Chester Willis, "Dost Thou Still Retain Thine Integrity?" (unpublished term paper, Andrews University, 1977), 18.
32. Ibid., 19.
33. Ibid., 22.
34. This account of J. K. Humphrey has been taken from Joe Mesar and Tom Dybdahl, "The Utopia Park Affair and the Rise of Northern Black Adventists," *Adventist Heritage* 1:1 (1974): 34–41, 53–54.
35. Authors' interview, Huntsville, Ala. Aug. 19, 1985.
36. Talbert O. Shaw detected an inherent racism in Adventist theology in a rather technical discussion, "Racism and Adventist Theology," *Spectrum* 3:4 (1971): 36.
37. A. W. Spalding, *Lights and Shades in the Black Belt* (unpublished manuscript, n.d.), 142.
38. Lincoln's famous passage on the inferiority of blacks can be found in Van den Berghe, *Race and Racism*, 79.
39. See Graybill, *E. G. White and Church Race Relations*, 71, 72, 77.
40. Ibid., 79–80.
41. EGW, "Proclaiming the Truth Where There Is Race Antagonism," p. 122.
42. EGW, 9*T*, p. 214.
43. Van den Berghe provides an excellent discussion of this process in *Race and Racism*, 85–91. See also Williamson, *Crucible of Race*, which is largely devoted to this thesis.
44. J. E. White, "In the South," *Review*, Apr. 23, 1901, p. 265.
45. For more details see Louis B. Reynolds, "She Fulfilled the Impossible Dream," *Review*, Jan. 4, 1973, pp. 15–17.
46. Story quoted in Lee Mellinger, "Racism? Not Here! Not Now!" *Campus Chronicle* (Pacific Union College student newspaper), Feb. 18, 1982, p. 13.
47. See Tom Dybdahl, "Prejudice in the Church," *Insight*, Jan. 21, 1975, pp. 13–14. Calvin Moseley also recalled such incidents in his interview with the authors.
48. See Durand, "Reporting the Big Event," 37–39.
49. F. D. Nichol, "Unity in the Faith," *Review*, Apr. 29, 1965, p. 12.
50. See "Actions of General Interest: Spring Meeting of the General Conference Committee," *Review*, Apr. 29, 1965, p. 8.
51. See Butler, "Race Relations in the Church," p. 10.
52. E. E. Cleveland, "Regional Union Conferences," *Spectrum* 2:2 (1970): 44.
53. Calvin B. Rock, "Cultural Pluralism and Black Unions," *Spectrum* 9:3 (1978): 4–12.
54. See Benjamin Reeves, "The Call for Black Unions," *Spectrum* 9:3 (1978): 2–3; and Butler, "Race Relations in the Church," 13–14.
55. See F. L. Peterson, *The Hope of the Race* (Nashville, Tenn.: SPA, 1934), especially 21–24, 72, 236.
56. E. E. Cleveland, *Free at Last* (Washington D.C.: RHPA, 1970). The special West African edition of the book especially emphasized black history in its presentation.

57. See Richard Wright, *Native Son* (New York: Harper & Bros., 1940).
58. See White, *The Life and Times of Little Richard*, 100–01, 183–89.
59. On the racial and apocalyptic influences in Prince's music see Hill, *Prince*, 194–213 and 108–25, respectively.
60. On Michael Jackson and George Benson see Penton, *Apocalypse Delayed*, 277–79.
61. Michael Banton provides a useful discussion of the work of Park and Burgess in *The Idea of Race* (London: Tavistock Publications, Ltd., 1977), 105–11.
62. Ibid., 125–29.
63. Ibid., 135–42.
64. Williamson, *Crucible of Race*, 505.

16. Ministers

Authors' note:
This chapter is also based on conversations with Adventist ministers over many years.

1. Researchers interested in more information on all the above individuals should consult the relevant entries in the *SDA Encyclopedia*.
2. See J. N. Loughborough, *The Rise and Progress of Seventh-day Adventists with Tokens of God's Hand in the Movement* (Battle Creek, Mich.: General Conference Association of the Seventh-day Adventists, 1892), 304.
3. A. W. Spalding, *Origin and History of Seventh-day Adventists*, vol 3 (Washington, D.C.: RHPA, 1962), 245, 247.
4. "Report of Committee on Course of Reading for Ministers," *Review*, Dec. 20, 1881, p. 395.
5. Schwarz, *Light Bearers*, 481.
6. For a good account of the professionalization of the Adventist ministry, including the establishment of the seminary, see Schwarz, *Light Bearers*, 481–93.
7. David S. Schuller, Merton P. Strommen, and Milo L. Brekke, eds., *Ministry in America: A Report and Analysis, Based on an In-Depth Survey of Forty-Seven Denominations in the United States and Canada* (San Francisco: Harper & Row, 1980), 60–70.
8. Ibid., 57, 60–64. see also pp. 355, 362.
9. Ibid., 64.
10. EGW, 4*T*, 372.
11. See, for example, EGW, 2*T*, 610.
12. Ibid., 568–69.
13. Roger L. Dudley et al., "The Personality of the Pastor as a Function of Church Growth" (unpublished research study commissioned by the North American Division of Seventh-day Adventists, Institute of Church Ministry, Andrews University, June 1982), 11, 19, 48–49.
14. Ibid., 12, 48.
15. Orley Berg, *The Work of the Pastor* (Nashville, Tenn.: SPA, 1966), 10.
16. Roger L. Dudley et al., "The Pastor as Person and Husband: A Study of Pastoral Morale" (unpublished research study commissioned by Ministerial Department of General Conference of Seventh-day Adventists, Institute of Church Ministry, Andrews University, May 1981), 13.
17. Ibid., 15.
18. Dudley et al., "Personality of the Pastor," 17, 11, 19, 48.
19. Dudley et al., "Pastor as Person and Husband," 15.
20. Schuller et al., *Ministry in America*, 102–3, 126–27, 130–31.
21. Ila Zbaraschuk, "Why Young Adventists Leave the Church," *Insight*, Sept. 11, 1973, pp. 13–14. See also Charles Bradford's discussion of this problem in *Preaching to the Times* (Washington, D.C.: RHPA, 1975), 14–15.
22. Dudley et al., "Pastor as Person," 15; cf. Schuller et al., *Ministry in America*, 210–11.
23. Dudley et al., "The Pastor as Person," 15; cf. Schuller et al., *Ministry in America*, 138–39. For a detailed discussion of the characteristics of the Adventist grouping, see

David Allan Hubbard and Clinton W. McLemare in the chapter "Evangelical Churches," in Schuller et al., *Ministry in America*, 351–94.

24. Dudley et al., "Pastor as Person and Husband," 15–16.
25. Ibid., 16, 19.
26. Ibid., 21.
27. Ibid., 5.
28. Ibid., 23–24.
29. Ibid., 24, 18.
30. Ibid., 5.
31. Ibid.
32. See Dudley et al., "Pastor as Person," 8–9; EGW, 1*T*, 137–40, 449–54; and, for example, Carlyle B. Haynes, *The Divine Art of Preaching* (Washington, D.C.: RHPA, 1939), 173–84.
33. Dudley et al., "Pastor as Person," 5.
34. Carole Luke Kilcher et al., "The Pastor's Wife as Person: A Study of Morale of the Pastor's Wife" (unpublished research study commissioned by the Ministerial Department of General Conference of Seventh-day Adventists, Institute of Church Ministry, Andrews University, Sept. 1981), 2, 10.
35. Ibid., 10.
36. Ibid., 5.
37. Ibid., 2.
38. James White, "The Ministry, No. 1" *Review*, July 18, 1865, p. 52.
39. James White, "The Ministry, No. 2" *Review*, July 25, 1865, p. 60.
40. EGW, 4*T*, pp. 402–3.
41. EGW, *GW*, 15.
42. Ibid., 451.
43. See EGW, 4*T*, 263 and 1*T*, 271–72.
44. Schwarz, "John Harvey Kellogg," 349.
45. EGW, 5*T*, 439.
46. EGW, 6*T*, 411.

17. Doctors

1. Kellogg to E. G. White, June 28, 1898; quoted in Richard Schwarz, "The Kellogg Schism: The Hidden Issues," *Spectrum* 4:4 (1972): 24.
2. An account of the development of Battle Creek Sanitarium can be found in Schwarz, "John Harvey Kellogg," 170–98.
3. Ibid., 355.
4. Ibid., 356–57.
5. G. I. Butler to Ellen G. White, Aug. 23 and Dec. 16, 1886; quoted in Richard Schwarz, "The Perils of Growth—1886–1905," in Gary Land, ed., *Adventism in America, A History* (Grand Rapids, Mich.: William B. Eerdmans, 1986), 133.
6. EGW, *MM*, 50.
7. Quoted in Schwarz, "John Harvey Kellogg," 312.
8. Ibid., 296.
9. Ibid., 335, 338.
10. Ibid., 296.
11. Ibid., 309–17, 321–37.
12. Ibid., 228.
13. Spalding, *Origin and History of Seventh-day Adventists*, vol. 3, 30, 31.
14. For the full story of Kellogg's break with the Adventist church, see Schwarz, "John Harvey Kellogg," 347–417.
15. See ch. 19.
16. For more details on Magan, see Merlin L. Neff, *Invincible Irishman: A Biography of Percy T. Magan* (Mountain View, Calif.: PPPA, 1964).

17. See Jerry Wiley, *Loma Linda University: Next Right* (Mountain View, Calif.: PPPA, 1968), 9–24.
18. The development of the church's health institutions in the period is discussed in James K. Davis, "The Bitter Taste of Prosperity: Sectarian Jeremiads and Adventist Medical Work in the 1920s," *Adventist Heritage* 8:2 (1983): 48–59.
19. See "Report of the Annual Council of the General Conference Committee," *Review*, Dec. 4, 1924, pp. 5–6.
20. Davis, "Bitter Taste of Prosperity," 55.
21. See F. D. Nichol, "Why Our Sanitariums Evolved into Hospitals," *Review*, Jan. 23, 1964, pp. 5–6. See also Ives Roberts et al., "Counsel for Adventist Health Systems" (unpublished research study commissioned by Adventist Health Systems North, Institute of Church Ministry, Andrews University, 1982), 13–16.
22. See *SDA Encyclopedia*, 1571–73.
23. Quoted in F. D. Nichol, "Recapturing, in Part, the Sanitarium Idea," *Review*, Jan. 30, 1964, pp. 3–4.
24. Nichol, "Why Our Sanitariums Evolved into Hospitals," p. 5.
25. On the development of the Adventist health network, see Larmar W. Young, "Building on a Vision: Foundations of the Adventist Health System, 1900–1986," *Review* Feb. 13, 1986, pp. 20–21; and Robin Duska, "Autumn Council Creates Seventh Largest Health System," *Spectrum* 13:2 (1982), 69–70.
26. The functions of AHS/US were given in an interview with the system's president, Donald W. Welch, in the *Review*, Feb. 13, 1986, p. 13.
27. For the recent changes in American health care and the Adventist response to them, see Joel W. Hass, "The Shape of Health Care to Come," *Review*, Feb. 13, 1986, pp. 22–23.
28. This was revealed in interviews the authors conducted with several Adventist hospital directors in 1985.
29. Figures obtained from Florida Hospital's public relations department in 1985.
30. For example, one of the public relations officers at Florida Hospital in 1985 was a Baptist.
31. See Richard A. Schaefer, *Legacy: The Heritage of a Unique International Medical Outreach* (Mountain View, Calif.: PPPA, 1977), 123–25.
32. See ch. 12.
33. The amalgamation question was immediately recognized by the editors of the *Review* (Dec. 13, 1984, pp. 16–17), who later published letters from members criticizing the operation on this basis (Jan. 31, 1985, p. 14).
34. See R. C. Bainer, "Medical-Ministerial Relationship in the Seventh-day Adventist Church" (unpublished paper, Andrews University, 1969).
35. See the General Conference's "Abortion Guidelines," *Ministry*, Mar. 1971, pp. 10–11. An example of a less compromising attitude came in Ralph Waddell's "Abortion Is Not the Answer" on pp. 7–9 of the same issue.
36. See ch. 6.
37. Bull and Lockhart, "Intellectual World of the Adventist Theologians."
38. A good account of the accreditation process can be found in William G. White, "Flirting with the World: How Adventist Colleges in North America Got Accredited," *Adventist Heritage* 8:1 (1983): 40–51.
39. Quoted in Davis, "Bitter Taste of Prosperity," 58.

18. Educators

1. James White, quoted in "Questions and Answers," *Review*, Dec. 23, 1862, p. 29.
2. Roy E. Graham, "James White: Initiator," in George R. Knight, ed., *Early Adventist Educators* (Berrien Springs, Mich.: Andrews University Press, 1983), 18, 20–21.
3. See George R. Knight, "Early Adventists and Education: Attitudes and Context"; and Graham, "James White," in Knight, ed., *Early Adventist Educators* 2 and 14, 18–20, respectively.

4. See ch. 8 and 13.
5. See Allan G. Lindsay, "Goodloe Harper Bell: Teacher," in Knight, ed., *Early Adventist Educators*, 50–71; and John O. Waller, "Adventist English Teachers: Some Roots," *Spectrum* 10:3 (1979): 38–41.
6. Quoted in Emmett K. VandeVere, *The Wisdom Seekers* (Nashville, Tenn.: SPA, 1972), 27.
7. Ibid.
8. Quoted in Joseph G. Smoot, "Sidney Brownsberger: Traditionalist," in Knight, ed., *Early Adventist Educators*, 81. More details on Brownsberger's contribution can be found in Leigh Johnsen, "Brownsberger and Battle Creek: The Beginning of Adventist Higher Education," *Adventist Heritage* 3:2 (1976), 30–41.
9. See Graham, "James White," 23.
10. George I. Butler, "Unpleasant Themes: The Closing of Our College," *Review*, Sept. 12, 1882, p. 586.
11. See for example, George R. Knight, "Ellen G. White: Prophet," in Knight, ed., *Early Adventist Educators*, 30–31, 32, 37–39.
12. Quoted in Waller, "Adventist English Teachers," 39.
13. Ibid.
14. EGW, 5*T*, 27.
15. Ibid., 21–36.
16. The most controversial of Mrs. White's early educational writings is the document "Proper Education," issued in 1872 (see *FE*, 15–46), which Adventist writers universally regard as the prophetess's ideal for Adventist education. However, the document failed to recognize the Bible as an essential educational tool, paid only cursory attention to ministerial training, and did not reject secular educational practices— aspects of Mrs. White's philosophy that developed only in reaction to Battle Creek College. A close analysis of the document reveals that it had really little to do with education, but rather with health reform. It was the regulation of the body that Mrs. White, at this stage, regarded as "proper education." Yet Adventist writers persist in viewing "Proper Education" as an educational statement and thus have had to construct hypotheses to explain why the pattern for Adventist education ignored the central elements of the pattern. See, for example, Knight, "Ellen G. White," 27–28.
17. EGW, *Ed*, 13.
18. Ibid., 30.
19. Smoot, "Sidney Brownsberger," 91.
20. VandeVere, *Wisdom Seekers*, 50.
21. On Prescott, see Gilbert M. Valentine, "William W. Prescott: Architect of a Bible-Centered Curriculum," *Adventist Heritage* 8:1 (1983): 18–24. On Sutherland, see Floyd O. Rittenhouse, "Edward A. Sutherland: Independent Reformer," *Adventist Heritage* 4:2 (1977): 20–34.
22. The Sutherland presidency is described in VandeVere, *Wisdom Seekers*, 80–118.
23. See Knight, "Ellen G. White," 43–44.
24. See White, "Flirting with the World," 40–51.
25. See Frederick Rudolph, *The American College and University: A History* (New York: Vintage Books, 1962), 470–71.
26. For the details of the development of the Theological Seminary, see Schwarz, *Light Bearers*, 485–93. See also ch. 16.
27. On Griggs, see Arnold C. Reye and George R. Knight, in Knight, ed., "Frederick Griggs: Moderate," *Early Adventist Educators*, 184–204.
28. The story of the denomination's two universities is told in the *SDA Encyclopedia*, 45–52 and 798–810, respectively.
29. For example, Keld J. Reynolds, "Some Observations on Academic Freedom," *The Journal of True Education* 27:4'(1965): 16–19; and Earle Hilgert, "Academic Freedom," *The Journal of True Education* 29:3 (1967): 16–19.
30. EGW, *Ed* 17.
31. See Richard C. Osborn, "The Establishment of the Adventist Forum," *Spectrum* 10:4

(1980): 49 and Malcolm Bull, "The Medicalization of Adventism," *Spectrum* 18:3 (1988): 18–19 and 21, n. 3.

32. See Osborn, "The Establishment of the Adventist Forum," 45–48; and the official statement of support of the organization in "Adventist Graduate Students Establish Organization," *Review*, Jan. 11, 1968, p. 21.

33. Quoted in Osborn, "Establishment of the Adventist Forum," 48.

34. Ibid, 51.

35. McAdams, "Shifting Views of Inspiration," 40.

36. See William G. Johnsson, "The *Review* in Your Future," *Review*, Dec. 9, 1982, 9–10.

37. For example, Wilfred M. Hillock, "Need for Organizational Change in the Adventist Church," *Spectrum* 4:3 (1972): 24–32; Raymond F. Cottrell, "The Case for an Independent North American Division," *Spectrum* 13:1 (1982): 2–14.

38. See the issue "A Call for an Open Church," *Spectrum* 14:4 (1984).

39. See Neal Wilson, "Statement on Association of Adventist Forums and *Spectrum*," *Spectrum* 15:4 (1984): 26. For the AAF's response, see pp. 28–30 of the same issue.

40. In the special issue of *Spectrum* devoted to Numbers's book, it was noticeable that the Adventist reviewers Richard Schwarz and Fritz Guy were markedly critical while the non-Adventist reviewers Fawn Brodie and Ernest Sandeen were much more favorably disposed to Numbers's work. See the issue "Ellen White and Health," *Spectrum* 8:2 (1977).

41. Donald R. McAdams, "Free the College Boards: Toward a Pluralism of Excellence," *Spectrum* 16:4 (1985): 30.

42. See the open letter to the church president Neal Wilson signed by thirty-nine Andrews University academics and the statement of church theologians in *Spectrum* 11:2 (1980), 61–62, 65.

43. See the reports on the two institutions in "Adventist Colleges Under Siege," *Spectrum* 13:2 (1982), 4–18.

44. Kenneth H. Wood, "Colleges in Trouble," *Review*, Feb. 21, 1980, p. 3.

45. An account of the sacking of the dissident Andrews University professor, Smuts van Rooyen, can be found in Lori Pappajohn, "Smuts van Rooyen Resigns Under Pressure," *Student Movement*, May 27, 1981, pp. 1, 11, and 5. The controversy over the seminary deanship is best related in Ray Foody, "Seminary Dean Selection Questioned: Why Hasel?" *Student Movement*, Oct. 28, 1981. (This report was incorrectly attributed to Hernan Visani.) See also Richard Emmerson, "The Continuing Crisis," *Spectrum* 12:1 (1981): 44.

46. On Hasel's resignation see Wendy Ripley, "Changing of the Guard at the SDA Seminary, *Spectrum* 19:2 (1988): 57–59.

47. See Emmerson, "Continuing Crisis," 41–43.

48. See Warren C. Trenchard, "In the Shadow of the Sancturary: The 1980 Theological Consultation," *Spectrum* 11:2 (1980): 26–30; and Alden Thompson, "Theological Consultation II," *Spectrum* 12:2 (1981): 40–52.

49. *Sudden Sound Songsheet* (n.p., n.d.), 1.

50. Bernard Ramm, *The Christian View of Science and Scripture* (Grand Rapids, Mich.: William B. Eerdmans, 1954), 180. Biographical information on Price can be obtained from Harold W. Clark, *Crusader for Creation: The Life and Writings of George McCready Price* (Mountain View, Calif.: PPPA, 1966).

51. See Ronald L. Numbers, " 'Sciences of Satanic Origin': Adventist Attitudes Toward Evolutionary Biology and Geology," *Spectrum* 9:4 (1979): 24.

52. See George McCready Price, *The New Geology*, (Mountain View, Calif.: PPPA, 1923), 278, 280, 627, 629, 298, 300, 164, 296.

53. George McCready Price, *The Modern Flood Theory of Geology* (New York: Fleming H. Revell, 1935), 61; cf. EGW, *Ed*, 129.

54. For example, Henri Blocher, *In the Beginning* (London: Inter Varsity Press, 1984), 213–14.

55. Clark, *Crusader for Creation*, 70.

56. Harold W. Clark, *The Battle over Genesis* (Washington, D.C.: RHPA, 1977), 141.

57. George McCready Price, "Theories of Satanic Origin" (n.p., n.d.), 6, 9.
58. See *1BC* (1978 rev. ed.), p. 87, and compare Price's statement rejecting the orderly arrangement of the geological column on p. 75 of the original 1953 edition. For a useful review of the debate between Price and Clark, see W. W. Hughes, "Shifts in Adventist Creationism," *Spectrum* 16:2 (1985): 47–51.
59. The origins of GRI are related in Richard Hammill, "Fifty Years of Creationism: The Story of an Insider," *Spectrum* 15:2 (1984): 34–36.
60. See the interview with P. E. Hare in Roy Benton, "Odyssey of an Adventist Creationist," *Spectrum* 15:2 (1984): 48; and Hammill, "Fifty Years of Creationism," 37. The scientists of, and the issues within, GRI in its initial years are also covered in Edward Lugenbeal, "The Conservative Restoration at Geoscience," *Spectrum* 15:2 (1984): 23–28.
61. See Lugenbeal, "Conservative Restoration," 23, 28–29.
62. See Harold G. Coffin, *Creation—Accident or Design?* (Washington D.C.: RHPA, 1969).
63. See Richard Ritland, *A Search for Meaning in Nature: A New Look at Creation and Evolution* (Mountain View, Calif.: PPPA, 1970), 157, 167, 168, 47.
64. Coffin, *Creation*, 6; and Ritland, *Search for Meaning*, 8.
65. See Lugenbeal, "The Conservative Restoration," 30. See also Ralph Blodgett, "Adventists Play Key Role in Creation Trial," *Review*, Feb. 18, 1982, pp. 4–7.
66. Unpublished 1980 survey conducted by Ervil D. Clark, late professor of biology, Pacific Union College.
67. George W. Reid, "The Issues at Stake," *Review*, Dec. 8, 1983, p. 16; and Benton, "Odyssey of an Adventist Creationist," 51.
68. McAdams. "Free the College Boards," 30–31.

19. The Self-Supporting Movement

1. See *Adventist-Laymen's Service and Industries: North American Directory* (Washington D.C.: General Conference of Seventh-day Adventists, 1980).
2. This account is based on the authors' visit to a self-supporting center in the mid-1980s.
3. See Standish and Standish, *Adventism Challenged*, vol. 1, 29–44.
4. Colin D. Standish and Russell R. Standish, *Adventism Imperiled: Education in Crisis* (Rapidan, Virg.: Historic Truth Publications, 1984); *Adventism Unveiled*, (Rapidan, Virg.: Historic Truth Publications, 1983).
5. The topic was repeatedly raised by Adventist academics during the authors' visits to denominational colleges in 1985.
6. On social movements, see Rudolf Heberle, *Social Movements: An Introduction to Political Sociology* (New York: Appleton, 1951).
7. See Louis A. Hansen, *From So Small a Dream* (Nashville, Tenn.: SPA, 1968); also William Cruzan Sandborn, "The History of Madison College" (unpublished Ed.D. thesis, George Peabody College for Teachers, 1953); also Ira Gish and Harry Christman, *Madison: God's Beautiful Farm: The E. A. Sutherland Story* (Mountain View, Calif.: PPPA, 1979).
8. EGW, *An Appeal for the Madison School* (n.p., 1908), 4.
9. Gish and Christman, *Madison*, 126.
10. Robert H. Pierson, *Miracles Happen Every Day: A Story of Self-Supporting Workers* (Mountain View, Calif.: PPPA, 1983), 16–35.
11. *SDA Encyclopedia*, 831.
12. Pierson, *Miracles*, 1–15.
13. Ibid., 124–34. See also Patty Ann Schwab, "A Brief Look at Weimar Institute" (unpublished paper, Andrews University, 1981); and Suzanne Schuppel-Frey, "Inside the Weimar Institute," *Spectrum* 15:1 (1984): 24–28. The institute publishes a newsletter, *The Weimar Bulletin*.
14. Raymond Moore, *Adventist Education at the Crossroads* (Mountain View, Calif.: PPPA, 1976).

15. Weimar Institute, "Weimar Institute Is . . ." (pamphlet); quoted in Schwab, "A Brief Look at Weimar Institute," 7.
16. E. A. Sutherland, *Living Fountains or Boken Cisterns: An Educational Problem for Protestants* (Battle Creek, Mich.: RHPA, 1900).
17. See Gish and Christman, *Madison*, 82.
18. Sutherland, *Living Fountains*, 344.
19. Ibid., 255.
20. Ibid., 228.
21. On contemporary fundamentalist schooling, see Alan Peshkin, *God's Choice: The Total World of a Fundamentalist Christian School* (Chicago: University of Chicago Press, 1986).
22. EGW, 6*T*, 179.
23. Standish and Standish, *Adventism Imperiled*, 67.
24. Sutherland, *Living Fountains*, 29.
25. W. D. Frazee, *Another Ark to Build* (Harrisville, N.H.: Mountain Missionary Press, 1979), 117.
26. On the Kellogg crisis, see ch. 17.
27. For a discussion of Douglas, see ch. 6.
28. *The Layworker*, Adventists Layworkers, Inc., P.O. Box 916, Hesperia, Calif. 92345.
29. See *The Layworker*, Fall 1973.
30. For a statement of purpose, see *"Watchman, What of the Night?"* 1:1 (1968): 1. (*The Layworker* pointed its readers to Grotheer's analysis of the 1985 General Conference session in its Fall 1985 issue.)
31. See *The Layworker*, Winter (1983), back cover.
32. Hoehn Research Library, Box 1270, Grand Forks, B.C., Canada, V0H 1H0.
33. *The Layworker*, Fall (1973): 13.
34. Frazee, *Another Ark to Build*, 168.
35. See Foster, "Had Prophecy Failed?"
36. See Everett Webber, *Escape to Utopia: The Communal Movement in America* (New York: Hastings House, 1959), 299–317.
37. Mesar and Dybdahl, "The Utopia Park Affair," 34–41, 53, 54.
38. Pierson, *Miracles*, 62.
39. F. D. Nichol, quoted in Pierson, *Miracles*, 84, 85.

20. Conclusion: The Revolving Door

1. Wade Clark Roof and Christopher Kirk Hadaway, "Denominational Switching in the Seventies: Going Beyond Stark and Glock," *Journal for the Scientific Study of Religion* 18 (1979): 367.
2. See Rodney Stark and Charles Y. Glock, *American Piety: The Nature of Religious Commitment* (Berkeley: University of California Press, 1968), 183–203.
3. See ch. 3.
4. Ronald Graybill, "Millenarians and Money: Adventist Wealth and Adventist Beliefs," *Spectrum* 10:2 (1979): 31–41.
5. W. R. Goldschmidt, "Class Denominationalism in Rural California Churches," *American Journal of Sociology* 49 (1944): 348–55.
6. "Population Sampling Report of the Seventh-day Adventists in the United States," statistical appendix to *SDA Youth at Mid-Century* (Washington D.C.: General Conference of Seventh-day Adventists, 1952), 25–29.
7. Ibid., 27.
8. North American Division Marketing Program, 142, 144.
9. Bull, "Eschatology and Manners."
10. See ch. 9.
11. "Population Sampling Report," 28.
12. EGW, 5*T*, 439, 578.
13. On professionlization and secularization, see Wilson, "Sect or Denomination."

14. On the status of the medical profession, see Bryan S. Turner: *The Body and Society* (Oxford: Basil Blackwell, 1985), ch. 9.
15. "Church Growth in the North American Division," 127, 128.
16. See *SDA Youth at Mid-Century*.
17. Osborn, "The Establishment of the Adventist Forum," 43.
18. James T. Borhek, "Social Bases of Participation in the Seventh-day Adventist Church" (unpublished M. A. thesis, University of California, Berkeley, 1960). See also "Role Orientations and Organizational Stability," *Human Organization* 24 (1965): 332–38.
19. See Schwartz, *Sect Ideologies and Social Status*.
20. The terminology is derived, rather loosely, from Ernst Troeltsch, *The Social Teaching of the Christian Churches*, trans. O Wyon (London: Allen & Unwin, 1931), and perhaps also approximates to the "world-rejecting," "world accommodating," and "world affirming" typology of Roy Wallis, in *The Elementary Forms of the New Religious Life* (London: Routledge & Kegan Paul, 1984), 35, 36.

Bibliographical Note

Bibliographical sources on Adventism include the bibliography of Millerism in Edwin Scott Gaustad, ed., *The Rise of Adventism: Religion and Society in Mid-Nineteenth Century America* (New York: Harper & Row, 1974), and William M. Schomburg's "Check List of Seventh-day Adventist Publications in the United States, 1850–1900" (M.S. thesis, Catholic University of America, 1972). The indices at the Heritage Rooms of Andrews University, Michigan, and Loma Linda University, California, provide a guide to the extensive holdings of these institutions, and researchers may also consult Gilberto Abella's bibliography of "Dissertations, Theses and Research Papers Related to the Seventh-day Adventist Church." The *SDA Periodicals Index* lists articles published in denominational journals since 1971. The Ellen G. White Research Center in Washington, D.C., houses all the published and unpublished writings of the prophetess and a comprehensive index. Similar facilities are available at the heritage rooms of Adventist universities and colleges. The church paper, the *Adventist Review* (formerly the *Review and Herald* and the *Advent Review and Sabbath Herald* 1850–) is an invaluable source. Of other denominational periodicals, the most useful are *The Ministry* (1928–), *Adventist Heritage: A Magazine of Adventist History* (1974–), and *Spectrum: Journal of the Association of Adventist Forums* (1969–). The *General Conference Statistical Report* has been published annually since 1908, and the *Seventh-day Adventist Yearbook* since 1882. *The Seventh-day Adventist Encyclopedia*, ed. Don F. Neufeld (Washington, D.C.: Review and Herald Publishing Association, rev. ed., 1976), is an important work of reference, as is *The Seventh-day Adventist Bible Commentary*, vols. 1–7, ed. Francis D. Nichol (Washington, D.C.: Review and Herald Publishing Association, rev. eds. 1976–80).

There are several general histories of the church written by Seventh-day Adventists. Of these, the most up to date are Gary Land, ed., *Adventism in America: A History* (Grand Rapids, Mich.: William B. Eerdmans, 1986), and Richard W. Schwarz, *Lightbearers to the Remnant* (Mountain View, Calif.: Pacific Press Publishing Association, 1979).

Earlier, less scholarly works include A. W. Spalding's *Origin and History of Seventh-day Adventists*, 4 vols. (Washington, D.C.: Review and Herald Publishing Association, 1961–62), M. Ellsworth Olsen's *A History of the Origin and Progress of Seventh-day Adventists* (Washington, D.C.: Review and Herald Publishing Association, 1925), and J. N. Loughborough's *The Great Second Advent Movement: Its Rise and Progress* (Washington, D.C.: Review and Herald Publishing Association, 1905).

The Millerite movement has been extensively investigated. Francis D. Nichol's *The Midnight Cry* (Washington, D.C.: Review and Herald Publishing Association, 1944) is openly apologetic, but a remarkable piece of amateur historical scholarship. The standard works by professionals are David L. Rowe's *Thunder and Trumpets: Millerites and Dissenting Religion in Upstate New York, 1800–1850* (Chico, Calif.: Scholars Press, 1985) and David T. Arthur's " 'Come Out of Babylon' A Study of Millerite Separatism and Denominationalism, 1840–1865" (Ph.D. dissertation, University of Rochester, 1970). The essays in Gaustad's *The Rise of Adventism* and Ronald L. Numbers and Jonathan M. Butler, eds., *The Disappointed: Millerism and Millenarianism in the Nineteenth Century* (Bloomington: Indiana University Press, 1987) relate Millerism to contemporary religious and social movements. Jerome Clark's *1844*, 3 vols. (Nashville, Tenn.: Southern Publishing Association, 1968), has similar aims but is heavily reliant on Whitney Cross's classic *The Burned-Over District: The Social and Intellectual History of Enthusiastic Religion in Western New York, 1800–1850* (Ithaca, N.Y.: Cornell University Press, 1950).

The early years of Adventism are discussed in P. Gerard Damsteegt's sober but pedestrian *Foundations of the Seventh-day Adventist Message and Mission* (Grand Rapids, Mich.: William B. Eerdmans, 1977) and Ingemar Linden's idiosyncratic *The Last Trump: A Historico-Genetical Study of Some Important Chapters in the Making and Development of the Seventh-day Adventist Church* (Frankfurt, Germany: Peter Lang, 1978). The official biography of Ellen White is by her grandson, Arthur L. White, *Ellen G. White*, 6 vols. (Washington, D.C.: Review and Herald Publishing Association, 1981–85). Sharper analysis is to be found in Ronald L. Numbers's *Prophetess of Health: A Study of Ellen G. White* (New York: Harper & Row, 1976) and Ronald Graybill's "The Power of Prophecy: Ellen G. White and the Women Religious Founders of the Nineteenth Century" (Ph.D. dissertation, Johns Hopkins University, 1983). D. M. Canright's *Life of Mrs. White* (Cincinnati, Ohio: Standard Publishing Company, 1919) is an early critique; Rene Noorbergen's *Prophet of Destiny* (Canaan, Conn.: Keats Publishing Company, 1972) is modern hagiography. Walter Rea's *The White Lie* (Turlock, Calif.: M & R Publications, 1982) attempts to undermine the prophetess's credibility; Roy E. Graham in *Ellen G. White: Co-founder of the Seventh-day Adventist Church* (New York: Peter Lang, 1985) shows how she gained that credibility. There are biographies of many other Adventist pioneers, the most scholarly of which are Godfrey T. Anderson's *Outrider of the Apocalypse: The Life and Times of Joseph Bates* (Mountain View, Calif.: Pacific Press Publishing Association, 1972) and Harry Leonard, ed., *J. N. Andrews: The Man and His Mission* (Berrien Springs, Mich.: Andrews University Press, 1985).

The history of Adventism in the twentieth century has been little explored. Developments at the turn of the century are chronicled in A. V. Olson's *Through Crisis to Victory, 1888–1901: From the Minneapolis Meeting to the Reorganization of the General Conference* (Washington, D.C.: Review and Herald Publishing Association, 1966). The fascinating character of Kellogg is cautiously but carefully explored in Richard W. Schwarz's "John Harvey Kellogg: American Health Reformer" (Ph.D. dissertation, University of Michigan, 1964). This forms the basis of the same author's popular biography *John Harvey Kellogg, M.D.* (Nashville, Tenn.: Southern Publishing Association, 1970). LeRoy Edwin Froom's *Movement of Destiny* (Washington, D.C.: Review and Herald Publishing Association, 1971) takes the history of Adventists up to the 1960s but focuses almost exclusively on the church's alignment with evangelicalism. Lowell Tarling in *The Edges of Seventh-day Adventism* (Barragga Bay, Australia: Galilee, 1981) provides a useful guide to twentieth-century dissident groups.

The development of Adventist theology has received some attention. Specific doctrines are discussed in Roy Adams's *The Sanctuary Doctrine: Three Approaches in the Seventh-day Adventist Church* (Berrien Springs, Mich.: Andrews University Press, 1981); Edwin H. Zackrison's "Seventh-day Adventists and Original Sin: A Study of the Early Development of the Seventh-day Adventist Understanding of the Effect of Adam's Sin on His Posterity" (Ph.D. dissertation, Andrews University, 1984); Eric C. Webster's *Crosscurrents in Adventist Christology* (Frankfurt, Germany: Peter Lang, 1984); Cosmas Rubencamp's "Immortality and Seventh-day Adventist Eschatology" (Ph.D. dissertation, Catholic University of America, 1968); and Jonathan Gallagher's "Believing Christ's Return: An Interpretative Analysis of the Dynamics of Christian Hope" (Ph.D. dissertation, University of St. Andrews, Scotland, 1983). Despite its evident bias, Geoffrey J. Paxton's *The Shaking of Adventism* (Grand Rapids, Mich.: Baker Book House, 1977) is a good presentation of theological disputes during the 1960s and 1970s.

Adventists' attempts to locate their theology within the Protestant tradition are represented by LeRoy Edwin Froom's *The Prophetic Faith of Our Fathers: The Historical Development of Prophetic Interpretation*, 4 vols. (Washington, D.C.: Review and Herald Publishing Association, 1954), and *The Conditionalist Faith of Our Fathers: The Conflict of the Ages over the Nature and Destiny of Man* (Washington, D.C.: Review and Herald Publishing Association, 1965–66). Froom's research is impressive but sometimes lacks an adequate historical framework. Narrower in scope are B. W. Ball's *The English Connection: The Puritan Roots of Seventh-day Adventist Belief* (Cambridge: James Clarke, 1981), which takes a somewhat anachronistic view of Adventist theology, and a more popular work, W. L. Emmerson's *The Reformation and the Advent Movement* (Washington, D.C.: Review and Herald Publishing Association, 1983). Adventism's relationship to modern evangelicalism has been investigated by non-Adventists. Walter R. Martin takes a positive approach in *The Truth about Seventh-day Adventism* (Grand Rapids, Mich.: Zondervan, 1960), while Norman F. Douty in *Another Look at Seventh-day Adventism* (Grand Rapids, Mich.: Baker Book House, 1962) and Anthony A. Hoekema in *The Four Major Cults* (Grand Rapids, Mich.: William B. Eerdmans, 1963) view the church more negatively.

Other aspects of Adventism are covered in Dores Eugene Robinson, *The Story of Our Health Message* (Nashville, Tenn.: Southern Publishing Association, 1943); George W. Reid, *The Sound of Trumpets: Americans, Adventists and Health Reform* (Washington, D.C.: Review and Herald Publishing Association, 1982); Borge Schantz, "The Development of Seventh-day Adventist Missionary Thought: A Contemporary Appraisal" (Ph.D. dissertation, Fuller Theological Seminary, 1983); Howard B. Weeks, *Adventist Evangelism in the Twentieth Century* (Washington, D.C.: Review and Herald Publishing Association, 1969); Roger G. Davis, "Conscientious Cooperators: The Seventh-day Adventists and Military Service, 1860–1945" (Ph.D. dissertation, George Washington University, 1970); Eric B. Syme, *A History of SDA Church-State Relations* (Mountain View, Calif.: Pacific Press Publishing Association, 1976); Robert C. Kistler, *Adventists and Labor Unions in the United States* (Washington, D.C.: Review and Herald Publishing Association, 1984); George Colvin, Jr., "The Women, the Church and the Courts: Sex Discrimination and the First Amendment" (Ph.D. dissertation, Claremont Graduate School, 1986); Michael Pearson, "Seventh-Day Adventist Responses to Some Contemporary Ethical Problems" (D.Phil thesis, Oxford University, 1986); Steven G. Daily, "The Irony of Adventism: The Role of Ellen White and Other Adventist Women in Nineteenth-Century America" (D.Min. project, School of Theology at Claremont, 1985); Louis B. Reynolds, *We Have Tomorrow* (Washington, D.C.: Review and Herald Publishing Association, 1984), a history of black Adventism; and George R. Knight, ed., *Early Adventist Educators* (Berrien Springs, Mich.: Andrews University Press, 1983). The Institute of Church Ministry at Andrews University has produced several unpublished studies on ministry and church growth, which are obtainable from the institute.

The church has received little attention from sociologists. The exceptions are James T. Borhek, "Social Bases of Participation in the Seventh-day Adventist Church" (M.A. thesis, University of California, Berkeley, 1960); Gary Schwartz, *Sect Ideologies and Social Status* (Chicago: University of Chicago Press, 1970); Robin Theobald, "The Seventh-day Adventist Movement: A Sociological Study with Particular Reference to Great Britain" (Ph.D. dissertation, University of London, 1979); Ronald Coffin, "Approche Sociologique d'un Groupe Minoritaire Religieux: L'Eglise Adventiste en France" (D.es Sc. Rel. thesis, University of Strasbourg, 1981); and Robert Wolfgramm, "Charismatic Delegitimation in a Sect: Ellen White and Her Critics" (M.A. thesis, Chisholm Institute of Technology, Australia, 1983). Of these works only the first two are directly concerned with Adventism in America.

Malcolm Bull and Keith Lockhart have jointly published "The Intellectual World of Adventist Theologians," *Spectrum* 18:1 (1987): 32–7. Malcolm Bull has also written several theoretical articles: "The Medicalization of Adventism," *Spectrum* 18:3 (1988): 12–21; "Eschatology and Manners in Seventh-day Adventism," *Archives de Sciences Sociales des Religions* 65:1 (1988): 145–59; "The Seventh-day Adventists: Heretics of American Civil Religion," *Sociological Analysis* 50:2 (1989): 177–87; "Secularization and Medicalization," *British Journal of Sociology*, forthcoming.

Index